SYNTAX and SEMANTICS

VOLUME 3

EDITORIAL BOARD

SYNTAX and SEMANTICS

VOLUME 3
Speech Acts

Edited by

PETER COLE and JERRY L. MORGAN

Department of Linguistics
University of Illinois
Urbana, Illinois

ACADEMIC PRESS   *New York   San Francisco   London*

A Subsidiary of Harcourt Brace Jovanovich, Publishers

COPYRIGHT © 1975, BY ACADEMIC PRESS, INC.
ALL RIGHTS RESERVED.
NO PART OF THIS PUBLICATION MAY BE REPRODUCED OR
TRANSMITTED IN ANY FORM OR BY ANY MEANS, ELECTRONIC
OR MECHANICAL, INCLUDING PHOTOCOPY, RECORDING, OR ANY
INFORMATION STORAGE AND RETRIEVAL SYSTEM, WITHOUT
PERMISSION IN WRITING FROM THE PUBLISHER.

ACADEMIC PRESS, INC.
111 Fifth Avenue, New York, New York 10003

United Kingdom Edition published by
ACADEMIC PRESS, INC. (LONDON) LTD.
24/28 Oval Road, London NW1

LIBRARY OF CONGRESS CATALOG CARD NUMBER: 72-9423

ISBN 0–12–785423–1

PRINTED IN THE UNITED STATES OF AMERICA

80 81 82   9 8 7 6 5 4

CONTENTS

List of Contributors   ix

Preface   xi

Contents of Previous Volumes   xiii

Meaning and Truth in the Theory of Speech Acts   1

DENNIS W. STAMPE

The Conventionalist or Performativist View   1
Constativism, or Back to the Truth   18
Saying and Illocutionary Acts   33
References   38

Logic and Conversation   41

H. PAUL GRICE

Implicature   43

Indirect Speech Acts   59

JOHN R. SEARLE

Introduction   59
A Sample Case   61
Some Sentences 'Conventionally' Used in the Performance
  of Indirect Directives   64
Some Putative Facts   67
An Explanation in Terms of the Theory of Speech Acts   71
Some Problems   75
Extending the Analysis   79
References   82

Conversational Postulates   83

DAVID GORDON and GEORGE LAKOFF

Introduction   83
Some Conversational Postulates   84
The Role of Conversational Postulates in Grammar   94
Concluding Remarks   104
References   106

How to Get People to Do Things with Words:
The Whimperative Question   107

GEORGIA M. GREEN

Four Approaches   108
How to Get People to Do Things   120
Impositives and Impostors   125
Implications of Gordon and Lakoff's Proposal   126
R.S.V.P.   137
Variations on a Theme   140
References   141

Indirect Speech Acts and What to Do with Them   143

ALICE DAVISON

Introduction   143
Semantic Properties   145
Descriptions   158
Replies   160
Sentence Adverbials   161
Reason Adverbials   162
So Pronominalization   164
Slifting   170
Negative Questions   174
Nonrestrictive Relative Clauses   175
Conclusion   177
References   184

Hedged Performatives   187

BRUCE FRASER

Introduction   187
A Taxonomy of Illocutionary Acts   189
An Explanation of Hedged Performatives   193
Conclusions   208
'eferences   210

Asymmetric Conjunction and Rules of Conversation   211

SUSAN F. SCHMERLING

Text   211
References   230

Where to Do Things with Words   233

JOHN R. ROSS

Text   233
References   255

The Synchronic and Diachronic Status of Conversational
Implicature   257

PETER COLE

Introduction   257
Uses of *Let's*   259
A Clear Case of Conversational Implicature   260
Criteria for Conversational Implicature   260
Some Additional Examples of Nonliteral *Let's*   261
Syntactic Evidence   263
The Status of Syntactic Evidence   271
Conversational Implicature and Language Change   273
Factors Leading to the Lexicalization of Contextual Meaning 276
A Cross-Linguistic Prediction   278
Summary of Conclusions   285
Appendix   286
References   288

Some Interactions of Syntax and Pragmatics   289

JERRY L. MORGAN

Text   289
References   303

'Meaning'   305

RICHARD T. GARNER

The Rejection of Meanings   305
Syntactic Considerations against Meanings   307
A Semantical Treatment of 'Mean'   313
Theories of Meaning as Attempts to Change the Subject   316
The "Basic" Meaning Formula   320

Treatments of the Basic Meaning Formula   321
The Use of the Basic Meaning Formula   335
The "Syntax" of the Basic Meaning Formula   346
The Uniqueness of 'Mean'   348
Quotation   352
Remarks about Identity Statements   357
References   359

Meaning$_{nn}$ and Conversational Implicature   363

RICHARD A. WRIGHT

Text   363
References   382

The Soft, Interpretive Underbelly of Generative Semantics   383

JERROLD M. SADOCK

Text   383
References   396

Author Index   397
Subject Index   399

LIST OF CONTRIBUTORS

Numbers in parentheses indicate the pages on which the authors' contributions begin.

PETER COLE (257), Department of Linguistics, University of Illinois, Urbana, Illinois

ALICE DAVISON (143), Program in Linguistics, State University of New York, Stony Brook, New York

BRUCE FRASER (187), Boston University, Boston, Massachusetts

RICHARD T. GARNER (305), Department of Philosophy, The Ohio State University, Columbus, Ohio

DAVID GORDON (83), Department of Psychology, University of California, Berkeley, California

GEORGIA M. GREEN (107), Department of Linguistics, University of Illinois, Urbana, Illinois

H. PAUL GRICE (41), Department of Philosophy, University of California, Berkeley, California

GEORGE LAKOFF (83), Department of Linguistics, University of California, Berkeley, California

JERRY L. MORGAN (289), Department of Linguistics, University of Illinois, Urbana, Illinois

JOHN R. ROSS (233), Department of Linguistics, Massachusetts Institute of Technology, Cambridge, Massachusetts

JERROLD M. SADOCK (383), Department of Linguistics, University of Chicago, Chicago, Illinois

SUSAN F. SCHMERLING (211), Department of Linguistics, The University of Texas, Austin, Texas

JOHN R. SEARLE (59), Department of Philosophy, University of California, Berkeley, California

DENNIS W. STAMPE (1), Department of Philosophy, University of Wisconsin, Madison, Wisconsin

RICHARD A. WRIGHT (363), Department of Philosophy, Talladega College, Talladega, Alabama

PREFACE

Until recently, the work of linguists and of philosophers of language appeared to be incommensurable. Linguists were concerned with predicting the distribution of morphemes in strings, while philosophers were interested in the meaning and use of various linguistic forms. As generative grammarians gradually turned their attention to semantics in the early 1960s, this situation began to change. In the mid-1960s, it became apparent that abstract, underlying syntactic structures, motivated primarily by nonsemantic matters of distribution and well-formedness of strings, tend also to represent meaning better than do superficial syntactic structures.

During the late 1960s and early 1970s, many syntacticians came to believe that the study of syntax is inseparable from the study of meaning. As a result, scholars trained in the methodology of abstract syntax have taken on many of the problems traditionally considered to be within the purview of philosophers of language. The approaches of philosophers and linguists have, however, remained reasonably distinct. This has led to a wide variety of analyses. Linguists and philosophers have attempted to take cognizance of each others' work, but it has not always been certain that the interpretation of linguistic research by philosophers, and of philosophic research by linguists, bears more than a superficial resemblance to the intent of the author of the research.

This volume is an attempt to explore an area of apparently shared concern: speech acts. The papers included center around two controversial aspects of the treatment of speech acts.

The first topic treated by a number of the authors is the performative hypothesis. The papers of A. Davison, J. R. Ross, and D. W. Stampe deal explicitly with the status of this hypothesis. In addition, P. Cole, B. Fraser, G. M. Green, and J. R. Searle touch on issues affecting the status of the hypothesis.

The second controversy addressed in many of the papers is the proper treatment of conversational implicature. H. P. Grice's "Logic and Conversation," the seminal work on this topic, appears in print for the first time here. R. A. Wright examines the relationship between Grice's theory of conversational implicature and Grice's earlier work on meaning. A wide range of related philosophical issues in the theory of meaning are treated by R. T. Garner. The problem of indirect speech acts per se is the subject of papers by P. Cole, B. Fraser, D. Gordon and G. Lakoff, G. M. Green, J. L. Morgan, J. M. Sadock, S. F. Schmerling, and J. R. Searle.

The interaction of philosophical and linguistic approaches to language can be seen in articles by both philosophers and linguists. It is to be hoped that this interaction will help to develop both fields.

The editors would like to thank Kathy Wise for her competent assistance in the preparation of the manuscript. We would also like to thank the staff of Academic Press for their patience and helpfulness.

CONTENTS OF PREVIOUS VOLUMES

Volume 1

Possible and Must
LAURI KARTTUNEN

The Modality of Conditionals — A Discussion of "Possible and Must"
JOHN P. KIMBALL

Forward Implications, Backward Presuppositions, and the Time Axis of Verbs
TALMY GIVÓN

Temporally Restrictive Adjectives
DAVID DOWTY

Cyclic and Linear Grammars
JOHN P. KIMBALL

On the Cycle in Syntax
JOHN GRINDER

Discussion
GEORGE LAKOFF

Action and Result: Two Aspects of Predication in English
MICHAEL B. KAC

Three Reasons for Not Deriving 'Kill' from 'Cause to Die' in Japanese
MASAYOSHI SHIBATANI

Kac and Shibatani on the Grammar of Killing
JAMES D. McCAWLEY

Reply to McCawley
MICHAEL B. KAC

Doubl-ing
JOHN ROBERT ROSS

Where Do Relative Clauses Come From?
JUDITH AISSEN

On the Nonexistence of Mirror Image Rules in Syntax
JORGE HANKAMER

The VP-Constituent of SVO Languages
ARTHUR SCHWARTZ

Lahu Nominalization, Relativization, and Genitivization
JAMES A. MATISOFF

Navaho Object Markers and the Great Chain of Being
NANCY FRISHBERG

The Crossover Constraint and Ozark English
SUZETTE HADEN ELGIN

Author Index—Subject Index

Volume 2

Explanation in Syntax
THEO VENNEMANN GENANNT NIERFELD

The Semantics and Syntax of Number and Numbers
RENATE BARTSCH

Opacity and Reference in Language: An Inquiry into the Role of Modalities
TALMY GIVÓN

Focus and Relativization: The Case of Kihung'an
ALEXIS TAKIZALA

On J. Emonds's Analysis of Extraposition
F. R. HIGGINS

Language Lateralization and Grammars
DIANA VAN LANCKER

Get
JOHN KIMBALL

Sentence and Predicate Modifiers in English
FRANK W. HENY

Deriving S from S + Is
JAMES R. HURFORD

Nonsources of Unpassives
DOROTHY SIEGAL

Index

MEANING AND TRUTH IN THE THEORY OF SPEECH ACTS

DENNIS W. STAMPE
University of Wisconsin

1   What one says determines what one may hope to do in so saying, and what one hopes to do determines what one may say in the effort to do it. In this truism there lies a rich opportunity to penetrate the nature of the acts we perform in speech, and to understand why sentences should have certain of the features they do. That opportunity is lost if we misunderstand the relationships between what one says and what one does in saying it, and between what one means by what he says and what he means what he says AS, or intends it to BE.

THE CONVENTIONALIST OR PERFORMATIVIST VIEW

2   Of course, many sentences, and thus many of the things one says, are not such as to determine uniquely what 'illocutionary' act[1] one is performing: For instance, *There is a bull in the field* is not such as to determine whether one, in uttering it, is issuing a warning, making a promise, or merely making a casual remark. It may seem a reasonable strategy, then, in seeking to understand the relationships between sentences and the various illocutionary forces with which they may be uttered, to begin not with sentences that are more or

---

[1] The term is, of course, Austin's (see Austin, 1962).

1

[handwritten marginalia: "speech act", "difficult to define", "illocutionary act —", "many things or be promised", "threat / observation preface", "explicit performative preface", "fully determined", "I worn you that"]

but, instead, with those sen-
at respect. Such sentences
rmative preface,' sentences
ull in the field. It may well
m which we can see clearly
iry force with which a sen-

king the features of a sen-
rce for the factor that *deter-*
has. It is obvious that it
hat the performative prefix
prefix that does the latter.
been made. For the proper

indicate or to say what one is doing in saying what he says, but variously to 'constitute' his saying of it the making of a promise, a request, or whatever it may be—that is, to be what MAKES IT THE CASE that one has performed this or that speech act. Or, if this determination of force cannot be attributed to the actual utterance of the preface, it may be attributed to the conformity of the utterance with those considerations that WOULD render the use of the preface proper, were it to be employed.

4 The more natural view would be to suppose that the function of the performative preface is simply to COMMUNICATE something, about what one is saying—specifically, to MAKE IT CLEAR what one is doing in saying what he is saying, and in that way to remove any possible ambiguity as to force. (Of course, the utterance of an expression that functions to make it clear whether something is this or that kind of thing does not MAKE that thing the kind of thing it is.) On this more natural view, the function of the performative preface would not differ essentially from the cooking demonstrator's *Now I beat the olive oil into the egg yolks.* Of course, as one might have beaten the oil into the egg yolks without saying that that was what he was doing, so likewise may one perform a certain speech act without saying, or otherwise indicating, that that is what he is doing. And it would be extraordinary to suppose that one's performing either the culinary act, or the illocutionary act, CONSISTS IN one's making certain motions, or noises, in accordance with those considerations that would have made it proper for him so to have described what he was doing as he did it.

5 Plainly, the fact that one need not employ the performative preface to perform a speech act is something wholly predictable in

the natural view. It is NOT readily predictable but, rather, poses an apparent problem for any view on which the explicit performative preface plays a central role. Such views include Searle's, on which the performance of an illocutionary act of a given kind CONSISTS IN the conforming of one's utterance to the semantic rules governing the ILLOCUTIONARY-FORCE-INDICATING DEVICE (hereafter, acronymously, the IFID; see Searle, 1970: chapter 3). Such a view immediately must contend with the fact that the ifid is apparently quite INESSENTIAL: One may perfectly well have made a promise without having uttered the words *I hereby promise* or having employed any other illocutionary-force-indicating device whatever. This is a fact perfectly well known, of course; but in the face of it the view in question is not discarded. At best, it is merely reformulated, rarefied through a process that may be called the sublimation of the ifid.

The Sublimation of the Ifid

6   The ifid, being required by the theory to figure in every sentence, ascends to the status of a theoretical entity, so that those factors thought to determine illocutionary force where the performative prefix occurs may be held to operate to determine force even where no prefix or other ifid occurs — i.e., where the ifid is not 'overt.' (This will bring to some minds the syntactic analysis of Ross and others, called the performative analysis; some remarks about this proposal are interspersed throughout this study.)

7   There are considerations thought to justify this position. If we inquire what EXPLAINS the capacity of *I hereby promise that I'll come* to make it the case that, upon uttering it, the utterer has promised to come (and all that that entails), we tend to consult our general conviction that it is owing to its MEANING, fundamentally, that a sentence has such powers as it has. And no doubt it IS in some sense owing to the meaning of the sentence *I hereby promise that I'll come* that, upon uttering it seriously and literally, I can have performed no illocutionary act other than that of promising to come. From this it is inferred that it is the meaning of that sentence that MAKES IT THE CASE that the utterance of that sentence has the force of a promise and, indeed, may constitute the making of a promise. Now once this doubtful step is made (see §32), one reasons further: IF it is the meaning of *I hereby promise* that determines the illocutionary force of that utterance, what can it be that determines the illocutionary force of an utterance of the ifidless sentence *I'll come* as being that of a promise, if that should happen to be its force? One

might hold that it was here some other factor altogether. But the course of theoretical simplicity would be to hold that it was the same thing in either case (ifid or no) that determines the force of the utterance.[2] And that is, by hypothesis, if not the admittedly unnecessary ifid, the MEANING of the ifid, of *I hereby promise*—and, thus, or alternatively, the semantic rules governing that phrase.

8   Now, what is it that determines that when I said to my son, *I'll go for a walk with you as soon as I finish this page*, I had made him a promise? IF it is determined by meaning, it must be not the meaning of the sentence I utter, which is indeterminate as to force, but rather what I mean BY what I say, my meaning, more fully expressed. What I mean, it will be held, is in fact the same as what is meant by the sentence *I hereby promise that I will go for a walk* (*etc.*). If so, the operation of semantic rules governing the phrase *I hereby promise* (the rules determining the meaning of the ifid) may be invoked to ACCOUNT for this—the rules operating not on an overtly occurring ifid but, instead, on its postulated counterpart, perhaps 'subsequently' deleted from the uttered sentence.

9   By now, one may as well jettison the very distinction between meaning and illocutionary force, as does Searle (1968), who contends that the 'distinction between the literal meaning of a sentence and the intended force of its utterance . . . is only a special case of the distinction between literal meaning and intended meaning, between what the sentence means and what the speaker means in its utterance, and it has no special relevance to the general theory of illocutionary forces . . . [p. 413].'

10   I will want to assail this philosophical view both root and branch. I have merely pointed to what might be the root (§3), but having got into them, we may as well skirmish in the branches first.

The Distinction between Meaning and Illocutionary Force

11   There are two well-known attempts to impeach the distinction between illocutionary force and meaning, issuing one in the claim that such forces 'do not exist' and the other in the charge that the distinction has been 'exaggerated' (whatever either claim might mean). In both studies, the arguments given turn on perfectly transparent equivocations on the term *mean*, on resolutely confusing and conflating the matter of WHAT ONE MEANS TO DO (i.e., intends to do)

---

[2] I accept this point, but hold that force is not in the relevant sense determined by meaning; still, whether the ifid occurs or not, the force of the utterance is a function of the SAME factors. I recur to this §33.

with the matter of WHAT ONE MEANS BY SOMETHING, e.g., by something he says. Thus, L. J. Cohen (1964), considering the locutionary act of uttering *Is it raining?*, asks, 'What on earth could be the meaning of your locutionary act other than to ask whether it is raining? [p. 124].' One may ask what on earth might be meant by 'the meaning of your locutionary act'[3]; but clearly what I mean, when I utter that sentence, is, presumably, Is there any rain coming down?, and that is what the sentence means. What I mean to do, i.e., intend to do, is another matter. I mean to ask whether it is raining.[4] (Thus, what I meant what I said AS — roughly, what I intended it to be TAKEN as, or better, intended it to BE — is: A QUESTION. Neither can THAT be what I meant, or the meaning of what I said.)

12   Searle (1968), engaging in the same equivocation, contributes an argument intended to minimize the distinction between force and meaning. This argument involves his 'Principle of Expressibility': 'Whatever can be meant can be said.' He says that 'a neglect of the Principle of Expressibility seems to be one of the reasons why Austin overestimated the distinction between meaning and force [p. 418],' that is, 'between uttering a sentence with a certain meaning in the sense of sense and reference, and uttering it with a certain force; but . . . ,' he continues:

> according to the Principle, whenever one wishes to make an utterance with force *F*, it is always possible to utter a sentence the meaning of which expresses exactly force *F*, since *if it is possible to mean (intend) that force it is possible to say that force literally* [ibid., p. 419; italics added].

This passage very nearly defies comment. But following the admonition of Searle's Principle, let us try to say what it might mean, partic-

---

[3] It is extremely tedious to trace and identify these equivocations, to supply the necessary interpretations of obscure and obfuscating language like ' . . . the warning is part of the meaning of the . . . utterance' (Cohen), or 'Every serious literal utterance contains some indicators of force as part of meaning' (Searle), and so on. It is merely futile to try to discuss these issues without some effort to speak precisely about meaning, and that requires a lively awareness of the various senses that *mean* may bear. (Incidentally, there is no excuse provided for such equivocations by the view, associated with Grice, that the relevant concept of meaning may be ANALYZED in terms of intentions. Needless to say, the proposal is not that *mean* just means the same thing as *intends*.) The rudimentary distinctions here are described in Stampe (1968: Section VIII).

[4] This sentence is ungrammatical: *°The meaning of what I did (said) was to do x.* The sentence *What I meant by what I said was to do x* serves to explicate what I meant when I uttered some IMPERATIVE sentence; thus, not *I* but *you* is the subject of *do x*.

ularly the doubly ungrammatical clause I have italicized. By *'to mean (intend) that force,' what is meant is presumably 'to mean (intend) one's utterance to HAVE that force.' But *'to say that force literally' is harder to construe.[5] Apparently, it finds its interpretation in this claim:

> For every illocutionary act one intends to perform, it is possible to utter a sentence the literal meaning of which is such as to determine that its serious literal utterance in an appropriate context will be a performance of that act [ibid., p. 418].

(There are well-known apparent exceptions to this, including insults and threats. But never mind that.) What is important to notice is that the statement presupposes the truth of the view characterized earlier (§7), that it is meaning that determines the illocutionary force with which a sentence is uttered, at least in the case of those sentences which contain an explicit ifid. And Searle argues from this fact for the general position, that it is meaning that everywhere determines force, even where no ifid occurs. I shall reject that argument, but I do not dispute the fact that there is a sense in which the meaning of ifid-containing sentences can be said to determine their force. Thus, the meaning of *I hereby promise that I'll be there* is such as to determine that, if one speaks literally, he must mean that, in saying that he will come, he is promising to come; and if he furthermore speaks seriously, then he must intend what he says to have the force of a promise — which, under certain conditions, will then be the force it does have. Now it may seem that this fact diminishes the importance of the difference between one's meaning a certain thing and his intending what he says to have a certain force, in the particular case of ifid-containing sentences. That is as it may be, but it tells us nothing about sentences without ifids. Thus, it does not diminish the difference between, e.g., what one means by *I will be there* and the illocutionary force one intends what he says to have, e.g., that of a promise. For while it is true that there is a sentence, *I promise that I will be there*, that is unambiguous as to force, it is NOT the case that that sentence is the 'literal' expression of WHAT ONE MEANS BY what he says when he says *I will be there*, meaning (intending) what he says as a promise, or intending it to have the force of a promise. So I contend against Searle.

[5] The fact is that the FORCE of an utterance is not something that COULD be 'meant,' 'intended,' 'expressed,' or 'said': It is the wrong kind of thing for any of these predicates.

13 The matter comes to rest on this unlikely issue: Are we to accept the view Searle (1968) expresses when he says, in commenting on his Principle of Expressibility:

> Often we mean more than we actually *say*. You ask me, "Are you going to the party?" I say, "Yes." But what I mean is "Yes, I am going to the party," not "Yes, it is a fine day." Similarly, I might say, "I'll come," *and mean it as a promise — that is, mean it as I would mean "I hereby promise I will come,"* if I were uttering that sentence seriously and meaning literally what I said [p. 415].

I italicize the crucial phrase, in which one's meaning what he says (*s*) AS an *F* (where '*F*' stands for the name of some specific kind of illocutionary act) is identified with meaning BY what he says what one would properly mean by another sentence, sc., one of the form *iFid* + *s*, (where the ifid indicates that the utterance is to have the force of an *F*). Let us call the thesis that these things are identical Thesis *J*. (Without this seemingly innocent contention, there is no way the Principle of Expressibility can be enlisted to support the reduction of the distinction between force and meaning to that of the distinction between the meaning of the sentence uttered and what one means when he utters it.[6])

14 We are concerned with the thesis that performative prefaces, or other ifids, express part of what may properly be MEANT by what one says in uttering a sentence that is inexplicit as to force. This is a thesis of some relevance to linguistic theory, for (among other reasons) it may be tied to the so-called performative analysis, on current views about the semantic properties of deep structure representations. These include the view that transformations 'preserve meaning' and the 'generative semanticist' thesis that representations of the underlying syntactic structure of sentences ARE 'semantic representations.' Thus, on the latter view, if *I hereby say to you that I'll*

---

[6] Thus, if we find *J* to be false, we will have found the Principle of Expressibility, in regard to the issues here in question, to be negligible in fact, and Austin to have been right to neglect it. For the Principle must yield Thesis *J* if the force–meaning distinction is successfully to be reduced [in Searle's way of putting it, on p. 421 (2)] to 'the distinction between the literal meaning of the sentence and what the speaker means (by way of illocutionary force) when he utters it.' When I say that this thesis is required to make the Principle of Expressibility relevant to the matter, I am talking about that Principle on an interpretation under which it is true. No doubt, the statement 'What can be meant can be said' can be subject to equivocation on *meant*. But it is not TRUE that 'what can be INTENDED can be said.'

come represents the syntactic structure of the simple sentence *I'll come*, then it also represents its meaning. That would SEEM to imply that the former sentence has the same meaning as the latter. I shall deny that they have the same meaning. If I am right about that, there is a prima facie case that EITHER (1) the performative analysis is wrong OR (2) it is false that deep structure represents meaning or that transformations preserve meaning.[7]

15 Thesis *J* claims that one who says *I'll come*, therein intending to promise to come, means the same thing that one means who says *I hereby promise that I'll come*, speaking seriously and literally. Now, what DOES the latter speaker mean? First, clearly, he means (1) that he will come—as does the speaker who says just *I'll come*. And indeed, each speaker SAYS that he will come (§42–43). But further, one who says *I hereby promise that I'll come* also MEANS that BY saying what he says he PROMISES that he will come. For the hypothesis is that he is speaking 'literally'; that is, that what he means does not deviate from the meaning of the sentence he utters, as that is determined by the meaning of its constituents, INCLUDING THE EXPRESSION *hereby*. *Hereby* is a reflexive demonstrative pronoun that properly makes reference to what one is doing by or in uttering that sentence.[8] The relevant thing that the speaker is doing in uttering that sentence is saying that something is so, sc., that he would come. Therefore, if he is speaking literally, it would seem that part of what he MEANS when he says *I hereby promise that I'll come* MUST be (2) *that* IN *saying or* BY *saying that he will come, he is promising that he will come.*[9] For if he does not mean that, the expression *hereby*, which surely means SOMETHING, would seem not to enter into the determination of what the speaker means. So (2) is part of what the speaker means. Now, unless every part of what he means is also part of what is meant by the man who says just *I'll come*, therein intending to promise to come, then it is not true that the two speakers mean the SAME thing. But plainly, the speaker who says just *I'll come* cannot have meant that BY saying or IN saying what he is saying, he is promising that he will come; he cannot mean that he

---

[7] There are in fact other possibilities, including (3): One sentence, owing to its superficial structure, may be held to constitute a REPRESENTATION of the meaning of a second, even though the two do NOT have the same meaning (see §51).

[8] Compare: '*I herewith extract a rabbit from the hat,*' he said, *and therewith he extracted a rabbit from the hat; 'I hereby promise that I'll come,*' he said, *and thereby he promised that he would come.*

[9] I do not assert, or require the premise, that in saying *I hereby promise that I'll come* the speaker SAYS that he is making a promise in or by saying that he will come.

hereby—i.e., BY THESE WORDS—promises: not if he is speaking 'literally.' For there is nothing in the sentence he utters (*I'll come*)—e.g., no such reflexive demonstrative expression as *hereby*—by which he might be referring to what he is saying or to his saying what he is saying. And indeed, obviously, one who says *I'll come* does not in any way make reference to what he says; nor could he do so. So he cannot intend to convey anything about the thing he is saying (including information about the intentions with which it is said) BY what he says.[10] So I conclude that one who says *I hereby promise that I'll come*, speaking seriously and literally, does *not* mean the same thing as what one means who says *I'll come*, speaking seriously and literally, and meaning what he says as, i.e., intending it to have the force of, a promise. And more generally, one's meaning what he says, *s*, as an *F* is not to be identified with meaning what one would properly mean by another sentence, one of the form *iFid + s*.

16 This argument depends upon the occurrence in the ifid of a reflexive demonstrative like *hereby*.[11] It is true that not all ifids involve that or any other EXPRESSION referring to what the speaker is doing or saying. For instance, there is the sentence *I promise to come*. But of course, THIS sentence has an ambiguity of meaning that makes it ambiguous with respect to force. For if it means what it would in answer to the question, *How do you get me to throw these parties?*, then *I promise you that I'll come* cannot have the force of a promise. It is the effect of reflexive demonstratives like *with these*

---

[10] It is true that the *way* one says what he says, e.g., the intonation with which one says it, may function as a conventionally determined vehicle via which something concerning those intentions might be being conveyed. But this is not to concede that by the intonation of my words I might properly mean that in saying what I am saying I am performing or intending to perform a certain speech act. If a person says *Give me a nickel* with a whining intonation contour, that fact may mean that, and he may intone it thus to convey the fact that, he wants you to comply out of pity. This is good EVIDENCE that the illocutionary force of his utterance is that of an entreaty rather than that of a command. But while the speaker intends to convey that fact about the intentions with which he utters the sentence and the illocutionary force of the utterance, it is not true that part of WHAT HE MEANS is that he is appealing to your sense of pity. Notice that the contexts 'By saying it the way he did, he meant . . . ' or 'By the intonation of his words, he meant . . . ' require completion by an infinitive clause (e.g., 'to express his apprehensiveness'); they cannot be completed by a *that*-clause (e.g., *'. . . that he was apprehensive' or *'. . . that he was issuing a warning'). This is a clear indication that the sense of the verb *mean* is here that of *intend*.

[11] There is a familiar similar line of reasoning distinguishing the meaning of the sentence *It is true that snow is white* from that of the sentence *Snow is white*, wherein it is maintained that the former sentence says something about the proposition that snow is white, whereas the latter does not do so.

words or *here and now* or *hereby* to eliminate this ambiguity—to block the 'continuous' reading of the verb—and therein to determine uniquely the force of the utterance.[12] But it is upon just such entirely unambiguous sentences that the argument being criticized depends, i.e., sentences the meaning of which UNIQUELY determines the illocutionary force with which they may be properly ('seriously and literally') uttered. For only they could be held to represent a point at which force is indistinguishable from meaning, thus to support the claim that force is determined by meaning fully expressed. But if, as I predict, some expression relevantly like demonstrative *hereby* is required to achieve such singularity of meaning, the argument in §15 is sufficiently general to refute Thesis *J*.

17 For that argument indicates that there IS no point at which intended illocutionary force collapses into meaning, and that there is no reason to suppose that there is not ALWAYS a distinction to be made between what one means by what he says and what illocutionary act one intends to perform in so saying.[13] It is, of course, nearly always possible explicitly to indicate what that intention is.

---

[12] In addition to these reflexive phrases, there are other ifids having a similar if not quite the same effect, among them *as I live and breathe, so help me God, cross my heart,* and *with God as my witness,* at least when taken in their idiomatic senses. I would predict that the argument of §15 applies also, mutatis mutandis, to cases involving SUCH ifids; e.g., there is something one means when he says *I'll come, so help me God* that one does not mean when he says *I'll come,* intending thereby to promise.

[13] Searle treats this matter as analogous to the situation in which what had been thought to be two distinct kinds of animals are found not to be distinct kinds upon the discovery of an animal that has the characteristics of both putative kinds. (The 'explicit performative' sentence, unambiguous as to force, plays the role of this animal.) But it is OBVIOUSLY wrong to represent Austin's distinction between locutionary and illocutionary acts as SUCH a distinction, that is, as Searle says he thinks it must be, a distinction between two 'mutually exclusive classes of acts [1968:413].' Searle says that there is no distinction of this sort '. . . between separate classes of acts, because just as every terrier is a dog, so every locutionary act is an illocutionary act [ibid.]'—as if this contradicted Austin, who said that 'to perform a locutionary act is in general, we may say, also and *eo ipso* to perform an illocutionary act . . . 1962:98].' Austin did not purport to distinguish two CLASSES of acts at all. Such a doctrine would require us to speak of acts as we speak of dogs, in respect of their 'arithmetic': Thus, if you have a dog that is a terrier, you have ONE dog—so dogs and terriers are not 'separate classes of dogs.' We should have to raise the question, analogously, If you SAY that you will come, therein promising to come, have you performed one act or two? (Searle apparently is clear that you've performed only one.) I should have thought that Austin, for HIS part, would have regarded this question itself as exactly the kind of question that gets a philosopher (deservedly) 'stared at as at an idiot,' as he put it. If I am right in this, he would scarcely have taken the position Searle imputes to him, which depends on believing the question to be answerable (and the correct answer to be that you have performed TWO acts).

But in doing so, what one makes explicit is neither what he means nor those intentions that constitute his meaning what he means, but, rather, certain intentions he has CONCERNING what he says. He makes it clear how he intends what he says to be taken, e.g., whether as a promise or as a warning. And to do that is to SAY something about what one says or has said or will say, OR, if not to say it, otherwise to give it to be understood that a certain thing is true OF what one says — e.g., that it is intended to be taken as, or to constitute, a promise. But if this is so, then what he says, thus to make known what he intends what he says to be taken as, must be DISTINCT FROM what he says (and what he means thereby) and further must pertain or REFER TO his saying of it. And therefore, the expression he uses to indicate illocutionary force must mean something, and by it he must mean something, other than — something 'more than' — what he means by what he said. Thus, I cannot BY what I say, should I say just that I will come, properly mean that by so saying, or in so saying, I intend to make a promise; for I cannot BY saying that I will come, mean that something is true of or about what I am saying.[14]

Searle's "Semantic Rule" Account of Force Determination

18   In framing this refutation of Thesis *J*, I have implicitly fallen in with what I earlier called the natural view of the semantic function of ifids (§4). The issue here, now at the root of the matter, is, What determines the illocutionary force of an utterance? When a speaker, speaking literally and seriously, utters a certain sentence, what makes it the case that that utterance constitutes the making of a promise, and all that that entails?

19   The conventionalist or performativist account holds that there is a CONVENTION, or RULE, owing to which the utterance of that sentence 'counts as' and constitutes the performance of a certain illocutionary act (cf. footnote to §29). This view, the progeny of Hume, is a not implausible one of the particular 'performative utterances' Austin first focused upon, whereby babies are christened and bids redoubled. (Here verbal 'formulae' ARE prescribed by, broadly speaking,

[14] For instance, I cannot, by what I say, mean that I shall be bound to doing this thing BY my saying this thing. What I mean by what I say is just that I will come, AND if I am promising that I will come, I further give it to be understood that I will be bound to come by the fact that I said that I would come. But this is no more part of what I MEAN by what I say than it is part of what the SENTENCE *I'll come* means. But if I say *I promise that I'll come*, there IS something I say, sc., I PROMISE *that I'll come*, by which I do mean, if I speak seriously and literally, that I will be bound to come BY the fact that I said that I would come.

convention — liturgical tradition or the rule book of bridge.) When we go over to plain 'illocutionary acts,' however — stating, requesting, remarking, promising, objecting — the plausibility of the view is left behind. Where are the 'rules' of making remarks? What have conventions to do with it? The doctrine of illocutions must work free of the conventionalist cocoon which encloses the initial 'performative utterance' stage of the inquiry. Searle's contribution would arrest the doctrine in its pupal stage, by this device: The RULES allegedly governing the utterance so as to determine its illocutionary force are identified with the semantic rules governing a certain linguistic (or paralinguistic) expression — the illocutionary-force-indicating device — in such a way as to determine the meaning thereof.[15] That there ARE such semantic rules, or at least that the meaning of an expression is determined by conventions, is a proposition almost universally accepted for independent reasons, and surely it holds good for such expressions as *I hereby request* and other ifids. So Searle's maneuver of identifying the alleged force-determining rules with the acknowledged meaning-determining rules — semantic rules — has the apparent virtue of requiring, thus far, no theoretical innovations, no novel apparatus. This is why the view will gain ready acceptance, and why it may be hard for the subject to move beyond it and conventionalism generally.

20 My argument is that this identification of force-determining with meaning-determining rules cannot be sustained, for the reasons I have elaborated; but since it cannot be sustained, the entire doctrine that illocutionary force is determined by convention is to be rejected, and with it the view that an illocutionary act is CONSTITUTED an act of its specific kind by certain 'constitutive' rules. [This is the fundamental thesis of Searle's book *Speech Acts* (Searle, 1970).][16]

---

[15] Searle's procedure (1970: Chapter 3) is to state a set of conditions necessary and jointly sufficient for the 'successful and non-defective performance of the act of promising [ibid., p. 54],' and he says then, 'if we get such a set of conditions we can extract from them a set of rules for the use of the illocutionary force indicating device.' One such necessary condition of 'non-defective' promising (ibid., p. 58) is, e.g., that the hearer 'would prefer' the speaker's doing the thing in question to his not doing it. (Thus, you cannot promise me a punch in the mouth.) From this condition Searle 'extracts' this 'semantical rule for the use of any illocutionary force indicating device *Pr*': 'Rule 2. *Pr* is to be uttered only if the hearer would prefer "the speaker's doing the thing," etc. [ibid., p. 63].'

[16] 'I have said that the hypothesis of this book is that speaking a language is performing acts according to rules. The form this hypothesis will take is that the semantic structure of a language may be regarded as a conventional realization of a series of sets

21 The identification cannot be sustained because it yields an utterly incoherent notion of a semantic rule. These rules must have the twin properties, first, of governing the use of the indicator of illocutionary force—*I hereby promise,* or whatever it may be—and, secondly, of thereby constituting any such utterances as do have the force of a promise as being utterances of that illocutionary force—and this whether the expression governed by the rule is in fact used or not. In this matter, we must keep clearly before us just what a 'semantic rule' might BE and what its powers might be. The only thing on earth that a rule can actually do is govern BEHAVIOR, here linguistic behavior—the UTTERANCE of expressions. A rule may govern utterance by specifying conditions under which expressions are to be uttered; thus, they may be expressed in the form, 'Utter *e* only if conditions *C* obtain.' It is thus that they determine the meaning of an expression, that is, what one may mean when he utters that expression properly—that is, in accordance with the dictates of that rule. But then, of course, the scope of that rule, the set of expressions that it governs, must be properly defined. Obviously, our knowledge of what may be meant by what expressions cannot be adequately represented as mastery of such rules unless that includes a knowledge of what RANGE of expressions are governed by a given rule—and thus what utterances are to be, and may be presumed to be, issued in accordance therewith. And, if it held to be true quite generally that the meaning of expressions is established by such rules, then EVERY expression that may properly be uttered with a given meaning, and no expression that may not be uttered with that meaning, must fall within the scope of such a rule.

22 Now Searle contends (falsely, according to me) that a speaker MAY utter a sentence of the form *s* (*I'll come*), properly meaning thereby the same thing that is properly meant by a sentence of the form *ifid* + *s* (*I promise that I'll come*). The fact that this is false is not the fundamental point. For suppose we waive that objection and

---

of underlying constitutive rules, and that speech acts are acts characteristically performed by uttering expressions in accordance with these sets of constitutive rules . . . The effort to state the rules for the performance of speech acts can also be regarded as a test of the hypothesis that there are constitutive rules underlying speech acts. If we are unable to give any satisfactory rule formulations, our failure could be construed as partially disconfirming evidence against the hypothesis [p. 36].' It is, however, not the FORMULATION of the rules that is unacceptable but, rather, the very CONCEPTION of such rules as these have to be. Indeed, it is my conviction—though I will not produce the argument here—that Searle's notion of a 'constitutive rule' (ibid., p. 34) is plainly incoherent, even as applied to his paradigm, certain rules of games.

pretend for the moment (as that view would require) that *s* is ambiguous in meaning, as between what is meant by *I promise that s* and *I
warn you that s*, and so on. Now the semantic rule determining 'the'
meaning of that sentence will determine not what MUST be meant
thereby but, rather, the several things that MAY be meant. The rule,
we may say, will be not a categorical but a DISJUNCTIVE imperative:
'Utter *s* only if you mean EITHER A OR B OR C OR D.' That, so far as
it goes, would perhaps be tolerable. But the rule is useless to the
purpose of determining illocutionary force. For obviously, the fact
that one utters *s* in obedience to this disjunctive imperative cannot
determine which of the permissible things one MAY mean by that
sentence is the one he DOES mean, in fact. We are allowing that one
might properly mean the same thing one must mean if he says *I
hereby promise that I'll come*. But if that is what he does mean, in
fact, it is impossible to discover that that is so from the semantic rule
allegedly governing his utterance. For it does not prescribe that that
is what he must mean. Therefore, it does not determine what he does
mean. Thus, if it WERE what a speaker means by what he says that
determines the force of his utterance, it would not be the semantic
rule governing his utterance that determines that force. For these
rules are not categorical imperatives that dictate, e.g., that the
expression *I'll come* ' . . . is to be uttered only if [the speaker]
intends to [come]' or that its utterance ' . . . counts as the undertaking of an obligation' to come (cf. Searle, 1970:63).[17] (And
obviously, there IS no such rule as that, since I may also properly
utter that sentence in making a prediction or expressing a mere intention.)

23   The insoluble task before this analysis is to specify the scope
of alleged rules that, in determining the meaning of certain utterances, thereby determine their illocutionary force. The scope must
on the one hand be defined sufficiently NARROWLY that it does not
apply to every utterance of the sentence *I'll come*, for that sentence
is INdeterminate as to force; and yet, if it is this rule that accounts for
its having the force of a promise, on such occasions as it does have
that force, that sentence must somehow come within its scope.
Plainly, one must somehow deny that the sentences, or the objects,

---

[17] Notice, as these formulations indicate, that Searle wants these semantic rules to
determine still more — in particular, in this case, to account for the fact that one who
makes a promise is often obligated to do what he said he would. That this is a too
heavy burden for SEMANTIC rules to play should be obvious enough. Happily, this part
of his view is separable from the aspects here under scrutiny, though they are certainly related.

that fall under the scope of this rule ARE indeterminate or ambiguous as to illocutionary force.

THE FAILURE OF THE "PERFORMATIVE ANALYSIS" TO VINDICATE SEARLE'S ACCOUNT

24   How can it be done? The most desperate move is just to deny that there IS any such indeterminacy about an uttered sentence completely described, with all its overt suprasegmental characteristics, intonation, etc. This is absurd (but cf. Searle, 1968:419). The move worth dwelling on is that which defines the scope of the rule in terms of unexpressed elements occurring in the deep structure of the sentence, but not necessarily in the uttered rendition of it. The rules then will govern not only the utterance of sentences with expressed ifids, like *I hereby promise to do it*, but also the utterances of sentences WITHOUT expressed ifids, like *I'll do it*, where that sentence has (allegedly) the same deep structure as the sentence with the overt ifid. If this can be made good, then rules of the categorical (nondisjunctive) imperative form required to make good the thesis that the rules DETERMINE the particular force of its utterance can be held to apply to certain utterances of *I'll come*, determining what the speaker may mean thereby (the same thing that one means by *I hereby promise*) and, thus, that the utterance has the force of a promise.[18]

25   But this is all confusion. Semantic rules govern the utterance

---

[18] Searle's only recognition of the problem his view faces comes in Searle (1970:64), where he asks the question, 'To which elements, in an actual description of a natural language would rules such as [the ones described] attach? . . . it seems to me extremely unlikely that illocutionary act rules would attach directly to elements (formatives, morphemes) generated by the syntactic component, except in a few cases such as the imperative. In the case of promising, the rules would more likely attach to some output of the combinatorial operations of the semantic component.' But Searle's 'illocutionary act rules' are allegedly 'semantical rules' 'for the use of the illocutionary force indicating device [ibid., p. 62].' Semantic rules surely generate the output of the 'semantic component' and can hardly operate upon it. (This is the point I raise in §25.) It is in Searle (1968) that Searle actually swallows the systematic implications of his position, as he embraces Thesis J. And there he says, ' . . . the meaning [sic] of every sentence already contains some determiners of illocutionary force [ibid., p. 418],' though this is, of course, not good enough to meet the point. He also emphasizes that 'deep syntactic structure, stress and intonation contour' are 'bearers of meaning' as well as the uttered sentence and its surface structure (ibid., p. 419), though this occurs in belaboring the noncontroversial point that the meaning of a sentence determines its illocutionary force POTENTIAL. By the end of the paragraph these factors are referred to as 'crucial determinants of illocutionary force.' The issue is whether such factors can be held to determine the particular illocutionary force of a particular utterance of a sentence.

of expressions, thereby to determine what may be meant by that expression and what the expression means. But if it is the application of the rule to that expression that determines what it means, it cannot be OWING to the expression's having a certain meaning that it falls within the jurisdiction of that rule. It must be owing to some other fact about the expression. Thus, the rule may govern, for instance, the utterance of any expression of a given PHONEMIC description, thereby determining its meaning. Or, it may govern the utterance of a homonymous expression in a certain syntactic environment, thereby uniquely determining its meaning. But there is no SYN-TACTIC (nor any phonemic) characteristic of the sentence *I'll come* that might bring it within the scope of the rule determining that one must mean by it that he promises to come, and thus that its force must be that of a promise. That is to say, there is no syntactic basis for postulating an underlying ifid clause, *I hereby promise.*

26   To enlarge on this, compare the classic case of the understood subject of imperative sentences, described in the language of se-mantic rules. The sentence *You go* is governed by a rule that dictates that it is to be uttered only if the speaker means that the referent of *you*, i.e., the addressee, is to go. But the subjectless sentence *Go* has syntactic characteristics in common with the sentence *You go;* i.e., it mirrors its 'distribution' in grammatical English sentences. For in-stance, both will occur with the tag question *will you?* or with the reflexive *yourself.* But generally, the simplest description of the con-ditions under which these elements may occur requires the pronoun to have an antecedent of the same person; and to retain this rule (and also the general proposition that every sentence consists of a noun phrase and a verb phrase), an unexpressed second-person subject is postulated in *Go.* Now we may observe that the same semantic rule that requires *You go* to be uttered with reference to the addressee also may be held to explain why it is that one must utter *Go* with that same reference, meaning that the addressee is to go. For that se-mantic rule applies to sentences with an expressed OR AN UNEX-PRESSED second-person subject. But this semantic rule, which DE-TERMINES that *Go* means that the addressee is to go, applies to a structure specified by its SYNTACTIC properties. The view is not the incoherent one that the rule applies to just those sentences that have a certain MEANING, thereby determining that they have that meaning.

27   The performative analysis is, as its proponents emphasize, based on very similar kinds of alleged facts regarding syntactic dis-tribution and theoretical simplicity. Thus, the sentence *As for my-self, I'll come* is acceptable, or preferable to **As for yourself, I'll* *come*, indicating the existence of a higher antecedent I[19]; the possibility of *Confidentially, I'll come* suggests the existence of an unexpressed verb of saying that the adverb *confidentially* might modify (cf. Schreiber, 1972). In such ways the case is built that the underlying structure of the sentence is something like that of *I hereby say confidentially to you that I'll come*. It is then further claimed that even such sentences as *I'll come*, which bear none of the evidence of any such higher structure, also have that same deep structural representation, just as it is claimed that *Go*, as well as *Go, will you?* has an underlying second-person subject.

28 Whatever the ultimate merits or defects of the performative analysis may be, it does not, at least, provide aid and comfort to the semantic rule analysis of illocutionary force determination. Specifically, it does not provide a deep structure index that would serve to signal the application of a rule to a sentence without an expressed ifid in such a way as to determine that its utterance has some particular illocutionary force. The postulated verb, whether construed as an 'abstract bundle of features' or as a concrete verb like *say* or *tell* (as argued in McCawley, 1968: pf 156), is, in any case, not associated with any particular ILLOCUTIONARY verb, nor is it representative of the distinctive abstract features thereof. Rather, it is the LOCUTIONARY verb, *say, tell, ask*, etc., or features that characterize such a verb, that is postulated.[20] With the support of the performative analysis, it might be maintained that a semantic rule governing *say* operates on the sentence *I'll come*. But it cannot be maintained that that sentence, given its deep structure description, can be brought within the scope and governance of the semantic rule governing the illocutionary verb *promise* or the phrase *I hereby promise*. So the performative analysis is useless to the purpose of defending the thesis that the illocutionary force of an utterance is determined by a rule governing the illocutionary-force-indicating device and determining its meaning.

29 The assignment was on the one hand to NARROW the scope of the application of the alleged semantic rules so that they would not apply indiscriminately to every utterance of, e.g., *I'll come* (requiring

[19] For this and a battery of other arguments, see Ross, (1970). I will express no opinion regarding the quality of the evidence for the performative analysis.

[20] Searle also rejects the distinction between locutionary and illocutionary acts (holding that saying is an illocutionary act), but this muddle is here irrelevant. For his thesis is that any illocutionary force an utterance has is determined by a semantic rule, and whether SAYING is 'illocutionary' (as Searle maintains) or not, promising and warning ARE illocutionary acts and suffice to refute the view.

each to have the force of a promise AND of a threat, etc.). We have seen no way to do this. On the other hand, it would also be necessary to WIDEN the scope of their application to include not just *I hereby promise* but also any other expression indicating that same illocutionary force, such as *you have my word that, you can count on me doing it, as God is my witness, Scout's honor, on my oath as an odd fellow,* or *cross my heart.* Now, many of these expressions may unambiguously indicate that what is being said is meant as a promise. Thus, Searle would have it that by any one of them one means the same thing. The problem here, of course, is that, obviously, none of them mean the same thing: I cannot by saying *You can count on my coming* mean the same thing that I mean by *You have my word that I'm coming.* But Searle has all these ifids (which plainly differ in meaning) governed by one and the same semantic rule[21] — that is, one rule determining their meaning. But since they all have different meanings and different phonetic and syntactic properties, it is impossible that this should be so.

30   But we have stalked the Searlish ifid far enough. I turn now to a more promising pursuit, the view that we may as well call CONSTATIVISM.[22]

CONSTATIVISM, OR BACK TO THE TRUTH

31   Why is it that the serious and literal utterance of that explicit performative sentence *iFid + s* makes it the case that that utterance has the force of an *F*? The constativist approaches this question from this indisputable fact: Somehow, the utterance of that sentence, given that one speaks literally and seriously, satisfies the truth conditions for the statement that the speaker's utterance has the force of an *F*, e.g., the force of an order. But what conditions are those? Let us suppose that they include the condition that the speaker means what he says AS an *F*, that is, that he intends it to be so taken. (This is a substantive assumption that removes us a certain distance from the performative utterance origins of the subject.[23]) If this supposition is correct, then the utterance, serious and literal, of that sentence sat-

---

[21] Or perhaps a battery of several such rules having the same effect.

[22] Opposing it to what might be called PERFORMATIVISM, an epithet that fits not only Austin's approach to the subject but also Searle's and Alston's, and others in which rules and conventions play a central role. For the term CONSTATIVE, see Austin (1962:3).

[23] It removes us from the cases of which it is most nearly actually TRUE that 'to say a few certain words' is actually to perform the act, where that statement requires no

isfies the truth conditions of the proposition that the speaker intends what he says as an *F*.

32 Now plainly, it is not owing to a CONVENTION that it does so. There is, for example, no convention to the effect that if one says *I promise that I will come,* speaking literally and seriously, one is to do so with the intention to be making a promise to come. For given what that sentence MEANS,[24] and given what literal and serious utterance IS, with what other intentions COULD one utter the sentence

---

qualifications about speaking seriously and literally. Thus, the act of marrying is accomplished whether one is serious or not when he says *I do,* and the ship is named whether one speaks literally and seriously or not; at an auction, one's uttering the words *I bid five dollars* constitutes making a bid, or an offer to buy, whether one is serious or not and even if he doesn't know what he is saying. That is to say, he is 'held' to have meant what he said as an offer, HELD to have intended to make an offer regardless of whether he did or did not have any such intention; and his utterance, according to the conventions of the auction, is held to constitute the making of an offer to buy. Now here it is particularly natural to say that his utterance 'has the force of' an offer to buy. I think this language actually implies a recognition of the fact that, while it has the force, and the effect, of an act of such a kind, it is not actually, or may not be actually, an act of such a kind. It may be not actually the case that the speaker was making an offer to buy the object. But by convention, even perhaps by law, it is regarded as such, that is to say, regarded as such an act is regarded; in particular, its effect and force is regarded as the same as that of a genuine offer, i.e. (I conjecture), an act wherein one intends to cause it to be known that one is willing to pay the mentioned amount. Again, I hear that recruits are informed that the REQUEST of a superior officer is 'equivalent to,' has the force of, or is to be regarded as an ORDER. Presumably, while the officer may intend that the private should shut the window if (but only if) it's no trouble, or he does not mind, and thus not merely because he is superior to him in rank (and all that that entails), nonetheless, the private is to REGARD the utterance as having the force of an order. Thus he is to regard himself as being REQUIRED to shut the window whether he minds doing it or not, and perhaps (depending how seriously this nonsense is taken) as subject to court-martial if he does not. What I wish to emphasize is that the language of illocutionary 'force,' speaking of one utterance as having the force OF an act of a given kind, is indeed language that implies the irrelevance of intentions, or of the seriousness and literalness with which one is speaking, to the determination of the illocutionary characterization of the utterance. As such, the language of forces is in fact tied up with conventions. For if an utterance that is not an *F* nonetheless has the force OF an *F*, is to be regarded as if it were an *F*, it may well to be true to say that is is precisely by virtue of some convention, rule, or law that it is to be regarded as such. But by the same token, what COUNTS AS, or is to be regarded AS, or has the force OF an order, etc., need not be actually an order. Thus, accidentally discharging your gun into the chest of the man you are robbing may COUNT AS deliberately murdering him, but it IS NOT deliberate murder.

[24] It may more reasonably be held that the meaning of the sentence is determined by convention, for the sentence could just as well mean something else. (To be accurate, the sentence could NOT 'as well' mean something else, but the sounds that constitute an utterance of the sentence could.)

seriously and literally? Yet it is only where 'it could as well be otherwise' that a state of affairs may said to be owing to convention. (It is owing to a convention that we drive on the right, for in this we 'could as well do otherwise.') To explain why a person must utter that sentence with the intention to make a promise, if he speaks literally and seriously, we need postulate no special convention governing the ifid, or the first-person noncontinuous-present, etc., tense. The fact is explainable by the systematically determined, nonidiomatic meaning of the ifid-containing sentence, taken together with certain general, independently established or perfectly obvious facts and principles of inference.

33   One such principle is this: If I am to speak literally, then what I mean by what I say may not deviate from the meaning of the sentence I utter. But then it is only in this sense, and only on that presumption, that the meaning of the performative sentence can be said to DETERMINE the illocutionary force of a particular utterance of that sentence—i.e., make it the case that it has the force it has (cf. §7). But this accords no special powers to the semantic rules governing the ifid. It does not retell the myth of rules that CONSTITUTE the utterance a promise. For we recognize only one way in which the meaning of any sentence or the semantic rules that govern its utterance can be held to determine that a certain state of affairs obtains, and this goes for sentences of any kind whatever. The meaning of a sentence directly determines only what may properly be meant by it, and so, indirectly, such states of affairs as must obtain if it is so used, and further, IS UTTERED SERIOUSLY. Thus, the meaning of a sentence can determine a state of affairs in this way: The conditions NECESSARY for one's having meant what one must mean by that sentence, if he speaks literally, and for his having been serious in so speaking, are either identical with or include conditions that are SUFFICIENT for the truth of what one says or, more generally, sufficient for the truth of some proposition that, in saying what he says, the speaker represents as being true. This includes the proposition that the speaker is, in saying what he says, intending to perform a certain act. In just the same way and for the same reason, one of the conditions necessary for my SERIOUSLY saying that ANYTHING is thus and so is that I BELIEVE it is so. In exactly the same way, if I say *It's a duck*, I give it to be understood (if I speak literally) that I think it is a duck, and if I am SERIOUS in so saying—that is, if I mean what I say[25]—then I do actually think that it is a duck.[26] Here, too, the

---

[25] One's seriously and literally uttering the sentence requires one's meaning what he says. But it also requires, where he does not say, but by CONVENTIONAL linguistic

meaning of the sentence I utter makes it the case that a certain thing is true — on the assumption that I speak seriously and literally. (If one is to hold that semantic rules 'constitute' an utterance a promise, one must be willing to say that it is the semantic rules governing *It's a duck* that constitute its utterance a veridical expression of belief.)

34 Let us say that an utterance of a suitable sentence, whether *I'll come* or *I promise I'll come*, has the force of a promise if[27] it is true that the speaker intends therein to be making a promise. On the constativist view, it is the condition that MAKES TRUE that proposition — that the speaker intends therein to be making a promise — that makes it the case that the utterance has the force of a promise. Thus, it may be the intention with which it is issued that makes it the case that an utterance has a given illocutionary force.[28] This accomplishes the theoretical desire (cf. §7) to hold that it is one and the same thing that determines the force of an utterance whether an ifid is employed or not. It does so while doing justice to the fact that sometimes (where an ifid is involved) the meaning of a sentence does determine the force of its literal serious utterance. For it does so BY determining that that intention (sufficient for the utterance to have that force) must be present. But where no ifid is present, it is just one's intention, not what he means, that determines the force of his utterance.

35 Whether the utterance intended to be a promise actually IS a promise is, of course, a matter of whether such other conditions as are necessary for having made a promise do in fact obtain. Again, this is so whether an ifid is employed or not. But if I DO say *I hereby promise that I'll come*, then in saying that I will come I have expressed the proposition that I am promising and, thus, have indicated that the conditions for its truth *do* obtain. It is, again, no CON-

---

means implies or presupposes or indicates ('implicates'), that *p*, that there, too, what the speaker gives his audience to understand about his believing, etc., that *p* should be true. Thus, if I say *I hereby warn you that, being a philosopher, John is dangerous*, and speak literally and seriously, I not only mean it, i.e., mean WHAT I SAY, sc., (a) that John is a philosopher — I also must believe what my statement PRESUPPOSES, (b), that John is a philosopher; and ALSO what I IMPLY, (c), (roughly) that philosophers are dangerous; and also that (d) I do in fact intend what I say AS I give it to be understood that it is intended, that is, as a warning, thus (e), that I believe you should beware of John. That I mean it, when I say this thing, does not entail the truth of (b) through (e), but only that (a) is true. The *it* in *mean it* refers to WHAT I SAY.

[26] Supposing that I know what I believe, as previously we supposed that the speaker knows what he intends to do.

[27] Provided that the required 'uptake' is forthcoming.

[28] This claim is subject to the caveats detailed in the footnote to §31.

VENTION that constitutes my utterance the making of a promise. Rather, what makes it a promise is just whatever states of affairs satisfy the truth conditions of the proposition that I am making a promise. And it is surely the fact that those SAME conditions obtain that constitute my saying just *I'll come* the making of a promise. The happenstance that in the former case I EXPRESS that proposition, by using the ifid *I hereby promise*, whereas in the latter case I do not express it, has no bearing whatever on the matter of what makes the two utterances promises. It is clear that we need postulate no convention nor constitutive rule to achieve a unified account of the matter. And so, we need postulate no unuttered ifid for that convention or rule to govern. What makes my utterance a promise is just what makes a certain proposition true: the proposition that I express, by the ifid, if I do employ one, and, if I do not employ an ifid, the proposition I expect to be understood to be true—i.e., in either case, the proposition that, in saying what I say, I am promising to do the thing I say I will do.

Explicit Performatives as Oratio Obliqua Sentences

36   A great virtue of the constativist view is its continuity with the general account of indirect speech, or oratio obliqua sentences. For, other things being equal, the better account will provide the same kind of view of oratio obliqua sentences in any PERSON, whether:

(1)   *John promised that he would come.*

or:

(2)   *I promised that I would come.*

and, further, in any TENSE, including the noncontinuous present, whether third person:

(3)   *John thereby promises that he will come.*[29]

or first person:

(4)   *I hereby promise that I will come.*

The constativist will point out that not only are (1) and (2) oratio obliqua sentences—expressing what someone said and the illocutionary act performed in so saying—but so, likewise, is (4), a first-person, noncontinuous-present-tense oratio obliqua sentence. In ut-

---

[29] A possible context for such a sentence: a radio announcer, covering an inaugural ceremony, as the oath is sworn in Latin.

tering (4), one says that he will come, and he indicates explicitly that in so saying he promises to come. The constativist will claim that the idiosyncrasies of sentences like (4) can be understood, predicted from the general semantic and logical principles required to account for oratio obliqua propositions in general.[30]

37 Regarded in this light, four main idiosyncrasies of explicit performative sentences—(i) through (iv)—are thrown into relief and made intelligible. Thus:

(i) *Whereas, in uttering (1), (2), or (3), the speaker does not therein say that someone will come, in uttering (4) he does say that someone (namely, he) will come.*

(ii) *Whereas, in uttering (1), (2), or (3), it is impossible that anyone should therein be making a promise, in uttering (4) it is possible that someone* (namely, the speaker) *is making a promise.*

Obviously, fact (ii) is a consequence of fact (i), on the premise that it is a necessary condition of someone's making a promise in uttering a sentence that in uttering it he should say that he will do some certain thing. Only in uttering (4) does the speaker do so. But why should (i) be the case? The explanation of that involves this third fact, that:

(iii) *Whereas in uttering (1), (2), or (3) the speaker is not therein indicating that a promise is thereby being made, he is so indicating when he utters (4).*

But then, since for a person to be promising that he will come he must be saying that he will come, this proposition (which the speaker indicates is true) will in fact be true only if the speaker is therein saying that he will come. (For it is by HIMSELF that the speaker of (4) indicates that a promise is being made.) But this proposition that he expresses MAY be true. If it is true, it is made true by the occurrence of those events, etc., that are necessary for its truth. One such event is that the person indicated should say that he will come. And further, the expression *hereby* serves to indicate that the events necessary for the truth of that proposition—i.e., for a promise to be being made—must occur IN, or by virtue of, the utterance of the sentence *I hereby promise that I will come.* So if that is true, i.e., that he THEREBY promises, then it must be the case that in uttering those words he is doing what that requires, sc., SAYING that he will come. Now that, so far, has to do just with the necessary conditions of the

[30] By the same token, accounts of oratio obliqua may be evaluated on their capacity to predict the facts about the explicit performative form.

truth of various propositions that the utterer of (4) expresses. What is to be explained—fact (i)—is specifically why the utterer of (4) therein SAYS that someone is coming, i.e., how it happens that it actually gets said that someone is coming.[31] Here one must keep in mind that it actually gets said only on the supposition that the speaker speaks literally and IS SERIOUS. It is evident that the conditions necessary for being serious when one utters sentence (4) are somehow sufficient for the truth of the proposition that the utterer says that he will come, just as the conditions necessary for being serious when one utters the sentence *I'll come* are evidently sufficient[32] for the truth of the proposition that the utterer says that he will come. The utterer of (4), again, expresses the proposition that he is making a promise, and if he is serious he must actually believe that he is making a promise and therefore must actually have such other beliefs and intentions, in uttering that sentence, as are necessary to believing that that is what he is doing. These constitute the beliefs and intentions sufficient for its being the case that he is saying that he is coming. And therefore, if he utters (4) seriously and literally, it is actually being said (by the speaker) that the speaker will come. Finally, there is this fact about explicit performatives:

(iv) *Whereas in uttering (1), (2) or (3) the speaker may report or assert or make the statement that someone promises to come, in uttering (4) he does not report, state, or assert that someone (he) promises to come.*

—even if (as I hold) he is INDICATING that someone (he) promises.

38   Throughout this, we hear crashing toward us through the bushes a veritable Frankenstein, the thesis that PERFORMATIVES HAVE NO TRUTH VALUE. How can the constativist maintain that what makes it the case that a promise has been made is that the truth conditions for *S has made a promise* have been satisfied, when the truth of this proposition has not been ASSERTED? But before meeting

---

[31] As Davidson, discussing this question, put it, the question is why it happens in such explicit performative sentences that the internal sentence *I will come* is not INSULATED from being asserted by its being embedded within the context *I hereby promise that . . .* , that being the usual effect of embedding a sentence in such a 'propositional attitude' context. (Davidson suggests that this is the major serious question that exercised Austin about performative utterances, although, as he also remarks, Austin never explicitly stated this problem.)

[32] I speak of these conditions abstractly here, without venturing to say more specifically what the required intentions and beliefs might be. On that question, see §54 and following.

Frankenstein face to face, it should be noted that the constativist has not needed to DENY that 'performatives have no truth value,' nor has he needed to maintain that the speaker of (4) SAID, much less asserted or reported, that he is promising to come. The view is that what determines the illocutionary force of his utterance to be that of a promise is that the truth conditions for that proposition are satisfied, not that the speaker has SAID that they are satisfied or that he has asserted that proposition. What the constativist has needed to hold is that in saying (4) a proposition is in SOME way expressed, that the speaker INDICATES, if he does not say, that that proposition is true, and that those conditions are satisfied, and he does this by what he says, given what the words mean.

The Truth Value of Performatives and the Performative Analysis

39   The question of whether performatives have truth value is important to the performative analysis for this reason: It is sometimes charged against that analysis that it cannot be correct, on common assumptions about the semantic properties of deep structure representation (cf. §14). For whereas *Grass is blue* has a truth value (FALSE), *I hereby say to you that grass is blue* has NO truth value, is NEITHER true NOR false. This is a typically performativist objection to the performative analysis. But the constativist view may also appear to present an insuperable difficulty, which, without putting a fine point on it, is this: *I hereby say to you that grass is blue* DOES have a truth value, since the speaker is indicating THAT HE SAYS that grass is blue. But THAT, i.e., that he says that grass is blue, is TRUE (or may be true). But then, *I hereby say to you that grass is blue* obviously has (or may have) a DIFFERENT truth value from the sentence *Grass is blue*. But if so, then the former sentence can hardly represent the meaning of the latter, for two sentences having the same meaning must have the same truth value, or express the same proposition. But then, IF representations of underlying syntactic representations are semantic representations, the sentence *I hereby say to you that grass is blue* cannot represent the underlying syntactic structure of *Grass is blue*. This constitutes a destructive dilemma for the performative analysis. Either (1) the sentence *I hereby say to you that grass is blue* does have a truth value or (2) it does not. If (1) it does have a truth value, it may have the value 'true.' But that is not the same as the truth value of *Grass is blue*. So the analysis is wrong. But suppose (2) that *I hereby say to you that grass is blue* does NOT have a truth value. Here again, it must differ in meaning from *Grass is*

blue, which DOES have a truth value. So the analysis is wrong. Therefore, either way, the analysis is wrong.

40 On this showing, so far as the performative analysis goes, it seems to matter not at all whether performatives do or do not have truth value. But there is a possible way out. To anticipate, the way out is to hold that what has truth value in the performative sentence is just the proposition expressed by the complement sentence, embedded to the ifid — that is, just the sentence from which the performative prefix may be deleted by the rule called performative deletion.

41 For consider. It is, of course, not properly a SENTENCE that has truth value, nor its utterance, but rather, something one says, or more generally, some proposition one expresses, when he utters a sentence. So to decide the question of whether performatives have truth value we must first decide whether, in uttering sentences of the form *I hereby* VERB$_{illoc}$ + C (where C is the complement construction), one is either saying that something is so or otherwise appropriately expressing a proposition: that is, whether there IS anything APPROPRIATELY ASSOCIATED[33] with such an utterance, which is properly subject to the predicates 'true' and 'false.'

Austin on the Truth of Performatives

42 Austin (1961) introduces his performative utterances as '. . . a kind of utterance which looks like a statement and grammatically, I suppose, would be classed as a statement, which is not nonsensical, and yet *is not true or false* [italics added].' and '. . . couldn't possibly be true or false'; and shortly he says that

> (A) . . . if a person makes an utterance of this sort we should say that he is doing something, rather than merely *saying* something [p. 222].

Now, this last statement, I think, serves as one REASON people think performatives are not or even cannot be true or false. And it plainly

---

[33] This is tricky, for all parties would agree that there are several propositions, variously associated with the utterance of the sentence, that are certainly either true or false, and these include certain IMPLICATIONS of one's uttering that sentence. Thus, the performativist may freely agree that when I utter the sentence *I hereby order you to take out that machine gun nest,* there are various implications of my so saying — e.g., that I think that you could possibly do that thing (perhaps) or that I am your commanding officer — which are either true or false; and there are certain presuppositions of what I say — e.g., that there is a machine gun nest to take out — that are true or false. But he will plausibly insist that that does not suffice to make the 'performative' true. (But we must ask, what is it that is not true or false?)

is not a good reason. For it is far from obvious why the fact that in uttering a sentence I am DOING something should be opposed in this way to my having SAID something. These are not, on the face of it, incompatible things. It may well be the case, and obviously often is the case, that it is precisely by saying something, even saying that something is so, that I do what I do. Indeed, so far from saying and doing being opposed, it is perfectly clear that in order to do some things one MUST say that something is so. For instance, in order to make a statement, one must say that something is so, and in order to make a promise, to perform that act, one must say that he will do something—though the text shows that Austin was not (yet) thinking of such 'illocutionary verbs' as these.

43 Sentences like (A), or (regarding my utterance *I promise that I will be there*) such as:

(5)   *I am not saying that I will be there, I am
        promising that I will be there.*

(6)   *I am not saying that I promise, I am making
        the promise.*

are sentences of a kind (Fillmore suggests calling them REJECTED-ALTERNATIVE SENTENCES) that must be handled with some caution in arguing philosophical issues. For some such sentences, e.g.:

(7)   *It's not a house, it's a mansion.*

do not express the proposition they seem superficially to express, i.e., the proposition that a certain thing is NOT TRUE. Thus, (7) does not mean, or at least what is meant is not, that it is false that the structure in question is a house. What is meant is that it is not MERELY a house but is FURTHERMORE a mansion: though it is, of course, a house.[34] We can conclude little from the fact that (A) sentences like (5) and (6) have their point, or even from the claim that what they say is true (it being unclear what exactly they do say). Thus, we cannot conclude from (A) that it is false that (in making an utterance of the performative sort) the speaker is SAYING something; or from (5) that it is false that I am saying that I will be there; or from (6) that it is false that I am saying that I promise. For all we know so far, (A), (5) and (6) may be like (7) in this respect, even to the point that, far from the speak-

[34] The example if Lehrer's (1968), who makes this same point in arguing that the instance of such remarks as *I don't believe it, I know it* does not refute the thesis that knowing that *p* entails believing that *p*. (The trouble with Lehrer's argument is that he does not consider the possibility that this sentence is like (8), and he has no argument that it is not.)

er's meaning that these things are false, it is actually an implication of what he does say, that they should be true. But let me add a cautionary note: By the same token, these sentences may be unlike (7) and, instead, like:

(8)   *I am not just **guessing** that she's married,*
             *I **know** that she is*

which DOES imply that it is false that I am guessing that she is married, since if I know it, it cannot be the case that I am guessing that it is so. So the issue is simply not to be decided thus by consideration of 'what we would say' as this is evidenced by rejected-alternative sentences.

44   Austin (1962) introduces the notion of a performative utterance with these four examples:

(9)   a. *I do* (sc., take this women to be my
                lawful wedded wife).
         b. *I name this ship the Queen Elizabeth.*
         c. *I give and bequeath my watch to my brother.*
         d. *I bet you sixpence it will rain tomorrow.* [5]

of which he says, 'None of these utterances cited is either true or false: I assert this as obvious and do not argue it. It needs argument no more than that "damn" is not true or false . . . [p. 6].' Now, of these sentences only (9d) has a SENTENTIAL COMPLEMENT. This is important. For whether one who says something of the form *I (hereby) Verb + C* has therein SAID that something is so depends upon the nature of the complement *C* and, further, on the particular verb it complements.[35] Now, in (9b), it does seem very doubtful whether the speaker said either that the ship was thereby named the Queen Elizabeth or that it was to be called the Q.E. And it seems that there is nothing here that might BE true or false. But in (9c), does the speaker not say that his watch is bequeathed to his brother, that he gives his watch to his brother, or anyway (surely this), that his brother IS TO HAVE his watch? And it does seem to me that this last can be said to be 'true': If the will is properly drawn, etc., his brother is to have his watch, and further, his watch is bequeathed to, given to his brother. Now, granted, the speaker is not saying that these things ARE TRUE: He is not in that way asserting the truth of propositions or reporting facts. Austin often emphasizes this last point, but it is not a

---

[35] Thus, in (9*a*) the verb is not a speech act verb at all. The speaker cannot, I think, be held to have said that he 'does' take this woman (or 'did'?); but did he not say that he takes this woman to be his lawful wedded wife? Perhaps not.

telling one. Thus, when he says of his performatives that ' . . . they do not "describe" or "report" or constate anything at all, are not "true or false" [1962:5],' he is running two things together. For certainly the man does not 'report' that his watch is to go to his brother, as if the fact that it is to go to his brother were there to be reported upon 'prior' to his utterance.[36] But this is quite consistent with his having SAID that it is to go to his brother. When, having forgotten what he had said about the watch, we again consult the will and find that it is to go to brother Harry, do we not find that it is so precisely because the departed SAID that the watch is to go to his brother? He did not say that that was true, of course, and indeed, it is the fact that he said what he said, in the circumstances, that makes what he said 'true.'[37]

45 If this is a bit hard, or doubtful, it is clearer as we approach the central illocutionary acts of Austin's later theory. This we begin to do already in (9d), where the sentence consists of a SENTENCE embedded to an illocutionary-force-indicating device. Sometimes, at least, the utterer of that sentence does SAY THAT it will rain tomorrow, and what he said may be true — or false, as I will point out when I come around to collect. But leaving behind even betting, which is a tricky case, we come here to the mass of illocutionary verbs. These are verbs that will form oratio obliqua sentences [cf. the verbs of (9a), (9b), and (9c) which will not do so], taking as complements SENTENCES transformationally related to the sentence uttered by the person referred to by the subject of the verb. Thus:

(10) $\begin{Bmatrix} I \\ John \end{Bmatrix}$ promised (announced, claimed, warned, insisted,

objected, etc.) that $\begin{Bmatrix} I \\ he \end{Bmatrix}$ would come.

It is plainly a necessary condition of the truth of these that the sub-

[36] Austin himself might have made this criticism retrospectively, from the standpoint of his later doctrine of illocutions. For *reporting* and *stating* are themselves names of specific illocutionary acts, different from one another and requiring for their performance that certain specific conditions obtain in *addition* to the speaker's performing what Austin called the locutionary act of saying that something is so. So the fact that one who says *I promise* or *I request* does not report that he promises or requests is quite consistent with the position that he does say that he promises or requests. And however that may be, the reason he is not reporting or stating may be this: What one reports or states is, if what one says be true, a fact that enters into the causal explanation of his uttering that sentence. Whether this conjecture about reports and statements is correct or not remains to be seen. But clearly, performatives are not related causally to facts in that 'direction.' For the idea of a performative is the idea of an utterance causes the fact to obtain that would make what the speaker says true.

[37] Compare my remarks on orders in §61.

ject should have SAID that he would come. Similarly, the truth conditions of:

(11) $\begin{Bmatrix} I \\ John \\ You \end{Bmatrix} \begin{Bmatrix} asked \\ wondered \ aloud \\ inquired \end{Bmatrix}$ whether Joe was alive.

require that the subject should have ASKED whether Joe was alive. And the truth conditions of:

(12) $\begin{Bmatrix} I \\ John \\ You \end{Bmatrix} \begin{Bmatrix} \begin{Bmatrix} insisted \ that \\ demanded \ that \end{Bmatrix} Joe \ was \ to \ come. \\ \\ \begin{Bmatrix} commanded \\ ordered \\ told \end{Bmatrix} Joe \ to \ come. \end{Bmatrix}$

require that the subject should have SAID THAT Joe was to come. So far, this is quite clear and in no way controversial. There remains only the explicit performative form, the first-person, noncontinuous present indicative (active or passive, singular or plural), *I hereby promise that I will come.* When I utter this sentence seriously and literally, I am certainly saying that I will come; and thus, I do certainly say SOMETHING that is either true or false.[38]

46   Now, if *I hereby promise that I will come* is a 'performative utterance,' then there are, indisputably, performative utterances in the issuing of which something is said, and that, i.e., WHAT IS SAID, may certainly have a truth value. If this leaves it unclear whether performative utterances have truth value or not, that is only because the meaning of the claim either that they do or that they do not is simply too unclear to pronounce it true or false. The foregoing sections have emphasized that it is principally what is said that is evaluable as to truth, and that if something is said, then the presumption of truth is to be made, and truth conditions are variously invoked. To recognize that something is being said, and what is being said, requires going beneath the superficial form of the uttered sentence. In particular, a speaker may SAY something, in the sense invoking considerations of truth, by uttering sentences of moods other than indicative.[39]

---

[38] Austin's later doctrine agrees in this, for the performance of an illocutionary act requires the performance of a 'locutionary' act, i.e., an act of saying something 'in the full normal sense' thereof, consisting in the performance of a 'rhetic' act, reported in oratio obliqua sentences (1962:96).

[39] The presumption of truth may be stated in its most general form in this way: It is presumed that a speaker will see to it that what he says shall be true. One can readily

47   The thrust of these remarks is clearly contrary to the views associated with the slogan that performatives lack truth value. In particular, it is contrary to a leading theme of Austin's, that truth is merely one among many evaluative concepts applicable to speech acts, and that, as such, truth has been the subject of a wrong-headed obsession among philosophers. The general doctrine of 'infelicities' was Austin's prescription against the obsession. But the diagnosis is wrong, and consequently, the doctrine of infelicities, while diverting indeed, is a fruitless diversion.

The Performative Analysis: Last Remarks

48   I shall now go back to the dilemma posed against the performative analysis in §39, and the suggestion made in §40. The suggestion is that one who says something of the form *I hereby Verb + Sentence* does, indeed, say something true or false—provided that, had he uttered just the complement *Sentence*, he would have said something true or false; and WHAT he says when he utters the 'performative' sentence is precisely what he would have said had he uttered just the complement *Sentence*. (Therefore, the deletion of the performative prefix does not alter the truth value of what is being said.)

49   Now, if that were the only thing the utterer says, or the only proposition otherwise 'appropriately associated' with, or expressed in, the utterance of the sentence *I hereby say to you that grass is blue*, then the performative analyst would be home free. (For then the only truth value relevantly associated with that sentence would be the same as that—sc., 'false'—associated with the sentence *Grass is blue*, which allegedly has the same deep structure.) But we must consider whether the objection I raised against Thesis *J* does not also defeat the performative analysis, where that analysis is wedded first to the thesis that transformations preserve meaning. Now, if that requires two sentences having the same deep structure to have the same meaning (and it is not OBVIOUS that it should require that; cf.

---

see that there are various possible ways in which this presumption may be satisfied. The speaker may, of course, conform what he says to the facts, as he expected to do in reporting or stating that something is the case. But, equally well, he may conform the facts to what he says, ensuring that what he has said shall have been true. This is what he is expected to do, and what he gives it to be understood that he will do, if he is making a vow or a promise or an offer to do something. And finally, should he say that someone else is to do something or will do it, therein issuing an order or a threat, he gives it to be understood that he will see to it, or more generally, that there is sufficient reason to believe, that what he says will be made true by the addressee's conforming the facts to what he has said.

Partee, 1971: pf 4 *et passim*), then the trouble is still with us. For again, surely it is part of the meaning of the sentence *I hereby say to you that grass is blue* that the speaker is, in saying *grass is blue*, saying to the addressee that grass is blue. And, equally surely, this is no part of the meaning of the sentence *Grass is blue*. So the two sentences do mean something different. Once again, to make this observation, we need not hold that, in uttering the former sentence, what I am SAYING is that I am saying that grass is blue. But I do MEAN by what I say that I am (actually) saying that grass is blue; but if I say just that grass is blue, I do not mean that I am saying that grass is blue. So clearly, the truth values of the propositions I express owing to the meaning of the sentence I utter differ, or may differ, between the two cases.

50   If the thesis that transformations preserve meaning requires something less than full synonymy to obtain between sentences assigned the same deep structures, then the issue is not settled by this.[40] In particular, if it should suffice that the two sentences should be identical with respect to what one SAYS, in a strict sense thereof, there is hope left. Moreover, it should be noticed that, in deleting the performative clause, there is in a sense no loss of INFORMATION, given the presumption that the speaker is speaking literally and seriously. For to presume that is to presume that when someone says *Grass is blue* he is therein (actually) saying that grass is blue. Of course, there is no easy identification of meaning with information. (And against this it may be argued that the information conveyed by the use of such a performative preface is just that one IS speaking seriously and literally in saying what he says.)

51   Consider, finally, the thesis that the deep structure of a sentence constitutes a 'semantic representation' of that sentence, the 'generative semanticist' position. It seems to me clear that the fact that performative deletion alters meaning is NOT inconsistent with this thesis, taken on its face. For such a thesis, I think, cannot be refuted by the fact that two sentences allegedly having the same deep structure do not have the same meaning. In saying this, I am simply taking seriously the notion of a 'representation.' For repre-

---

[40] The version of the claim that Partee (1971) 'tends toward' will, however, not do for these purposes: 'All those parts of meaning that have to do with truth-value (in all possible worlds) are determined at the deep structure level and preserved by transformational rules; what can change in the course of a transformational derivation are just those subtler aspects of "meaning" which are suggested by such terms as "topicalization." "focus/presupposition" . . . ,' etc. The difference in meaning upon which I have insisted DOES affect truth value; but the issue outstanding is this: Exactly what is it that transformations do not affect the truth value OF?

sentations by their nature involve trading distortions in one respect for perspicuity in another—as a Mercator projection provides a plane representation of the surface of a sphere at the cost of distorted representations of areas removed from the equator. It should therefore not be surprising that a representation perspicuously representing the syntactic categorization and relations of the constituents of sentences should—perhaps as a consequence of that gain in perspicuity—constitute a somewhat distorted representation of the semantic content of those sentences. This might well be the case even while there IS a relation between the syntactic and semantic facts of a sentence that makes it true that a theoretical representation of the one necessarily represents the other.

SAYING AND ILLOCUTIONARY ACTS

52   In §44, I remarked that whether one who says something of the form *I (hereby) Verb + C* has therein said that something is so (therein producing something evaluable for truth) depends upon the character of the COMPLEMENT, *C*. This fact suggests that:

(G) *Whenever one seriously utters a sentence of the form I (hereby) Verb$_{illoc}$ + Sentence$_{indicative}$, one is thereby saying that p, where p represents an appropriate form of the complement sentence of that construction.*

This generalization holds true for *warn, state, promise, assert, maintain, insist, repeat, affirm, answer, testify, report, swear, announce, claim,* and other illocutionary verbs. But it fails for at least these:

1. *grant, concede, acknowledge*—i.e., something someone ELSE is saying;

2. *deny*—where what the speaker says is, of course, that *p* is false;

3. *suggest*—where what the speaker says is that it MAY be true that *p*, not that it *is* true.

These facts show that whether the speaker says that something is so, and WHAT he says, is a function also of the particular illocutionary VERB involved.

53   This stands to reason on the constativist approach to the matter, on which the preface *I hereby Verb* functions to indicate that the speaker is, in the utterance of the sentence, performing the act of *Verb*-ing and, thus, to indicate that the truth conditions of that proposition are satisfied. Whether the speaker will have said that something is so will then depend on the specific truth conditions of the proposition that the speaker is (thereby) performing that act. (Thus, that S *stated that p* entails that S *said that p;* but that S *suggested that Nixon planned it himself* does not entail that S *said that Nixon planned it himself.*) Consideration of such facts as these furnish evidence bearing in one direction on the question, What is it to perform some certain illocutionary act? and also, in the other direction, on the question, What is it to say (or mean) that something is so? Investigation works back and forth between the two theoretical concerns, within the developing framework of the total theory of language.

54 Thus, to revert to (G), the conditions under which it fails are instructive as to the nature of SAYING that something is so. For (G) seems to fail when one's sincerely uttering a sentence of the relevant form is NOT understood as his representing himself as being (let us say tentatively) CONFIDENT that p is the case. Schematically, it suggests this hypothesis:

(H) *A person* **says** *that p only if he utters something therein giving it to be understood that he stands in a certain cognitive state,* **K,** *with respect to the proposition that p.*

The question may then be pursued, What cognitive state or state might K denote?

55 By way primarily of illustrating this pursuit, we may continue to reason as follows. It seems clear that K is something more than BELIEF (that p is the case). For if I am asked who planned the burglary and I merely BELIEVE Nixon planned it, I am not in a position to SAY that Nixon planned it. Something constrains me to say not that but that I BELIEVE Nixon did it or (if my belief is based on inconclusive evidence), to say that Nixon PROBABLY planned it or (though this is different still), to say that he MAY have done it. This would be explained on the view that in saying that p I am giving it to be understood that I am CERTAIN that p — i.e., that K = certainty — or equally well on the hypothesis that I give it to be believed that I know that p — that K = knowledge.

56 Now, working up the other way, we may test such hypotheses against the evidence afforded by conditions required for the performance of various illocutionary acts. Consider, first, the evidence provided by SUGGESTING. When I say *I suggest that Nixon planned it himself,* I have not SAID that Nixon planned it himself. Conversely, if I wish to SUGGEST that Nixon did it, I must stop short of SAYING that he did it. Therefore, if the suggestion is to be made without the use of the explicit ifid, it cannot be done clearly and felicitously by uttering the sentence *Nixon planned it himself.* I must say, instead,

Maybe Nixon planned it himself if I am properly to have expressed myself in making the suggestion. How is this to be explained? If we embrace (H) and let *K* be certainty, or knowledge, then we may proceed as follows: The act of suggesting that something is so is an act of such a nature that in performing it one does NOT give it to be understood that he is certain (or that he knows) that *p*. And it is owing to that fact about the nature of the act of making a suggestion, that one cannot felicitously perform such an act by saying that *p* — on the indicated interpretations of the hypothesis *H*.[41]

57   This illustrates the way I think we should proceed. Notice the 'blank' reference to the nature of the act of making a suggestion — it is an act of such a nature that such and such is true. This is not yet to say what the nature of that act IS, but it gives us something to go on. Our hypothesis about the nature of a thing has got to explain its phenomenal characteristics — such as the possibility of a given performance of the act taking various forms, consisting in the utterance of sentences of various descriptions. Analogously, water occurs in various forms, i.e., solid, liquid, or gaseous, under various conditions; our hypothesis about the nature of water — that it is H_2O — explains these phenomena. Similarly, a suggestion can be variously expressed under various conditions in various environments. Such facts can tell us what it is to make a suggestion, if we attempt to understand those facts in terms of the specific nature of the act.

58   For instance, we may suppose that, like other speech acts, the act of making a suggestion is one way in which a certain thing may be done by the means of speech.[42] It is, on one conjecture, one way of — one tactic for — getting people to consider something AS BEING A

[41] Why is it that I can suggest that *p* by saying *I suggest that p* but not by saying *p*? Why do I not HAVE to say *I suggest that maybe p*? Evidently, the higher verb *suggest* determines the modality of the lower or complement sentence *p*. Only sentences with *may be* in their structure can be embedded to the verb *suggest*. Sentences like °*I suggest that he is schizophrenic, and I know that for a fact* are out. And sentences like *I suggest that he is definitely (obviously) schizophrenic* must be construed as suggesting that it MAY BE the case that he is definitely schizophrenic, or that it MAY be obvious that he is so.

[42] For a full-dress treatment of a particular speech act within this framework of investigating the distinctive strategies underlying various speech acts, and also other aspects of the case against conventionalism, see Stampe (forthcoming). (In that work, the various characteristics of or conditions for making a promise that Searle construes as conditions for the proper use of the ifid *Pr* are shown to be consequences of, or conditions for, the utilization of that strategy for causing belief that is called promising. For instance, I explain there why you cannot promise to punch me in the mouth — but can threaten to do so — without appealing to a 'rule' to the effect that one can promise only what the promisee would like to have done.)

(Continued on page 36)

POSSIBILITY. One cannot do this by giving it to be believed that one is certain that p or that one knows that p. For if the hearer accepts that—that the speaker knows that p—then he believes that p is an actual fact and therefore cannot consider it as being a possibility. This, again, would explain why one cannot suggest that p by saying that p, on the hypothesis that K is knowledge or certainty.

59 This conception of the way to do speech act theory, I must emphasize, is entirely contrary to the program of research that might be associated with Searle's account of speech acts. It will not be enlightening to say that there is some RULE governing the illocutionary-force-indicating device involved in making a suggestion, which applies to both *I hereby suggest that* p and *Maybe* p, but not to p, constituting their utterance the making of a suggestion. These phenomena are no more arbitrary, no more a matter of convention, than the fact that both ice and steam constitute forms of the substance water. In either case there is a REASON for it, which lies in the specific underlying nature of the substance, or the act.[43]

60 To repair to those illocutionary verbs discussed in §47, which conform to (G)—that is, those such that when one says *I hereby Verb that* p one has SAID that p—this fact, too, is to be understood as a function of what it is to perform these various acts. That is, I expect

---

My view of this matter is connected with a general conception of the semantics of common nouns (including *promise, suggestion*, etc.) as NAMES of KINDS of things (or acts). In this view the extension of the term is not fixed by its 'meaning,' or by any semantic rule, but rather, through the concept of a KIND of thing, by taxonomic principles essentially independent of linguistic or semantic considerations (see Stampe, 1972).

[43] And the reason is NOT that the two sentences have the same meaning. They clearly do not have the same meaning. The correct account is, rather, that the meaning of *I suggest that* p is such that the best explanation of its being uttered is that the speaker intends to be making a suggestion, and that is one possible explanation of the utterance of *Maybe* p, given what THAT means. (Of course, it is not the only one: The speaker may instead be making a concession.) The problem raised for the semantic rule account in §27 presents no difficulty for the view I advocate. The meanings of the phrases *Scout's honor, You have my word*, and *You can count on it* are all different, and different from that of *I promise*. But in each case the meaning is such that their utterance invites the inference that the speaker, in saying what he says, is making a promise. There is no evident reason to suppose that we must cite a CONVENTION relating these phrases to the act of promising to account for these inferences. (It may be argued that *you have my word for it* and *so help me God* are IDIOMS, and that a special convention IS required to interpret these particular phrases. This is certainly true for SOME ifids. But it is not true for all of them by any means, so the general point is not affected.)

such acts to constitute ways of doing various specific things in specific ways, all of which require for one or another reason (as part of the several strategies, as it were) that the speaker should give it to believed that he knows or is certain that something is the case. For instance, issuing a person a warning that p—which may be done by saying p—is a strategy for bringing it about that that person is warned that p, i.e., is made aware of a certain danger associated with a certain fact. This may be done by bringing it about that he KNOWS that p, provided that he knows that there are dangers associated with that fact. What is it about the act of saying that p that explains the fact that one can issue a warning by saying that p? Evidently, by saying that p, one can bring it about that a person knows that p. This is explainable on the hypothesis that K is knowledge; for if he will believe that you know that p, and you do know it, then under certain conditions that knowledge will a fortiori be imparted to him.[44]

61 Consider requests and orders. I can issue an order by saying either *Do x!* (imperious intonation) or *You will do x* (e.g., *You will proceed to the depot and blow up the ammunition stores*), but NOT by saying *Will you please do x?* or *If you don't mind, do x.*[45] The latter two sentences can be used to make a request, while the former two cannot be. Requesting and ordering represent specific distinct tactics for accomplishing the same end, the purpose of getting someone to do something. To this end, the request appeals to and depends upon the hearer's willingness to accommodate the speaker: It is represented as left to him to determine whether he will do the

---

[44] On the possibility of bringing it about that someone knows that p by saying that p, see Stampe (to appear).

[45] If I am a general and you are a private, my saying *If you don't mind, do x* or *Would you mind doing x?* may be equivalent in force to the issuance of an order and may count as the issuance of an order. (This is surely not ACTUALLY the case, but never mind.) But again, while what I may say may be IN EFFECT an order, that is precisely NOT to say that it is an order in point of actual fact. Notice, in this connection, that we should NOT say that in saying *It's cold in here* the master has ordered OR requested his butler to close the window. To say that the utterance has the force of, i.e., is in effect, an order, is just to say that it has the same consequences, in the circumstances, as an order would have. (This is a perfectly straightforward state of affairs, and it can only be obscured by talk of, e.g., the utterance 'conveying a request.' A fairly reliable test of the request-making potential of a sentence is its capacity to accept modification by *please*. For instance, we cannot have °*It's cold in here, please*, whereas we do have *Shut the window, please*, *Would you mind shutting the window, please?*, and perhaps *How would you like to shut the window, please*, as well as indicatives (*I'd like that window shut, please*) and optatives (*Oh, please, to have that window shut!*).

thing or not. Thus, he is not to understand that he MUST do it. If this is correct, it follows that the speaker will not proceed on this strategy to give the hearer to understand that he KNOWS or is certain that the hearer will do the thing that he wants him to do. For that would not be leaving it to him to decide. And so, if saying that p — that something is to be so — is giving it to be understood that one knows or is certain that p (that is, if K is knowledge or certainty), we have explained why one does not make a request by saying something is, or is to be the case.[46] But an order, unlike a request, is a strategy predicated on the premise that the hearer MUST do what the speaker indicates that he wants him to do. Therefore, an order may be given by saying *You will do x:* For the hearer MUST do x, i.e., must make what the speaker says true. Now, even this is consistent with the hypothesis that in saying that p the speaker gives it to be believed that he knows or is certain that p. Consequently, too, when the speaker says *Do x*, therein issuing an order, the speaker is saying that the hearer will do, or is to do, x. But if he is issuing a request, he has not said that the hearer is to do x.

REFERENCES

Austin, J. *How to do things with words.* New York and London: Oxford University Press, 1962.

Austin, J. Performative utterances. In *Philosophical papers.* New York and London: Oxford University Press, 1961.

Cohen, L. J. Do illocutionary forces exist? *Philosophical Quarterly,* 1964, **14** (55).

Lehrer, K. Belief and knowledge. *The Philosophical Review,* 1968, **77** (4).

[46] Notice that he will not have said that you are to pass the salt, even if he requests the salt with the imploringly intoned sentence *Pass the salt.* Perhaps to make a request one must represent himself as NOT knowing whether the hearer would mind shutting the window and, thus, not knowing whether he will or will not shut the window; for if he knows, it is determined that he will (or will not) do it and therefore cannot be up to the hearer himself to determine as he wishes. This is perhaps why questions are good for making requests (*Will you shut the window?*). Notice here, also, that the conditional *If you don't mind, shut that door behind you* is only AP-PARENTLY a conditional imperative, saying that you are to shut that door if the antecedent condition is satisfied. Certainly, if one intends to be making a request it may not be interpreted in that way. It is interesting that in fact many of what pose as such antecedents cannot be interpreted in that way. For IS there a state of affairs that consists in your not minding shutting the door, or its not being too much trouble for you to shut the door, to be assessed apart from and independently of the suggestion that, e.g., you might accommodate someone's desire to have it shut? Contrast *If there's any beer in the cooler, bring me one*, which could be an order. But I doubt whether *If you don't mind, do x* CAN be interpreted as a conditional ORDER.

McCawley, J. The role of semantics in a grammar. In E. Bach and R. Harms (Eds.), *Universals in linguistic theory*. New York: Holt, 1968.

Partee, B. H. On the requirement that transformations preserve meaning. In C. J. Fillmore and D. T. Langendoen (Eds.), *Studies in linguistic semantics*. New York: Holt, 1971.

Ross, J. R. On declarative sentences. In R. A. Jacobs and P. S. Rosenbaum (Eds.), *Readings in English transformational grammar*. Waltham, Mass.: Ginn, 1970.

Schreiber, P. A. Style disjuncts and the performative analysis. *Linguistic Inquiry*, 1972, 3 (3).

Searle, J. Austin on locutionary and illocutionary acts. *The Philosophical Review*, 1968, 77 (4).

Searle, J. *Speech acts*. New York and London: Cambridge University Press, 1969.

Stampe, D. W. Making promises. Unpublished manuscript, forthcoming.

Stampe, D. W. On the meaning of nouns. In D. Cohen (Ed.), *On limiting the domain of linguistics*. University of Wisconsin at Milwaukee Symposium I, 1972.

Stampe, D. W. Show and tell. In *Forms of representation*. Proceedings of the 1972 University of Western Ontario Colloquium, to appear.

Stampe, D. W. Toward a grammar of meaning. *The Philosophical Review*, 1968, 77 (2).

LOGIC AND CONVERSATION*

H. P. GRICE
University of California, Berkeley

It is a commonplace of philosophical logic that there are, or appear to be, divergences in meaning between, on the one hand, at least some of what I shall call the FORMAL devices— $\sim$, $\wedge$, $\vee$, $\supset$, (x), $\exists(x)$, $\int x$ (when these are given a standard two-valued interpretation)—and, on the other, what are taken to be their analogs or counterparts in natural language—such expressions as *not, and, or, if, all, some* (or *at least one*), *the*. Some logicians may at some time have wanted to claim that there are in fact no such divergences; but such claims, if made at all, have been somewhat rashly made, and those suspected of making them have been subjected to some pretty rough handling.

Those who concede that such divergences exist adhere, in the main, to one or the other of two rival groups, which for the purposes of this article I shall call the formalist and the informalist groups. An outline of a not uncharacteristic formalist position may be given as follows: Insofar as logicians are concerned with the formulation of very general patterns of valid inference, the formal devices possess a decisive advantage over their natural counterparts. For it will be possible to construct in terms of the formal devices a system of very general formulas, a considerable number of which can be regarded as, or are closely related to, patterns of inferences the expression of which involves some or all of the devices: Such a system may consist of a

* Used by permission of the author and publisher from H. Paul Grice's William James Lectures, delivered at Harvard University in 1967, and to be published by Harvard University Press. Copyright 1975 by H. Paul Grice.

41

certain set of simple formulas that must be acceptable if the devices have the meaning that has been assigned to them, and an indefinite number of further formulas, many of them less obviously acceptable, each of which can be shown to be acceptable if the members of the original set are acceptable. We have, thus, a way of handling dubiously acceptable patterns of inference, and if, as is sometimes possible, we apply a decision procedure, we have an even better way. Furthermore, from a philosophical point of view, the possession by the natural counterparts of those elements in their meaning, which they do not share with the corresponding formal devices, is to be regarded as an imperfection of natural languages; the elements in question are undesirable excrescences. For the presence of these elements has the result that the concepts within which they appear cannot be precisely/clearly defined, and that at least some statements involving them cannot, in some circumstances, be assigned a definite truth value; and the indefiniteness of these concepts is not only objectionable in itself but leaves open the way to metaphysics—we cannot be certain that none of these natural language expressions is metaphysically 'loaded'. For these reasons, the expressions, as used in natural speech, cannot be regarded as finally acceptable, and may turn out to be, finally, not fully intelligible. The proper course is to conceive and begin to construct an ideal language, incorporating the formal devices, the sentences of which will be clear, determinate in truth value, and certifiably free from metaphysical implications; the foundations of science will now be philosophically secure, since the statements of the scientist will be expressible (though not necessarily actually expressed) within this ideal language. (I do not wish to suggest that all formalists would accept the whole of this outline, but I think that all would accept at least some part of it.)

To this, an informalist might reply in the following vein. The philosophical demand for an ideal language rests on certain assumptions that should not be conceded; these are, that the primary yardstick by which to judge the adequacy of a language is its ability to serve the needs of science, that an expression cannot be guaranteed as fully intelligible unless an explication or analysis of its meaning has been provided, and that every explication or analysis must take the form of a precise definition that is the expression/assertion of a logical equivalence. Language serves many important purposes besides those of scientific inquiry; we can know perfectly well what an expression means (and so a fortiori that it is intelligible) without knowing its analysis, and the provision of an analysis may (and usually does) consist in the specification, as generalized as possible, of the conditions that count for or against the applicability of the expression being analyzed. Moreover, while it is no doubt true that the formal devices are especially amenable to systematic treatment by the logician, it remains the case that there are very many inferences and arguments, expressed in natural language and not in terms of these devices, that are nevertheless recognizably valid. So there must be a place for an unsimplified, and so more or less unsystematic, logic of the natural counterparts of these devices; this logic may be aided and guided by the simplified logic of the formal devices but cannot be supplanted by it; indeed, not only do the two logics differ, but sometimes they come into conflict; rules that hold for a formal device may not hold for its natural counterpart.

Now, on the general question of the place in philosophy of the reformation of natural language, I shall, in this article, have nothing to say. I shall confine myself to the dispute in its relation to the alleged divergences mentioned at the outset. I have, moreover, no intention of entering the fray on behalf of either contestant. I wish, rather, to maintain that the common assumption of the contestants that the divergences do in fact exist is (broadly speaking) a common mistake, and that the mistake arises from an inadequate attention to the nature and importance of the conditions governing conversation. I shall, therefore, proceed at once to inquire into the general conditions that, in one way or another, apply to conversation as such, irrespective of its subject matter.

IMPLICATURE

Suppose that A and B are talking about a mutual friend, C, who is now working in a bank. A asks B how C is getting on in his job, and B replies, *Oh quite well, I think; he likes his colleagues, and he hasn't been to prison yet.* At this point, A might well inquire what B was implying, what he was suggesting, or even what he meant by saying that C had not yet been to prison. The answer might be any one of such things as that C is the sort of person likely to yield to the temptation provided by his occupation, that C's colleagues are really very unpleasant and treacherous people, and so forth. It might, of course, be quite unnecessary for A to make such an inquiry of B, the answer to it being, in the context, clear in advance. I think it is clear that whatever B implied, suggested, meant, etc., in this example, is distinct from what B said, which was simply that C had not been to prison yet. I wish to introduce, as terms of art, the verb *implicate* and the related nouns *implicature* (cf. *implying*) and *implicatum* (cf. *what is implied*). The point of this maneuver is to avoid having, on each occasion, to choose between this or that member of the family of verbs for which *implicate* is to do general duty. I shall, for the time being at least, have to assume to a considerable extent an intuitive understanding of the meaning of *say* in such contexts, and an ability to recognize particular verbs as members of the family with which *implicate* is associated. I can, however, make one or two remarks that may help to clarify the more problematic of these assumptions, namely, that connected with the meaning of the word *say*.

In the sense in which I am using the word *say*, I intend what someone has said to be closely related to the conventional meaning of the words (the sentence) he has uttered. Suppose someone to have uttered the sentence *He is in the grip of a vice.* Given a knowledge of the English language, but no knowledge of the circumstances of the utterance, one would know something about what the speaker had said, on the assumption that he was speaking standard English, and speaking literally. One would know that he had said, about some particular male person or animal x, that at the time of the utterance (whatever that was), either (1) x was unable to rid himself of a certain kind of bad character trait or (2) some part of x's person was caught in a certain kind of tool or instrument (approximate account, of course). But for a full identification of what the speaker had said, one would need to know (a) the identity of x, (b) the time of utterance, and (c) the meaning, on the particular occasion of utterance, of the phrase *in the grip of a vice* [a decision between (1) and (2)]. This brief indication of my use of *say* leaves it open whether a man who says (today) *Harold Wilson is a great man* and another who says (also today) *The British Prime Minister is a great man* would, if each knew that the two singular terms had the same reference, have said the same thing. But whatever decision is made about this question, the apparatus that I am about to provide will be capable of accounting for any implicatures that might depend on the presence of one rather than another of these singular terms in the sentence uttered. Such implicatures would merely be related to different maxims.

In some cases the conventional meaning of the words used will determine what is implicated, besides helping to determine what is said. If I say (smugly), *He is an Englishman; he is, therefore, brave,* I have certainly committed myself, by virtue of the meaning of my words, to its being the case that his being brave is a consequence of (follows from) his being an Englishman. But while I have said that he is an Englishman, and said that he is brave, I do not want to say that I have SAID (in the favored sense) that it follows from his being an Englishman that he is brave, though I have certainly indicated, and so implicated, that this is so. I do not want to say that my utterance of this sentence would be, STRICTLY SPEAKING, false should the consequence in question fail to hold. So SOME implicatures are conventional, unlike the one with which I introduced this discussion of implicature.

I wish to represent a certain subclass of nonconventional implicatures, which I shall call CONVERSATIONAL implicatures, as being essentially connected with certain general features of discourse; so my next step is to try to say what these features are.

The following may provide a first approximation to a general principle. Our talk exchanges do not normally consist of a succession of disconnected remarks, and would not be rational if they did. They are characteristically, to some degree at least, cooperative efforts; and each participant recognizes in them, to some extent, a common purpose or set of purposes, or at least a mutually accepted direction. This purpose or direction may be fixed from the start (e.g., by an initial proposal of a question for discussion), or it may evolve during the exchange; it may be fairly definite, or it may be so indefinite as to leave very considerable latitude to the participants (as in a casual conversation). But at each stage, SOME possible conversational moves would be excluded as conversationally unsuitable. We might then formulate a rough general principle which participants will be expected (ceteris paribus) to observe, namely: Make your conversational contribution such as is required, at the stage at which it occurs, by the accepted purpose or direction of the talk exchange in which you are engaged. One might label this the COOPERATIVE PRINCIPLE.

On the assumption that some such general principle as this is acceptable, one may perhaps distinguish four categories under one or another of which will fall certain more specific maxims and submaxims, the following of which will, in general, yield results in accordance with the Cooperative Principle. Echoing Kant, I call these categories Quantity, Quality, Relation, and Manner. The category of QUANTITY relates to the quantity of information to be provided, and under it fall the following maxims:

1. Make your contribution as informative as is required (for the current purposes of the exchange).
2. Do not make your contribution more informative than is required.

(The second maxim is disputable; it might be said that to be overinformative is not a transgression of the CP but merely a waste of time. However, it might be answered that such overinformativeness may be confusing in that it is liable to raise side issues; and there may also be an indirect effect, in that the hearers may be misled as a result of thinking that there is some particular POINT in the provision of the excess of information. However this may be, there is perhaps a different reason for doubt about the admission of this second maxim, namely, that its effect will be secured by a later maxim, which concerns relevance.)

Under the category of QUALITY falls a supermaxim — 'Try to make your contribution one that is true' — and two more specific maxims:

1. Do not say what you believe to be false.
2. Do not say that for which you lack adequate evidence.

Under the category of RELATION I place a single maxim, namely, 'Be relevant.' Though the maxim itself is terse, its formulation conceals a number of problems that exercise me a good deal: questions about what different kinds and focuses of relevance there may be, how these shift in the course of a talk exchange, how to allow for the fact that subjects of conversation are legitimately changed, and so on. I find the treatment of such questions exceedingly difficult, and I hope to revert to them in a later work.

Finally, under the category of MANNER, which I understand as relating not (like the previous categories) to what is said but, rather, to HOW what is said is to be said, I include the supermaxim — 'Be perspicuous' — and various maxims such as:

1. Avoid obscurity of expression.
2. Avoid ambiguity.
3. Be brief (avoid unnecessary prolixity).
4. Be orderly.

And one might need others.

It is obvious that the observance of some of these maxims is a matter of less urgency than is the observance of others; a man who has expressed himself with undue prolixity would, in general, be open to milder comment than would a man who has said something he believes to be false. Indeed, it might be felt that the importance of at least the first maxim of Quality is such that it should not be included in a scheme of the kind I am constructing; other maxims come into operation only on the assumption that this maxim of Quality is satisfied. While this may be correct, so far as the generation of implicatures is concerned it seems to play a role not totally different from the other maxims, and it will be convenient, for the present at least, to treat it as a member of the list of maxims.

There are, of course, all sorts of other maxims (aesthetic, social, or moral in character), such as 'Be polite', that are also normally observed by participants in talk exchanges, and these may also generate nonconventional implicatures. The conversational maxims, however, and the conversational implicatures connected with them, are specially connected (I hope) with the particular purposes that talk (and so, talk exchange) is adapted to serve and is primarily employed to serve. I have stated my maxims as if this purpose were a maximally effective exchange of information; this specification is, of course, too narrow, and the scheme needs to be generalized to allow for such general purposes as influencing or directing the actions of others.

As one of my avowed aims is to see talking as a special case or variety of purposive, indeed rational, behavior, it may be worth noting that the specific expectations or presumptions connected with at least some of the foregoing maxims have their analogues in the sphere of transactions that are not talk exchanges. I list briefly one such analog for each conversational category.

1. **Quantity.** If you are assisting me to mend a car, I expect your contribution to be neither more nor less than is required; if, for example, at a particular stage I need four screws, I expect you to hand me four, rather than two or six.

2. **Quality.** I expect your contributions to be genuine and not spurious. If I need sugar as an ingredient in the cake you are assisting me to make, I do not expect you to hand me salt; if I need a spoon, I do not expect a trick spoon made of rubber.

3. **Relation.** I expect a partner's contribution to be appropriate to immediate needs at each stage of the transaction; if I am mixing ingredients for a cake, I do not expect to be handed a good book, or even an oven cloth (though this might be an appropriate contribution at a later stage).

4. **Manner.** I expect a partner to make it clear what contribution he is making, and to execute his performance with reasonable dispatch.

These analogies are relevant to what I regard as a fundamental question about the CP and its attendant maxims, namely, what the basis is for the assumption which we seem to make, and on which (I hope) it will appear that a great range of implicatures depend, that talkers will in general (ceteris paribus and in the absence of indications to the contrary) proceed in the manner that these principles prescribe. A dull but, no doubt at a certain level, adequate answer is that it is just a well-recognized empirical fact that people DO behave in these ways; they have learned to do so in childhood and not lost the habit of doing so; and, indeed, it would involve a good deal of effort to make a radical departure from the habit. It is much easier, for example, to tell the truth than to invent lies.

I am, however, enough of a rationalist to want to find a basis that underlies these facts, undeniable though they may be; I would like to be able to think of the standard type of conversational practice not merely as something that all or most do IN FACT follow but as something that it is REASONABLE for us to follow, that we SHOULD NOT abandon. For a time, I was attracted by the idea that observance of the CP and the maxims, in a talk exchange, could be thought of as a quasi-contractual matter, with parallels outside the realm of discourse. If you pass by when I am struggling with my stranded car, I no doubt have some degree of expectation that you will offer help, but once you join me in tinkering under the hood, my expectations become stronger and take more specific forms (in the absence of indications that you are merely an incompetent meddler); and talk exchanges seemed to me to exhibit, characteristically, certain features that jointly distinguish cooperative transactions:

1. The participants have some common immediate aim, like getting a car mended; their ultimate aims may, of course, be independent and even in conflict—each may want to get the car mended in order to drive off, leaving the other stranded. In characteristic talk exchanges, there is a common aim even if, as in an over-the-wall chat, it is a second-order one, namely, that each party should, for the time being, identify himself with the transitory conversational interests of the other.

2. The contributions of the participants should be dovetailed, mutually dependent.

3. There is some sort of understanding (which may be explicit but which is often tacit) that, other things being equal, the transaction should continue in appropriate style unless both parties are agreeable that it should terminate. You do not just shove off or start doing something else.

But while some such quasi-contractual basis as this may apply to some cases, there are too many types of exchange, like quarreling and letter writing, that it fails to fit comfortably. In any case, one feels that the talker who is irrelevant or obscure has primarily let down not his audience but himself. So I would like to be able to show that observance of the CP and maxims is reasonable (rational) along the following lines: that any one who cares about the goals that are central to conversation/communication (e.g., giving and receiving information, influencing and being influenced by others) must be expected to have an interest, given suitable circumstances, in participation in talk exchanges that will be profitable only on the assumption that they are conducted in general accordance with the CP and the maxims. Whether any such conclusion can be reached, I am uncertain; in any case, I am fairly sure that I cannot reach it until I am a good deal clearer about the nature of relevance and of the circumstances in which it is required.

It is now time to show the connection between the CP and maxims, on the one hand, and conversational implicature on the other.

A participant in a talk exchange may fail to fulfill a maxim in various ways, which include the following:

1. He may quietly and unostentatiously VIOLATE a maxim; if so, in some cases he will be liable to mislead.

2. He may OPT OUT from the operation both of the maxim and of the CP; he may say, indicate, or allow it to become plain that he is unwilling to cooperate in the way the maxim requires. He may say, for example, *I cannot say more; my lips are sealed.*

3. He may be faced by a CLASH: He may be unable, for example, to fulfill the first maxim of Quantity (Be as informative as is required) without violating the second maxim of Quality (Have adequate evidence for what you say).

4. He may FLOUT a maxim; that is, he may BLATANTLY fail to fulfill it. On the assumption that the speaker is able to fulfill the maxim and to do so without violating another maxim (because of a clash), is not opting out, and is not, in view of the blatancy of his performance, trying to mislead, the hearer is faced with a minor problem: How can his saying what he did say be reconciled with the supposition that he is observing the overall CP? This situation is one that characteristically gives rise to a conversational implicature; and when a conversational implicature is generated in this way, I shall say that a maxim is being EXPLOITED.

I am now in a position to characterize the notion of conversational implicature. A man who, by (in, when) saying (or making as if to say) that *p* has implicated that *q*, may be said to have conversationally implicated that *q*, PROVIDED THAT (1) he is to be presumed to be ob-

serving the conversational maxims, or at least the cooperative principle; (2) the supposition that he is aware that, or thinks that, q is
required in order to make his saying or making as if to say p (or doing
so in THOSE terms) consistent with this presumption; and (3) the
speaker thinks (and would expect the hearer to think that the speaker
thinks) that it is within the competence of the hearer to work out, or
grasp intuitively, that the supposition mentioned in (2) IS required.
Apply this to my initial example, to B's remark that C has not yet
been to prison. In a suitable setting A might reason as follows: '(1) B
has apparently violated the maxim 'Be relevant' and so may be
regarded as having flouted one of the maxims conjoining perspicuity,
yet I have no reason to suppose that he is opting out from the operation of the CP; (2) given the circumstances, I can regard his irrelevance as only apparent if, and only if, I suppose him to think that C
is potentially dishonest; (3) B knows that I am capable of working out
step (2). So B implicates that C is potentially dishonest.'

The presence of a conversational implicature must be capable of
being worked out; for even if it can in fact be intuitively grasped,
unless the intuition is replaceable by an argument, the implicature
(if present at all) will not count as a CONVERSATIONAL implicature; it
will be a CONVENTIONAL implicature. To work out that a particular
conversational implicature is present, the hearer will reply on the
following data: (1) the conventional meaning of the words used,
together with the identity of any references that may be involved; (2)
the CP and its maxims; (3) the context, linguistic or otherwise, of the
utterance; (4) other items of background knowledge; and (5) the fact
(or supposed fact) that all relevant items falling under the previous
headings are available to both participants and both participants
know or assume this to be the case. A general pattern for the working
out of a conversational implicature might be given as follows: 'He has
said that p; there is no reason to suppose that he is not observing the
maxims, or at least the CP; he could not be doing this unless he
thought that q; he knows (and knows that I know that he knows) that
I can see that the supposition that he thinks that q IS required; he has
done nothing to stop me thinking that q; he intends me to think, or is
at least willing to allow me to think, that q; and so he has implicated
that q.'

Examples

I shall now offer a number of examples, which I shall divide into
three groups.

GROUP A: *Examples in which no maxim is violated, or at least in which it is not clear that any maxim is violated*

A is standing by an obviously immobilized car and is approached by B; the following exchange takes place:

(1)   A: *I am out of petrol.*
        B: *There is a garage round the corner.* (Gloss: B would be infringing the maxim 'Be relevant' unless he thinks, or thinks it possible, that the garage is open, and has petrol to sell; so he implicates that the garage is, or at least may be open, etc.)

In this example, unlike the case of the remark *He hasn't been to prison yet,* the unstated connection between B's remark and A's remark is so obvious that, even if one interprets the supermaxim of Manner, 'Be perspicuous,' as applying not only to the expression of what is said but also to the connection of what is said with adjacent remarks, there seems to be no case for regarding that supermaxim as infringed in this example. The next example is perhaps a little less clear in this respect:

(2)   A: *Smith doesn't seem to have a girlfriend these days.*
        B: *He has been paying a lot of visits to New York lately.*

B implicates that Smith has, or may have, a girlfriend in New York. (A gloss is unnecessary in view of that given for the previous example.)

In both examples, the speaker implicates that which he must be assumed to believe in order to preserve the assumption that he is observing the maxim of relation.

GROUP B: *An example in which a maxim is violated, but its violation is to be explained by the supposition of a clash with another maxim*

A is planning with B an itinerary for a holiday in France. Both know that A wants to see his friend C, if to do so would not involve too great a prolongation of his journey:

(3)   A: *Where does C live?*
        B: *Somewhere in the South of France.* (Gloss: There is no reason to suppose that B is opting out; his answer is, as he well knows, less informative than is required to meet A's needs. This infringement of the first maxim of Quantity can be explained only by the supposition that B is aware that to be more informative would be to say something that infringed the maxim of Quality, 'Don't say

what you lack adequate evidence for', so B implicates that he does not know in which town C lives.)

GROUP C: *Examples that involve exploitation, that is, a procedure by which a maxim is flouted for the purpose of getting in a conversational implicature by means of something of the nature of a figure of speech*
In these examples, though some maxim is violated at the level of what is said, the hearer is entitled to assume that that maxim, or at least the overall Cooperative Principle, is observed at the level of what is implicated.

(1a) *A flouting of the first maxim of Quantity*
A is writing a testimonial about a pupil who is a candidate for a philosophy job, and his letter reads as follows: 'Dear Sir, Mr. X's command of English is excellent, and his attendance at tutorials has been regular. Yours, etc.' (Gloss: A cannot be opting out, since if he wished to be uncooperative, why write at all? He cannot be unable, through ignorance, to say more, since the man is his pupil; moreover, he knows that more information than this is wanted. He must, therefore, be wishing to impart information that he is reluctant to write down. This supposition is tenable only on the assumption that he thinks Mr. X is no good at philosophy. This, then, is what he is implicating.)
Extreme examples of a flouting of the first maxim of Quantity are provided by utterances of patent tautologies like *Women are women* and *War is war*. I would wish to maintain that at the level of what is said, in my favored sense, such remarks are totally noninformative and so, at that level, cannot but infringe the first maxim of Quantity in any conversational context. They are, of course, informative at the level of what is implicated, and the hearer's identification of their informative content at this level is dependent on his ability to explain the speaker's selection of this PARTICULAR patent tautology.

(3b) *An infringement of the second maxim of Quantity, 'Do not give more information than is required', on the assumption that the existence of such a maxim should be admitted*
A wants to know whether p, and B volunteers not only the information that p, but information to the effect that it is certain that p, and that the evidence for its being the case that p is so-and-so and such-and-such.
B's volubility may be undesigned, and if it is so regarded by A it may raise in A's mind a doubt as to whether B is as certain as he says

he is ('Methinks the lady doth protest too much'). But if it is thought of as designed, it would be an oblique way of conveying that it is to some degree controversial whether or not *p*. It is, however, arguable that such an implicature could be explained by reference to the maxim of Relation without invoking an alleged second maxim of Quantity.

(2a) *Examples in which the first maxim of Quality is flouted*

1. *Irony.* X, with whom A has been on close terms until now, has betrayed a secret of A's to a business rival. A and his audience both know this. A says 'X *is a fine friend*'. (Gloss: It is perfectly obvious to A and his audience that what A has said or has made as if to say is something he does not believe, and the audience knows that A knows that this is obvious to the audience. So, unless A's utterance is entirely pointless, A must be trying to get across some other proposition than the one he purports to be putting forward. This must be some obviously related proposition; the most obviously related proposition is the contradictory of the one he purports to be putting forward.)

2. *Metaphor.* Examples like *You are the cream in my coffee* characteristically involve categorial falsity, so the contradictory of what the speaker has made as it to say will, strictly speaking, be a truism; so it cannot be THAT that such a speaker is trying to get across. The most likely supposition is that the speaker is attributing to his audience some feature or features in respect of which the audience resembles (more or less fancifully) the mentioned substance.

It is possible to combine metaphor and irony by imposing on the hearer two stages of interpretation. I say *You are the cream in my coffee,* intending the hearer to reach first the metaphor interpretant 'You are my pride and joy' and then the irony interpretant 'You are my bane.'

3. *Meiosis.* Of a man known to have broken up all the furniture, one says *He was a little intoxicated.*

4. *Hyperbole.* Every nice girl loves a sailor.

(2b) Examples in which the second maxim of Quality, 'Do not say that for which you lack adequate evidence', is flouted are perhaps not easy to find, but the following seems to be a specimen. I say of X's wife, *She is probably deceiving him this evening.* In a suitable context, or with a suitable gesture or tone of voice, it may be clear that I have no adequate reason for supposing this to be the case. My partner, to preserve the assumption that the conversational game is still being played, assumes that I am getting at some related proposition for the acceptance of which I DO have a reasonable basis. The related proposition might well be that she is given to deceiving her husband, or possibly that she is the sort of person who would not stop short of such conduct.

(3) *Examples in which an implicature is achieved by real, as distinct from apparent, violation of the maxim of Relation* are perhaps rare, but the following seems to be a good candidate. At a genteel tea party, A says *Mrs. X is an old bag.* There is a moment of appalled silence, and then B says *The weather has been quite delightful this summer, hasn't it?* B has blatantly refused to make what HE says relevant to A's preceding remark. He thereby implicates that A's remark should not be discussed and, perhaps more specifically, that A has committed a social gaffe.

(4) *Examples in which various maxims falling under the supermaxim 'Be perspicuous' are flouted*

1. *Ambiguity.* We must remember that we are concerned only with ambiguity that is deliberate, and that the speaker intends or expects to be recognized by his hearer. The problem the hearer has to solve is why a speaker should, when still playing the conversational game, go out of his way to choose an ambiguous utterance. There are two types of cases:

(a) Examples in which there is no difference, or no striking difference, between two interpretations of an utterance with respect to straightforwardness; neither interpretation is notably more sophisticated, less standard, more recondite or more far-fetched than the other. We might consider Blake's lines: 'Never seek to tell thy love, Love that never told can be.' To avoid the complications introduced by the presence of the imperative mood, I shall consider the related sentence, *I sought to tell my love, love that never told can be.* There may be a double ambiguity here. *My love* may refer to either a state of emotion or an object of emotion, and *love that never told can be* may mean either 'Love that cannot be told' or 'love that if told cannot continue to exist.' Partly because of the sophistication of the poet and partly because of internal evidence (that the ambiguity is kept up), there seems to be no alternative to supposing that the ambiguities are deliberate and that the poet is conveying both what he would be saying if one interpretation were intended rather than the other, and vice versa; though no doubt the poet is not explicitly SAYING any one of these things but only conveying or suggesting them (cf. 'Since she [nature] pricked thee out of women's pleasure, mine be thy love, and thy love's use their treasure.)

(b) Examples in which one interpretation is notably less straightforward than another. Take the complex example of the British General who captured the town of Sind and sent back the message *Peccavi*. The ambiguity involved ('I have Sind'/'I have sinned') is phonemic, not morphemic; and the expression actually used is unambiguous, but since it is in a language foreign to speaker and hearer, translation is called for, and the ambiguity resides in the standard translation into native English.

Whether or not the straightforward interpretant ('I have sinned') is being conveyed, it seems that the nonstraightforward must be. There might be stylistic reasons for conveying by a sentence merely its nonstraightforward interpretant, but it would be pointless, and perhaps also stylistically objectionable, to go to the trouble of finding an expression that nonstraightforwardly conveys that p, thus imposing on an audience the effort involved in finding this interpretant, if this interpretant were otiose so far as communication was concerned. Whether the straightforward interpretant is also being conveyed seems to depend on whether such a supposition would conflict with other conversational requirements, for example, would it be relevant, would it be something the speaker could be supposed to accept, and so on. If such requirements are not satisfied, then the straightforward interpretant is not being conveyed. If they are, it is. If the author of *Peccavi* could naturally be supposed to think that he had committed some kind of transgression, for example, had disobeyed his orders in capturing Sind, and if reference to such a transgression would be relevant to the presumed interests of the audience, then he would have been conveying both interpretants; otherwise he would be conveying only the nonstraightforward one.

2. *Obscurity.* How do I exploit, for the purposes of communication, a deliberate and overt violation of the requirement that I should avoid obscurity? Obviously, if the Cooperative Principle is to operate, I must intend my partner to understand what I am saying despite the obscurity I import into my utterance. Suppose that A and B are having a conversation in the presence of a third party, for example, a child, then A might be deliberately obscure, though not too obscure, in the hope that B would understand and the third party not. Furthermore, if A expects B to see that A is being deliberately obscure, it seems reasonable to suppose that, in making his conversational contribution in this way, A is implicating that the contents of his communication should not be imparted to the third party.

3. *Failure to be brief or succinct.* Compare the remarks:

(a)   *Miss X sang 'Home sweet home.'*
(b)   *Miss X produced a series of sounds that corresponded
        closely with the score of 'Home sweet home'.*

Suppose that a reviewer has chosen to utter (b) rather than (a). (Gloss: Why has he selected that rigmarole in place of the concise and nearly synonymous *sang?* Presumably, to indicate some striking difference between Miss X's performance and those to which the word *singing* is usually applied. The most obvious supposition is that Miss X's performance suffered from some hideous defect. The reviewer knows that this supposition is what is likely to spring to mind, so that is what he is implicating.)

I have so far considered only cases of what I might call particularized conversational implicature — that is to say, cases in which an implicature is carried by saying that *p* on a particular occasion in virtue of special features of the context, cases in which there is no room for the idea that an implicature of this sort is NORMALLY carried by saying that *p*. But there are cases of generalized conversational implicature. Sometimes one can say that the use of a certain form of words in an utterance would normally (in the ABSENCE of special circumstances) carry such-and-such an implicature or type of implicature. Noncontroversial examples are perhaps hard to find, since it is all too easy to treat a generalized conversational implicature as if it were a conventional implicature. I offer an example that I hope may be fairly noncontroversial.

Anyone who uses a sentence of the form *X is meeting a woman this evening* would normally implicate that the person to be met was someone other than X's wife, mother, sister, or perhaps even close platonic friend. Similarly, if I were to say *X went into a house yesterday and found a tortoise inside the front door,* my hearer would normally be surprised if some time later I revealed that the house was X's own. I could produce similar linguistic phenomena involving the expressions *a garden, a car, a college,* and so on. Sometimes, however, there would normally be no such implicature ('I have been sitting in a car all morning'), and sometimes a reverse implicature ('I broke a finger yesterday'). I am inclined to think that one would not lend a sympathetic ear to a philosopher who suggested that there are three senses of the form of expression *an X:* one in which it means roughly 'something that satisfies the conditions defining the word X,' another in which it means approximately 'an X (in the first sense) that is only remotely related in a certain way to some person indicated by the context,' and yet another in which it means 'an X (in the first sense) that is closely related in a certain way to some person indicated by the context.' Would we not much prefer an account on the following lines (which, of course, may be incorrect in detail):

When someone, by using the form of expression *an X*, implicates that the X does not belong to or is not otherwise closely connected with some identifiable person, the implicature is present because the speaker has failed to be specific in a way in which he might have been expected to be specific, with the consequence that it is likely to be assumed that he is not in a position to be specific. This is a familiar implicature situation and is classifiable as a failure, for one reason or another, to fulfill the first maxim of Quantity. The only difficult question is why it should, in certain cases, be presumed, independently of information about particular contexts of utterance, that specification of the closeness or remoteness of the connection between a particular person or object and a further person who is mentioned or indicated by the utterance should be likely to be of interest. The answer must lie in the following region: Transactions between a person and other persons or things closely connected with him are liable to be very different as regards their concomitants and results from the same sort of transactions involving only remotely connected persons or things; the concomitants and results, for instance, of my finding a hole in MY roof are likely to be very different from the concomitants and results of my finding a hole in someone else's roof. Information, like money, is often given without the giver's knowing to just what use the recipient will want to put it. If someone to whom a transaction is mentioned gives it further consideration, he is likely to find himself wanting the answers to further questions that the speaker may not be able to identify in advance; if the appropriate specification will be likely to enable the hearer to answer a considerable variety of such questions for himself, then there is a presumption that the speaker should include it in his remark; if not, then there is no such presumption.

Finally, we can now show that, conversational implicature being what it is, it must possess certain features:

1. Since, to assume the presence of a conversational implicature, we have to assume that at least the Cooperative Principle is being observed, and since it is possible to opt out of the observation of this principle, it follows that a generalized conversational implicature can be canceled in a particular case. It may be explicitly canceled, by the addition of a clause that states or implies that the speaker has opted out, or it may be contextually canceled, if the form of utterance that usually carries it is used in a context that makes it clear that the speaker IS opting out.

2. Insofar as the calculation that a particular conversational implicature is present requires, besides contextual and background infor-

mation, only a knowledge of what has been said (or of the conventional commitment of the utterance), and insofar as the manner of expression plays no role in the calculation, it will not be possible to find another way of saying the same thing, which simply lacks the implicature in question, except where some special feature of the substituted version is itself relevant to the determination of an implicature (in virtue of one of the maxims of Manner). If we call this feature NONDETACHABILITY, one may expect a generalized conversational implicature that is carried by a familiar, nonspecial locution to have a high degree of nondetachability.

3. To speak approximately, since the calculation of the presence of a conversational implicature presupposes an initial knowledge of the conventional force of the expression the utterance of which carries the implicature, a conversational implicatum will be a condition that is not included in the original specification of the expression's conventional force. Though it may not be impossible for what starts life, so to speak, as a conversational implicature to become conventionalized, to suppose that this is so in a given case would require special justification. So, initially at least, conversational implicata are not part of the meaning of the expressions to the employment of which they attach.

4. Since the truth of a conversational implicatum is not required by the truth of what is said (what is said may be true—what is implicated may be false), the implicature is not carried by what is said, but only by the saying of what is said, or by 'putting it that way.'

5. Since, to calculate a conversational implicature is to calculate what has to be supposed in order to preserve the supposition that the Cooperative Principle is being observed, and since there may be various possible specific explanations, a list of which may be open, the conversational implicatum in such cases will be disjunction of such specific explanations; and if the list of these is open, the implicatum will have just the kind of indeterminacy that many actual implicata do in fact seem to possess.

INDIRECT SPEECH ACTS*

JOHN R. SEARLE
University of California, Berkeley

INTRODUCTION

The simplest cases of meaning are those in which the speaker utters a sentence and means exactly and literally what he says. In such cases the speaker intends to produce a certain illocutionary effect in the hearer, and he intends to produce this effect by getting the hearer to recognize his intention to produce it, and he intends to get the hearer to recognize this intention in virtue of the hearer's knowledge of the rules that govern the utterance of the sentence. But notoriously, not all cases of meaning are this simple: In hints, insinuations, irony, and metaphor—to mention a few examples—the speaker's utterance meaning and the sentence meaning come apart in various ways. One important class of such cases is that in which the speaker utters a sentence, means what he says, but also means something more. For example, a speaker may utter the sentence *I want you to do it* by way of requesting the hearer to do something. The utterance is incidentally meant as a statement, but it is also meant primarily as a request, a request made by way of making a statement. In such cases a sentence that contains the illocutionary force indicators for one kind of illocutionary act can be uttered to perform, IN ADDITION, another type of illocutionary act. There are also cases in which the speaker may utter a sentence and mean what he says and also mean another illocution with a different

* © John R. Searle

propositional content. For example, a speaker may utter the sentence *Can you reach the salt?* and mean it not merely as a question but as a request to pass the salt.

In such cases it is important to emphasize that the utterance is meant as a request; that is, the speaker intends to produce in the hearer the knowledge that a request has been made to him, and he intends to produce this knowledge by means of getting the hearer to recognize his intention to produce it. Such cases, in which the utterance has two illocutionary forces, are to be sharply distinguished from the cases in which, for example, the speaker tells the hearer that he wants him to do something; and then the hearer does it because the speaker wants him to, though no request at all has been made, meant, or understood. The cases we will be discussing are indirect speech acts, cases in which one illocutionary act is performed indirectly by way of performing another.

The problem posed by indirect speech acts is the problem of how it is possible for the speaker to say one thing and mean that but also to mean something else. And since meaning consists in part in the intention to produce understanding in the hearer, a large part of that problem is that of how it is possible for the hearer to understand the indirect speech act when the sentence he hears and understands means something else. The problem is made more complicated by the fact that some sentences seem almost to be conventionally used as indirect requests. For a sentence like *Can you reach the salt?* or *I would appreciate it if you would get off my foot*, it takes some ingenuity to imagine a situation in which their utterances would not be requests.

In Searle (1969: chapter 3) I suggested that many such utterances could be explained by the fact that the sentences in question concern conditions of the felicitous performance of the speech acts they are used to perform indirectly — preparatory conditions, propositional content conditions, and sincerity conditions — and that their use to perform indirect speech acts consists in indicating the satisfaction of an essential condition by means of asserting or questioning one of the other conditions. Since that time a variety of explanations have been proposed, involving such things as the hypostatization of 'conversational postulates' or alternative deep structures. The answer originally suggested in Searle (1969) seems to me incomplete, and I want to develop it further here. The hypothesis I wish to defend is simply this: In indirect speech acts the speaker communicates to the hearer more than he actually says by way of relying on their mutually shared background information, both linguistic and nonlinguistic, together with the general powers of rationality and inference on the part of the hearer. To be more specific, the apparatus necessary to explain the indirect part of indirect speech acts includes a theory of speech acts, certain general principles of cooperative conversation [some of which have been discussed by Grice (this volume)], and mutually shared factual background information of the speaker and the hearer, together with an ability on the part of the hearer to make inferences. It is not necessary to assume the existence of any conversational postulates (either as an addition to the theory of speech acts or as part of the theory of speech acts) nor any concealed imperative forces or other ambiguities. We will see, however, that in some cases, convention plays a most peculiar role.

Aside from its interest for a theory of meaning and speech acts, the problem of indirect speech acts is of philosophical importance for an additional reason. In ethics it has commonly been supposed that *good, right, ought,* etc. somehow have an imperative or 'action guiding' meaning. This view derives from the fact that sentences such as *You ought to do it* are often uttered by way of telling the hearer to do something. But from the fact that such sentences can be uttered as directives[1] it no more follows that *ought* has an imperative meaning than from the fact that *Can you reach the salt* can be uttered as a request to pass the salt it follows that *can* has an imperative meaning. Many confusions in recent moral philosophy rest on a failure to understand the nature of such indirect speech acts. The topic has an additional interest for linguists because of its syntactical consequences, but I shall be concerned with these only incidentally.

A SAMPLE CASE

Let us begin by considering a typical case of the general phenomenon of indirection:

(1)   *Student X: Let's go to the movies tonight.*

(2)   *Student Y: I have to study for an exam.*

The utterance of (1) constitutes a proposal in virtue of its meaning, in particular because of the meaning of *Let's*. In general, literal utter-

---

[1] The class of 'directive' illocutionary acts includes acts of ordering, commanding, requesting, pleading, begging, praying, entreating, instructing, forbidding, and others. See Searle (forthcoming) for an explanation of this notion.

ances of sentences of this form will constitute proposals, as in:

(3)   *Let's eat pizza tonight.*

or:

(4)   *Let's go ice skating tonight.*

The utterance of (2) in the context just given would normally constitute a rejection of the proposal, but not in virtue of its meaning. In
virtue of its meaning it is simply a statement about Y. Statements of
this form do not, in general, constitute rejections of proposals, even
in cases in which they are made in response to a proposal. Thus, if Y
had said:

(5)   *I have to eat popcorn tonight.*

or:

(6)   *I have to tie my shoes.*

in a normal context, neither of these utterances would have .been a
rejection of the proposal. The question then arises, How does X
know that the utterance is a rejection of the proposal? and that question is a part of the question, How is it possible for Y to intend or
mean the utterance of (2) as a rejection of the proposal? In order to
describe this case, let us introduce some terminology. Let us say that
the PRIMARY illocutionary act performed in Y's utterance is the rejection of the proposal made by X, and that Y does that by way of performing a SECONDARY illocutionary act of making a statement to the
effect that he has to prepare for an exam. He performs the secondary
illocutionary act by way of uttering a sentence the LITERAL meaning
of which is such that its literal utterance constitutes a performance of
that illocutionary act. We may, therefore, further say that the secondary illocutionary act is literal; the primary illocutionary act is not literal. Let us assume that we know how X understands the literal secondary illocutionary act from the utterance of the sentence. The
question is, How does he understand the nonliteral primary illocutionary act from understanding the literal secondary illocutionary
act? And that question is part of the larger question, How is it possible for Y to mean the primary illocution when he only utters a sentence that means the secondary illocution, since to mean the primary
illocution is (in large part) to intend to produce in X the relevant understanding?

A brief reconstruction of the steps necessary to derive the primary
illocution from the literal illocution would go as follows. (In normal con-

versation, of course, no one would consciously go through the steps involved in this reasoning.)

STEP 1: *I have made a proposal to Y, and in response he has made a statement to the effect that he has to study for an exam (facts about the conversation).*

STEP 2: *I assume that Y is cooperating in the conversation and that therefore his remark is intended to be relevant (principles of conversational cooperation).*

STEP 3: *A relevant response must be one of acceptance, rejection, counterproposal, further discussion, etc. (theory of speech acts).*

STEP 4: *But his literal utterance was not one of these, and so was not a relevant response inference from Steps 1 and 3).*

STEP 5: *Therefore, he probably means more than he says. Assuming that his remark is relevant, his primary illocutionary point must differ from his literal one (inference from Steps 2 and 4).*[2]

This step is crucial. Unless a hearer has some inferential strategy for finding out when primary illocutionary points differ from literal illocutionary points, he has no way of understanding indirect illocutionary acts.

STEP 6: *I know that studying for an exam normally takes a large amount of time relative to a single evening, and I know that going to the movies normally takes a large amount of time relative to a single evening (factual background information).*

STEP 7: *Therefore, he probably cannot both go to the movies and study for an exam in one evening (inference from Step 6).*

STEP 8: *A preparatory condition on the acceptance of a proposal, or on any other commissive, is the ability to perform the act predicated in the propositional content condition (theory of speech acts).*

STEP 9: *Therefore, I know that he has said something that has the consequence that he probably cannot consistently accept the proposal (inference from Steps 1, 7, and 8).*

STEP 10: *Therefore, his primary illocutionary point is probably to reject the proposal (inference from Steps 5 and 9).*

It may seem somewhat pedantic to set all of this out in 10 steps; but if anything, the example is still underdescribed—I have not, for example, discussed the role of the assumption of sincerity, or the ceteris paribus conditions that attach to various of the steps. Notice,

---

[2] For an explanation of the notion of 'illocutionary point' and its relation to illocutionary force, see Searle (forthcoming).

also, that the conclusion is probabilistic. It is and ought to be. This is because the reply does not necessarily constitute a rejection of the proposal. Y might have gone on to say:

(7)   *I have to study for an exam, but let's go to the movies anyhow.*

(8)   *I have to study for an exam, but I'll do it when we get home from the movies.*

The inferential strategy is to establish, first, that the primary illocutionary point departs from the literal, and second, what the primary illocutionary point is.

The argument of this chapter will be that the theoretical apparatus used to explain this case will suffice to explain the general phenomenon of indirect illocutionary acts. That apparatus includes mutual background information, a theory of speech acts, and certain general principles of conversation. In particular, we explained this case without having to assume that sentence (2) is ambiguous or that it is 'ambiguous in context' or that it is necessary to assume the existence of any 'conversational postulates' in order to explain X's understanding the primary illocution of the utterance. The main difference between this case and the cases we will be discussing is that the latter all have a generality of FORM that is lacking in this example. I shall mark this generality by using bold type for the formal features in the surface structure of the sentences in question. In the field of indirect illocutionary acts, the area of directives is the most useful to study because ordinary conversational requirements of politeness normally make it awkward to issue flat imperative sentences (e.g., *Leave the room*) or explicit performatives (e.g., *I order you to leave the room*), and we therefore seek to find indirect means to our illocutionary ends (e.g., *I wonder if you would mind leaving the room*). In directives, politeness is the chief motivation for indirectness.

SOME SENTENCES 'CONVENTIONALLY' USED IN THE PERFORMANCE OF INDIRECT DIRECTIVES

Let us begin, then, with a short list of some of the sentences that could quite standardly be used to make indirect requests and other directives such as orders. At a pretheoretical level these sentences naturally tend to group themselves into certain categories.[3]

---

[3] In what follows, I use the letters *H*, *S*, and *A* as abbreviations for 'hearer,' 'speaker,' and 'act' or 'action.'

GROUP 1:   *Sentences concerning H's ability to perform A:*

> **Can you reach the salt?**
> **Can you pass the salt?**
> **Could you be a little more quiet?**
> **You could be a little more quiet.**
> **You can go now** (this may also be a
>   permission = *you may go now*).
> **Are you able to reach the book on the**
>   **top shelf?**
> **Have you got change for a dollar?**

GROUP 2:   *Sentences concerning S's wish or want that H will
do A:*

> **I would like you to go now.**
> **I want you to do this for me, Henry.**
> **I would/should appreciate it if you**
>   **would/could do it for me.**
> **I would/should be most grateful if**
>   **you would/could help us out.**
> **I'd rather you didn't do that any more.**
> **I'd be very much obliged if you would**
>   **pay me the money back soon.**
> **I hope you'll do it.**
> **I wish you wouldn't do that.**

GROUP 3:   *Sentences concerning H's doing A:*

> **Officers will henceforth wear ties at**
>   **dinner.**
> **Will you quit making that awful racket?**
> **Would you kindly get off my foot?**
> **Won't you stop making that noise soon?**
> **Aren't you going to eat your cereal?**

GROUP 4:   *Sentences concerning H's desire or willingness to do A:*

> **Would you be willing to write a letter**
>   **of recommendation for me?**
> **Do you want to hand me that hammer over**
>   **there on the table?**
> **Would you mind not making so much noise?**
> **Would it be convenient for you to come**
>   **on Wednesday?**
> **Would it be too much (trouble) for you**
>   **to pay me the money next Wednesday?**

GROUP 5:   *Sentences concerning reasons for doing A:*

> *You ought to be more polite to your mother.*
> *You should leave immediately.*
> *Must you continue hammering that way?*
> *Ought you to eat quite so much spaghetti?*
> *Should you be wearing John's tie?*
> *You had better go now.*
> *Hadn't you better go now?*
> *Why not stop here?*
> *Why don't you try it just once?*
> *Why don't you be quiet?*
> *It would be better for you (for us all)*
>   *if you would leave the room.*
> *It wouldn't hurt if you left now.*
> *It might help if you shut up.*
> *It would be better if you gave me the*
>   *money now.*
> *It would be a good idea if you left town.*
> *We'd all be better off if you'd just*
>   *pipe down a bit.*

This class also contains many examples that have no generality of form but obviously, in an appropriate context, would be uttered as indirect requests, e.g.:

> *You're standing on my foot.*
> *I can't see the movie screen while*
>   *you have that hat on.*

Also in this class belong, possibly:

> *How many times have I told you (must I*
>   *tell you) not to eat with your fingers?*
> *I must have told you a dozen times not*
>   *to eat with your mouth open.*
> *If I have told you once I have told you*
>   *a thousand times not to wear your hat in*
>   *the house.*

GROUP 6:   *Sentences embedding one of these elements inside another; also, sentences embedding an explicit directive illocutionary verb inside one of these contexts.*

> *Would you mind awfully if I asked you*
>   *if you could write me a letter of*
>   *recommendation?*

> *Would it be too much if I suggested*
> *that you could possibly make a little*
> *less noise?*
> *Might I ask you to take off your hat?*
> *I hope you won't mind if I ask you if*
> *you could leave us alone.*
> *I would appreciate it if you could*
> *make less noise.*[4]

This is a very large class, since most of its members are constructed by permitting certain of the elements of the other classes.

SOME PUTATIVE FACTS

Let us begin by noting several salient facts about the sentences in question. Not everyone will agree that what follows are facts; indeed, most of the available explanations consist in denying one or more of these statements. Nonetheless, at an intuitive pretheoretical level each of the following would seem to be correct observations about the sentences in question, and I believe we should surrender these intuitions only in the face of very serious counterarguments. I will eventually argue that an explanation can be given that is consistent with all of these facts.

FACT 1: *The sentences in question do not have an imperative force as part of their meaning.* This point is sometimes denied by philosophers and linguists, but very powerful evidence for it is provided by the fact that it is possible without inconsistency to connect the literal utterance of one of these forms with the denial of any imperative intent, e.g.:

> *I'd like you to do this for me, Bill, but I am not asking you*
> *to do it or requesting that you do it or ordering you to do it*
> *or telling you to do it.*
> *I'm just asking you, Bill: Why not eat beans? But in asking*
> *you that I want you to understand that I am not telling you*
> *to eat beans; I just want to know your reasons for thinking*
> *you ought not to.*

FACT 2: *The sentences in question are not ambiguous as between an imperative illocutionary force and a nonimperative illocutionary force.* I think this is intuitively apparent, but in any case, an ordinary application of Occam's razor places the onus of proof on those who wish to claim that these sentences are ambiguous. One does not mul-

---

[4] This form is also included in Group 2.

tiply meanings beyond necessity. Notice, also, that it is no help to say they are 'ambiguous in context,' for all that means is that one cannot always tell from what the sentence means what the speaker means by its utterance, and that is not sufficient to establish sentential ambiguity.

FACT 3: *Notwithstanding Facts 1 and 2, these are standardly, ordinarily, normally — indeed, I shall argue, conventionally — used to issue directives.* There is a systematic relation between these and directive illocutions in a way that there is no systematic relation between *I have to study for an exam* and rejecting proposals. Additional evidence that they are standardly used to issue imperatives is that most of them take *please*, either at the end of the sentence or preceding the verb, e.g.:

> *I want you to stop making that noise, please.*
> *Could you please lend me a dollar?*

When *please* is added to one of these sentences, it explicitly and literally marks the primary illocutionary point of the utterance as directive, even though the literal meaning of the rest of the sentence is not directive.

It is because of the combination of Facts 1, 2, and 3 that there is a problem about these cases at all.

FACT 4: *The sentences in question are not, in the ordinary sense, idioms.*[5] An ordinary example of an idiom is *kicked the bucket* in *Jones kicked the bucket.* The most powerful evidence I know that these sentences are not idioms is that in their use as indirect directives they admit of literal responses that presuppose that they are uttered literally. Thus, an utterance of *Why don't you be quiet, Henry?* admits as a response an utterance of *Well, Sally, there are several reasons for not being quiet. First, ...* Possible exceptions to this are occurrences of *would* and *could* in indirect speech acts, and I will discuss them later.

Further evidence that they are not idioms is that, whereas a word-for-word translation of *Jones kicked the bucket* into other languages will not produce a sentence meaning 'Jones died,' translations of the sentences in question will often, though by no means always, produce sentences with the same indirect illocutionary act potential of the English examples. Thus, e.g., *Pourriez-vous m'aider?* and *Können Sie mir helfen?* can be uttered as indirect requests in French

---

[5] There are some idioms in this line of business, however, for example *How about* as used in proposals and requests: *How about going to the movies tonight? How about giving me some more beer?*

or German. I will later discuss the problem of why some translate with equivalent indirect illocutionary force potential and some do not.

FACT 5: *To say they are not idioms is not to say they are not idiomatic.* All the examples given are idiomatic in current English, and—what is more puzzling—they are idiomatically used as requests. In general, nonidiomatic equivalents or synonyms would not have the same indirect illocutionary act potential. Thus, *Do you want to hand me the hammer over there on the table?* can be uttered as a request, but *Is it the case that you at present desire to hand me that hammer over there on the table?* has a formal and stilted character that in almost all contexts would eliminate it as a candidate for an indirect request. Furthermore, *Are you able to hand me that hammer?*, though idiomatic, does not have the same indirect request potential as *Can you hand me that hammer?* That these sentences are IDIOMATIC and are IDIOMATICALLY USED AS DIRECTIVES is crucial to their role in indirect speech acts. I will say more about the relations of these facts later.

FACT 6: *The sentences in question have literal utterances in which they are not also indirect requests.* Thus, *Can you reach the salt?* can be uttered as a simple question about your abilities (say, by an orthopedist wishing to know the medical progress of your arm injury). *I want you to leave* can be uttered simply as a statement about one's wants, without any directive intent. At first sight, some of our examples might not appear to satisfy this condition, e.g.:

> *Why not stop here?*
> *Why don't you be quiet?*

But with a little imagination it is easy to construct situations in which utterances of these would be not directives but straight-forward questions. Suppose someone had said *We ought not to stop here.* Then *Why not stop here?* would be an appropriate question, without necessarily being also a suggestion. Similarly, if someone had just said *I certainly hate making all this racket,* an utterance of (*Well, then*) *Why don't you be quiet?* would be an appropriate response, without also necessarily being a request to be quiet.

It is important to note that the intonation of these sentences when they are uttered as indirect requests often differs from their intonation when uttered with only their literal illocutionary force, and often the intonation pattern will be that characteristic of literal directives.

FACT 7: *In cases where these sentences are uttered as requests,*

*they still have their literal meaning and are uttered with and as
having that literal meaning.* I have seen it claimed that they have
different meanings 'in context' when they are uttered as requests, but
I believe that is obviously false. The man who says *I want you to do
it* means literally that he wants you to do it. The point is that, as is
always the case with indirection, he means not only what he says but
something more as well. What is added in the indirect cases is not
any additional or different SENTENCE meaning, but additional
SPEAKER meaning. Evidence that these sentences keep their literal
meanings when uttered as indirect requests is that responses that are
appropriate to their literal utterances are appropriate to their indirect
speech act utterances (as we noted in our discussion of Fact 4), e.g.:

> *Can you pass the salt?*
> *No, sorry, I can't, it's down there at the end of the table.*
> *Yes, I can. (Here it is.)*

FACT 8:   *It is a consequence of Fact 7 that when one of these sentences is uttered with the primary illocutionary point of a directive,
the literal illocutionary act is also performed.* In every one of these
cases, the speaker issues a directive BY WAY OF asking a question or
making a statement. But the fact that his primary illocutionary intent
is directive does not alter the fact that he is asking a question or
making a statement. Additional evidence for Fact 8 is that a subsequent report of the utterance can truly report the literal illocutionary act.

Thus, e.g., the utterance of *I want you to leave now, Bill* can be
reported by an utterance of *He told me he wanted me to leave, so I
left.* Or, the utterance of *Can you reach the salt?* can be reported by
an utterance of *He asked me whether I could reach the salt.*
Similarly, an utterance of *Could you do it for me, Henry; could you
do it for me and Cynthia and the children?* can be reported by an
utterance of *He asked me whether I could do it for him and Cynthia
and the children.*

This point is sometimes denied. I have seen it claimed that the literal illocutionary acts are always defective or are not 'conveyed'
when the sentence is used to perform a nonliteral primary illocutionary act. As far as our examples are concerned, the literal illocutions are always conveyed and are sometimes, but not in general,
defective. For example, an indirect speech act utterance of *Can you
reach the salt?* may be defective in the sense that S may already
know the answer. But even this form NEED not be defective. (Con-

sider, e.g., *Can you give me change for a dollar?*.) Even when the literal utterance is defective, the indirect speech act does not depend on its being defective.

AN EXPLANATION IN TERMS OF THE
THEORY OF SPEECH ACTS

The difference between the example concerning the proposal to go to the movies and all of the other cases is that the other cases are systematic. What we need to do, then, is to describe an example in such a way as to show how the apparatus used on the first example will suffice for these other cases and also will explain the systematic character of the other cases.

I think the theory of speech acts will enable us to provide a simple explanation of how these sentences, which have one illocutionary force as part of their meaning, can be used to perform an act with a different illocutionary force. Each type of illocutionary act has a set of conditions that are necessary for the successful and felicitous performance of the act. To illustrate this, I will present the conditions on two types of acts within the two genuses, directive and commissive (Searle, 1969: Chapter 3).

A comparison of the list of felicity conditions on the directive class of illocutionary acts and our list of types of sentences used to perform indirect directives show that Groups 1–6 of types can be reduced to three types: those having to do with felicity conditions on the performance of a directive illocutionary act, those having to do with reasons for doing the act, and those embedding one element inside

	Directive (Request)	Commissive (Promise)
Preparatory condition	H is able to perform A.	S is able to perform A. H wants S to perform A.
Sincerity condition	S wants H to do A.	S intends to do A.
Propositional content condition	S predicates a future act A of H.	S predicates a future act A of S.
Essential condition	Counts as an attempt by S to get H to do A.	Counts as the undertaking by S of an obligation to do A.

another one. Thus, since the ability of H to perform A (Group 1) is a preparatory condition, the desire of S that H perform A (Group 2) is the sincerity condition, and the predication of A of H (Group 3) is the propositional content condition, all of Groups 1–3 concern felicity conditions on directive illocutionary acts. Since wanting to do something is a reason par excellence for doing it, Group 4 assimilates to Group 5, as both concern reasons for doing A. Group 6 is a special class only by courtesy, since its elements either are performative verbs or are already contained in the other two categories of felicity conditions and reasons.

Ignoring the embedding cases for the moment, if we look at our lists and our sets of conditions, the following generalizations naturally emerge:

GENERALIZATION 1: *S can make an indirect request (or other directive) by either asking whether or stating that a preparatory condition concerning H's ability to do A obtains.*

GENERALIZATION 2: *S can make an indirect directive by either asking whether or stating that the propositional content condition obtains.*

GENERALIZATION 3: *S can make an indirect directive by stating that the sincerity condition obtains, but not by asking whether it obtains.*

GENERALIZATION 4: *S can make an indirect directive by either stating that or asking whether there are good or overriding reasons for doing A, except where the reason is that H wants or wishes, etc., to do A, in which case he can only ask whether H wants, wishes, etc., to do A.*

It is the existence of these generalizations that accounts for the systematic character of the relation between the sentences in Groups 1–6 and the directive class of illocutionary acts. Notice that these are generalizations and not rules. The rules of speech acts (or some of them) are stated in the list of conditions presented earlier. That is, for example, it is a rule of the directive class of speech acts that the directive is defective if the hearer is unable to perform the act, but it is precisely not a rule of speech acts or of conversation that one can perform a directive by asking whether the preparatory condition obtains. The theoretical task is to show how that generalization will be a consequence of the rule, together with certain other information, namely, the factual background information and the general principles of conversation.

Our next task is to try to describe an example of an indirect request

with at least the same degree of pedantry we used in our description
of the rejection of a proposal. Let us take the simplest sort of case: At
the dinner table, X says to Y, *Can you pass the salt?* by way of asking
Y to pass the salt. Now, how does Y know that X is requesting him to
pass the salt instead of just asking a question about his abilities to
pass the salt? Notice that not everything will do as a request to pass
the salt. Thus, if X had said *Salt is made of sodium chloride* or *Salt is
mined in the Tatra mountains*, without some special stage setting, it
is very unlikely that Y would take either of these utterances as a
request to pass the salt. Notice further that, in a normal conversational situation, Y does not have to go through any conscious process
of inference to derive the conclusion that the utterance of *Can you
pass the salt?* is a request to pass the salt. He simply hears it as a
request. This fact is perhaps one of the main reasons why it is
tempting to adopt the false conclusion that somehow these examples
must have an imperative force as part of their meaning or that they
are 'ambiguous in context,' or some such. What we need to do is offer
an explanation that is consistent with all of Facts 1–8 yet does not
make the mistake of hypostatizing concealed imperative forces or
conversational postulates. A bare-bones reconstruction of the steps
necessary for Y to derive the conclusion from the utterance might go
roughly as follows:

STEP 1:   *Y has asked me a question as to whether I have the ability to pass the salt (fact about the conversation).*

STEP 2:   *I assume that he is cooperating in the conversation and
that therefore his utterance has some aim or point (principles of conversational cooperation).*

STEP 3:   *The conversational setting is not such as to indicate a
theoretical interest in my salt-passing ability (factual background
information).*

STEP 4:   *Furthermore, he probably already knows that the answer
to the question is yes (factual background information). (This step
facilitates the move to Step 5, but is not essential.)*

STEP 5:   *Therefore, his utterance is probably not just a question.
It probably has some ulterior illocutionary point (inference from
Steps 1, 2, 3, and 4). What can it be?*

STEP 6:   *A preparatory condition for any directive illocutionary
act is the ability of H to perform the act predicated in the propositional content condition (theory of speech acts).*

STEP 7:   *Therefore, X has asked me a question the affirmative
answer to which would entail that the preparatory condition for*

requesting me to pass the salt is satisfied (inference from Steps 1 and 6).

STEP 8: *We are now at dinner and people normally use salt at dinner; they pass it back and forth, try to get others to pass it back and forth, etc. (background information).*

STEP 9: *He has therefore alluded to the satisfaction of a preparatory condition for a request whose obedience conditions it is quite likely he wants me to bring about (inference from Steps 7 and 8).*

STEP 10: *Therefore, in the absence of any other plausible illocutionary point, he is probably requesting me to pass him the salt (inference from Steps 5 and 9).*

The hypothesis being put forth in this chapter is that all the cases can be similarly analyzed. According to this analysis, the reason I can ask you to pass the salt by saying *Can you pass the salt?* but not by saying *Salt is made of sodium chloride* or *Salt is mined in the Tatra mountains* is that your ability to pass the salt is a preparatory condition for requesting you to pass the salt in a way that the other sentences are not related to requesting you to pass the salt. But obviously, that answer is not by itself sufficient, because not all questions about your abilities are requests. The hearer therefore needs some way of finding out when the utterance is just a question about his abilities and when it is a request made by way of asking a question about his abilities. It is at this point that the general principles of conversation (together with factual background information) come into play.

The two features that are crucial, or so I am suggesting, are, first, a strategy for establishing the existence of an ulterior illocutionary point beyond the illocutionary point contained in the meaning of the sentence, and second, a device for finding out what the ulterior illocutionary point is. The first is established by the principles of conversation operating on the information of the hearer and the speaker, and the second is derived from the theory of speech acts together with background information. The generalizations are to be explained by the fact that each of them records a strategy by means of which the hearer can find out how a primary illocutionary point differs from a secondary illocutionary point.

The chief motivation—though not the only motivation—for using these indirect forms is politeness. Notice that, in the example just given, the *Can you* form is polite in at least two respects. Firstly, X does not presume to know about Y's abilities, as he would if he issued an imperative sentence; and, secondly, the form gives—or at least appears to give—Y the option of refusing, since a yes–no question allows *no* as a possible answer. Hence, compliance can be made to appear a free act rather than obeying a command.[6]

SOME PROBLEMS

It is important to emphasize that I have by no means demonstrated the thesis being argued for in this chapter. I have so far only suggested a pattern of analysis that is consistent with the facts. Even supposing that this pattern of analysis could be shown to be successful in many more cases, there are still several problems that remain:

PROBLEM 1:   The biggest single problem with the foregoing analysis is this: If, as I have been arguing, the mechanisms by which indirect speech acts are meant and understood are perfectly general—having to do with the theory of speech acts, the principles of cooperative conversation, and shared background information—and not tied to any particular syntactical form, then why is it that some syntactical forms work better than others. Why can I ask you to do something by saying *Can you hand me that book on the top shelf?* but not, or not very easily, by saying *Is it the case that you at present have the ability to hand me that book on the top shelf?*
Even within such pairs as:

> *Do you want to do A?*
> *Do you desire to do A?*

and:

> *Can you do A?*
> *Are you able to do A?*

there is clearly a difference in indirect illocutionary act potential. Note, for example, that the first member of each pair takes *please* more readily than the second. Granting that none of these pairs are exact synonyms, and granting that all the sentences have some use as indirect requests, it is still essential to explain the differences in their indirect illocutionary act potential. How, in short, can it be the case that some sentences are not imperative idioms and yet function as forms for idiomatic requests?
The first part of the answer is this: The theory of speech acts and the principles of conversational cooperation do, indeed, provide a framework within which indirect illocutionary acts can be meant and

---

[6] I am indebted to Dorothea Franck for discussion of this point.

understood. However, within this framework certain forms will tend to become conventionally established as the standard idiomatic forms for indirect speech acts. While keeping their literal meanings, they will acquire conventional uses as, e.g., polite forms for requests.

It is by now, I hope, uncontroversial that there is a distinction to be made between meaning and use, but what is less generally recognized is that there can be conventions of usage that are not meaning conventions. I am suggesting that *can you, could you, I want you to,* and numerous other forms are conventional ways of making requests (and in that sense it is not incorrect to say they are idioms), but at the same time they do not have an imperative meaning (and in that sense it would be incorrect to say they are idioms). Politeness is the most prominent motivation for indirectness in requests, and certain forms naturally tend to become the conventionally polite ways of making indirect requests.

If this explanation is correct, it would go some way toward explaining why there are differences in the indirect speech forms from one language to another. The mechanisms are not peculiar to this language or that, but at the same time the standard forms from one language will not always maintain their indirect speech act potential when translated from one language to another. Thus, *Can you hand me that book?* will function as an indirect request in English, but its Czech translation, *Můžete mi podat tu Knížku?* will sound very odd if uttered as a request in Czech.

A second part of the answer is this: In order to be a plausible candidate for an utterance as an indirect speech act, a sentence has to be idiomatic to start with. It is very easy to imagine circumstances in which: *Are you able to reach that book on the top shelf?* could be uttered as a request. But it is much harder to imagine cases in which *Is it the case that you at present have the ability to reach that book on the top shelf?* could be similarly used. Why?

I think the explanation for this fact may derive from another maxim of conversation having to do with speaking idiomatically. In general, if one speaks unidiomatically, hearers assume that there must be a special reason for it, and in consequence, various assumptions of normal speech are suspended. Thus, if I say, archaically, *Knowest thou him who calleth himself Richard Nixon?*, you are not likely to respond as you would to an utterance of *Do you know Richard Nixon?*

Besides the maxims proposed by Grice, there seems to be an additional maxim of conversation that could be expressed as follows: *Speak idiomatically unless there is some special reason not to.* For this reason, the normal conversational assumptions on which the possibility of indirect speech acts rests are in large part suspended in the nonidiomatic cases.

The answer, then, to Problem 1 is in two parts. In order to be a plausible candidate at all for use as an indirect speech act, a sentence has to be idiomatic. But within the class of idiomatic sentences, some forms tend to become entrenched as conventional devices for indirect speech acts. In the case of directives, in which politeness is the chief motivation for the indirect forms, certain forms are conventionally used as polite requests. Which kinds of forms are selected will, in all likelihood, vary from one language to another.

PROBLEM 2: Why is there an asymmetry between the sincerity condition and the others such that one can perform an indirect request only by asserting the satisfaction of a sincerity condition, not by querying it, whereas one can perform indirect directives by either asserting or querying the satisfaction of the propositional content and preparatory conditions?

Thus, an utterance of *I want you to do it* can be a request, but not an utterance of *Do I want you to do it?* The former can take *please,* the latter cannot. A similar asymmetry occurs in the case of reasons: *Do you want to leave us alone?* can be a request, but not *You want to leave us alone.*[7] Again, the former can take *please,* the latter cannot. How is one to explain these facts?

I believe the answer is that it is odd, in normal circumstances, to ask other people about the existence of one's own elementary psychological states, and odd to assert the existence of other people's elementary psychological states when addressing them. Since normally you are never in as good a position as I am to assert what I want, believe, intend, and so on, and since I am normally not in as good a position as you to assert what you want, believe, intend, and so on, it is, in general, odd for me to ask you about my states or tell you about yours. We shall see shortly that this asymmetry extends to the indirect performance of other kinds of speech acts.

PROBLEM 3: Though this chapter is not intended as being about English syntactical forms, some of the sentences on our lists are of enough interest to deserve special comment. Even if it should turn out that these peculiar cases are really imperative idioms, like *how about . . . ?*, it would not alter the general lines of my argument; it would simply shift some examples out of the class of indirect speech acts into the class of imperative idioms.

One interesting form is *why not plus verb,* as in *Why not stop here?* This form, unlike *Why don't you?*, has many of the same syn-

---

[7] This point does not hold for the etymologically prior sense of *want* in which it means 'need.'

tactical constraints as imperative sentences. For example, it requires a voluntary verb. Thus, one cannot say *Why not resemble your grandmother? unless one believes that one can resemble someone as a voluntary action, whereas one can say Why not imitate your grandmother? Furthermore, like imperative sentences, this form requires a reflexive when it takes a second-person direct object, e.g., Why not wash yourself? Do these facts prove that the Why not . . . ? (and the why . . . ?) forms are imperative in meaning? I think they are not. On my account, the way an utterance of why not? works is this: In asking Why not stop here? as a suggestion to stop here, S challenges H to provide reasons for not doing something on the tacit assumption that the absence of reasons for not doing something is itself a reason for doing it, and the suggestion to do it is therefore made indirectly in accordance with the generalization that alluding to a reason for doing something is a way of making an indirect directive to do it. This analysis is supported by several facts. First, as we have already seen, this form can have a literal utterance in which it is not uttered as a suggestion; second, one can respond to the suggestion with a response appropriate to the literal utterance, e.g., Well, there are several reasons for not stopping here. First . . . . And third, one can report an utterance of one of these, without reporting any directive illocutionary forces, in the form He asked me why we shouldn't stop there. And here the occurrence of the practical should or ought (not the theoretical should or ought) is sufficient to account for the requirement of a voluntary verb.

Other troublesome examples are provided by occurrences of would and could in indirect speech acts. Consider, for example, utterances of Would you pass me the salt? and Could you hand me that book? It is not easy to analyze these forms and to describe exactly how they differ in meaning from Will you pass me the salt? and Can you hand me that book? Where, for example, are we to find the if clause, which, we are sometimes told, is required by the so-called subjunctive use of these expressions? Suppose we treat the if clause as if I asked you to. Thus, Would you pass me the salt? is short for Would you pass me the salt if I asked you to?

There are at least two difficulties with this approach. First, it does not seem at all plausible for could, since your abilities and possibilities are not contingent on what I ask you to do. But second, even for would it is unsatisfactory, since Would you pass me the salt if I asked you to? does not have the same indirect illocutionary act potential as the simple Would you pass me the salt? Clearly, both forms have uses as indirect directives, but, equally clearly, they are not equivalent. Furthermore, the cases in which would and could interrogative forms DO have a nonindirect use seem to be quite different from the cases we have been considering, e.g., *Would you vote for a Democrat?* or *Could you marry a radical?* Notice, for example, that an appropriate response to an utterance of these might be, e.g., *Under what conditions?* or *It depends on the situation*. But these would hardly be appropriate responses to an utterance of *Would you pass me the salt?* in the usual dinner table scene we have been envisaging.

Could seems to be analyzable in terms of *would* and possibility or ability. Thus, *Could you marry a radical* means something like *Would it be possible for you to marry a radical? Would*, like *will*, is traditionally analyzed either as expressing want or desire or as a future auxiliary.

The difficulty with these forms seems to be an instance of the general difficulty about the nature of the subjunctive and does not necessarily indicate that there is any imperative meaning. If we are to assume that *would* and *could* have an imperative meaning, then it seems we will be forced to assume, also, that they have a commissive meaning as well, since utterances of *Could I be of assistance?* and *Would you like some more wine?* are both normally offers. I find this conclusion implausible because it involves an unnecessary proliferation of meanings. It violates Occam's razor regarding concepts. It is more economical to assume that *could* and *would* are univocal in *Could you pass the salt?*, *Could I be of assistance?*, *Would you stop making that noise?*, and *Would you like some more wine?*. However, a really satisfactory analysis of these forms awaits a satisfactory analysis of the subjunctive. The most plausible analysis of the indirect request forms is that the suppressed *if* clause is the polite *if you please* or *if you will*.

EXTENDING THE ANALYSIS

I want to conclude this chapter by showing that the general approach suggested in it will work for other types of indirection besides just directives. Obvious examples, often cited in the literature, are provided by the sincerity conditions. In general, one can perform any illocutionary act by asserting (though not by questioning) the satisfaction of the sincerity condition for that act. Thus, for example:

> *I am sorry I did it.* (an apology)
> *I think/believe he is in the next room.*
>   (an assertion)

I am so glad you won. (congratulations)
I intend to try harder next time, coach.
(a promise)
I am grateful for your help. (thanks)

I believe, however, that the richest mine for examples other than directives is provided by commissives, and a study of the examples of sentences used to perform indirect commissives (especially offers and promises) shows very much the same patterns that we found in the study of directives. Consider the following sentences, any of which can be uttered to perform an indirect offer (or, in some cases, a promise).

I.   Sentences concerning the preparatory conditions:

    A.   that S is able to perform the act:

> *Can I help you?*
> *I can do that for you.*
> *I could get it for you.*
> *Could I be of assistance?*

    B.   that H wants S to perform the act:

> *Would you like some help?*
> *Do you want me to go now, Sally?*
> *Wouldn't you like me to bring some more*
>   *next time I come?*
> *Would you rather I came on Tuesday?*

II. Sentences concerning the sincerity condition:

> *I intend to do it for you.*
> *I plan on repairing it for you next week.*

III. Sentences concerning the propositional content condition:

> *I will do it for you.*
> *I am going to give it to you next time*
>   *you stop by.*
> *Shall I give you the money now?*

IV. Sentences concerning S's wish or willingness to do A:

> *I want to be of any help I can.*
> *I'd be willing to do it (if you want me to).*

V.   Sentences concerning (other) reasons for S's doing A:

> *I think I had better leave you alone.*
> *Wouldn't it be better if I gave you some*
>   *assistance?*
> *You need my help, Cynthia.*

Notice that the point made earlier about the elementary psychological states holds for these cases as well: One can perform an indirect illocutionary act by asserting, but not by querying, one's own psychological states; and one can perform an indirect illocutionary act by querying, but not by asserting, the presence of psychological states in one's hearer.

Thus, an utterance of *Do you want me to leave?* can be an offer to leave, but not *You want me to leave.* (Though it can be, with the tag question *You want me to leave, don't you?*) Similarly, *I want to help you out* can be uttered as an offer, but not *Do I want to help you out?*

The class of indirect commissives also includes a large number of hypothetical sentences:

> *If you wish any further information, just*
>   *let me know.*
> *If I can be of assistance, I would be most*
>   *glad to help.*
> *If you need any help, call me at the office.*

In the hypothetical cases, the antecedent concerns either one of the preparatory conditions, or the presence of a reason for doing A, as in *If it would be better for me to come on Wednesday, just let me know.* Note also that, as well as hypothetical sentences, there are iterated cases of indirection. Thus, e.g., *I think I ought to help you out* can be uttered as an indirect offer made by way of making an indirect assertion. These examples suggest the following further generalizations:

GENERALIZATION 5: *S can make an indirect commissive by either asking whether or stating that the preparatory condition concerning his ability to do A obtains.*

GENERALIZATION 6: *S can make an indirect commissive by asking whether, though not by stating that, the preparatory condition concerning H's wish or want that S do A obtains.*

GENERALIZATION 7: *S can make an indirect commissive by stating that, and in some forms by asking whether, the propositional content condition obtains.*

GENERALIZATION 8: *S can make an indirect commissive by stating that, but not by asking whether, the sincerity condition obtains.*

GENERALIZATION 9: *S can make an indirect commissive by stating that or by asking whether there are good or overriding reasons for doing A, except where the reason is that S wants or desires to do A, in which case he can only state but not ask whether he wants to do A.*

I would like to conclude by emphasizing that my approach does not fit any of the usual explanatory paradigms. The philosopher's paradigm has normally been to get a set of logically necessary and sufficient conditions for the phenomena to be explained; the linguist's paradigm has normally been to get a set of structural rules that will generate the phenomena to be explained. I am unable to convince myself that either of these paradigms is appropriate for the present problem. The problem seems to me somewhat like those problems in the epistemological analysis of perception in which one seeks to explain how a perceiver recognizes an object on the basis of imperfect sensory input. The question, How do I know he has made a request when he only asked me a question about my abilities? may be like the question, How do I know it was a car when all I perceived was a flash going past me on the highway? If so, the answer to our problem may be neither 'I have a set of axioms from which it can be deduced that he made a request' nor 'I have a set of syntactical rules that generate an imperative deep structure for the sentence he uttered.'

ACKNOWLEDGMENTS

I am indebted for comments on earlier drafts of this study to Julian Boyd, Charles Fillmore, Dorothea Franck, Georgia Green, George Lakoff, Dagmar Searle, and Alan Walworth.

REFERENCES

Searle, J. R. A taxonomy of illocutionary acts. In K. Gunderson (Ed.), *Minnesota studies in the philosophy of language.* Minneapolis: University of Minnesota Press (forthcoming).
Searle, J. R. *Speech acts.* New York and London: Cambridge University Press, 1969.

CONVERSATIONAL POSTULATES*

DAVID GORDON AND GEORGE LAKOFF

University of California, Berkeley

INTRODUCTION

In everyday speech, we very often use one sentence to convey the meaning of another. For example, if the Duke of Bardello says to his butler, *It's cold in here,* he may be giving an order to close the window. This does not mean that the meaning of *It's cold in here* is the same as the meaning of *Close the window.* It only means that, under certain circumstances, saying one thing may entail the communication of another. What we would like to say about such a case is that *It's cold in here* has its usual literal meaning. In such a situation, it is an expression of discomfort and is said by a person in authority to a person whose job it is, in part, to relieve the discomforts of his employer as far as possible. If, in a context, the most obvious way to relieve the discomfort cited is to close the window, then an order to do that is what is being communicated.

Grice (this volume) has shown that cases in which saying one thing entails the communication of another are instances of certain general principles of conversation. Our purpose in this chapter is twofold: first, to outline a way in which conversational principles can begin to

° Originally published in D. Adams, M. A. Cambell, V. Cohen, J. Lovins, E. Maxwell, C. Nygren, and J. Reighard (Eds.), *Papers from the seventh regional meeting of the Chicago Linguistic Society.* Chicago: University of Chicago Department of Linguistics, 1971, 63–84. Reprinted by permission.

be formalized and incorporated into the theory of generative semantics; and, second, to show that there are rules of grammar, rules governing the distribution of morphemes in a sentence, that depend on such principles. Our strategy for beginning to incorporate such observations into a theory of grammar and for stating rules of grammar in terms of them is based on the notions of natural logic and of transderivational rules (G. Lakoff, 1970 and to appear). Natural logic characterizes the class of entailments of a sentence. Given the logical structure L of a sentence, we will call the entailments of L (given the axioms and meaning postulates of natural logic) $E(L)$:

(1) $L \Vdash E(L)$ ['L entails each member of $E(L)$.']

We will formulate conversational principles as postulates, called CONVERSATIONAL POSTULATES, which can be stated in the same format as meaning postulates. Let us call the set of conversational postulates CP. Since the application of conversational postulates depends on contexts, we will need to represent a class of contexts, CON_i, as a finite consistent set of logical structures. CON_i can be thought of as characterizing those contexts in which each logical structure in CON_i is true. In a given class of contexts, CON_i, a sentence with logical structure L will, in general, entail more than simply $E(L)$, and even more when conversational postulates are taken into account. That is, $CON_i \cup CP \cup \{L\}$ will entail much more than $E(L)$. For example, given the context (actually a class of contexts) described in the first paragraph, and given the conversational postulate informally stated there, *It's cold in here* entails *Close the window*. Thus, we can characterize the notion 'conversational implication in a class of contexts CON_i' as follows:

(2) *L conversationally implies P in CON_i IFF $CON_i \cup$ CP $\cup$*
     $\{L\} \Vdash P$ ('In context CON_i, given conversational postulates CP, L entails P.')

We will refer to L as the 'primary' or 'literal' meaning; and we will refer to P as the 'conversationally implied' or 'conveyed' meaning.

SOME CONVERSATIONAL POSTULATES

Sincerity Conditions

Let us begin by looking at some of the principles governing the sincerity of requests:[1]

---

[1] '$\rightarrow$' stands for material implication.

(3)   a.   SINCERE(a,REQUEST(a,b,Q)) → WANT(a,Q)
       b.   SINCERE(a,REQUEST(a,b,Q)) →
             ASSUME(a,CAN(b,Q))
       c.   SINCERE(a,REQUEST(a,b,Q)) →
             ASSUME(a,WILLING(b,Q))
       d.   SINCERE(a,REQUEST(a,b,Q)) → ASSUME($a,-Q$)
             where Q is of the form FUT(DO(b,R))
             ['b *will do act R*']

Thus, if *a* sincerely requests of *b* that *b* do *R*, then *a* wants *b* to do *R*,
a assumes that *b* can do *R*, *a* assumes that *b* would be willing to do *R*,
and *a* assumes that *b* will not do *R* in the absence of the request. We
assume that (3) is a set of meaning postulates in part characterizing
the concept of sincerity, in this case what sincerity means in the case
of requests.[2] What is interesting about these meaning postulates is
that they determine a set of conversational postulates, for English
and for a great many other languages as well.[3] Consider, first, the following sentences:

(4)   a.   *I want you to take out the garbage.*
         b.   *Can you take out the garbage?*
         c.   *Would you be willing to take out the garbage?*
         d.   *Will you take out the garbage?*

Each of these sentences can convey a request to take out the garbage. Compare (4) with (5), in which we have similar sentences that
do not convey such a request:

(5)   a.   *I suppose you're going to take out the
                   garbage.*
             b.   *Must you take out the garbage?*
             c.   *Are you likely to take out the garbage?*
             d.   *Ought you to take out the garbage?*

   How can we account for the fact that the sentences of (4) convey a
request to take out the garbage, but those of (5) do not. Note that
there is a systematic relation between the sentences of (4) and the

---

[2] Actually, each line in (3) should be a theorem, following from a single meaning
postulate giving if-and-only-if conditions for sincere requests.

[3] We do not know whether or not the conversational postulates discussed here are
universal. However, we have checked with a number of speakers of widely divergent
languages, and each of them finds that direct translations of the sentences of (4) can
convey requests in his language. We would not be at all surprised to find that these
postulates were universals.

postulates of (3). Look at the right-hand side of the arrows in (3). Sentence (4a) is the assertion of WANT(a,Q), where $a = I$ and $b = you$. Sentences (4b), (4c), and (4d) are the questions corresponding to CAN(b,Q), WILLING(b,Q), and $-Q$.[4] In the former case, the subject of WANT is a, the speaker. Let us call (3a) a speaker-based sincerity condition. In the latter cases, b is the subject of the sentence indicating what is assumed by the speaker. We will call these hearer-based sincerity conditions. Thus, we see that:

(6) *One can convey a request by* (*a*) *asserting a speaker-based sincerity condition or* (*b*) *questioning a hearer-based sincerity condition.*

That is, (6) characterizes the following conversational postulates:[5]

(7)   a.   SAY(a,b,WANT(a,Q))* → REQUEST(a,b,Q)
            b.   ASK(a,b,CAN(b,Q))* → REQUEST(a,b,Q)

---

[4] We are assuming that the question corresponding to a negative sentence is a positive question. Interestingly enough, there is no way of expressing a negative request by a question about the future. That is, one cannot convey 'Don't take out the garbage' by either *Won't you take out the garbage?* or *Will you take out the garbage?* We do not know why this should be the case.

Be this as it may, the fact that a positive question corresponds to a negative condition can be used to account for an otherwise mysterious fact, as Robin Lakoff has observed. Suppose you want to convey a negative request like 'Do not make that noise' by a use of postulate (7b). The result is the awkward *Can you not make that noise?* However, given that $\Box - = - \Box$, by a modal equivalence, and given that the $\Box$ corresponding to *can* is *must*, it follows that we can express the above-mentioned negative request by the positive question *Must you make that noise?*

As should be obvious, we are fudging in representing 'assumes that $-Q$ otherwise' by ASSUME (a,$-Q$); we are leaving out the 'otherwise.' Hopefully, we will someday be able to do without this fudge, but at present this is the best we can do.

[5] Actually, we predict additional conversational postulates:

(i)   a.   SAY(a,b,ASSUME(a,CAN(b,Q))) → REQUEST(a,b,Q)
            b.   SAY(a,b,ASSUME(a,WILLING(b,Q))) → REQUEST(a,b,Q)
            c.   SAY(a,b,ASSUME(a,$-Q$)) → REQUEST(a,b,Q)

Sentences (ia) and (ib) do in fact yield a semicorrect result.

(ii)   a.   *I assume you can take out the garbage.*
            b.   *I assume you'd be willing to take out the garbage.*
            c.   *I assume you won't take out the garbage.*

Sentences (iia) and (iib) are requests, but like all statements of hearer-based conditions, they convey imperious (or just plain snotty) requests. We do not know how to account formally for this. Sentence (ic) is wrong for our dialects, though correct in others. And (2c), for us, cannot be a request, but there are speakers for whom it does convey a request. We do not know why such variation should exist, but it does.

    c.   ASK$(a,b,\mathrm{WILLING}(b,Q))^* \rightarrow \mathrm{REQUEST}(a,b,Q)$

    d.   ASK$(a,b,Q)^* \rightarrow \mathrm{REQUEST}(a,b,Q)$

    where Q is of the form $FUT(DO(b,R))$ ['*b will do act R'*]
    (the asterisks will be discussed)

Note that each postulate in (7) has a performative verb on both the left-hand and the right-hand sides of the arrow. It is by means of such postulates that we can get one speech act to entail another.

Strictly speaking, (7) (without asterisks) is inadequate in an important way. A sentence like *Can you take out the garbage?* is ambiguous in context: It can be a real question, that is, a request for information about your ability to take out the garbage, or it can convey a request to do so. However, it can convey a request only if it is assumed by the hearer that the speaker does not intend to convey the question. In this case, the conversationally implied meaning (the request) can be conveyed only if the literal meaning (the question) is not intended to be conveyed and if the hearer assumes that it is not. We will indicate this notationally by putting an asterisk after the illocutionary content:

$$(8)\, V_p(a,b,S)^* = V_p(a,b,S) \text{ AND } -\mathrm{INTEND}(a,\mathrm{CONVEY}(a,b,V_p(a,b,S)))$$
$$\text{AND ASSUME}(b,-\mathrm{INTEND}(a,\mathrm{CONVEY}(a,b,V_p(a,b,S))))$$

    where V_p *is a performative predicate*

The preceding analysis has interesting consequences for the analysis of the logical form of questions. It has been suggested (by Postal, G. Lakoff, Ross, and others) that the logical form of questions should be REQUEST$(a,b,$ TELL$(b,a,S))$ instead of ASK(a,b,S); in other words, *I request that you tell me . . .* instead of *I ask you . . .* This proposal is confirmed, not surprisingly, by the preceding analysis of requests. Compare (9) with (4):

(9)   a.   *I want you to tell me whether Harry left.*[6]

           b.   *Can you tell me where the bus stops?*

           c.   *Would you be willing to tell me why*
                 you left your wife?

           d.   *Will you tell me how to adjust the TV?*

---

[6] A more common way of expressing this is *I want to know whether Harry left.* This is an automatic consequence of the meaning of *tell.* It will be a theorem of any adequate natural logic that TELL$(a,b,whether\ S) \rightarrow$ CAUSE$(a,\mathrm{KNOW}(b,whether\ S))$. Since CAUSE$(a,S) \rightarrow$ is a meaning postulate, it follows that TELL$(a,b,whether\ S) \rightarrow$ KNOW$(b,whether\ S)$ is a theorem. Therefore, since it is the case that:

(*Continued on page 88*)

Each of the sentences in (9) conveys a question. If questions are analyzed in accordance with our suggestion, as a type of request, this follows automatically.

It is not known at present to just what extent the analysis of requests given here extends to other performatives; however, it does extend in certain ways. For example, consider the following speaker-based sincerity conditions:[7]

(10)   a.   SINCERE(a,REQUEST(a,b,Q)) → WANT(a,Q)
        b.   SINCERE(a,SAY(a,b,Q)) → BELIEVE(a,Q)
        c.   SINCERE(a,PROMISE(a,b,Q)) → INTEND(a,Q)

Conditions (10b) and (10c) say that if you are sincere in saying something, then you believe it; and if you are sincere in promising to do something, then you intend to do it. As in the case of requests, one can convey statements and promises by asserting the corresponding speaker-based sincerity conditions.

SINCERE(a,REQUEST(a,b,TELL($b,a,whether\ Q$))) →
                          WANT(a,TELL($b,a,whether\ Q$))

will be a theorem, it will follow that:

SINCERE(a,REQUEST(a,b,TELL($b,a,whether\ Q$))) →
                          WANT(a,KNOW($a,whether\ Q$))

is also a theorem. By (6), it follows that:

SAY(a,b,WANT(a,KNOW($a,whether\ Q$)))° →
                          REQUEST(a,b,TELL($b,a,whether\ Q$))

This is why *I want to know whether Harry left* conveys a request for information.

[7] For other examples, consider the following hearer-based sincerity conditions:

(i)   a.   SINCERE(a,OFFER(a,b,Q)) → ASSUME(a,WANT(b,Q))
        b.   SINCERE(a,THREATEN (a,b,Q)) → ASSUME(a,−WANT(b,Q))

Condition (ia) says that if you are sincerely offering something to somebody, you assume that he wants it. Condition (ib) says that if you are sincerely threatening somebody with something, you assume that he does not want it. As in the case of requests, one can convey offers and threats by questioning the corresponding hearer-based sincerity conditions. What is especially interesting about this case is that since the content of the assumption in (ib) is negative, the corresponding positive question conveys the threat, which turns out to have the same syntactic form as an offer:

(ii)   *Do you want me to leave now?*

Sentence (ii) can be used as either a threat or an offer, and is ambiguous in many contexts. Examples that are unambiguous in normal real-world situations are:

(iii)   a.   *Do you want some cake?*   (an offer)

(11)   a. *I want you to shut the door.*
              b. *I believe it's time to go home.*[8]
              c. *I intend to pay you back.*[9]

Sentence (11b) can be a statement of the complement of *believe*, and (11c) can be a promise. This suggests that we have the following set of postulates:

(12)   a. SAY(a,b,WANT(a,Q))* → REQUEST(a,b,Q)
              b. SAY(a,b,BELIEVE(a,Q))* → SAY(a,b,Q)
              c. SAY(a,b,INTEND(a,Q))* → PROMISE(a,b,Q)

These postulates are predicted from (10) by (6a) or, rather, an extension of (6a) to cover speech acts other than requests. The conditions in (10) provide a formal account for the observation by Austin that sentences like those in (13) can never be said sincerely:

(13) a. *Please close the window, though I don't want you to.*
     b. *Harry is sleeping with Sheila, but I don't believe it.*
     c. *I promise to pay you back, but I don't intend to.*

Reasonableness Conditions

In addition to asking when a speech act is sincere, we need to ask when it is reasonable, since if it is not reasonable, it will normally be open to challenges of certain fixed types. We want to begin to characterize the grounds on which a speech act can be challenged, since challenges constitute a large and important class of replies to speech acts. In general, for each sincerity condition on a speech act, there is

---

     b. *Do you want your candy store to burn down, Mr. Schwartz?* (a threat)

This suggests that we have the following set of conversational postulates:

(iv)   a. ASK(a,b,WANT(b,Q))° → OFFER(a,b,Q)
              b. ASK(a,b,WANT(b,Q))° → THREATEN (a,b,Q)

Which postulate applies in which contexts will depend on the assumptions made in the various contexts.

   [8] Sentence (11b), though it conveys a statement, conveys it with less conviction than a direct statement. We do not know whether this is a defect in the postulate of (10b) or whether it will follow from other, independently motivated postulates.

   [9] There seems to be a dialect split in (11c). For some speakers (11c) constitutes a promise, while for others it does not.

a corresponding reasonableness condition, namely, that the speaker has a reason for maintaining the sincerity condition:

(14)   REASONABLE$(a,V_p(a,b,Q)) \rightarrow$
                           $(\exists r)$REASON$(r,a,[\text{sincerity condition}])$

For example, take the sincerity conditions given earlier:

(15)   a. SINCERE$(a,$REQUEST$(a,b,Q)) \rightarrow$ WANT(a,Q)
       b. SINCERE$(a,$REQUEST$(a,b,Q)) \rightarrow$
           ASSUME$(a,$CAN$(a,Q))$
       c. SINCERE$(a,$REQUEST$(a,b,Q)) \rightarrow$
           ASSUME$(a,$WILLING$(b,Q))$
       d. SINCERE$(a,$REQUEST$(a,b,Q)) \rightarrow$ ASSUME$(a,-Q)$
       e. SINCERE$(a,$SAY$(a,b,Q)) \rightarrow$ BELIEVE(a,Q)
       f. SINCERE$(a,$PROMISE$(a,b,Q)) \rightarrow$ INTEND(a,Q)

Given the schema in (14), (15) yields the following reasonableness conditions:

(16)   a. REASONABLE$(a,$REQUEST$(a,b,Q)) \rightarrow$
           $(\exists r)$REASON$(r,a,$WANT$(a,Q))$
       b. REASONABLE$(a,$REQUEST$(a,b,Q)) \rightarrow$
           $(\exists r)$REASON$(r,a,$ASSUME$(a,$CAN$(b,Q))$
       c. REASONABLE$(a,$REQUEST$(a,b,Q)) \rightarrow$
           $(\exists r)$REASON$(r,a,$ASSUME$(a,$WILLING$(b,Q)))$
       d. REASONABLE$(a,$REQUEST$(a,b,Q)) \rightarrow$
           $(\exists r)$REASON$(r,a,$ASSUME$(a,-Q))$
       e. REASONABLE$(a,$SAY$(a,b,Q)) \rightarrow$
           $(\exists r)$REASON$(r,a,$BELIEVE$(a,Q))$
       f. REASONABLE$(a,$PROMISE $(a,b,Q)) \rightarrow$
           $(\exists r)$REASON$(r,a,$INTEND$(a,Q))$

In other words:

(17)   a. *A request is reasonable only if the speaker has a reason for wanting it done.*
       b. *A request is reasonable only if the speaker has reason for assuming that the hearer can do it.*
       c. *A request is reasonable only if the speaker has reason for assuming that the hearer would be willing to do it.*
       d. *A request is reasonable only if the speaker has a reason for assuming that the hearer would not do it otherwise.*

e. *A statement is reasonable only if the speaker has reason to believe it.*

f. *A promise is reasonable only if the speaker has a reason for intending to do it.*

These conditions characterize some of the types of challenges to speech acts. Some examples are given in (18), in which the reasons are asked for:

(18) a. *Why do you want me to do that?*
b. *What makes you think I can do that?*
c. *What makes you think I would be willing to do that?*
d. *Why do you think I wouldn't do that anyway?*
e. *What makes you think that?*
f. *Why do you intend to do that?*

Other challenges can be given by denials of the reasonableness conditions:

(19) a. *You don't really want me to do that—it's against your best interests.*
b. *I can't do that—I hurt my arm.*
c. *I'd never be willing to do that—it's against my religion.*
d. *I was going to do that anyway.*
e. *There isn't any reason to believe that.*
f. *You don't have any reason for intending to do that—why make a promise?*

The general idea is that if you cast doubt on one of the reasonableness conditions, you cast doubt on the reasonableness of the act itself. In a later section, we will deal with the general problem of how, by asking for a reason, you can be making a negative suggestion.

There are, of course, many other reasonableness conditions besides those predicted by principle (14). For example, it is unreasonable to ask someone to do something if it does not need to be done. Hence, the challenges *Does it need to be done?* and *It's been done already.* Undoubtedly, there are many more such conditions.

Some Other Examples

Grice has written at considerable length about what he calls the Cooperative Principle, and he cites various principles of conversa-

tion that hold for normal speech situations in which the participants
are cooperating. In such situations, Grice has observed, it is assumed
that one will say as much as one knows that is assumed to be relevant to the concerns of one's audience. For example, suppose that at
a party all the guests leave early and this upsets the host. If someone
asked you what had happened, it would be uncooperative to reply
Someone left early, though strictly speaking, it would be true. Or
suppose you are witness to a murder and someone asks you what
happened; it would be uncooperative to reply *Someone tried to
kill Harry*. You would not have said anything false. If someone mur-
dered somebody, then surely he tried to murder him. But you would
be giving the misleading impression that the attempt was unsuc-
cessful.

Let us attempt an initial formalization of this principle of conversation:

(20)   [REP(a,b,SAY(a,b,Q)) AND COOP(a,b,SAY(a,b,Q))
          AND AS($a,P \rightarrow Q$)] $\rightarrow$ [$-$TRUE(KNOW(A,P))
          OR AS($a,-$REL(b,P))
          OR AS(a,SAY(a,b,Q)) $\rightarrow$ CONV(a,b,P)]

If a is replying to b in saying Q, and if a is cooperating with b in
saying Q, and if a assumes that P implies Q, then either it is not the
case that a knows P or a is assuming that P is not relevant or a is
assuming that, in saying Q to b, he is conveying P to b. This depends, of course, on the notion of relevance. When, for instance, is a
reply relevant to a question? It also depends on the notion of a reply.
What, in general, counts as a reply? Both notions will require considerable study. But if we ever come to understand precisely what constitutes a reply and a relevant reply, then (20) will be a reasonable
first approximation to a valid conversational postulate.

Let us take another example. Suppose I come up to an acquaintance on the street and say to him:

(21)   *Your wife is faithful.*

Chances are he would do a double-take or become angry with me.
The reason is fairly clear. In a conversational situation in which one
is not making small talk, that is, in situations in which statements are
meant to inform, you do not normally say something that the person
you're talking to presumably knows or takes for granted.[10] That is

---

[10] There are other situations besides small talk in which statements are not meant to
inform. For instance, in displaying an argument to someone, one normally states
premises that one anticipates are already known, e.g., *The Pope's a Catholic, right? So
why should he be celebrating Passover?*

part of what it means to intend to inform:

(22) $SAY(a,b,Q)^+ \rightarrow INTEND(a,CAUSE(a,COME$
$ABOUT(KNOW(b,Q))))$

> where + is a fudge to rule out small talk and other conversational situations in which one does not intend to inform

Given the meaning postulate for CAUSE:

(23) $\qquad\qquad CAUSE(a,S) \rightarrow S$

it follows from (22) that:

(24) $SAY(a,b,Q)^+ \rightarrow INTEND(a,COME\ ABOUT(KNOW(b,Q)))$

Then (25) should follow from the meaning of INTEND (though that has not been investigated in detail formally):

(25) $\qquad INTEND(a,COME\ ABOUT(R)) \rightarrow ASSUME(a,-R)$

From (22), (23), (24), and (25), it should follow that:

(26) $\qquad SAY(a,b,Q)^+ \rightarrow ASSUME(a,-KNOW(b,Q))$

Thus, in saying (21) to an acquaintance, I am assuming that he does not know whether his wife is faithful. This, of course, could precipitate a double take or anger on his part.

As (21) shows, one can say something whose primary meaning is innocuous in a given context, though the conversationally entailed meaning is far from innocuous. Another case of this sort has been given by Searle (1969: 124). It is usually taught in beginning logic courses that sentences of the form *P or not P* are tautologies and so do not convey anything. But, as Searle points out, sentences like the following can convey quite a bit:

(27) *Either Senator Quirk is a Communist or he isn't.*

In general, when one states a disjunction, one assumes that both of the disjuncts are possible:

(28) $\qquad SAY(a,b,P\ OR\ Q) \rightarrow [ASSUME(a,POSSIBLE(P))$
$AND\ ASSUME(a,POSSIBLE(Q))]$

If someone says (27), then he is assuming that it is possible that Senator Quirk is a Communist. In present-day America, since it is bad to be a Communist and since a senator should be above suspicion, someone saying (27) is questioning the loyalty of Senator Quirk. Interestingly enough, (29) has the same effect:

(29) *Either Senator Quirk is a loyal American or he isn't.*

Here, the speaker is assuming that it is possible that Senator Quirk is not a loyal American, and so is again questioning his loyalty.

THE ROLE OF CONVERSATIONAL POSTULATES IN GRAMMAR

Why Questions

Consider a question like (30):

(30)   *Why are you painting your house purple?*

This can be a normal question. You see someone painting his house purple and you ask why. On the other hand, it can be construed as a suggestion that he should not be painting his house purple. Thus, we can expect appropriate replies like either (31a) or (31b):

(31)   a.   *I don't have much money and there was a sale on*
              purple paint at the hardware store.
         b.   *What's wrong with purple?*

We will be interested in the reading in which this is not a straight-forward question. How can we account for this reading, taking context into account? What conversational postulates will be required?

Let us assume that the logical form of (30) is (32), or something of the sort:

(32)   REQUEST(a,b,TELL($b,a,(Tr)$REASON(r,b,DO(b,Q))))
           where (Tr)REASON(r,b,DO(b,Q)) stands for the r
           such that r is a reason for b to do Q'

When someone asks for a reason, either he is making a simple request for information and has no intention of judging whether or not the reason given is a good or bad reason, or he may be asking for justification and therefore be intending to judge whether or not the reason given is a good one. Thus, the following will be true in any such situation:

(33)   INTEND(a,JUDGE(a,WHETHER(SHOULD
          (REASON(r,b,DO(b,Q)))))) OR
          $-$INTEND(a,JUDGE(a,WHETHER(SHOULD
          (REASON(r,b,DO(b,Q))))))
             where SHOULD(REASON(r,b,DO(b,Q))) stands for
             '*r should be a reason for b to do Q*' *or, in other*
             words, '*r is a good reason for b to do Q.*'

If it is assumed that the speaker is just asking for information and has no intention of making a judgment, then we get a straightforward *why* question. But if it is assumed that the speaker will be making a judgment as to whether the reason is a good one, then other factors enter the situation. Suppose that *b* gives *a* his reason for doing *Q*, and suppose that *a* judges that it is a bad reason, that is, that it should not be a reason for *b* to do *Q*, then it will almost invariably be the case that *a* will believe that perhaps *b* should not do *Q*:

(34)   STANDARD ASSUMPTION
        [REASON(r,b,DO(b,Q)) AND
            JUDGE(a,−SHOULD(REASON(r,b,DO(b,Q))))
            BELIEVE(a,POSSIBLE(−SHOULD(DO(b,Q))))

Now, suppose that the speaker performs some speech act, and that that speech act conversationally implies that the speaker believes that it is possible that the hearer should not do *Q*; then the speaker is suggesting that the hearer should not do *Q*. This is a way of conveying a 'softened suggestion.' For example, suppose the speaker says:

(35)   *Maybe you shouldn't paint your house purple.*

In saying (35) sincerely, he is conveying the suggestion that the addressee should not paint his house purple. The general form of the appropriate conversational postulate is:

(36)   SOFTENED SUGGESTION POSTULATE
        $V_p(a,b,R)$ AND [$V_p(a,b,R)$ →
            BELIEVE(a,POSSIBLE(S))] → SUGGEST(a,S)
            where V_p *stands for any performative predicate,
            and R and S are any propositions.*

Then (37) will be a special case of (36):

(37) $V_p(a,b,R)$ AND [$V_p(a,b,R)$ →
        BELIEVE(a,POSSIBLE(−SHOULD (DO(b,Q)))))] →
        SUGGEST(a,−SHOULD (DO(b,Q)))

Now, if we let $V_p(a,b,R)$ = (32), and if we assume that that speaker is going to judge whether or not the addressee's reason is a good one, then the following will be conveyed by the utterance of (30):

(38)   JUDGE(a,−−SHOULD(REASON(r,b,DO(b,Q)))) →
        SUGGEST(a,−DO(b,Q))

Informally, (38) says:

(39)   *Unless you have a good reason for doing Q,
            you shouldn't do Q.*

It is for this reason that (30) conveys (40) in a context in which a straightforward nonjudgment *why* question is ruled out:

(39')   *Unless you have a good reason for painting your*
          house purple, you shouldn't paint your house purple.

Let us suppose that the preceding analysis is plausible, minor details aside. What is especially interesting about it is that the ambiguity of (30), that is, the fact that (30) can convey two very different meanings, is not due to its having two different logical structures. Rather, the ambiguity is one of conveyed meaning, depending on context. In one class of contexts, the normal meaning of the question is conveyed. In another class of contexts, given certain conversational postulates, a very different meaning can be conveyed.

This sort of ambiguity, where there is no difference of logical structure, is more than a mere linguistic curiosity. It turns out that there are grammatical phenomena that can disambiguate in such cases. Consider:

(40)   *Why paint your house purple?*

In (40), *you* and the tense marker are deleted. Presumably, (40) has the same logical structure as:

(41)   *Why do you paint your house purple?*

or something close to (41). But (41) is ambiguous in the same way that (30) is. What is interesting about (40) is that it is not ambiguous. Sentence (40) can never be a straightforward question. It always conveys:

(39'') *Unless you have some good reason for painting your*
       house purple, you should not paint your house purple.

That is, the rule that deletes *you* + tense can apply only if (39'') is conveyed. If our analysis is correct and (39') is conveyed by conversational implication, and then only in certain contexts, then it follows that the conditions for the correct application of *you* + tense deletion are dependent on context and on conversational implication.

An informal, first approximation to such a rule would be:

(42)   *With respect to a class of contexts CON_i and a set of*
        conversational postulates CP, WHY YOU TENSE
        $x \Rightarrow$ WHY x, if and only if, letting L be the logical struc-
        ture of the sentence, $CON_i \cup CP \cup \{L\}$ ⊩ ('Unless
        you have some good reason for doing x, you should not
        do x').

One can invent various notations for representing rules of this kind, factoring out the sort of thing that will appear in all such rules. Another informal but somewhat more compact way might be:

(43) WHY YOU TENSE $x \Rightarrow$ WHY x ONLY IF C
      $\Vdash$ ('*Unless you have some good reason for doing x, you should not do x.*')

In (43), C $\Vdash$ indicates that the application of the rules is relative only to those contexts and conversational postulates such that they together with the logical structure of the sentence entail what is on the right-hand side of C $\Vdash$. Such a rule would, of course, be trans-derivational. As logical structures and transderivational rules are studied in more detail, further formalization will be possible.

We have argued as follows: In *why* questions like (30), the ambiguity is due not to different logical structures for the same sentence but to the fact that the sentence can be uttered in different contexts. In some contexts, one gets a normal question meaning, while in other contexts, certain conversational postulates result in another meaning being conveyed, in particular, one of the form (38). Given such an account, one can use it for setting up a rule to describe what is going on in sentences like (40), in which the deletion results in disambiguation.

Some Other Cases

If the proposal made earlier is essentially correct, that is, if it is headed in the right direction, then it may be possible to use the same sort of apparatus to account for other recalcitrant phenomena. Let us consider a small catalogue of examples that are likely cases.

Sadock has noticed that the word *please* has a different distribution in final position than in initial position:

(44) *In initial position, please goes with any sentence that conversationally conveys a request in the given context, regardless of the superficial grammatical form of the sentence.*[11]

[11] Actually, this condition needs to be much more restricted. For example, *please* generally goes with requests that are for the speaker or someone he is representing. It does not go with requests to carry out something that the addressee is already obligated to do, e.g., *Shouldn't you close the door, please?* (Sadock's example.)

In general, there is much more going on in conveyed requests than we understand. As Wilbur Haas (personal communication) has observed, a statement conveying a request may be conjoined with a true imperative: *I want two hamburgers, and put*

(*Continued on page 98*)

In final position, *please* goes with any sentence whose logical structure conveys a direct request and which conversationally conveys a request in the given context.

Consider the following examples:

(45)   a.   *Please, can you open a window?*
              b.   *Please, will you get me a glass of water?*
              c.   *Please, it's cold in here.*
              d.   *Please, my daughter's a virgin.*
              e.   *Please, it's 10 o'clock.*
              f.   *Please, be glad that they didn't fire you.*
              g.   *Please, get me a drink.*

Compare (45) with:

(46)   a.   *Can you open a window, please?*
              b.   *Will you get me a glass of water, please?*
              c.   **It's cold in here, please.*
              d.   **My daughter's a virgin, please.*
              e.   **It's 10 o'clock, please.*
              f.   **Be glad that they didn't fire you, please.*
              g.   *Get me a drink, please.*

In (45), all of the sentences with *please* omitted could, in the appropriate contexts, convey requests. With *please* added initially, the sentences remain grammatical, but the sentences are now appropriate only to those contexts in which they convey requests. In (46), overt requests like (46g) and questions, which as we saw above are types of requests, like (46a) and (46b), permit *please* in final position. Statements that convey requests do not permit final *please*, nor do advice imperatives, such as (46f), which do not convey requests directly in their logical structure. Similarly, there are questions that can never convey requests for information or any other type of request in any context, and these do not take *please*, either initially or finally:

---

mustard on both. But this is not always possible. Recall that, in certain contexts, *It's cold in here* may convey *Close the window.* Although we can get *Close the window and get out*, we cannot in those contexts get *It's cold in here and get out.*

As Steve Straight (personal communication) has observed, it is sometimes possible to address one person and convey a request to another. For example, if at a meeting someone in the audience says to the speaker in a loud voice, *Don't you think the people in the back of the room should shut up?*, he is conveying a request to the people in the back of the room.

(47)   a.   *Who has ever lifted a finger to help me?*
       b.   **Please, who has ever lifted a finger to help me?*
       c.   **Who has ever lifted a finger to help me, please?*

Rhetorical questions like (47b) and (47c) can convey only statements, and so can never take *please*.

Thus, it would appear that the distribution of the morpheme *please* is, in part, determined by context and conversational implication.

Here works in a somewhat similar fashion. When prefixed to a sentence and followed by a pause, *here* has two distinct uses, both of which involve conversational implication:

(48)   a.   **Here** *with a following pause may be prefixed to any sentence that, in context, conversationally implies a request and in which the speaker is trying to get the attention of the addressee.*
       b.   **Here** *with a following pause may be prefixed to any sentence that, in context, conversationally implies an offer by the speaker to the addressee.*

Consider the following examples. First, examples of (48a):

(49)   a.   *Here, I want a roast beef special to go.*
           b.   *Here, I need that wrench.*
           c.   *Here, can you take care of me?*
           d.   *Here, let me through.*

In each case, the speaker is trying to get the attention of the addressee and is making a request. In (49a) and (49c), the request is not direct, but is conveyed conversationally according to postulates given earlier. In each case, the request can be conveyed without *here,* though then the sentences are ambiguous. *Here* disambiguates, and is permitted only with conversationally conveyed requests, not with true statements or questions. Now, consider examples of (48b):

(50)   a.   *Here, pass me that wrench.*
           b.   *Here, that's no way to fix a flat tire.*
           c.   *Here, can you get me a large wrench?*
           d.   *Here, I know how to do that.*

Suppose you come upon someone trying to fix a flat tire, and you say any of the sentences of (50). They can be construed only as offers. It would be rather inappropriate to say (50b) or (50d) and then walk away. Each of the sentences without *here* is, of course, ambiguous and can either be an offer or not, depending on context and conversational implication. *Here* disambiguates, and is permitted with offers, not statements or questions. In the case of requests, there is an ambiguity depending on whether or not the speaker is trying to get the hearer's attention. If he already has the hearer's attention, then a sentence like (50a) can only be an offer. Of course, suppose the speaker is also fixing a flat tire and does not have the hearer's attention, then (50a) is ambiguous and can be either a request or an offer.

Another case involves the rule of verb–subject inversion. In most dialects, inversion of the verb to second position is obligatory in embedded questions, but nonapplicable in questions that are unembedded in surface structure:

(51)   a.   *I am asking you where Harry went.*
              b.   *Where did Harry go?*

As we would expect, given the preceding discussion, requests for information can be conveyed by statements indicating a desire for knowledge:

(52)   *I want to know where Harry went.*

Sentence (52) either can be taken literally as a statement of a desire for knowledge or, in contexts in which it is not taken literally, can convey a request by the speaker that the hearer tell him where Harry went. The request-for-information reading will follow from conversational postulates given earlier.

Although verb–subject inversion is usually obligatory in sentences like (52), there are dialects in which both of the following are possible:

(53)   a.   *I want to know where Harry went.*
              b.   *I want to know where did Harry go.*

Sentence (53a) is ambiguous in these dialects, as in the others, and can convey either a literal statement of desire or a request for information. But (53b) in these dialects can convey only a request for information. It is inappropriate in contexts in which one is just stating a desire for knowledge and not requesting information. The nonapplication of verb–subject inversion is a disambiguating factor. But if the ambiguity of (53a) results not from a difference of logical structure but from the application of conversational postulates in given contexts, then it follows that the environment for the application or nonapplication of verb–subject inversion mentions not the literal content of the sentence but the conversationally implied content. Note that, in this dialect, verb–subject inversion is obligatory if no request for information is being conveyed, as in a past-tense statement.

(54)   a.   *Yesterday I wanted to know where Harry went.*
       b.   **Yesterday I wanted to know where did Harry go.*

The difference between these dialects and the standard dialect can
be expressed as follows:

(55)   a.   STANDARD DIALECT
            *Verb–subject inversion is nonapplicable in literal
            requests for information that are not embedded in
            surface structure.*
       b.   NONSTANDARD DIALECT
            *Verb–subject inversion is nonapplicable in requests
            for information (either literal or conveyed).*

Here, as is often the case, the nonstandard rule is the more general.

Some Problems

We have seen that there are regular rules, conversational postulates, that determine what meaning an utterance conveys, given the
literal content of the utterance and the context in which it is uttered.
We have also seen that there are rules of grammar, rules determining
the distribution of morphemes, that depend on the conveyed, not the
literal, meaning of sentences. We have attempted in a handful of
cases to provide a primitive analysis of some relatively transparent
cases in these terms. We would now like to consider some problems,
on which we have not been able to make much headway, but which
seem to be generally similar to those considered earlier.

The question in (56) can be construed in various ways, depending
on the context, and so it can be answered in various ways:

(56)   *Do you know who lives next door to you?*
       a.   *Yes.*
       b.   *No, tell me.*
       c.   *Sylvia Vigones.*

These correspond to the following conveyed meanings:

(57)   a.   (literal)
       b.   *If you don't know who lives next door to you, I'll
            tell you.*
       c.   *I request that you tell me who lives next door to
            you.*

It is possible for there to be contexts in which (56) is to be taken literally, and a yes or no answer would suffice. But this is very rare.
Usually, either (57b) or (57c) is conveyed. How does this come

about? The contexts that bring about the differentiation seem fairly clear:

(58) a. *I make no assumptions as to whether you know who lives next door to you.*
      b. *I assume that you probably don't know who lives next door to you.*
      c. *I assume that you probably do know who lives next door to you.*

These assumptions determine mutually exclusive classes of contexts. The problem is what, exactly, are the conversational postulates that, given the literal meaning and the assumptions of (58), enable one to convey the meanings of (57)? Precisely how can they be formulated?

A similar problem arises in:

(59) a. *I don't know whether the frying pan goes in the closet or not.*
      b. *Either the frying pan goes in the closet or not.*

If you are drying the dishes, you can turn to your spouse and say (59a), and it can convey the question:

(60)   *Does the frying pan go in the closet or not?*

But (59b), at least with normal intonation, cannot be used to convey that question. Why not? And why can (59a) be used in such a situation to convey (60)? Again the question is, What are the right postulates and how, exactly, can they be formulated?

A particularly interesting problem has been brought to our attention by Robin Lakoff. Consider the following examples:

(61) a. *May I offer you some of this brandy?*   (an offer)
      b. *Must I offer you some of this brandy?*   (not an offer)

(62) a. *I may offer you some of this brandy.*   (not an offer)
      b. *I must offer you some of this brandy.*   (an offer)

Sentence (61a) is an offer, but (61b) is not. Clearly, the offer reading is possible only with the *may* of permission and not with the *may* of possibility. Why does asking permission to convey an offer, as in (61a), convey the offer? Why does a question with *must*, as in (61b) fail in this respect? In (62) the situation reverses. Why does a statement of a requirement to make an offer convey the offer, as in (62b)? Note, incidentally, that in (62a), the *may* can only be the *may* of possibility, not the *may* of permission, as is *always* the case with first-person statements; so the question of why (62a) does not convey an offer does not arise, since (62a) does not correspond to (62a) in the appropriate respect.

As one might expect, this phenomenon holds, not simply for offers but for other speech acts as well. It is a fairly general phenomenon:

(63)   a.   *May I tell you that I love you?*   (a statement)
       b.   *May I ask you how you got in here?*   (a question)
       c.   *May I warn you that my pet wombat is dangerous?*   (a warning)
       d.   *May I suggest that you accept the nomination?*   (a suggestion)
       e.   *May I apologize for dripping ice cream on your dress?*   (an apology)

(64)   a.   *I may tell you that I love you.*   (not a statement of affection)
       b.   *I may ask you how you got in here.*   (not a question)
       c.   *I may warn you that my pet wombat is dangerous.*   (not a normal warning)
       d.   *I may suggest that you accept the nomination.*   (not a suggestion)
       e.   *I may apologize for dripping ice cream on your dress.*   (not an apology)

But this is by no means completely general:

(65)   *May I accuse you of murder?*   (not an accusation)

(66)   a.   *May I ask you to move your car?*   (a request)
       b.   *May I tell you to move your car?*   (not a request)

(67)   a.   *May I offer to marry you?*   (an offer)
       b.   *May I promise to marry you?*   (not a promise)

Why is it that in some, but not all, cases a question of permission for a performative utterance conveys that performative utterance? And why is it sometimes possible that a statement of obligation for a performative utterance [as in (62b)] conveys that performative utterance, but the corresponding question does not?

In each of these cases, an embedded performative is conveyed, presumably by virtue of some still unformulated conversational postulates. There are, of course, many other cases in which embedded performatives are conveyed. For example:

(68)   a.   *I am obligated to warn you that unless you pay up,*
           your car will be repossessed.   (a warning)
       b.   *I'm supposed to tell you that Billy won't be home*
           until six.   (a statement)
       c.   *I regret that I must ask you to leave.*   (a request)

Such examples raise the more general question of what principles of
conversation permit embedded performatives to be conveyed. Of
course, for each example cited here it is possible to set up an ad hoc
postulate to handle that example. But the real question is, What are
the correct generalizations? From what independently motivated
principle does it FOLLOW that (67a) is an offer but (67b) is not a
promise?

CONCLUDING REMARKS

   What we have proposed is a very small addition to the theory of
generative semantics, but one that should be able to handle a very
large range of linguistic phenomena previously beyond formal description. It has been shown that the theory of grammar requires a
natural logic and a set of transderivational rules. Natural logic will
characterize the notion of entailment. In particular, it will characterize entailments of a sentence, given a class of contexts characterized
by a finite, consistent set of logical structures. What we have done is
to take the notion of entailment relative to a class of contexts and add
conversational postulates to get conversational implications relevant
to a class of contexts. The notion of entailment is the same; the notion of a class of contexts is the same; and the notion of logical structure is the same. All that is new is the addition of conversational
postulates formulated in terms of ordinary logical structures. With
respect to rules of grammar, the theory of grammar already requires
transderivational rules. Transderivational rules characterize what
happens in one derivation on the basis of what is the case in one or
more other, related derivations. Transderivational rules, as previously conceived, could mention a small number of possible relations between derivations. For example, consider derivations D^a and
D^b.

(69) D^a: S^a, . . . L^a *(where S^a is surface structure and*
         D^b: S^b, . . . L^b *L^a is logical structure).*

Among the various relations between derivations D^a and D^b hitherto
considered in transderivational rules have been:

(70) L^a entails L^b
                         L^a is equivalent to L^b
                         L^a presupposes L^b
                         L^a assumes L^b
                         $t(S^a) = t(S^b)$
                            where $t(S^i)$ is the terminal
                            string of surface structure S^i

We are proposing that one additional relation be added to those
already used in transderivational rules, namely:

(71) L^a conversationally entails L^b

We are suggesting that, given just the addition of conversational
postulates and the addition of the relation of conversational implication to transderivational rules, it will ultimately be possible to
handle adequately the range of phenomena discussed here, depending, of course, on the further development of natural logic and
transderivational grammar.

Since not much is known about natural logic, all of the proposed
logical structures used in this chapter were approximations. In other
words, like all trees drawn in discussions of syntax, our logical structures are fudges, the best we can do at present, but certainly subject
to change. And like all rules of grammar mentioned in discussions of
syntax, our proposed postulates are approximations at best. But they
are sufficiently precise approximations to have a predictive value and
to be refutable. Like rules of grammar, they apply recursively and so
make extensive predictions, which can be shown to be wrong. In
fact, we would be surprised if the tentative postulates proposed in
this chapter were not found very soon to be inadequate in a great
many ways.

ACKNOWLEDGMENTS

This work was partially supported by grant GS-2939 from The National Science
Foundation to The University of Michigan. It was inspired by the work of philosophers J. L. Austin, H. P. Grice, John Searle, and Stephen Schiffer, and by the work of
linguists Robin Lakoff, Dwight Bolinger, Jerrold Sadock, and Georgia Green. We are
grateful to the following people for numerous lengthy discussions: Susan Andres, Ann
Borkin, Deborah James, Robin Lakoff, John Lawler, Brian Loar, John Miyamoto, Paul
Neubauer, Edward Stephenson, and Sabahat Tura.

REFERENCES

Austin, J. L. *How to do things with words.* New York and London: Oxford University Press, 1962.

Bolinger, D. The imperative in English. In *To Honor Roman Jakobson.* The Hague: Mouton, 1967.

Green, G. WH imperatives. Unpublished manuscript, 1970.

Lakoff, G. Some thoughts on transderivational constraints. University of Michigan mimeo, 1970. In B. Kachru *et al.* (Eds.), *Papers in linguistics in honor of Henry and Renee Kahane.* Edmonton, Ill.: Linguistic Research, Inc., to appear.

Lakoff, R. Questionable answers and answerable questions. In B. Kachru *et al.* (Eds.), *Papers in linguistics in honor of Henry and Renee Kahane.* Edmonton, Ill.: Linguistic Research, Inc., to appear.

Sadock, J. WH imperatives. In *Studies presented to Robert B. Lees by his students.* Edmonton, Ill.: Linguistic Research, Inc., 1970.

Schiffer, S. Meaning. Ph. D. dissertation, Oxford University, 1970.

Searle, J. *Speech acts.* New York and London: Cambridge University Press, 1969.

HOW TO GET PEOPLE
TO DO THINGS WITH WORDS
The Whimperative Question*

G. M. GREEN
University of Illinois

The analysis of sentences that have so-called imperative force, but a form other than the subjectless, tenseless, active verb phrase construction normal for so-called imperatives, was all but ignored during the classical period of transformational grammar, the sole exception being Bolinger's heretical article on English imperatives (Bolinger, 1967). In 1969, Sadock, intrigued, I imagine, by the implications of this phenomenon for the theory of performative hypersentences, took a close look at one subset of such sentences, that exemplified by (1)–(5):

(1)   *Will you close the door please?*
(2)   *Can you lend me a dime please?*
(3)   *Won't you have a seat please?*
(4)   *Could you move over please?*
(5)   *Do you want to set the table now?*

The question Sadock raised was this: How should a grammar account for native speakers' intuitions about sentences like (1)–(5)? In particular, how should a grammar explain the fact that these sentences

* ©G. M. Green

with the form of questions are intended and understood not as requests for information but as requests for action, just as the corresponding imperative forms (1')–(5') are:

(1')   *Close the door please.*
(2')   *Lend me a dime please.*
(3')   *Have a seat please.*
(4')   *Move over please.*
(5')   *Set the table now.*

In this chapter, I will consider four approaches to answering this question and discuss the merits of each, pointing out important classes of data that an adequate theory will have to account for.

FOUR APPROACHES

Sadock, reasoning that forms like (1)–(5) had the superficial form and intonation of questions but the cooccurrence restrictions and illocutionary force of so-called imperatives, called these forms WHIM-PERATIVES and proposed to analyze them as a conjunction of a question and an imperative, as in (6):

(6)

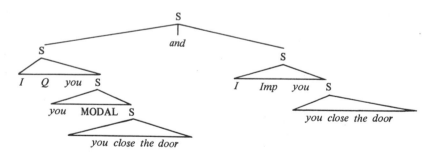

In Sadock's theory, embedded hypersentences are claimed to underlie various kinds of echo utterances, so they would not be available as the source of whimperatives. According to Sadock, a structure like (7) underlies a question echo of an imperative, e.g., *Wash myself?*, and a structure like (8) underlies an exhortation to ask a question of specified content, e.g., *Am I tired*, meaning 'Ask me if I'm tired.'

(7)   (8)

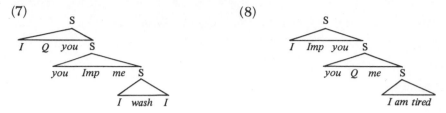

In the derivation of, say, (1) from (6), conjunction reduction would yield a clause that was dominated by two performative verbs, the first of which, it was argued, would account for the form, and the second of which would account for the force and cooccurrence restrictions on these sentences.

One can take issue with this analysis on the grounds that conjunction reduction and performative deletion would have to be obligatory for these structures (despite the fact that in no other cases do they seem to be governed), since the conjunction of a question and an order or request for action is ill-formed and does not have the force of the whimperative, as shown in (9) and (10). Furthermore, the proposed conjunction seems to be semantically ill-formed, even when each of the clauses is well-formed and even though there might be a connection between them that would be plausible enough to permit conjoining. Thus the ungrammaticality of (11) and (12):

(9)   *I ask you if you can open the door, and I order you to do it/so.
(10)   *Can you open the door, and do it/so.
(11)   *I ask you whether you like bagels, and I order you to tell me quick.
(12)   *Do you like bagels and tell me quick.

When one adds whimperatives of the form of (13) to the class of cases to be considered:

(13)   Why don't you put a different record on?

it becomes clear that the appropriate answers to a whimperative are neither those appropriate to a question nor those appropriate to an order or a request. That is, the appropriate answer to a yes–no question is yes or no. Yes and no may be followed by some vocative form of address, and by a pronoun referring to the subject of the question and a reduced form of the predicate phrase, as in (14):

(14)   Q: *Does John like creamed spinach?*
                                  A: *Yes/*OK/*All right.*
                                       Yes, he does/*might.
                                       Well, he might/*does.[1]
                                       Yes, ma'am/stupid.
                                       No, ma'am, he doesn't (like it).
                                       No, he doesn't, Captain.

The appropriate answer to a *why* question is a *because* clause. The *because* may be elliptically suppressed, and may be followed by a vocative form, as in (15):

(15):   Q: *Why didn't John kiss his Aunt Harriet?*
            A: *(Because) she has bad breath (ma'am/stupid).*

The appropriate verbal response to an 'imperative' utterance depends on whether or not there is an intention to comply. If the addressee attempts immediately to comply, he need not say anything, although failure to respond verbally will be interpreted as hostility unless the speaker and addressee are on very intimate terms. If the addressee does not intend to comply immediately, he may indicate that he IS going to comply by the use of such formulas as *OK* and *All right*, but if he wants to use *yes*, he must follow it with a respectful form of vocative address, as in (16), and the permitted modal auxiliary is limited to *will:*

(16)   I: *Take out the garbage (please).*
                   R: *OK/All right/Sure.*
                        *Yes.
                        Yes, ma'am/*(you) killjoy, I will/*can.

If the addressee intends to refuse, he is socially obligated to respond verbally. He may refuse straight out, by saying *no*; but if he wants to be polite, adding some respectful form of address does not help. Instead, he must offer an explanation for his refusal, and perhaps an apology, as in (17):

(17)   I: *Take out the garbage (please).*
                   R: *No.*
                        I will not
                        ?I won't.
                        *No ma'am/you big meanie.

---

[1] For a discussion of the interesting properties of affirmative answers beginning with *Well*, which explains why you get *might*, but not *does*, here, see R. Lakoff (1971).

(I'm sorry) I can't (I've broken both my arms).
**No (I'm sorry) I can't (I've broken both my arms).*

The appropriate response to a whimperative likewise depends on whether the addressee intends to comply. As with imperatives, if he does, he must say so unless he is on very intimate terms with the speaker. He may use any one of the formulas mentioned in (16), including *yes* plus a vocative of some sort. It need not be respectful, but some form of address must be there. Thus, the examples in (18) contrast somewhat with those in (14)–(16):

(18)   a.   W: *Would you take out the garbage please.*
               R: *OK/All right/Sure.*
                    Yes, dear/you lazy bum.
                    **Yes.*
                    **Well, I could.*
         b.   W: *Why don't you clean up that mess.*
               R: *OK/All right.*
                    Yes, ma'am/??you lazy bum.
                    **Yes.*

If the addressee intends not to comply, he must offer some explanation, as in (19). *No* is not an appropriate response, nor is *no sir/ma'am/dear*, etc., and *No I can't/won't/wouldn't*, etc., is a very rude way of responding.[2]

(19)   a.   W: *Would you take out the garbage please.*
               R: *(I'm sorry) I can't/It's not my job/I've broken*
                         both my arms.
                    ??No dear.
                    (No) it's not my job.
                    No, I won't/?wouldn't.
         b.   W: *Why don't you clean up that mess.*
               R: *(I'm sorry) It's not my job/I can't; I've*
                         broken both my arms.
                    **No (dear/bitch).*
                    *No, it's not my job/*I can't.*

   [2] Actually, there are whimperatives like *Do/would you mind opening the window* and *Would it be too much trouble to open the window* for which, for some speakers, compliance is accompanied by *No* with or without a respectful vocative. Noncompliance is conventionally accompanied by an explanation, and *yes sir* and *yes ma'am* are as rude as a mere *yes*. For other speakers, *sure* (but probably not *OK*, and definitely not *yes*) accompanies compliance, and noncompliance is accompanied by some kind of negative with an apology or explanation, e.g., *I'm afraid I do* or *I'm sorry, I can't.*

Since there is ample justification for deriving questions from requests or orders to give information anyway (Katz and Postal, 1964; Langacker, 1969), one could attempt to account for the semantic and conventional properties of whimperatives by deriving them from structures in which the ordered disjunction of the activity requested and the 'tell me' request (the question) are embedded as the complement of a verb of requesting or whatever, that is, something schematically of the form of (20):

(20)

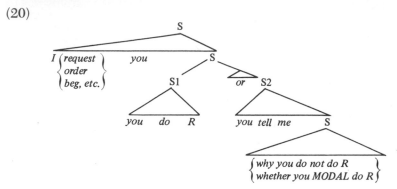

On semantic grounds such a structure works fine for *why don't you* whimperatives. It predicts that the response will either be compliance (R), which can be accompanied by an expression appropriate to agreeing to a request or will be a reason for noncompliance. Unfortunately, aside from the deletions and/or incorporations of performatives and conjunctions required, which are not significantly more or less plausible than those required for Sadock's proposal, there are difficulties with claiming such an analysis for yes-no whimperatives like (1)–(5). The analysis indicated in (20) incorrectly predicts that the speaker would be as satisfied with a mere linguistic response like *yes I will* or *yes I can* as he would be with compliance, but of course he would not.[3] If someone says *Will you give me a hand,* he is not going to accept *Yes I will* as complying with his request.[4]

On the other hand, Grice's maxims of conversation offer an explanation for this fact: When addressed with either a whimperative or an utterance closer to the form of (20), i.e., *Either close the door or*

---

[3] *Yes, I will, but I don't want to* is an appropriate response, but it accompanies compliance, not refusal. *Yes, I could/can, but I don't want to* are appropriate also, but do not indicate either compliance or refusal. *Yes, I would, but I don't want to* is not even grammatical, I don't think, much less appropriate.

[4] One might suppose that this form of analysis could be saved by changing the de-

say whether or not you will (can), a respondent would be being un-cooperative if he made any response other than the following:

1. compliance (with or without verbal sign of acquiescence);
2. promise of compliance at a definite time (e.g., *Yes, I will, in about 10 minutes or Sure, but not until I finish my pipe*);
3. announcement of intention not to comply.

To announce in response to a whimperative like (1), *Yes, I will* and then not give any sign of complying would be to violate the maxim of quality (Do not speak falsely or insincerely), as would it to announce intention not to comply and then comply. Apparently people use and take imperative-force utterances to be requests to do something RIGHT NOW, unless some time further in the future is specified. Thus, using a whimperative is equivalent to saying something like:

(21)   *Do R now, or tell me whether or not you'll do R, and if so, when (and if not, why not).*

Notice that if a future time is specified, as in:

(22)   *Can you turn off the oven in half an hour?*

then *Mm hmmm* and *Yes, I will* are perfectly good complete responses and indicate intent to comply. In fact, they are the only possible ways to comply, since to turn off the oven right away would be uncooperative. Likewise, they are appropriate to signify compliance when compliance is silence or inaction, for example, if the request is *Will you let me finish?* or *Be still.*

Notice, also, that assuming an underlying structure like (20) and

---

tails to something like:

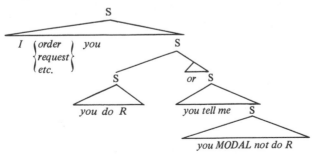

where the complement of 'tell me' is a negative clause with the appropriate modal. However, it is not obvious how 'you tell me that you MODAL not do R' could be considered the source for a positive surface question.

Grice's maxim of relevance correctly predicts that a response to a whimperative of *Yes, I can*,[5] unaccompanied by any attempt to comply, will (in cases other than those just discussed) be taken as signifying that the respondent will not comply, since it is a response to the 'otherwise' horn of the disjunction in (20).

One thing that a structure like (20) DOES NOT predict is that, although *Sure I can* is not a well-formed verbal response to *Will you* and *Would you* whimperatives, *Yes, I will* is as good a compliance affirmer for *Can you, Could you*, and *Would you* whimperatives as it is for *Will you* whimperatives; but this, again, would seem to follow from Grice's maxims.

However, one might wish to abstain from admitting evidence, and thus explanations, based on discourse, and, deprecating underlying structures as clumsy and syntactically ad hoc as (20), turn to something a little closer to the surface for a source for whimperatives. Notice that the complex-underlying-structure approaches just discussed claim, or at least suggest, that imperatives with question tags, such as:

(23)   a.   *Open the window, will you?*
              b.   *Sit down, won't you?*
              c.   *Push harder, can't you?*
              d.   *Open it a little wider, could you?*
              e.   *Add some salt, why don't you?*

are derived from whimperatives by a process analogous to sentence raising (Sadock has called this process FRACTURING), the rule that produces sentences like (24) from structures underlying sentences like (25):

(24)   a.   *John lives in Los Angeles, she thinks.*
              b.   *John will arrive on the Panama Limited, I bet.*

(25)   a.   *She thinks John lives in Los Angeles.*
              b.   *I bet John will arrive on the Panama Limited.*

One might, instead, claim that forms like (1)–(5) are merely simple imperatives to which tags have been added and then preposed, as in (26), making the question form of such 'imperatives' no more than coincidence:

(26)   a.   *Shut up:* → *Shut up, will you?* → *Will you shut up?*
          b.   *Close the window.* → *Close the window, why don't*
               you? → *Why don't you close the window?*

_____
[5] And in many circumstances, *Yes, I will.*

I am not sure whether anyone has made this particular proposal, although the claim that the underlying structure of a whimperative is the same as that of an imperative has been made by Heringer (1972).

Initial plausibility is lent to the analysis of whimperatives as imperatives with preposed tags by the fact that, in general, these tags occur attached only to expressions that alone would have the same illocutionary force as the composite, regardless of which end the 'tag' is found at. Thus, we have, in addition to (23) and (24), sentences like those in (27), which have the same force as the sentences in (28), in which the 'tags' are not present.

(27)   a. *I'll help you, I promise.*
            b. *Who did John invite, I wonder.*
            c. *Is John here, do you suppose?*
            d. *I defended you, I swear.*

(28)   a. *I'll help you.*
            b. *Who did John invite?*
            c. *Is John here?*
            d. *I defended you.*

But we do not find sentences like (29)–(34), which would be predicted by the most general form of an analysis that treated tagged imperatives like (23) as being derived from whimperatives by a fracturing process akin to sentence raising:

(29)   *I helped you, I promise.*
(30)   *Who John invited, I wonder.*
(31)   *He is here, does John think?*
(32)   *Go out and play, may I?*
(33)   *Going out and playing, I am considering.*
(34)   *John kiss my foot, I made.*

To take one case, sentence (32) is predictably ungrammatical according to the tag-addition analysis, since *Go out and play* cannot function as a request for permission to go out and play; similarly (33). The tag-addition analysis predicts that (30) and (31) will be ill-formed as requests for information because subject–verb inversion has not applied, as it should in questions. A fracturing analysis would have to specify that if fracturing (or sentence raising) applies to a question, subject–verb inversion must apply to the complement, even though it normally applies only to the highest clause or (from another point of view) only to the complement of the (possibly deleted or suppressed) performative.

However, there are severe difficulties with this analysis. First of all, if whimperatives are to be derived by preposing independently formed tags, as in (26), and sentences like *I wonder who John invited* and *Do you suppose John is here?* as questions about John are derived similarly from (29b) and (29c), then an independently unmotivated rule will be needed that is the inverse of subject–verb inversion. Second, even ignoring the fact that the identity of the infinitive verb form that follows the modals and the form that is used for imperatives is a peculiarity of English, we should take note of the fact that most languages seem to have whimperatives, but deriving them the same way the English ones would be derived would be very difficult. Some languages, like Hebrew, have neither sentence-raising tags with declaratives nor tagged imperatives. Others, like German, have sentence-raising tags with declaratives, but no tagged imperatives. Spanish has very restricted sentence raising with declaratives, and imperatives tagged only with *quieres* 'do you want.' Thus, the Hebrew translations of both (35a) and (35b) are ungrammatical. Sentence (36a) is well-formed, but (36b) is not. Sentences (37a) and (37b) are not acceptable Spanish, but (37c) is just as grammatical as (37d):

(35)   a.   *'John's a doctor, I think.'
          b.   *'Give me a match, do you want to?'

(36)   a.   *Hans ist ein Arzt, glaub ich.*
          b.   *Geben Sie mir ein Streichholz, wollen Sie?*

(37)   a.   *Juan es médico, creo.*
          b.   *Dame un fósforo, podrías.*
          c.   *Dame un fósforo, quieres.*
          d.   *Quieres darme un fósforo.*

I suppose that an adherent of this third proposal could claim that these languages differ from English in that the tag-formation and preposing rules are obligatory in Hebrew, and in German preposing is obligatory for imperatives that have undergone the optional rule of tag formation; but one would be hard put to explain the situation in Spanish without a global derivational constraint to the effect that tag formation on imperatives is inapplicable except with *querer*, unless preposing is going to occur.

Actually, English itself offers a veritable tar pit of problems for the whimperative-via-tag-formation proposal. First of all, there are a number of whimperatives that do not have corresponding tagged imperatives. Thus:

(38) a. *Do you want to get me a Scotch.*
      b. *Would you like to set the table now.*
      c. *Would it be too much trouble to remove your hat.*
      d. *Do you suppose you could let me finish.*

(39) a. **Get me a Scotch, do you want (to).*
      b. **Set the table now, would you like (to).*
      c. **Remove your hat, would it be too much trouble (to).*
      d. **Let me finish, do you suppose you could.*

(40) a. *Shouldn't you place your feet farther apart.*
      b. *Mightn't you slip a little arsenic in his tea.*
      c. *?Might you open a charge account in your own name.*

(41) a. **Place your feet farther apart, shouldn't you.*
      b. **Slip a little arsenic in his tea, mightn't you.*
      c. **Open a charge account in your own name, might you.*

The analysis of whimperatives as derived from imperatives via tag formation would predict the ungrammaticality of the forms in (39); tags would be defined to consist of a modal plus a pronominal copy of the subject (*you*) and, with some fudging, a *why* in front. However, there would have to be an entirely unrelated source for the imperative force of sentences like (38), and this analysis could account for the ungrammaticality of (41) only by a global derivational constraint to the effect that tag formation with *shouldn't, mightn't,* and *might* is inapplicable unless preposing is going to apply, or by having two rules of preposing, an obligatory one for *might, mightn't,* and *shouldn't,* and an optional one for other modals. Notice that a fracturing analysis could predict the ungrammaticality of (39), if fracturing is limited to whimperatives with modals and *why don't you,* but such an analysis would not readily predict the ungrammaticality of (41).

Furthermore, there are whimperatives like (42) whose 'imperative content' is expressed in a phrase that does not have 'imperative' form, providing counterexamples to the generalization that best supports the whimperative-via-tag-formation-and-preposing analysis: that the tags only occur with phrases that by their form indicate their illocutionary force:

(42)   a. *Would you mind closing the window.*
              b. *Do you mind removing your hat.*
              c. *How about setting the table.*

If these occur as 'imperatives' with tags (I find them all a bit dubious), they are morphologically dissimilar:

(43)   a. *Close the window, would you mind.*
              b. *Take off your hat, do you mind.*
              c. *Set the table, how about* $\begin{Bmatrix} *\emptyset \\ \text{it} \end{Bmatrix}$.

Finally, the proposal embodied in (26) would have to be supplemented with auxiliary hypotheses that would account for the appropriate responses, and ones that would provide a source for such modals in tags and whimperatives as *can, can't, would, wouldn't, could,* and *couldn't,* and at the same time, hopefully, explain the absence of whimperative requests, orders, and suggestions with *may you* and *mayn't you.*

Taking a wholly different approach to the matter, David Gordon and George Lakoff (this volume) proposed to treat whimperatives uniformly with a great number of other classes of sentences that systematically do not 'mean' exactly what they 'say'. Gordon and Lakoff claimed that the underlying or logical structure of a whimperative is not an imperative but a question. They claimed, that is, that the underlying logical form of a sentence like *Can you pass the salt,* regardless of its illocutionary force, is the underlying logical form of a question, something like 'I request that you tell me whether you can pass the salt'. They claimed that whimperatives get their 'imperative' force by means of rules that describe conventions of conversation — their conversational postulates — such as (44) and (45):

(44) *You can ask someone to do something by asking him if it will be the case in the future that he does it.*

(45) *Saying that you want someone to do something conversationally entails asking him to do it.*

Insofar as Gordon and Lakoff claim that their conversational postulates are systematic and follow from more general principles of conversation such as (46) [their (2)–(4)], they have a theory with great explanatory potential:

(46) *One can convey a request by (a) asserting a speaker-based*

> *sincerity condition or (b) questioning a hearer-based sincerity condition.*[6]

(The sincerity conditions they refer to are statements of states of affairs that must hold for a speaker to perform a sincere and felicitous speech act.) Their theory will be even more explanatory if they can discover the principles of natural logic that lead speakers to assume and accept principles like (46). Gordon and Lakoff's framework is theoretically capable of predicting, rather than just describing, or worse, merely listing, the set of all utterances that can convey requests—something well beyond the power of all three other theories. Sadock's proposal and mine both treated whimperatives as unrelated to sentences like (47a–d) that could be used to convey requests:

(47) a. *It would be nice if you would close the window.*
      b. *I want you to close the window.*
      c. *You better close the window right now.*
      d. *You will please remove your hat.*

and mine certainly could not be generalized to cover such cases. Furthermore, even if condition (46) is untenable (Gordon and Lakoff note some difficulties with it), and the notion of conversational postu-

---

[6] Actually, I believe one can convey a request also by asserting a hearer-based sincerity condition. Thus, (1) and (2) seem to be requests just as much as (3):

(i)   *You can open the door now, Jeeves.*
(ii)   *You will be so kind as to remove your hat.*
(iii)   *I want you to open the door.*

There are also, by the way, sentences that convey requests that one might describe as questioning possible addressee-based challenges. These are accurately described as loaded questions or traps that remove the recipient's grounds for an excuse to refuse to comply. For instance:

(iv)   *Are you too tired to take out the garbage?*
(v)   *Would it be too much trouble to take out the garbage.*
(vi)   *Would it be too much of a bother (for you) to take out the garbage.*
(vii)   *Would you mind (please) taking out the garbage.*
(viii)   *Do you mind (please?) taking out the garbage.*
(ix)   *Do you think it would be too much trouble to . . . etc.*

However, I am not sure how to classify them by their illocutionary force (cf. 'How to Get People to Do Things'). Only a few take *please,* and they are not reported by *ask to,* but at least (4)–(8) are reported as questions, by *ask if,* for example, *She asked me if it would be too much trouble to take out the garbage, so I did.* In any case, none of them have the intonation of real requests for information.

lates is reduced to a list of postulates like (44) and (45) in logico-semantic form (i.e., without reference to specific lexical items), it still has great explanatory potential, since it claims that the membership of the class of whimperatives, say, is a function of the speaker's natural logic, rather than a function of the grammatical rules that generate the class of well-formed underlying and surface structures in his idiolect.

I would like to consider next the implications of treating whimperatives in this paragrammatical manner, and to raise some objections to it; but before I do so, it will be necessary to embark on a minor digression to distinguish various ways of getting people to do things, with words, and to justify my use of the disclaimer 'so-called imperative.'

HOW TO GET PEOPLE TO DO THINGS

Doing It

There are several approaches one can take to getting people to do things; one can order, demand, request, plead, and suggest, to name just a few. Even the most directly phrased ones, to which I will restrict myself here, are distinct in terms of grammar as well as social context.

In social terms, orders are distinct from demands, requests, and pleas in that the giver of the order believes that he has the authority to control the intentional behavior of the recipient and expects to be obeyed—orders are, thus, typically given by military commanders, employers, parents, teachers, and bullies, but not by persons in a position of no power with respect to the addressee. Grammatically, they have the falling intonation typical of statements, not the level or level–rising intonation of sincere (nonrhetorical) yes–no questions. They do not permit a close initial or a final *please*, and they do permit a number of rude idiomatic expressions that occur only uninflected, such as *kiss off, flake off, butt out, bug off, lay off,* and *pipe down.* They are reported with *tell* rather than *ask,* and they may have a *why don't you* tag. Orders may be expressed as whimperatives, but even so, they have the same intonational properties as imperative-form orders, the same possibilities for reports, for occurrence with *please,* and with expressions like *bug off:*

<u>Pick up that butt,</u>|<u>soldier.</u>
*Pick up that butt, soldier.

> *Bug off, please.
> *Please bug off.
> She told/*asked/*expected him to bug off.
> Butt out, why don't you.
> Will you butt out (*please).
> Could you pipe down.
> Why don't you butt out.

Demands differ socially and psychologically from orders in that the giver has no institutionalized authority or circumstantial power over the addressee, nor as much of an expectation that he will get what he wants from him, although the demand may be made with more insistence than an order. Grammatically, demands have the same intonation as orders, and the same nonoccurrence with *please;* but they cannot be reported with *tell* or *ask,* but only with *demand,* and cannot have the *why don't you* tag which orders may have. I am not certain whether there are any whimperative demands. Something like *Will you let my people go, or won't you* is about as close as I can get:

> Let my people│go!   *Let my people go.
> *Moses asked/told Pharaoh to let his people go.
> Moses demanded that Pharaoh let his people go.
> *Let my people go, why don't you. (not a demand)

Requests are the method used in polite society for getting someone to do something. In the culture of this country, the utterer of a request is someone who has or is acting as if he has no authority or power to compel compliance. Although the speaker expects the addressee to grant his request, perhaps in the spirit of the golden rule, he is not insistent, and will not be enraged by refusal. Grammatically, requests are characterized by a level or only slightly falling intonation, an ability to occur with *please* in final position, and with no pause or separate intonation in initial position. They permit an *if you will* tag, which orders and demands do not permit, and they are reported with *ask* rather than *tell* or *demand:*

> Get me a Grant's.
> Please get me a Grant's.   Get me a Grant's if you will.
> *Please pipe down.   *Pipe down if you will.
>   *Let my people go if you will.
> She asked/*told him to get her a Grant's.
> *She demanded that he get her a Grant's.

Requests are probably more often whimperatives than not. Whimperative requests have the same intonation as imperative-form requests, the same ability to take final *please,* and the same ability to be reported with *ask* but not *tell.*

Pleas seem to bear about the same relation to requests as demands bear to orders. They are polite, though perhaps not 'cool,' and are made from a position of subordinacy, and with no real expectation that they will be granted. Grammatically, they have a slightly rising intonation and occur with an initial or final *please* that need not be separated from the plea by a pause and may have its own rather high-pitched (whining) intonation. A plea is the only imperative form that occurs with *for x's sake,* where *x* is a real person, e.g., *for mý sake, for Pául's sake, for the sake of your little bróther,* but not *for Christ's sáke,* or *for Pete's sáke,* which occur with more order-like imperatives. Pleas may be reported with *beg, plead,* and *ask,* but not with *tell* or *demand,* and, unlike orders and demands, permit *won't you* tags. Whimperative pleas are easy to find. They may occur with *won't you.* They have the same intonation and report possibilities as imperative-form pleas, and may be accompanied by the same whining *please* and by the same *for x's sake:*

Please take me with you.   Take me with you, please.
??Bug off, please.
  For the baby's sake, keep your voice down.
  *For the baby's sake, pipe down.
  *For the baby's sake, get me some Milltown
      if you will.
  For Pete's sáke, shut up.
??For Pete's sáke, take me with you.

  I begged him to take me with him.
  I asked him to take me with him.
  *I told him to take me with him.
  *I demanded that he take me with him.

  *Butt out, won't you.
  *Let my people go, won't you.
  Take me with you, won't you.

  Won't you take me with you.
  *Won't you let my people go.
  *Won't you butt out.
  Will you take me with you, for the baby's sake.

A fifth way of getting someone to do something by using an imperative form is to make a suggestion. The maker of a suggestion assumes no special authority over or subservience to the addressee,
and does not care quite as much whether the action he suggests is
carried out as does the giver of an order, demand, plea, or even
request; but like orders, suggestions are reported with *tell, say
for . . . to,* or *say that . . . should,* rather than *ask.* Actually,
suggestions are meant and understood as *should* statements
regarding an action that is in the interest of the (understood) subject
rather than in the interest of the speaker, and they differ in this
respect from orders, pleas, demands, and requests. The intonation of
a suggestion falls slightly, although probably not as much as that of a
statement. Suggestions cannot be followed by any kind of a
modal + *you* tag, although they can be followed by *why don't you*
tags. Their whimperative forms are the only ones that can occur with
might and *mightn't.* Other grammatical peculiarities of suggestions
show up in their whimperative forms, too, where *why don't* forms
reduce to *why not,* which is not possible for orders, pleas, and the
like. Suggestions also have forms in *why* plus infinitive that are
equivalent to negative *should* statements, again impossible for
orders, and so on. All of these nonimperative forms (modal whimperatives, *why don't you* whimperatives, *why not* whimperatives,
and *why* whimperatives) can have third-person as well as second-
person subjects, overt in the first two types and understood in the
others, while third-person subjects are not reconstructible for orders,
pleas, etc.:

> Put the meat on first, so it will be done in time.
> Put the meat on first, why don't you?
> *Put the meat on first, can/can't/will/won't/could/
>   couldn't/would/wouldn't/should/shouldn't you?
> Might (n't) you put the meat on first.
> *Might (n't) you bug off/get me a Grant's please/let my peo-
>   ple go.
> Why not put the meat on first.
> *Why not pipe down?
> *Why not get me a Grant's please.
> *Why not keep your voice down, for the baby's sake.
> Why put the vegetables on first.
> *Why raise your voice at me, you lout.
> *Why leave me alone, please.

Why doesn't she be a choreographer.
?Why doesn't she butt out, for Pete's sáke.
*Why doesn't she get me a Grant's please.
Why not wake you when she leaves.
    (= She should wake you . . .)
Why take you seriously if she doesn't have to.
    (= She shouldn't take you seriously . . .)
Can't she put the meat on first.
*Wake you when she leaves.⎫
*Make up her own mind.   ⎭   (OK only as frag-
                              ment responses
                              to direct ques-
                              tions, not as un-
                              solicited
                              suggestions)

Warnings like *Drive carefully, Beware of the dog,* and *Don't forget your galoshes* appear at first to be a kind of suggestion. Like suggestions, warnings are reported with *tell* or *say that . . . should* rather than *ask,* and warnings are made in the interest of the addressee rather than the speaker. What distinguishes warnings from suggestions is that the giver of the warning assumes that some ill will befall the addressee if he doesn't heed it; that warnings do not occur with *why don't, why not,* or *why;* and that they are unambiguously interpreted as having second-person subjects. Although warnings can have modal tags, as far as I know they have no whimperative forms, while suggestions have just about the full range of whimperatives:

    *Why don't you beware of the dogs.
    *Why not beware of the dogs.
    *Beware of the dogs, why don't you.
     Beware of the dogs, won't you.
    *Won't you beware of the dogs.

So-called imperative forms are also found as offers such as *Have some more cookies* and *Take the wheel if you like,* and as wishes like *Have a good time, Be well,* and *Break a leg!* Offers have whimperative forms in *will you* and *won't you,* and wishes are the only speech acts with imperative form that have whimperatives in *may you,* which is the only whimperative form they have. Offers are reported with *offer, say,* or *tell (. . .) that . . . could/might;* wishes with *wish* or *tell . . . to:*

Will/*can/*may you have some more cookies.
She offered us (*to have) some more cookies.
She said we could have some more cookies.
May/*will/*can you have a good time.
She wished us (*to have) a good time.
She told us to have a good time.

I would like to introduce the general term *impositive* to cover speech acts, regardless of their form, by which the speaker's desire or opinion is imposed on the addressee as an order, demand, request, plea, warning, or suggestion.

IMPOSITIVES AND IMPOSTORS

It will be useful to exclude from discussion certain forms which have the subjectless infinitive form characteristic of English 'imperatives' but which neither give nor imply any sort of instructions. For example, consider the sentences of (48).

(48)　　a.　*Cry and you cry alone.*
　　　　b.　*Realize what you've said, and you'll never be able to finish the speech.*
　　　　c.　*Show that air pollution increases soil fertility and General Motors will love you.*

The understood subject is generic second person, not the addressee. These forms have the force of *if . . . then* statements, and they are not reported like impositives with *She told me to, She asked me to, She said I should, She said for me to,* etc., but rather like statements, with *She said that if one* or *She said that if you.* Furthermore, as (48b) shows, they do not have the same constraints as orders and requests; it would be absurd to say to someone, *Realize what you've said, right now!*

Conditional threats and promises such as (49) and (50) are likewise *if . . . then* statements whose antecedents imply that the speaker wants the addressee to do or not do the activity described therein, and whose consequents spell out a threat or promise that will be carried out upon failure to do so or successful achievement, respectively:

(49)　　　　a.　*Clean up your room or I'll take away your teddy bear.*
　　　　　　b.　*Cry and I'll smack you again.*
(50)　　　　*Clean up my room and I'll give you a dollar.*

These forms may be reported like impositives with *tell* (threats) and *say for . . . to* (promises), but threats must be reported with an *or* conjunction, even if this involves making explicit what was merely implied; and promises must be reported with *and*. Thus, (49) and (50) are reported as in (51) and (52):

(51) a. *She told me to clean up my room or she'd take away my teddy bear.*
      b. *She told me not to cry or she'd smack me again.*
          (Not: *She told me to cry and she'd smack me again.*)

(52) a. *She told me to clean up her room and she'd give me a dollar.*
      b. *She said for me to clean up her room and she'd give me a dollar.*

IMPLICATIONS OF GORDON AND LAKOFF'S PROPOSAL

Returning now to Gordon and Lakoff's proposal that whimperatives have the underlying logical form of questions and may be interpreted as impositives by the grace of conversational postulates, they were correct in their prediction that many of the specifics of their analysis would be found to be incorrect. However, I do not wish just to point out such errors as their claim that final *please* never occurs with statements that imply requests—cf. (53) and similar cases:

(53)   *I'd like two Big Macs please.*[7]

Rather, what I would like to do is to consider some general properties and implications of a theory that treats the meaning and use of whimperatives not as a direct function of their underlying syntactic or logical structure but as a function of the logical form that ordinarily underlies the surface syntactic form they have, along with certain rules of conversation.

Whimperatives That Would Be Ungrammatical As Questions

Gordon and Lakoff's analysis claims that the underlying structure of a whimperative is the underlying structure of the question whose form it has, and that it has its own impositive meaning because of

---

[7] But not *I'd adore two Big Macs please* or *I'm hoping you'll pay for them please.* I do not know why.

specifiable rules of conversation that say that certain kinds of questions can be used with the same meaning as certain kinds of imperatives. This implies that, out of context, a given whimperative will always be ambiguous between a question meaning and an impositive meaning. I have just pointed out that whimperatives do not have the same intonation as questions but, rather, have approximately the same intonation as the corresponding imperative forms. The speaker's intention, therefore, will almost always be obvious to the hearer from the intonation. Still, we must note that there is a stumbling block for this theory in the existence of orders, requests, and suggestions which have the surface word order of questions but never their intonation, and which would be ungrammatical as questions. Thus, (54a–c) are all unambiguously whimperatives, and (55a–c) are all unambiguously questions:

(54)   a. *Why don't you be quiet!*
          b. *Why don't you be nice to your brother*
               for a change.
          c. *Why don't you (doesn't she) be a doctor.*
          d. *Why don't you have given her the ring*
               before I get there.
(55)   a. *Why aren't you quiet?*
          b. *Why aren't you nice to your brother?*
          c. *Why aren't you (isn't she) a doctor?*
          d. **Why haven't you given her the ring*
               before I get there?

I suppose that one could claim that the sentences of (54a–c) and those of (55a–c) have the same logical structure. A syntactic rule would then be necessary which said, in effect, 'Make sure there is a *do* before the subject in a *why* question, just in case the question isn't a question.' Actually, Gordon and Lakoff would have a harder time stating the rule than that, because they would, I suspect, want to claim that (55a–c) convey 'requests' in the same way that (54b) does, so that they cannot draw a clear distinction in semantic or pragmatic terms between the cases in which you have *do* and those in which you do not, and given their assumptions, they certainly cannot draw such a distinction in syntactic terms. I do not deny that an addressee might infer from (55a) that he was supposed to be quiet, but he could hardly interpret it as an order.

There is a further difference between *why not* whimperatives with *do* and *why not* questions with *be* which can be used to make implications. Both forms like (56) and forms like (57) can be answered by noncomplying addressees with statements like (58) giving reasons for noncompliance:

(56)   *Why don't you cook dinner. It's 8:30.*
(57)   *Why aren't you cooking dinner? It's 8:30.*
(58)   *The stove's broken.*

If the reason is introduced by *because*, as in (59), it is conversationally and socially equivalent to (58) if it is an answer to (57):

(59)   *Because the stove's broken.*

And this should not be surprising, since sincere *why* questions may be responded to with statements that give relatively direct reasons, regardless of whether or not they are introduced by *because*. All of the responses represented in (61) are appropriate responses to (60):

(60)   *Why is Roosevelt purring?*
(61)   a.   *(Because) he likes your lap.* (motivation)
                b.   *(Because) he can't help it.* (cause)

However, (59) is not an appropriate answer to (56). This is especially clear if *why don't you* is pronounced [wainčə]. If someone responds to (56) with (59), he has taken (56) the wrong way. From differences like this it is clear to me that whimperatives like (56) must be distinguished from HINTS like (57).[8]

It seems to me that there are important distinctions, which Gordon and Lakoff ignore, between intentional hints and unintentional clues like (55a) and (57), on the one hand, and true orders, requests, suggestions, etc., such as (54a–d) and (56), on the other. Whimperative orders, requests, suggestions, etc., have the syntactic properties and intonation of corresponding imperative forms. Hints have the syntax and intonation of questions, or statements if they are in statement form.[9] A form like *Have you taken out the garbage?* can convey the speaker's desire to have the garbage taken out (brides often think this is a subtle way to nag), but notice that it has question intonation

---

[8] *Because* clause responses to whimperatives are facetious, hostile, or smart-alecky, even if the reason is a direct denial of one of the felicity conditions for requests. Thus, (i–iv) are not appreciably better as answers to (56) than (59) is:

(i)   *Because I don't want to.*
(ii)   *Because you don't really want me to.*
(iii)   *Because I can't cook.*
(iv)   *Because I already have.*

[9] There is one exception to this, but even it serves to distinguish between hints and whimperatives. As C.-J. Bailey has pointed out to me, real questions, imperatives, and

and can function as a request only if the addressee knows that he is expected to have done whatever he is asked about. Notice also that adding *please* to a hint like (55b) would make it a politer request for an answer, not a politer request that the addressee be nice to his brother.

---

statements may have smooth intonation curves, as described, or, with varying kinds of emphasis, the intonation may go up or down in bounces, as in (i–iii):

```
(i)                      Where              chil
                              are      the
                              all
                                            dren?
```

```
(ii)               Take
                            hands off
                     your
                                   of me!
```

```
(iii)                                coo
                  I
                        he'd     a
                     think
                           like
                                   kie.
```

Whimperatives may have this sort of intonation [cf. (iv)], but hints may not; (v) is unambiguously a question, (vi) unambiguously a statement:

```
(iv)                              doc
                  Why
                              be a
                        you
                     don't         tor?
```

```
(v)           Why        qui
                     you
                  aren't     et?
```

```
(vi)                              win
                  I
                     you     o
                  think   can  pen a
                                   dow.
```

Gregory Lee has suggested that this difference between hints and whimperatives may have something to do with the 'emotional' intonation being a normal alternative for direct speech acts (including whimperatives), while true hints are, logically, only pre-liminaries to direct (emotional) speech acts.

Thus, hints seem to call for a Gricean treatment of the sort Gordon and Lakoff propose, but whimperatives, although they may have had their historical origin in true Gricean hints, for many reasons seem to be synchronically a horse of a different color.

To echo some remarks of Butters (1973), calling hints like *It's cold in here* and (57) 'commands' because they may sometimes have the same effect that unambiguous commands would have is like calling Coca-Cola 'coffee' if it keeps you up at night. They are simply not the same thing, not even in the same class. Notice again how, as Butters observes, whimperatives and hints are responded to in different ways: It is conversationally and socially perfectly appropriate to respond to hints like (62) with a question like (63), which brings the real issue out in the open:

(62)   a.   *Are you going to cook dinner tonight?*
            b.   *Have you started dinner yet?*
            c.   *I'm hungry.*
            d.   *It's not too early to eat, is it?*

(63) $\left(\left\{\begin{matrix} Yes_a \\ No_{b,d} \end{matrix}\right\}\right)$ *Do you want me to start dinner now?*

But if someone makes such a response to a whimperative like (64a) or (64b), he will be assumed to have misunderstood the request, and taken it as a real question (either innocently or because he wants to be difficult). And if he makes a response like (65) to (64c) or (64d), it will simply be assumed that he does not speak the language properly:

(64)   a.   *Could you start dinner now.*
            b.   *How about starting dinner now.*
            c.   *Why don't you be a honey and start dinner now.*
            d.   *Wyncha start dinner now, so you can watch*
                 the movie with me.

(65) $(Sure_{a,b})$ *Do you want me to (start dinner now)?*

The Consequences of the Gordon–Lakoff Analysis of Whimperatives for the Abstract Performative Analysis

Another case in which whimperatives have forms that would be ungrammatical as questions concerns internal *please*. Thus, (66a) is unambiguously a request, and (66b) is ungrammatical as a question:

(66)   a.   *Could you please be quiet.*
            b.   **Could John please be attractive to your sister?*

Presumably, Gordon and Lakoff could attempt to explain this with a quasi-transderivational rule that said, in effect:

please may be inserted before the first verb after a modal expression in a question just in case the question (1) conversationally entails a request for the action described by that verb and/or (2) will have the intonation of a request.

Gordon and Lakoff do in fact bring up such a case (a somewhat more complicated one), and claim a parallel solution for it.[10] They maintain their claim that speech acts with different illocutionary force, different intonation, and different grammatical properties, but similar gross surface structure, do not encode different logical or 'deep' structures. But it seems to me that this claim seriously undermines many of the rather convincing arguments given in support of abstract performative verbs — a concept that lies at the basis of a number of valuable insights into the nature of language, including several contributions by George and Robin Lakoff. In fact, the possibility of having global syntactic rules that refer to conversational entailments of deep structures removes the basis for all arguments in favor of generative semantics and makes 'generative semantics' an interpretive theory.[11]

---

[10] Gordon and Lakoff's example concerns reduced *why* questions with negative suggestion force, such as *Why paint your house purple?* Their 'informal, first approximation' to the rule that performs this reduction is:

> *With respect to a class of contexts CON_i and a set of conversational postulates CP, WHY YOU TENSE x → WHY x, if and only if, letting L be the logical structure of the sentence, $CON_i \cup CP \cup \{L\} \Vdash$ (Unless you have some good reason for doing x, you should not do x').*

A number of phenomena that would have to be treated in parallel fashion are discussed in Sadock (1972).

[11] This was pointed out to me by Jerry Morgan. In particular, Gordon and Lakoff's claim that sentences with different illocutionary forces, different intonations, and/or different grammatical properties can have the same logical or 'deep' structure and be derived one from the other by rules that depend on speaker's intent and conversational convention invalidates all arguments of the following form:

OBSERVATION 1:   *x expressions cooccur with (or refer to) only y expressions in sentences of form z in language L.*

OBSERVATION 2:   *In the surface structure SS_i there is an x expression but no y expression.*

CONCLUSION A: *SS_i is derived from an underlying structure U_i, in which there is a y expression in the appropriate position, and it is later deleted or suppressed.*

(Continued on page 132)

Gordon and Lakoff's theory claims that the meaning in context of a whimperative is an entailment of its logical structure. I pointed out earlier some of the difficulties such a theory encounters in whimperatives that would be ungrammatical as questions. But there is something that would have even worse consequences for such a theory. This would be the existence of whimperatives whose 'literal, question meaning' is nonsensical. It is, to my mind at least, nonsense to even speak of the entailments of nonsense. A candidate for such a case is any whimperative with *would*. In requests for information and statements, *would* either (1) asserts repeated or habitual past action, and is meaningful only if there is some explicit or previously mentioned definite stretch of time for it to refer to, or (2) refers to hypothetical or contingent activity in the future—in which case it is meaningful only if there is (expressed or previously mentioned) an *if* clause (or the equivalent) stating the condition under which this event or activity would take place. Whimperatives such as (67a) and (67b) certainly do not make any reference to the past:

(67)   a. *Would you get me a glass of water.*
            b. *Would you be so kind as to let me through.*

And not only do they not require a condition, explicit or otherwise,

---

Arguments of this type include Morgan's (1969) *again* and *almost* arguments for the decomposition of causative verbs and R. Lakoff's (1968) arguments for abstract optative, imperative, and potential verbs in Latin, quoted in G. Lakoff (1971). Gordon and Lakoff's claim entails that arguments of this type are open to the following interpretation:

CONCLUSION B: *There are conversational postulates such that the logical structure L_i of SS_i is conversationally entailed by the logical structure L_i of SS_i, in which a y expression occurs, so x may occur in SS_i without there being a y in SS_i or L_i.*

Since Gordon and Lakoff provide no principled way to decide whether to draw Conclusion A or Conclusion B, the syntactic arguments given in support of any semantically motivated underlying form could equally well be taken as arguments for conversational postulates relating underlying or logical forms.

To call a theory of grammar a generative semantic theory when in that theory the logical form of an utterance intended and unambiguously understood as a request is the logical form of a morphologically related question is, to my mind, stretching the term GENERATIVE SEMANTICS far beyond what it was originally intended to cover. Such a theory is interpretive insofar as certain semantic properties (e.g., illocutionary force) are not represented directly in the underlying form, but are determined by rules that look at the surface structure and the underlying structure and give an interpretation distinct from the interpretation that would be made on the basis of the underlying structure alone. This is exactly what Chomsky's interpretive rules do.

to make sense, but they lose the illocutionary force of an impositive if a condition is expressed; the sentences of (68) are unambiguously questions, although, of course, they may be taken as hints, since almost anything can be a hint:

(68)

$$\textit{Would you get me a glass of water} \begin{cases} \textit{if I asked you?} \\ \textit{if I wanted one?} \\ \textit{if I was asking you?} \\ \textit{if I didn't ask you?} \\ \textit{if I wasn't asking you?} \\ \textit{if I was(n't) speaking} \\ \quad \textit{English?} \end{cases}$$

Thus, the logical forms Gordon and Lakoff would have to have would lack either a condition or a past time reference and would thus be logically ill-formed as questions. Nonetheless, they would have to say that the meanings of the whimperatives (67a) and (67b) were entailed by them.

Alternatively, since past time references would be semantically unjustifiable, the logical forms of (67a) and (67b) would have to have condition clauses that were obligatorily and in an ad hoc fashion deleted just in case they were intended to convey direct requests.

Semantic Support for Lexical Idiosyncrasy?

Miscellaneous Cases

Gordon and Lakoff's view that the use of whimperatives is explained by reference to general principles of conversation such as (46) is rendered quite attractive by its claim that the set of possible whimperatives is a function of a speaker's assumptions about context and felicity conditions for specific speech acts. The 'logical aberration' of using a question, say, to convey a desire or a request, is described as lawful and, in fact, to be expected, given principles of conversation like (46). Principle (46) thus predicts that *Can you lend me a dime please* may be a request, since a speaker can make a request sincerely only if he assumes that the addressee can do what he asks him to, and claims that the fact that *Did you give me a cigarette please* may not be a request for a cigarette is relatable to the fact that, to make a sincere request, a speaker does not have to assume that the addressee has performed the act in the past. It might even be claimed that (46) predicts the absence of whimperative requests and orders with *may you:* One does not necessarily assume that the person to whom one gives orders or requests must be permitted to do what compliance entails. A person can easily ask another to disobey some injunction without committing an ungrammatical act. Of course, there is another possible explanation for this absence of *may you* whimperatives, and it might take logical precedence in a theory in which the underlying structures of whimperatives are questions: There are (in most dialects of American English) no real questions with *may you*, either, such as *May you give me a dime*, meaning 'Is it possible you'll give me a dime?' or 'Are you permitted to give me a dime?' or 'Will you permit yourself to give me a dime?'

In any case, it is hard to see what sort of analysis in terms of felicity conditions would predict the absence of whimperatives with *should*. Presumably, when someone sincerely tells, asks, begs, etc., someone to do something, it is because he thinks that person should do that thing. This is, thus, a hearer-based condition and, according to (46), should result in whimperatives like:

(69)   a.   *Should you pipe down.*
              b.   *Should you get me a Grant's please.*
              c.   *Should you let my people go!*
              d.   *Should you put the meat on first.*

But (69a–c) are ungrammatical as impositives, and (69d) can only be a suggestion or a hint, where the 'should' force is weakest! This is an especially vexing problem, since *should* shows up in other whimperative forms, and always only with suggestions:

(70)   a.   *Shouldn't you/she put the meat on first.*
        b.   **Shouldn't you pipe down/get me a Grant's please/let my people go.*
        c.   *Don't you think you/she should put the meat on first.* (n.b. falling intonation)
        d.   **Don't you think you should flake off/get me a Grant's please/let my people go.*

Gordon and Lakoff attempt to explain the possibility of expressing a 'negative request by the positive question [(71)]':

(71)   *Must you make that noise.*

by referring to a logical equivalence between NECESSARY THAT NOT and NOT POSSIBLE THAT. I would not deny that (71) invites an inference that the addressee should cease making noise, or that the cited equivalence is the basis for this inference; but (71) is not a request but, rather, something closer to a hint. *Must you* forms of this sort do not occur with *please*, although requests do:

(72)   a.   *Must you make that noise please.
            b.   *Must you please leave so soon.
            c.   Could you not make that noise please.
            d.   Could you please not leave so soon.

and they permit third-person subjects:

(73)   a.   Must she make that noise.
                 b.   Must she leave so soon.

Sentences like (71) differ also from suggestions, which I argue are distinct from hints, in that suggestions are made by a party who purports to be disinterested, whereas when someone uses a *must you* 'hint', one concludes that he cares. In the best of all possible worlds, a linguistic explication of natural logic would explain why *must you* 'hints' have only suggestion force from the addressee's point of view, although logically they refer to a necessity. Presumably, such an explanation would simultaneously explain the distribution of *do you have to* forms, which have exactly the same distribution, even to the possibility of third-person subjects, and connotations of concern on the part of the speaker. I do not know what principles of conversation or logic, natural or philosophical, would predict the nonexistence of whimperative hints with *mustn't you*, especially in the face of the existence of parallel forms with *don't you have to;* one could remind someone to mail letters by saying *Don't you have to mail some letters* but not by saying *Mustn't you mail some letters.*

Synonym Cases

The parallel distributions of the synonyms *must* and *have to* raises another important point: If conversational postulates are phrased in terms of semantic rather than lexical elements, and whimperative phenomena are a function of conversational postulates, then synonyms should be substitutable for each other in whimperatives without affecting their illocutionary force. However, this predicted substitutability occurs only rarely in the whimperatives Sadock and I have attempted to account for, although they are quite common in the conveyed desires I have referred to as hints. Thus, (74a), (74b), and (75a–d) are equivalent, and the challenges of (76a–e) are equivalent:

(74)   a.   Why aren't you quiet?
                 b.   How come you aren't quiet?

(75)   a.   *I assume you can take out the garbage.*
           b.   *I assume you are able to take out the garbage.*
           c.   *I assume you are capable of taking out*
                   the garbage.
           d.   *I assume it's possible for you to take*
                   out the garbage.
(76)   a.   *I was going to do that anyway.*
           b.   *I had planned to do that anyway.*
           c.   *I had plans to do that anyway.*
           d.   *I had intended to do that anyway.*
           e.   *I would have done that anyway.*

But *how come* cannot be used in a whimperative in the ways *why
don't you* can:

(77)   a.   *Why don't you flake off/shut up/put the meat on*
                   first.
           b.   *How come you don't flake off/shut up/put the meat*
                   on first.

The sentences of (77b) are either ungrammatical or unambiguously
requests for information. Similarly, *be able, be capable,* and *be possible* cannot substitute freely for *can* in direct whimperative
requests,[12] although the last may occur in suggestions; the sentences
of (78b) and (78c) are unambiguously requests for information,
although, of course, such questions can be used (rather sarcastically)
to hint:

(78)   a.   *Can you get me a Grant's please/put the meat on*
                   first.
           b.   *Are you able to get me a Grant's please/put the*
                   meat on first.
           c.   *Are you capable of getting me a Grant's please/put-*
                   ting the meat on first.
           d.   *Is it possible for you to get me a Grant's please/put*
                   the meat on first.

Likewise, questions with *be going to* cannot be pronounced or understood in the ways questions with *will* can:

---

[12] In English and in Hebrew, the "inherent capability' and 'possibility' meanings of
can occur in all kinds of whimperatives. In Hebrew, the 'kennen' sense, which is literally 'know how', has a different distribution.

(79)   a. *Will you get me a Grant's please.*
                Will you take me with you, please.
            b. *Are you going to get me a Grant's please.*
                Are you going to take me with you, please.

Given these nonequivalences, a conversational-postulates explanation for whimperatives is in grave danger of degenerating into a list
of idiosyncratic conversational properties of lexical items. Granted,
there are systematic distinctions to be made among the expressions I
have been calling synonymous (cf., for example, R. Lakoff, 1970; Antinucci and Parisi, 1971; Binnick, 1971, 1972), but I have been
unable to come up with very much that would show how these distinctions predict the differences in distribution. One suspicious distribution that might be explainable in terms of such distinctions is
that of *might* and *can*. The fact that *might* expresses contingent possibility as opposed to the capability expressed by *can* is perhaps
related to the fact that *might* and *mightn't* occur only in suggestions,
although *can* and *can't* occur in a greater number of whimperative
types.

Negative Questions

A particularly hairy problem that an adequate semantic and logical
account of whimperatives should elucidate is the fact that negative
questions are sometimes polite whimperatives and, in other cases,
rather impolite. Thus, (80a) is a polite suggestion, but (80b) is an
impolite order, especially compared to the positive form (80c), which
can be only a request or a suggestion, while (80d) is a polite request,
even more deferential than (80e):

(80)   a. *Can't you put the meat on first.*
            b. *Can't you be a little quieter.*
            c. *Can you be a little quieter.*
            d. *Won't you close the window please.*
            e. *Will you close the window please.*

R.S.V.P.

Turning now to a fourth kind of implication of a conversational-
postulates analysis, let us consider Gordon and Lakoff's claim that
'the conversationally implied meaning (the request) can be conveyed
only if the literal meaning (the question) is not intended to be conveyed and if the hearer [i.e., the addressee] assumes that it isn't
[this volume: 87].' This is a claim that these whimperatives are

grammatically questions, but pragmatically requests and not questions. In other words, it is a claim that whimperatives do not function as both impositives and questions. Thus, it is absolutely incapable of explaining the fact that whimperatives have some of the pragmatic characteristics of questions; in particular, they demand verbal responses in a way typical of questions but not typical of requests in their 'canonical' 'imperative' form, or in forms with overt performative verbs. A cooperating recipient of a request like (81a) or (81b) need not make any verbal response:

(81)   a. *Please take your aluminum cans to the*
              Recycling Center.
          b. *I hereby request that you take your*
              aluminum cans to the Recycling Center.

Such remarks are, thus, appropriate to an address to an unemotional (and therefore silent) audience. But the recipient of (81c) is being uncooperative if he does not make some kind of affirmative or negative verbal response or gesture. Sentences like (81c) are, thus, appropriate to addressing intimates or emotional mobs, from which the speaker can expect an immediate audible or visible response, regardless of whether or not the request will actually be carried out:

          c. *Will you please take your aluminum cans*
              to the Recycling Center.

If Gordon and Lakoff's analysis is correct, and the individual(s) to whom (81c) is addressed assume that it is not a question, then there is no reason for him (or them) to feel compelled to react to it as a question, and answer.

Universality

An important question that raises itself whenever claims like Gordon and Lakoff's are made about meaning postulates (statements that give the intension and implication of atomic predicates, the smallest semantic units necessary for linguistic analysis) is whether they are universal and hold for all languages. Gordon and Lakoff say that they have checked with speakers of widely divergent languages and would not be surprised to find that their postulates equivalent to (44) and (45) hold for all languages. We apparently checked speakers of complementary sets of languages, because four out of the five languages I checked did not seem to have a principle like (44), and one of them was German. In fact, my data show considerable variation as to what question can function as what kind of impositive speech act.

The conditional form equivalent to English *would* cannot introduce an order in Spanish, Hebrew, or Japanese, according to my informants, although it can in English, German, and Finnish; forms meaning 'are you ready' and 'are you interested' can introduce requests in Hebrew, but not in any other language I checked. Only in exceptional cases could a given expressional type function as a given speech act in all six of the languages I considered, but it was rare for a question to lack whimperative uses across the board in a given language, if it had them in other languages. The situation is quite different for utterances of the type I have called hints, e.g., those of (82):

(82)   a. *The rain that's coming in the window*
              will ruin the rug.
       b. *I want to audit this course.*
       c. *If I was in your shoes, I'd tell him*
              where to go.

In all of the languages, these could be interpreted as indicating the speaker's desire for action, the speaker's desire for permission, and the speaker's suggestion, respectively. This is strong support, I think, for my claim that hints and whimperatives are indeed different, something that follows from my treatment but not from Gordon and Lakoff's. They claim that the sentences of (1)–(5) and those of (82) are essentially the same in use and interpretation.

The cross-linguistic distribution of whimperatives and hints raises another question: Given that there is variation from language to language, if whimperatives are based on conversational postulates and natural logic deductions from them, one would expect the forms resulting from the simplest deductions to be the most prevalent among the languages of the world, and forms that required more assumptions and more complex deductions to be rarer and more scattered. Unfortunately, our knowledge of the logic and assumptions that generate the set of English whimperatives is less than sketchy, so no claim can be made about the translations of English whimperatives as whimperatives in other languages. However, I would think that the hints of (82), which are more nearly universal as possible hints than the forms of (1)–(5) seem to be as possible whimperatives, involve considerably more complex deductions than the whimperatives of (1)–(5).

I have presented evidence that Gordon and Lakoff's analysis, ambitious and attractive as it might be, not only entails the abandonment of all principled support for abstract predicates of just about

any sort but also predicts the occurrence of various kinds of whimperatives that fail to occur, and fails to provide a well-formed source
for various kinds of whimperatives whose corresponding questions
are ungrammatical or nonsensical. It thus appears to be incorrect, not
only in many details but in its fundamental claim as well.

VARIATIONS ON A THEME

I had hoped to be able to subtitle this paper 'Variations on a
theme' and spend most of it describing language-specific and cross-
linguistic variation as to which modals and so on can be used in
which kinds of questions in the performing of which kinds of impositive speech acts, and showing how this variation was determined by
subtle aspects of the meaning of the questioned semantic predicates,
grammatical and semantic properties of the lexical items used as lexical predicates, cultural values, and culture-specific assumptions, and
interactions of these. However, it soon became apparent that an
incredible amount of work remains to be done before such an explanation can be attempted. Questions to be answered include the following:

1. Is it possible to characterize the whole set of whimperatives in
    a language in terms of independently motivated concepts such
    as sincerity conditions and reasonableness conditions, or will
    such attempts always degenerate into unmotivated lexical idio-
    syncracies?
2. If this is possible, how much variation is there from culture to
    culture, from language to language, from speaker to speaker
    within a language, and from subculture to subculture within a
    language? Are the variations in conversational postulates only,
    or in felicity conditions as well?
3. Is it necessary to take into account language-specific homon-
    ymies? Does the fact that *ask* is ambiguous in English between
    'request' and 'inquire' contribute to the relatively large set of
    possible whimperatives in English? Is the fact that *may* in
    English is used for both permission and possibility related to
    the fact that *may* does not occur in impositives, or do neither of
    these expressions ever occur in impositives in natural lan-
    guages anyway?

Semantic, pragmatic, and logical considerations must be at the
basis of an adequate explanation for whimperative phenomena—and
all other systematic phenomena involving sincere utterances that do

not mean exactly what they literally say. Fortunately for those who fear that all the important questions have already been answered, we have no viable account for the systematicity of these utterances.

REFERENCES

Antinucci, F., and Parisi, D. On English modal verbs. In D. Adams, M. A. Cambell, V. Cohen, J. Lovins, E. Maxwell, C. Nygren, and J. Reighard (Eds.), *Papers from the seventh regional meeting of The Chicago Linguistic Society*. Chicago: Chicago Linguistic Society, University of Chicago, 1971, 28–39.

Binnick, R. *Will* and *be going to*. In D. Adams, M. A. Cambell, V. Cohen, J. Lovins, E. Maxwell, C. Nygren, and J. Reighard (Eds.), *Papers from the seventh regional meeting of the Chicago Linguistic Society*. Chicago: Chicago Linguistic Society, University of Chicago 1971, 40–52.

Binnick, R. *Will* and *be going to* II. In P. M. Peranteau, J. M. Levi, and G. C. Phares (Eds.), *Papers from the eighth regional meeting of The Chicago Linguistic Society*. Chicago: Chicago Linguistic Society, University of Chicago, 1972, 3–9.

Bolinger, D. The imperative in English. In *To honor Roman Jakobson I*. The Hague: Mouton, 1967, 335–362.

Butters, R. What is 'data' in the expanding domain? Unpublished paper, 1973.

Heringer, J. Some grammatical correlates of felicity conditions and presuppositions. Columbus: The Ohio State University, Department of Linguistics, *Working papers in linguistics no.* 11, 1972, iv–110.

Katz, J., and Postal, P. *An integrated theory of linguistic descriptions*. Cambridge, Mass.: MIT Press, 1964.

Lakoff, G. On generative semantics. In D. Steinberg and L. Jakobovits (Eds.), *Semantics: An interdisciplinary reader in philosophy, linguistics, and psychology*. New York and London: Cambridge University Press, 1971, 232–296.

Lakoff, R. *Abstract syntax and Latin complementation*. Cambridge, Mass.: MIT Press, 1968.

Lakoff, R. The ineluctable visibility of the modal. Speech to the University of Illinois Linguistics Club, 1970.

Lakoff, R. Questionable answers and answerable questions. In B. Kachru *et al.* (Eds.), *Papers in linguistics in honor of Henry and Renée Kahane*. Urbana: University of Illinois Press, 1973, 453–467.

Langacker, R. English question intonation. In J. Sadock and A. Vanek (Eds.), *Studies presented to Robert B. Lees by his students*. Edmonton, Ill.: Linguistic Research, Inc., 1970, 139–162.

Morgan, J. On arguing about semantics. *Papers in linguistics* 1, 1969, 49–70.

Sadock, J. Whimperatives. In J. Sadock and A. Vanek (Eds.), *Studies presented to Robert B. Lees by his students*. Edmonton, Ill.: Linguistic Research, Inc., 1970, 223–238.

Sadock, J. Speech act idioms. In P. M. Peranteau, J. M. Levi, and G. C. Phares (Eds.), *Papers from the eighth regional meeting of the Chicago Linguistic Society*. Chicago: Chicago Linguistic Society, University of Chicago, 1972, 329–339.

INDIRECT SPEECH ACTS AND WHAT TO DO WITH THEM

ALICE DAVISON
State University of New York, Stony Brook

INTRODUCTION

A puzzling topic of much interest to linguists in recent years is the nature and source of what Heringer (1972) has felicitously called INDIRECT SPEECH ACTS. A satisfactory syntactic and semantic analysis must account in some general and motivated way both for the surface syntactic structure and for the meaning and illocutionary force. These are not related in the way they are for other speech acts, which we might call 'direct' speech acts by contrast. For example, sentences (1)–(3) have the surface syntactic form normally associated with the general class of illocutionary acts they belong to semantically, while sentences (4)–(7) do not have the expected surface form:

(1)   *Move your car.*

(2)   *The attorney general may have acted unwisely.*

(3)   *Do you intend to sue?*

(4)   *I must ask you to move your car.*[1]

---

[1] Indirect speech acts sound most natural with little stress on the first and higher clause. *Ĭ mŭst śay that* S is a statement of S (indirectly expressed), while *Ĭ mŭst śay*

(Continued on page 144)

(5)   *Let me say that the attorney general may have*
           acted unwisely.

(6)   *May I ask if you intend to sue?*

(7)   *Would you move your car?*

The surface syntactic structure of indirect speech acts may contain a
verb of saying, subject and indirect object pronouns, and various
predicates including modals and verbs such as *allow* and *like,* in addition to what one might call the 'core' of the speech act, or the
expression of the action or proposition involved. The additional elements other than the core do not contribute in any obvious way to
the meaning of the sentence, though I will present evidence to show
that they provide some additional features not shared by corresponding direct speech acts. The surface form of indirect speech acts
may also be syntactically marked, with, for example, the inverted
word order characteristic of questions, while the actual illocutionary
force might be that of a request, as in sentence (7).

It is unlikely that all sentences that indirectly convey a speech act
are of the same linguistic nature, so it is not surprising that a given
analysis is not totally satisfactory for all of them. Discussion here will
be confined to three or four illocutionary types (statements, questions, requests, and occasionally others) and a narrow range of distinct surface forms, mainly declarative, interrogative, and imperative
sentences containing modals, verbs of saying or others, and pronouns. Interesting properties of speech acts can be revealed by con-

---

that S is a statement of obligation to say S, directly expressed, and not semantically
equivalent to the destressed version. The lack of stress relative to direct speech acts is
probably an important fact about indirect speech acts, but I do not know all its implications or any explanation for it.

A few general remarks should be made about the sentences used in this chapter.
Some of the sentences may sound odd to some speakers, though I do not think that a
speaker will reject all sentences of a given type. Because of the idiomatic nature of
indirect speech acts (which has not been much discussed), a speaker may accept a sentence if one modal is substituted for another, or if the position of some element is
changed. In other cases, it may be that sentences that are intended to illustrate and
locate the borderline of the possible simply fall on the other side of the border for
some speakers.

Some of these sentences may seem strange as written sentences rather than spoken
ones. Examples found in renderings of spoken English or in linguistics papers bring
out a significant fact, which is that it is hard for native speakers of English to decide on
the right punctuation. Punctuation based on the surface syntactic form is often absurd,
but a plain period may also seem odd. I will use periods in most cases unless a question mark or exclamation point is clearly more justified.

sidering a controlled range of indirect acts in conjunction with the corresponding direct speech act and with other syntactic structures. These properties, expected or unexpected, constitute useful evidence with which to weigh the various theories advanced about their remote structure.

Attempts to deal with indirect speech acts have chosen as the remote structure or source a representation based on the illocutionary act suggested by the surface form (Gordon and Lakoff, 1971), or on the actual illocutionary force of the speech act (Heringer, 1972; Davison, 1973), or on some combination of the two (Sadock, 1969, 1971; Green, 1970, 1971). The first type of analysis fails to note or predict the semantic differences between indirect speech acts and corresponding direct ones, differences that I will consider here. The second kind (particularly my first attempts) fails to note the relationship between the surface form and the conditions on performing the act conveyed, and treats the appearance of the surface form as a case of idiomatic substitution. The relationship was admirably captured in Gordon and Lakoff's elegant paper—which I cannot totally accept, however, for reasons discussed in the concluding section of this one. The third kind of analysis runs into trouble in getting exactly the right surface form to be derived from the underlying semantic components without resorting to ad hoc syntactic processes. In other sections of this chapter, I will note ways in which indirect speech acts are very much like corresponding direct speech acts having the same meaning, or subset of the same meaning, and also ways in which indirect speech acts are unique and unlike semantically related speech acts. I will consider the analyses mentioned earlier in relation to the properties of indirect speech acts. I am sorry to say that, after casting aspersions and doubts on other people's theories, I will not be able to propose a more satisfactory analysis but only to point to the properties such an analysis might have.

SEMANTIC PROPERTIES

The aspect of indirect speech acts that is absent from ordinary direct speech acts seems to consist of two relations. The first is between the speaker and the hearer, which is to be expected. The second concerns the proposition or action involved in the speech act and the attitudes of the speaker and the hearer toward it. These relationships become much clearer when speech acts of many types are considered, in addition to the much-discussed requests; I will argue that indirect questions and statements involve propositions of some immediate personal relevance to the hearer, an importance that the speaker must share or at least be aware of. This condition is not an intrinsic condition on making statements and asking questions, though requests do have such a requirement in that the speaker must want the requested action done.

As for the first relation, I will characterize the situation in which indirect statements and questions are normally used as one in which some conflict exists between the speaker's intention to say something and the anticipated reaction of the hearer. The indirect speech act form serves as a signal of the intrusion of a disturbing topic into the discourse, and as an acknowledgment of that fact, which the speaker makes with the purpose of forestalling criticism or some other kind of resistance from the hearer.

In the following examples, I include both propositions whose emotional value to the speaker and hearer is easily imagined, and ones for which it is not so evident, unless the situation in which the sentence is uttered could be imagined. When the importance to the hearer is not evident, the sentence is odd. The corresponding ordinary speech act could, of course, have the same value attached to it but need not necessarily have it:

(8)   a.   *I have just won the Nobel Prize.*

       b.   *I* $\left\{ \begin{array}{l} \textit{have to} \\ \textit{must} \end{array} \right\}$ *tell you I have just won the Nobel Prize.*

       c.   *May I* $\left\{ \begin{array}{l} \textit{say} \\ \textit{tell you} \end{array} \right\}$ *that I have just won the Nobel Prize?*

       d.   *Allow me to tell you that* $\left\{ \begin{array}{l} \textit{?I} \\ \textit{you} \end{array} \right\}$ *have just won the Nobel Prize.*

       e.   *Let me say that I have just won the Nobel Prize.*

(9)   a.   *David is walking alone down Orange Street.*

       b. $\left\{ \begin{array}{l} \textit{I have to} \\ \textit{must} \end{array} \right\}$ *tell you that David is walking alone down Orange Street.*

       c.   *May I tell you that David is walking alone down Orange Street?*

       d.   *Allow me to tell you that David is walking alone down Orange Street.*

       e.   *Let me say that David is walking alone down Orange Street.*

(10) a. *John Lord O'Brien died yesterday.*
   b. *I must tell you that John Lord O'Brien died yesterday.*
   c. *May I tell you that John Lord O'Brien died yesterday?*
   d. *Allow me to* $\left\{\begin{array}{l}\text{tell you}\\\text{say}\end{array}\right\}$ *that John Lord O'Brien died yesterday.*
   e. *Let me tell you that John Lord O'Brien died yesterday.*

(11) a. *Your slip is showing.*
   b. *I must* $\left\{\begin{array}{l}\text{tell you}\\\text{?say}\end{array}\right\}$ *that your slip is showing.*
   c. *May I* $\left\{\begin{array}{l}\text{tell you}\\\text{?say}\end{array}\right\}$ *that your slip is showing?*
   d. *?Allow me to tell you your slip is showing.*
   e. *Let me* $\left\{\begin{array}{l}\text{tell you}\\\text{?say}\end{array}\right\}$ *your slip is showing.*

   The preceding statements of information are clearly ones which could be of great importance to the hearer. The following, which are statements of universal truths or historical facts, require more imagination to find a reasonable context for their utterance:

(12) a. *The Battle of Agincourt was fought in 1415.*
   b. *?*I must tell you that the Battle of Agincourt was fought in 1415.*
   c. *?May I* $\left\{\begin{array}{l}\text{say}\\\text{tell you}\end{array}\right\}$ *that the Battle of Agincourt was fought in 1415?*
   d. $\left\{\begin{array}{l}\text{?Let me say}\\\text{?Allow me to tell you}\end{array}\right\}$ *that the Battle of Agincourt was fought in 1415.*

(13) a. *Hollandaise sauce curdles if the heat is too high.*
   b. *?I must tell you that Hollandaise sauce curdles if the heat is too high.*
   c. *?May I tell you that Hollandaise sauce curdles if the heat is too high?*
   d. *?Let me tell you that Hollandaise sauce curdles if the heat is too high.*

(14) a. *Newsprint is usually made of wood pulp.*

    b.   ??*I must tell you that newsprint is usually made of wood pulp.*

    c.   ??*Can I tell you that newsprint is usually made of wood pulp.*

    d.   ?*Let me tell you that newsprint is usually made of wood pulp.*

Sentences (12)–(14) would be very strange in discourse initial position, without a preceding context to justify them. Sentences (8)–(11) could well be the first in a discourse, at least in the (b) and (c) versions. Sentences (12)–(14) express propositions of which it is hard to see the personal importance, though some argument over facts or an imminent danger to the sauce might well serve as contexts for the reasonable utterance of these sentences.

    Matters of opinion as well as facts can be stated in indirect statements:

(15) a. *That movie never had quite enough substance to justify its technical brilliance.*

      b. *I must* $\begin{Bmatrix} say \\ ?tell\ you \end{Bmatrix}$ *that that movie never had enough substance to justify its technical brilliance.*

      c. *May I* $\begin{Bmatrix} say \\ ?tell\ you \end{Bmatrix}$ *that that movie never had enough substance to justify its technical brilliance?*

      d. $\begin{Bmatrix} Let\ me\ say \\ Allow\ me\ to\ \begin{Bmatrix} Say \\ ?tell\ you \end{Bmatrix} \end{Bmatrix}$ *that that movie never had enough substance to justify its technical brilliance.*

Tell is generally odd in an expression of an opinion, as it seems to be the means of imparting information and facts. The distinction between *say* (or *state*) and *tell* is not apparent in direct speech acts, which are dominated by some declarative performative verb without any surface reflex.

    As with statements, some questions are easier to imagine as having the appropriate emotional value when asked as indirect questions:

(16) a. *Are these real diamonds?*

      b. *I must ask you if these are real diamonds.*

      c. *May I ask if these are real diamonds?*

      d. *Allow me to ask if these are real diamonds.*

(17)   a.   *Is this person a friend of yours?*
       b.   *I must ask you if this person is a friend of yours.*
       c.   *May I ask if this person is a friend of yours?*
       d.   *Allow me to ask if this person is a friend of yours.*

(18)   a.   *Have you seen David recently?*
       b.   *I must ask if you've seen David recently.*
       c.   *Can I ask if you've seen David recently?*
       d.   *Let me ask if you've seen David recently.*

In contrast, the following sentences are odd except in contexts that take some stretching of the imagination:

(19)   a.   *Did Leif Ericson land in Rhode Island?*
       b.   *??I must ask if Leif Ericson landed in Rhode Island.*
       c.   *??May I ask if Leif Ericson landed in Rhode Island?*
       d.   *?Let me ask if Leif Ericson landed in Rhode Island.*

(20)   a.   *Is cochineal a red dye?*
       b.   *??I must ask you if cochineal is a red dye.*
       c.   *?May I ask if cochineal is a red dye?*
       d.   *?Let me ask if cochineal is a red dye.*

They might be used in some heated argument over facts, of course, but they can be used in contexts much more limited than the ones in which the direct forms (a) could be said.

The extra factor in indirect speech acts is often described as politeness (for example, in Heringer, 1972), but politeness is hard to define narrowly enough to be of use. Webster's dictionary mentions good breeding and polished manners, and then courtesy, tact, and consideration for others. These are more or less permanent attributes of individuals, rather than factors present in situations involving a speaker, a hearer, and a proposition. Individuals possessing these attributes do not use indirect speech acts exclusively and in all situations. Utterances can be said politely without being overtly (syntactically) marked for politeness, and in a discourse in which the participants are continuously polite, the sentences used are not all indirect speech acts. In fact, a number of consecutive indirect speech acts in a discourse gives an impression of excess, which is mitigated, however, by interspersing requests of the *would you* variety, as in (23):

(21)   ??**May I say that I doubt that these maps are entirely
        accurate. Can I tell you that the distances between
        Srom and Seraneb are not consistent on several
        maps, and I must say that I cannot see how the
        projections from the first angle match those from the
        second. Let me say that I am not sure that you ob-
        served all this at first hand.*

(22)   ??*I must request you to do me a favor. Could I ask you
        to get me a quart of milk and half a dozen eggs, and
        may I ask you to pick my dress up at the cleaner and
        mail this letter? Why don't I give you a $5 bill now,
        and could I ask you to give me the change when you
        return?*

(23)   ?*Would you do me a favor? Would you get me a quart of
        milk and half a dozen eggs? And could I ask you to
        pick up my dress at the cleaner and mail this letter?
        Why don't I give you a $5 bill now, and could you give
        me the change later?*

Examples (21) and (22) are pretty strange, though (23) could be said
by a very determined person politely imposing on someone who is
presumably not unwilling. But (23) is still pretty excessive. If the
only function of the indirect expression of a speech act is to indicate
politeness, it is strange that sequences of polite sentences (or sentences uttered by polite people) cannot occur as sequences of indirect speech acts. It is closer to linguistic reality to view indirect
speech acts as having a signaling function of some sort rather than
just an expresive function. If indirect speech acts are used as signals
of some psychological state, then it would not be at all strange that
they are used intermittently rather than continuously, and tend to
occur in the beginning of a discourse, if at all.

Indirect speech acts can be used to express anger and extreme
rudeness. For example:

(24)   a. *I must say that I never want to come back here
            again.*
        b. *I must ask if you have ever sailed anything but a
            bathtub before now.*

(25)   a. *Can I say that this is the worst party I have ever
            been to.*
        b. *May I ask if you have ever considered giving up
            writing plays?*

(26) a. *May I inform you that you have bad breath.*
  b. *Can I ask what you are going to do about my smashed headlights?*

(27) a. *Let me say that your brother-in-law is a creep.*
  b. *Let me ask if you are planning to do that again.*

I do not think (24)–(26) are cases of irony, of impolite things said politely as a form of sarcasm. If they were ironic, however, the problem is merely reduced to another, the so far unresolved problem of how one can say something and mean its opposite or something entirely different.

Genuine irony cannot be expressed in an indirect speech act uttered with normal intonation and stress. For example, (28) could be ironic:

(28)   a. *I love walking five miles in the rain.*
      b. *It's a gorgeous morning.*

If (28a) or (28b) is uttered while plodding through mud, rain, and cold, one might assume that the speaker meant that the morning was miserable and so was she. Even so, some speakers might sincerely mean what they said if, for example, they were fond of long walks in the rain. But (29) and (30) can only be taken nonironically:

(29) a. *I must say that I love walking five miles in the rain.*
  b. *May I say that I love walking five miles in the rain?*
  c. *Let me say that I love walking five miles in the rain.*

(30) a. *I must say it's a gorgeous morning.*
  b. *May I say it's a gorgeous morning?*
  c. *Allow me to say that it's a gorgeous morning.*

Indirect statements seem to express only sincerely believed propositions as their complements. Indirect questions also are sincere requests for information, rather than rhetorical questions:

(31)   a. *Are we going to submit to this sort of blackmail?*
      b. *Who would do such a thing?*

(32)   a. *We will not submit to this sort of blackmail.*
      b. *No one would do such a thing.*

(33)   a. *May I ask if you are going to submit to this sort of blackmail?*
      b. *I must ask you who would do such a thing.*

The sentences of (31) imply that the speaker knows the answers, (32). The sentences of (33) could have other replies, and do not strongly imply (32). They do have some implications, for instance that the speaker of (33a) thinks they ought not to submit or that the speaker of (33b) believes the hearer is unwilling to give the answer unless there is some good reason to do so. Irony and nonliteral meaning thus seem to be absent from indirect statements and questions,[2] if normal intonation is used. Both direct and indirect speech acts can be used nonliterally with heavy contrastive stress, a sort of emphatic timing in the words and/or special sarcastic intonation. But this unmistakably sarcastic mode is not necessarily used in uttering the rude remarks (24)–(27). These sentences can be said quite rudely with straightforward normal intonation and stress. If irony is the explanation, it must be a very special and idiomatic irony of form. To account for it, we must resort to something more than the conven-

---

[2] The conditions on nonliteral requests and commands are somewhat harder to deal with, as it is less obvious when the need for such requests would arise. I can think of several cases, mostly used to disrupt some situation that the speaker does not like. Sentences (1) and (3) might also be literal:

(1)   *Bertha, peel me a grape.*

(2)   a.   *Go jump in the lake.*
               b.   *Go buy yourself a hearse.*
               c.   *Go boil your head.*
               d.   *Go to hell.*

(3)   a.   *Oh, shut up!*
               b.   *Stop it!*   (used to interrupt a string
                          of flattering remarks)
               c.   *Watch it!*

If expressed indirectly, these imperatives are more or less literal. The 'whimperative' forms in (4a)–(6a) [the term for imperatives having a question form and a modal, invented by Sadock (1970)] are slightly less odd for me than the others, if nonliteral meaning is intended:

(4)   a.   *Bertha, would you peel me a grape.*
               b.   *Bertha, may I ask you to peel me a grape?*

(5)   a.   *Would you go jump in the lake?*
               b.   *I must ask you to go jump in the lake.*

(6)   a.   *Oh, would you shut up!*
               b.   *Oh, may I ask you to shut up?!*

Sentences (4)–(6) are perfectly well-formed requests if the speaker really wants the hearer to perform the action specified.

tions of politeness and the ways (whatever they are) in which one says something and means another.[3]

Politeness involves both pleasant and unpleasant things, thanking one's host for a pleasant time and apologizing for causing inconvenience, for example. But indirect speech acts seem to be associated most of the time with bad news, unfavorable opinions, and intrusive questions. They can be used for informing people of tragic events, at one end of the spectrum, and for talking about things that are only mildly disturbing or might have painful implications for the hearer, though what is actually said is not obviously unpleasant. For instance, (34a) and (35a) might have the implications in (34b) and (35b):

(34)   a. *May I say that you look lovely.*
             b. *You don't always look lovely.*

(35)   a. *May I tell you that I love you.*
             b. *Perhaps you don't love me, and*
                 will have to tell me so.

In the case of (8b) and (8c), telling one's colleagues of one's good fortune reminds them that they did not win the prize, and so the indirect form would be appropriate. It would be much less appropriate for informing members of one's family, who would not be considered professional rivals.

Politeness is subsumed in the following description of the function of indirect speech acts.[4] In making a statement or asking a question, and often when making a request or offer, the speaker introduces a topic that the speaker thinks the hearer will find painful or disturbing, and that the speaker does not feel really entitled to talk about. The intrusion, signaled by the form of the speech act, is overridden by some other factor, the speaker's anger or the importance of the hearer's acting on some piece of information, for example.

[3] In claiming that the primary function of indirect speech acts is not to express conventional politeness, I disagree with the position taken by R. Lakoff (1973 and personal communication). She analyzes indirect speech acts in terms of rules of politeness based on Gricean conversational postulates and, as I understand her, concludes that indirect speech acts that have the intended effect of being rude are cases of a pretence of politeness, a sort of formal irony.

[4] Discussion with Thomas Wehr made me aware of the function of indirect speech acts in distancing oneself from a conflict.

Other means exist for signaling intrusion. *Excuse me, but,* and *I'm sorry, but* often serve the function of signaling intrusion and making apology. The speaker apologizes, or appears to, in order to forestall the hearer's criticism of the speaker's act or the hearer's expression of resistance to what has been said. For example, the use of (9), which concerns possible danger to a small child, would suggest that the speaker does not want to interfere by commenting on the behavior of the child but feels that someone should know what is happening. In other words, the speaker says anyway what he shows he is aware is not welcome to the hearer.

Such attitudes are found in milder forms with whimperative requests and with offers. The surface syntactic form signals an acknowledgment of a certain personal distance between the speaker and the hearer:

(36)   a. *May I offer you some lemonade?* (A *yes* answer
             means that the offer is accepted)
        b. *Do you want some lemonade?*
        c. *Have some lemonade.*

Sentences (36b) and (36c) could certainly be used if the speaker knows the hearer's taste in drinks, but (36a) acknowledges that the speaker does not necessarily know if the hearer likes lemonade and that an unsolicited offer of lemonade would presume some personal acquaintance that does not exist. Sentence (36a) might be used to create distance between a speaker and hearer who are angry at one another, if said AS THOUGH possibility of intrusion existed. These are similar circumstances to the ones in which rude indirect questions and statements can be used without sounding odd.

The function of signaling a conflict in the speaker–hearer situation explains, better than the function of signaling politeness, the condition that the speech act must be literally meant and of some personal relevance to the hearer. The fact that the proposition involved is disturbing and must be apologized for would naturally guarantee its relevance to the hearer.[5] Politeness is also not sufficient to explain why some illocutionary acts may be performed indirectly and other illocutionary types may not. A person who is considerate and tactful (and empowered to marry people) nevertheless may not say:

---

[5] The same restriction applies to adverbial clauses modifying the speech act rather than the propositional contents of the speech act:

(1)   a. *It's going to be a beautiful day, if I may say so.*
       b. *It's going to be a beautiful day, because it said so on the radio.*

(37)   a.   ??*I must pronounce you man and wife.*
         b.   ??*May I pronounce you man and wife?*
         c.   ??*Allow me to pronounce you man and wife.*

when (38) is meant:

(38)   *I hereby pronounce you man and wife.*

It is true that the judge is under no compulsion to be polite to the criminal, nor to apologize for intrusion:

(39)   a.   ??*May I sentence you to thirty days?*
              b.   ??*Let me sentence you to thirty days.*[6]

But it is not immediately obvious why promises on the one hand and thanks or congratulations on the other differ in being able to be expressed indirectly. All these acts can be performed in polite ways and in situations calling for politeness.

(40)   a.   *I must advise you to think it over.*
         b.   *Let me advise you to think it over.*

(41)   a.   *May I warn you that Finlay is not to be trusted.*
         b.   *I must warn you that Finlay is not to be trusted.*
         c.   *Let me warn you that Finlay is not to be trusted.*

(42)   a.   *I must thank you for pulling me out of the pond.*
         b.   *May I express my gratitude for your help?*
         c.   *Allow me to thank you for your kind help.*

(43)   a.   *I must congratulate you.*
         b.   *May I congratulate you.*
         c.   *Allow me to congratulate you.*

---

(2)   a.   *Are we going to allow this, if I may ask?*
         b.   *Are we going to allow this? because I'm leaving if we are.*
         c.   *Are we going to allow this? because if we do, then we'll really be in trouble.*

Sentences (1) and (2) must be taken as sincere statements and questions, rather than ironic statements [in (1)] or rhetorical questions [in (2)]. Sentence (1b) might have ironic meaning, but only if said with special sarcastic intonation.

[6] I have not included the declarative form, as it is hard to distinguish, except by stress, between the act of sentencing (1) and a statement of obligation to sentence (2):

(1)   *I mŭst séntence you to thirty days on the County Farm.*

(2)   *I mús̀t séntence you to thirty days on the County Farm*
              (*in view of the nature of the offense*).

(44)   a.   *I must confess I have never read the novel.*
            b.   *Let me confess that I forgot to call them.*[7]

Sentences (45)–(49), however, are not well-formed instances of promises, appointments, and so forth. They have only the literal meaning of a direct speech act:

(45)   a.   *I must promise you I will pay you back on Thursday.*
            b.   *May I promise I will stop smoking?*
            c.   *Allow me to promise that I won't forget.*

(46)   a.   *I must appoint you acting chief.*
            b.   *May I appoint you Ambassador to Graustark?*
            c.   *Let me name you Prime Minister of Samavia.*

(47)   a.   *I must decree that the fourth Thursday of February will be Liberation Day.*
            b.   *May I decree that dogs must wear leashes?*
            c.   *Allow me to decree that no one may go outside today.*

(48)   a.   *I must christen this ship* **Thalassa.**
            b.   *May I christen this ship the U.S.S.* **Wasp?**
            c.   *Let me christen this ship the U.S.S.* **Stupendous.**

(49)   a.   *May I find the defendant guilty?*
            b.   *Allow me to conclude that this is genuine English Channel 1923.*

The preceding sentences all contain performative verbs for acts that might be described as having one of two properties. One is that the speaker performing the verbal act must have special qualifications of some sort—for instance, that of having been appointed judge or legally entitled to perform marriages. A second characteristic is one of formal procedure, which is most apparent by contrast with the speech acts exemplified in (40)–(44). Warning, advising, and the others, including stating, asking questions, and requesting, are gen-

---

[7] These confessions express the speaker's embarrassment. Perhaps for this reason, the question in indirect form sounds less plausible than the others:

(1)   *Can I confess that I haven't read your paper?*

(2)   *May I confess that it was I that broke the hatstand?*

Sentences (1) and (2) at least have a sort of pleading intonation and an arch style not found in the others. They seem to do more semantically, in apologizing for both the act (or omission) and the confession.

erally unsolicited acts, at least in the strict sense of the word. But acts by duly constituted authorities, which occur through normal procedures of society or which are specifically asked for, cannot reasonably be apologized for by the speaker, even if the hearer is not pleased with the act.[8]

So far, I have treated the differences between direct and indirect speech acts as a single factor for which some single component in linguistic representation is responsible. Indirect speech acts are not all alike, and not all members of just one class of linguistic structures. In SOME sense, indirect speech acts are the speech acts suggested by their surface forms, in addition to being some other speech act. The question that now plagues linguists is whether indirect speech acts are two illocutionary acts, simultaneously, or whether they are primarily one illocutionary act, and secondarily or relatedly some other act. If the former possibility is the case, it must be explained how one illocutionary component determines the surface form and some emotional value, and the other the semantic aspect of its actual illocutionary force. If the latter is the case, then it must be demonstrated that one illocutionary act is primary and that the other can be related to it in some general way.

The surface syntactic structure does reflect some real variable in indirect speech acts. The question form is clearly more abject and apologetic than the others, while the imperative form is more peremptory. Both have the effect of asking permission, unlike the statement form. The latter does convey an apology by implying that what the speaker does is not intentional, since it is the result of outside compulsion.[9]

---

[8] The distinction between unsolicited speech acts and others does not predict in an obvious way which type of act promises will belong to. It is true that the maker of the promise does not have to be endowed with special promissory powers, nor does the hearer have to ask for the promise to be made, though it is often the case that the hearer has let it be known in some way that the promised action would be desirable. The conditions on sincere and successful promises do include special powers and solicitation in a general way, however; the maker of the promise must have the means and intention to carry it out, and must believe that the recipient of the promise desires it.

[9] In other cases, the expression of the speaker's attitude toward what he says is integrated into the utterance itself. Many instances of *I think, I'm afraid*, and so forth, do not have literal meaning and are incidental to what is said:

(1)   *I have to go home now, or else I'm* $\begin{Bmatrix} afraid \\ {}^{\circ}terrified \end{Bmatrix}$ *my mother will be mad at me.*

(continued on page 158)

I will argue in the following sections that it is the actual illocutionary force of indirect speech acts that is important for the statement of syntactic restrictions and of well-formed semantic combinations, and not the surface structure or the illocutionary act that the surface structure suggests. The apologetic element expressed by the surface structure reflects the speaker's attitude about the speech act actually performed, but the actual illocutionary force of the utterance seems to me to be central to an adequate account of it. (Descriptions of indirect speech acts, for instance, focus on what was done rather than the way it was said.)

In the next six sections, I will describe ways in which indirect speech acts resemble the corresponding direct speech act with the same illocutionary force, rather than the speech act corresponding to the surface structure taken in its literal meaning. The sections after that will deal with ways in which indirect speech acts are syntactically unique and, finally, what implications these have for the linguistic structure of indirect speech acts.

DESCRIPTIONS

While speech acts can be described in other sentences in a variety of ways, most speech acts have a description that specifies what kind of illocutionary act is performed. The complement contains indirect discourse:

(50)   a.   'It was a Wurlitzer.'

$$
\text{b.} \quad She \begin{Bmatrix} said \\ stated \\ told\ them \end{Bmatrix} that\ it\ was\ a\ Wurlitzer.
$$

(51)   a.   'What was that?'
            b.   *He asked what that was.*

---

(2)   *We should sue them, because I* $\begin{Bmatrix} suppose \\ {}^{*}hypothesize \end{Bmatrix}$ *they'll refuse to settle out of court.*

(3)   *Get the cat out of here, or else I'm afraid Bernie will give us a lot of trouble.*

Mark Liberman (1973) discusses many interesting cases of 'transparent' predicates like these, which present complex problems in analysis. He suggests that two structures are combined into one, though he does not say how; such an analysis would explain why the transparent predicate, like the indirect speech act surface form, is mysteriously absent from the structure at some levels of derivation.

(52)   a.   'Put your hands up over your head.'

  b.   *He* $\begin{Bmatrix} told\ me \\ commanded\ me \\ requested\ me \end{Bmatrix}$ *to put my hands up over my head.*

Indirect speech acts have exactly the same description as direct speech acts; a description of the surface syntactic form describes only the literal meaning and not the verbal act that actually occurred:

(53)   a.   'I must tell you that John has been arrested.'
  b.   *She told me that John had been arrested.*
  c.   **She said that she was obliged to tell me that John had been arrested.*

(54)   a. $\begin{Bmatrix} \text{`May I say} \\ \text{`Let me say} \end{Bmatrix}$ that Karen behaved beautifully tonight.'
  b.   *She told me that Karen had behaved beautifully tonight.*
  c.   **She requested permission to tell me that Karen had behaved beautifully tonight.*

(55)   a.   'I must ask you if you have seen my aunt.'
  b.   *Charlie asked us if we had seen his aunt.*
  c.   **Charlie said that he had to ask us if we had seen his aunt.*

(56)   a. $\begin{Bmatrix} \text{`May I ask} \\ \text{`Let me ask} \end{Bmatrix}$ if you bought this on sale?'
  b.   *She asked if I had bought it on sale.*
  c.   **She asked permission to ask if I had bought it on sale.*

(57)   a.   'I must request you to move your car.'
  b.   *He requested them to move their car.*
  c.   **He said he was under obligation to ask them to move their car.*

(58)   a. $\begin{Bmatrix} \text{`May I request} \\ \text{`Let me ask} \end{Bmatrix}$ you not to do that.'
  b.   *She asked them not to do that.*
  c.   **She asked permission to ask them not to do that.*

Sentences (53b)–(59b) are possible descriptions of the speech acts in (53a)–(58a). The (c) sentences are not possible descriptions of the indirect speech acts.

REPLIES

Questions and requests of various sorts have a limited range of normal replies. If asked a question, the hearer must either provide the information or say that he or she is unable to do so. In the case of requests, there are four kinds of satisfactory responses: (1) agreement, (2), refusal, (3) explanation of why the request cannot or will not be complied with, and (4) compliance.[10] Indirect speech acts have the same range of possible responses as the corresponding direct speech acts. One cannot reply to a question with imperative surface structure in the ways one would respond to a request; a request with interrogative surface structure has the responses appropriate to requests and not questions:

(59)   a.   *Let me ask the questions this time.*
            b.   *All right, I'll let you.*
            c.   *No, I won't allow it.*

(60)   a.   *Let me ask if you noticed anything odd*
                  about it.
            b.   **All right.*
            c.   **No, I won't allow it.*

(61)   a.   *Can I ask them to send me free samples?*
            b.   *Yes you can.*
            c.   *No, you can't.*

(62)   a.   *Can I ask you to turn down the radio.*
            b.   **Yes, you can.*[11]
            c.   **No, you can't.*

The responses allowed for the request for permission in (59) are not possible for the question in (60), and the *yes* and *no* answers to the question in (61) will not do for the indirectly expressed request in (62). Sentences (60) and (62) would have just the same possible replies if they were directly expressed questions and requests. Again, the surface form of the utterance is disregarded in choosing an appropriate reply.

[10] Possible replies are used to great advantage in Green (1970) to define differences among speech acts having the form of questions.

[11] An uncooperative addressee can stonewall a request by treating it as a question. Generally, such an interpretation is a result of refusal to cooperate rather than misunderstanding.

SENTENCE ADVERBIALS

It is a well-known fact that adverbials like *fortunately, obviously, happily, unfortunately, sad to say,* and so on, do not occur with questions and requests. Such an adverbial, set off by pauses, occurs in (63) but is quite odd if introduced into (64) and (65):

(63)
> The anarchists, $\begin{cases} unfortunately, \\ fortunately, \\ obviously, \end{cases}$ have no organization.

(64)
> *Do the anarchists, $\begin{cases} unfortunately, \\ fortunately, \\ obviously, \end{cases}$ have any organization?[12]

(65)
> *Get, $\begin{cases} unfortunately, \\ fortunately, \\ obviously,[13] \end{cases}$ an organization, you silly, misguided boy.

These sentence adverbials may occur with indirect statements, regardless of their surface syntactic form:

(66) a. *Unfortunately, our spy at the eggplant cannery was caught.*
   b. *I must tell you that, unfortunately, our spy at the eggplant cannery was caught.*
   c. *I have to tell you that, unfortunately, our spy at the eggplant cannery was caught.*
   d. *May I say that our spy at the eggplant cannery was caught, unfortunately.*
   e. *Can I tell you that our spy at the eggplant cannery was, unfortunately, caught by the guards.*
   f. *Allow me to tell you that our spy at the cannery was caught, unfortunately.*
   g. *Let me say that, unfortunately, our spy there was caught.*

[12] Even without pauses around the adverbial, the question is not quite grammatical; in any case, the adverbial constituent would be what is questioned in (64), while in (63) the adverbial is not what is asserted by the statement. Sentences (63) and (64) consequently are not parallel semantically.

[13] *Obviously* is possible in imperatives only if they are suggestions of the sort that answers the question *What should I do?*.

(67)   a.   *Obviously, a listening device disguised as a lady-
             bug is going to be spotted immediately.*
       b.   *I must say that a listening device disguised as a
             ladybug is going to be discovered, obviously.*
       c.   *I have to tell you that, obviously, a listening device
             disguised as a ladybug is going to be spotted
             immediately.*
       d.   *May I say that, obviously, a listening device
             disguised as a ladybug is going to be spotted
             immediately.*
       e.   *Can I tell you that such a device is going to be
             spotted, obviously, if there is any search.*
       f.   *Allow me to say that, obviously, a bug like that
             is going to be spotted in no time.*
       g.   *Let me tell you that a bug like that is going to be
             discovered in no time, obviously.*

All varieties of indirect statements allow sentence adverbials, as in
(66) and (67). Nonstatements expressed in statement form do not
allow sentence adverbials:

(68)   a.   *?I must ask you if, unfortunately, you have any
             contraband in your duffle bag.*
       b.   *?I have to ask if, obviously, you have embezzled
             any money.*
       c.   *?I must ask you to hand in your resignation, prob-
             ably.*
       d.   *?I have to ask that you give us an application, for-
             tunately, so that we can hire you immediately.*

The adverbials *fortunately, unfortunately,* and the others do, of
course, occur also with statements about obligation, but not with
indirect questions and requests expressed as statements. This is
another case, like the preceding section on replies, in which a
restriction applies to the actual rather than the surface verbal act.

REASON ADVERBIALS

Reason adverbials, like those in (69)–(71), which do not very plausibly modify the propositional content of the utterance, are linked in
some way with the performative verb defining the illocutionary force
of the utterance:

(69) *The game had already started, because nobody was home when I arrived.*

(70) *Is that them over there? because I thought they weren't coming.*

(71) *Mail this letter for me, please, as I won't be going by a mailbox today.*

As I have argued elsewhere (Davison, 1973a and 1973b), the reason clause is actually related to presuppositions associated with the performative verb, the conditions that must hold, in the belief of the speaker, in order for the speech act to be sincere and successful. (These are discussed in much detail in Searle, 1969.) In (69), the reason clause gives grounds for believing that the asserted proposition is true, and implies in a rather loose way that it is true. In (70), the reason clause implies that the speaker expected them not to have come, and thus gives grounds for not knowing definitely whether they were or were not here. In (71), the reason clause implies that the hearer is better able than the speaker to perform the action, and gives a reason for the speaker's wanting the hearer to do what is requested.

Reason clauses of this sort, being linked to the constituent defining the illocutionary force of the utterance, can be used as tests for illocutionary force, particularly of sameness or difference of force. If the force of two utterances being compared is not the same, the reason clause that is well-formed with one will sound odd with the other, or have a different meaning:

(72) a. *Has the game started yet? because I don't have a copy of the schedule.*
      b. **The game has started already, because I don't have a copy of the schedule.*

(73) a. *Is that John over there? because it looks exactly like him.*
      b. **Tell me if that's John over there, because it looks exactly like him.*

In (72a), the reason clause implying that the speaker does not know the answer is well-formed, as it shows that a felicity condition on questions has been fulfilled. The same reason clause is ludicrous with statements, as in (72b), because the condition that the speaker does not know the answer does not hold for statements. The condition that the questioned proposition is possibly true holds for questions, as in (73a), but not for commands to answer questions, as in (73b).[14]

Indirect speech acts allow the same reason clauses as their direct counterparts, with the surface structure form irrelevant to the choice of well-formed reason clause combinations. This is curious, in the light of what was said about the shades of meaning expressed by the surface form (see page 157). Nevertheless, a reason clause appropriate to a statement is appropriate with a statement with the surface form of a question, as in (74b), while the clause in (74c), appropriate to a question about permission, is not possible with (74a):

(74) a. *May I say there is evidence of activity across the river,*

      b. *as I have just read the reconnaissance reports.*

      c. **because you usually don't like to hear bad news.*

(75) a. *Let me ask if you have been taking any drugs recently,*

      b. *since your eyes are extremely dilated.*

      c. **because it's for your own good that I ask.*

The question in (75a), which has the form of an imperative, allows a reason clause appropriate to questions, one that implies that the questioned proposition is possible, but does not allow (75c), which would be appropriate to the literal request meaning of (75a). This is yet another case in which the surface form is irrelevant and the well-formedness of a combination of clauses is determined on the basis of the actual illocutionary force of the utterance.

SO PRONOMINALIZATION

The restrictions discussed in previous sections concerned possible well-formed combinations, in discourse or within an utterance. In this section, I will discuss a syntactic rule, *so* pronominalization of sentences, that serves to distinguish statements and questions from all other illocutionary acts.[15] Some examples follow:

[14] This is partial evidence that questions are not always just requests to give the speaker some information. Some of the conditions on questions are specific cases of general conditions on requests, but questions differ from requests in allowing fewer possible replies, and in having additional conditions having to do with the truth or possible truth of a proposition.

[15] The apparent exceptions to this restriction are suggestions and instructions, which may have imperative form. But they may be phrased also as statements of obligation or

(76)   *Jonathan is back, because Bernie told me so.*

(77)   *Is Jonathan back today? because it said so in
            his note.*

(78)   *Is Jonathan back today? because if so,
            I want to talk to him.*

So pronominalization replaces an entire sentential complement with
so on the basis of identity to the complement of some preceding
statement or question.[16] The identity is one of sense rather than
form; in (78), the antecedent of *so* is the inverted interrogative form
of the proposition, while the complement of *if* would be declarative
if not reduced to *so;* and in (77), the antecedent is interrogative,
while the S replaced by *so* might be *I will be back Thursday,* identical only in reference to the antecedent.

   So pronominalization is not possible if the antecedent is in the
complement of a command, though other reduction rules may
operate, as in the following sentences:

(79)   a.   *Shut up then,*
            b.   *°as your Dad told you so.*
            c.   *since your Dad told you to (do so).*
            d.   *as that's what your Dad told you to do.*

---

conditional sentences, unlike real requests and commands:

(1)   *Attach the winch aft of the mast, because it said so in the instructions.*

(2)   *Put the red one on the negative terminal, because John told me so.*

(3)   *To attach the winch properly, (you should) put the winch aft of the mast,
      because it said so in the instructions.*

(4)   *To make it work, put the red one on the negative terminal, because John
      told me so.*

Other tests, such as *please,* discussed in Sadock (1970), show that instructions and
suggestions are not true requests:

(5)   *Get your foot off my dress, please.*

(6)   *°To get to the station, go down Quaker Path, please.*

(7)   *What should I do?   °Write your congressman, please.*

Sentence (5) is a request, and allows *please.* The directions in (6) and the suggestion
in (7) do not. I have profited greatly from discussion of these points with Jerry Sadock
and James McCawley.

   [16] The complements of some verbs of mental activity also undergo *so* replacement,
as in (1), in which *so* could mean *The earth is flat:*

(1)   *John thinks that the earth is flat,* $\left\{ \begin{array}{l} \textit{because he said so.} \\ \textit{because I told him so.} \end{array} \right\}$

(Continued on page 166)

(80)   a.   *Let him go,*
            b.   **since the boss said so.*
            c.   *since the boss said to.*
            d.   *because it would be a good idea to (do so).*
            e.   *because that's what the boss said (to do).*

The other reduction rules replace the verb phrase with *do* or delete it entirely, and replace whole sentential constituents with the pronouns *it* and *that.*

The following are examples of speech acts, in addition to commands, that do not allow the identity conditions for *so* pronominalization to be met:

(81)   **Let the cat out, please, because my aunt said so.*

(82)   ??*Honestly, I'll be there at 4:15, because Martin said so.*

(83)   ??*I sincerely promise to abstain totally from alcohol, because Alcoholics Anonymous told me so.*

(84)   ??*I hereby appoint you attorney general, because it said so in the New York Times.*

(85)   ??*You'd better get out of range of the H-bomb test tomorrow, because the Army told me so.*

(86)   ??*Thank you for the lovely birthday present, because my mother told me so.*

So has as its antecedent the complement of verbs of stating and asking questions, both descriptively and performatively used. It may also have as an antecedent the complement of certain other predicates like *seem, be afraid, think* (but not *suppose, suggest,* or *assume*), which might form a subset of the 'transparent' predicates mentioned in note 9.

Anderson (1972) assumes that sentential *so* is derived by the same rule that replaces verbs of activity and their objects by *do so.* If this is so, and the arguments about the respective orderings of the rules of replacement are correct, then an ordering paradox arises. The correct ordering for *do so* replacement is quite unclear, (discussed in Bouton, 1969), and it is also unclear what the status of other instances of *so* is:

(1)   a.   *Do you swear to tell the truth?*
                     b.   *Do you swear that this is the truth?*
                     c.   *I (do) so swear.*
                     d.   **I swear so.*

Sentence (1c) is a proper reply to both (1a) and (1b), while (1d) is not possible at all. If this is the same *so* as the one in reason clauses, it will be hard to treat *so* as a pronominal complement of verbs of mental state, and *do so* as its counterpart for verbs of activity.

(87)   ??*Congratulations on winning the prize, because it said
        so in the Three Village Herald.*

Some of these sentences might be well-formed if said with contrastive stress, or taken as statements (with declarative surface form) or
suggestions (if imperative in form). But as requests, promises, thanks,
etc., they are odd. They cannot be ruled out on semantic grounds.
The illocutionary acts represented here usually are not done
BECAUSE of what someone else says; but many of these acts require
that the speaker hold some belief, which has propositional form, and
the reason clause could justify the speaker's holding this belief. For
instance, in warning someone, as in (85), one must believe that some
bad event will occur, and this belief could be based on what the
Army said. In fact, this is the case in sentences in which *so*
pronominalization has not occurred:[17]

(88)   *You'd better get out of range of the test, because the
        Army said it's scheduled for tomorrow.*

There is a specific condition on the rule of *so* pronominalization that
distinguishes between speech acts.

   This fact provides a test to discriminate between those verbal acts
which really are statements or questions and those which are questions or statements only in surface form.[18] Sentences (89)–(94) are
requests having the form of questions and statements. The first
reason clause is well-formed, but the second included with each
speech act contains *so* pronominalization and is not well-formed:

(89) a.   *May I ask you to remit $100 by the end of the month,*

---

[17] The reason clause is to be pronounced without contrastive stress. Other sentences
are possible with contrastive stress and *so* replacement:

(1)   *Get out of here — because Ì say so!*

Sentence (1) is more fully expressed as a sequence of sentences:

(2)   *Get out of here!*

(3)   *Why should I?*

(4)   *Because Ì say so.*

Sentence (1) has contrastive stress because of the real or anticipated objections of the
hearer. I do not think such objections are factors to be considered in the cases of
reason clauses discussed in the main body of the chapter.

[18] The suggestion meaning of imperatives need not be considered here because the
literal meaning of imperative indirect speech acts (*allow me, let me*) would be a
demand for permission rather than a suggestion.

b.   *because that's what the contract stipulates.*
c.   **?because it says so in the contract.*

(90) a.   *Could I request that you refund my money for the electric fork I bought,*
b.   *since your advertisement contains a money-back guarantee.*
c.   **?because it says so in your advertisement.*

(91) a.   *May I ask you to keep your dog on a leash,*
b.   *because the city code requires it.*
c.   *??because it says so in the city code.*

(92) a.   *I must ask you to appear before a magistrate next week,*
b.   *because the law requires your appearance within a short time.*
c.   **because the law says so.*

(93) a.   *I'd like to request that you keep your dog on a leash,*
b.   *because the tenants have said they would prefer that you do.*
c.   *??the tenants have said so.*

Requests in imperative indirect form also, as the restriction would predict, do not allow *so* pronominalization:

(94) a.   *Let me ask you to give me your address in Mannheim,*
b.   *because Jonathan reminded that I had better do so, before you leave.*
c.   **because Jonathan said so.*

Sentence (94c) is bad because (94a) is a request in actual illocutionary force, not because it has imperative surface form.

So pronominalization is possible if the antecedent is contained in a statement or question expressed in indirect form. This should be expected, in light of the facts about reason clauses discussed in the previous section, as the reason clauses in which *so* pronominalization occur are cases of reason clauses qualifying the conditions on the performative verb. Following are examples of statements and questions:

(95)   *May I ask if thunderstorms are predicted for next week? because it doesn't say so in the newspaper prediction.*[19]

---

[19] The indirect object pronoun *you* could have been included in these sentences, but it would have complicated the discussion because the presence of *you* introduces

(96)   *I must ask if John is definitely coming next week; be-*
       cause I thought he said so but I've muddled things
       recently.

(97)   *Can I ask if you've tinted your hair recently? because*
       somebody, I don't remember who, told me so.

(98)   *Let me ask if that's a real sable coat; because the person*
       I was talking to just said so.

(99)   *May I say that thunderstorms are predicted for D-Day;*
       because the meteorologists just told me so.

(100) *Allow me to say that we can expect trouble from the*
       other side; because my spies have just told me so.

(101) *I must say that Smedley has made a poor showing in*
       Suffolk county; because the poll-takers have just told
       me so.

The clauses with *so* pronominalization are well-formed, regardless of
the surface form of the sentences, because (95)–(98) are questions,
while (99)–(101) are statements.

The same reason clauses differentiate between statements and
questions having the same surface syntactic form. The question in
(102a) allows both reason clauses, while the statement in (103a)
allows only one.

(102) a.   *Can I ask if the British are gathering in large*
           numbers on the other side of the Hudson,
       b.   *because General Arnold has received no reports that*
           say so.
       c.   *because General Arnold has received reports that*
           say so.

(103) a.   *Can I say that it appears the British are gathering*
           on the other side of the Hudson,
       b.   *because General Arnold just told me so.*
       c.   **because General Arnold hasn't told me so.*

Sentence (103c) is incompatible with a statement, as it implies that
the speaker does not know if a proposition is true or not; a statement
with the surface form of a question is a statement for the purposes of
the syntactic rule involved here.

---

ambiguity. The literal meaning, request for permission [or statement of obligation],
would also be possible.

SLIFTING

In this section, I will discuss a restriction involving requests and the rule of SENTENCE LIFTING, or SLIFTING, discussed in Ross 1973b). If the slifting analysis of sentences like (104b) should run into insuperable objections, the restriction would have to be stated as a semantic one.

The rule, as Ross presents it, operates on postverbal sentential complements of verbs like *say, ask, think, believe, be afraid, seem,* and *appear:*

(104)   a. *I believe John's here.*
                         b. *John's here, I believe.*

(105)   a. *I wonder if John's here.*
                         b. *Is John here, I wonder.*

The rule moves the complement of *believe* to the left of *I believe.* The complement is then conjoined with *I believe,* with the normal phrase break between them.[20] Sentences (104b) and (105b) are the result of Slifting operating on (104a) and (105a).

Slifting is subject to numerous restrictions, discussed by Ross (1973a,b).[21] In addition to these, it is subject to a restriction that distinguishes between structures containing verbs of requesting and commanding, and all other illocutionary types. Indirect requests do not undergo Slifting, nor do descriptive uses of requests. More generally, it might explain the absence of verbs of requesting in emphatic tags.

---

[20] The tag is separated from the slifted complement in two ways. It may have stress, in which case it is separated by a pause:

(1)   a. *I believe John's here.*
                         b. *John's here, I believe.*

(2)   a. *I'm afraid they're not coming.*
                         b. *They're not coming, I'm afraid.*

The stress is also present in the unslifted version, and indicates some sort of disclaimer of definite knowledge. As *be afraid,* when stressed, does not assert fear, in (2), the stress does not emphasize the literal meaning of the predicate.

If the tag is unstressed, it is also set off by a drop in pitch followed by level intonation:

(3)   a. *I bĕlĭeve John's hére.*
                         b. *John's hére, I bĕlĭeve.*

The predicate *believe* is unstressed in the unslifted version also.

[21] Slifting does not apply to the complements of formal performatives of the kind that may have *hereby* combined with them:

Indirect questions and statements, whatever their surface structure, do undergo Slifting freely, although some speakers find the result more plausible as a sentence if the tag is parenthetical rather than final. The positions of tags internal to a slifted complement are the result of another rule called NICHING (Ross, in preparation). The following (b) sentences are derived by slifting from the (a) sentences:

(106)   a. *May I say that the soufflé is delicious.*
          b. *The soufflé is delicious, may I say.*

(107)   a. *I must say that the movie was a bummer.*
          b. *The movie was a bummer, I must say.*

(108)   a. *Let me say that Iodine's behavior was*
              to be expected.
          b. *Iodine's behavior was to be expected,*
              let me say.

Indirect questions also undergo the rule:

(109)   a. *May I ask if those are real diamonds?*
          b. *Are those real diamonds, may I ask?*

---

(1)   a. *I hereby state that I was in New York that day.*
       b. *°I was in New York that day, I hereby state.*

(2)   a. *I hereby ask you whether you have any knowledge*
           of the crime.
       b. *°Do you have any knowledge of the crime, I hereby*
           ask you.

(3)   a. *I hereby request you to perform with your bear*
           for the King.
       b. *°Perform with your bear for the King, I hereby request you.*

Promise with *hereby* does not allow Slifting, as we would expect:

(4)   a. *°I'll be there at 10, I hereby promise.*
             b. *I'll bé there at 10, I prómise.*
             c. *°I'll be there at 10, I prŏmĭse.*

With heavy stress, emphasizing the promise in the face of disbelief, the complement of *promise* can be slifted, as in (4b). If the tag is unstressed and has lowered pitch, the sentence is ungrammatical. Lexically expressed verbs used performatively, like *promise*, *suggest*, and *warn*, allow Slifting in their complements only if *hereby* is not present. Performative verbs are never destressed, so that the destressed tag with lowered pitch is not to be expected as the output of the rule. As verbs used performatively constitute a crucial part of an act, one would not expect them to be transparent, in the sense mentioned in note 9, expressing the speaker's attitude toward a speech act with independent existence. Predicates mentioned in the preceding note, like *be afraid*, do allow destressing and are transparent.

(110)   a.   *I must ask how you expect to support yourself.*
            b.   *How do you expect to support yourself,*
                I must ask.

(111)   a.   *Let me ask if you think we haven't noticed*
                anything.
            b.   *Do you think we haven't noticed anything,*
                let me ask.

Indirectly expressed requests, however, never undergo the rule, even if they have the surface form of statements or questions:

(112)   a.   *May I ask you to be a little more quiet?*
            b.   ??*Be a little more quiet, may I ask you.*

(113)   a.   *I must request you to move your car.*
            b.   ??*Move your car, I must request you.*

(114)   a.   *Let me request that you lock the door when*
                 you leave.
            b.   ??*Lock the door when you leave, let me request.*

Descriptively used verbs of requesting may have their complements extracted by Slifting:

(115)   *'Walk aft until your cap floats,' he* $\begin{cases} \textit{requested.} \\ \textit{commanded.} \end{cases}$

The slifted complement in (115) is an example of direct discourse; complements of requests and questions in indirect discourse do not undergo slifting under most conditions [but Ross discusses exceptions (Ross, 1973a)].[22]

Statements and questions have emphatic postposed tags, *I téll you* and *I ask you.* They have the function of reminding the hearer that the speaker has already stated something, and of lending urgency to a question. Tags can appear with requests and commands only if they do not contain a verb of requesting:

(116)   a.   *John's here, I tell you.*
              b.   *John's here, I said.*

(117)   a.   *What time does the train léave, I ask you!*
              b.   *Now, I ask you, did you actually see*
                 the defendant at that time?

---

[22] For example, the sentence cited by Ross (1973a) is an example of direct discourse inversion and indirect discourse tense shift:

(1)   *Would dinner be late, Archie wondered?*

(118)

a. $\left\{\begin{array}{l} \textit{Would you} \\ \textit{Won't you} \\ \textit{Could you} \\ \textit{Can you} \end{array}\right\}$ *pass the pheasant, please?*

b. *Pass the pheasant, please,* $\left\{\begin{array}{l} \textit{would you} \\ \textit{won't you} \\ \textit{could you} \\ \textit{?can you} \end{array}\right\}$?

(119)   a. *Pass the bútter, I tell you.*
           b. *Pass the bútter, I told you.*
           c. *Get óut of here, I say.*
           d. *Get óut of here, I said.*

Examples (118), which contains requests, and (119), which contains emphatic commands, are well-formed with normally stressed tags, that is, unstressed tags in (118) and relatively unstressed tags in (119), by contrast with the heavy stresses in the preceding clause.

No cases exist of emphatic tags containing a verb of requesting:[23]

(120)   a.   ??*Pass the bútter, I ask you.*
           b.   *Lock the door when you léave, I request.
           c.   *Get lóst, I order you.
           d.   *Take out the garbage, I demand.
           e.   *Take your hat off when you speak, I command.*

This is not surprising, if the restrictions on indirectly expressed requests indicate a general restriction that, taken with another restriction that prevents extraction of the complements of nontransparent performative verbs, prevents the creation of tags or parenthetical constituents containing verbs of requesting. In the case of indirect speech acts, the restriction applies only to sentences that are actually requests, regardless of their surface form.

---

[23] An imperative tag containing a verb of linguistic communication is possible, as in:

(1)   *The reason why Ethel Smyth is so repulsive, tell Nessa, is her table manners.*
     [From Bell, 1972: II, 170n]

Only verbs like *tell, inform, say,* etc., are possible:

(2)

   John will be there, $\left\{\begin{array}{l} \textit{tell them} \\ \textit{inform them} \\ \textit{*convince them} \\ \textit{*confound them with the fact} \end{array}\right\}$, *as soon as he returns.*

These tags do not, however, contain any overt verb of requesting.

NEGATIVE QUESTIONS

In the next two sections I will discuss properties of indirect speech acts not shared by the corresponding direct speech act or the literal meaning of the surface structure. The first restriction prevents negative questions from being expressed indirectly.

Indirect questions may be either yes–no or *wh-* questions but not yes–no questions, which like tag questions, assume that the questioned proposition is probably the case:

(121) a. *May I ask if John's here?*
       b. *May I ask who's coming?*

(122) a. *Those are real diamonds, aren't they?*
       b. *Aren't those real diamonds?*

(123) a. *May I ask if those are real diamonds?*
       b. *??May I ask if those aren't real diamonds?*
       c. **?Aren't those real diamonds, may I ask?*

(124) a. *I must ask if that is cannabis on your windowsill.*
       b. *??I must ask if that isn't cannabis on your windowsill.*
       c. *??Isn't that cannabis on your windowsill, I must ask.*

(125) a. *Let me ask if you have lost weight recently.*
       b. *??Let me ask if you haven't lost weight recently.*
       c. **?Haven't you lost weight recently, let me ask.*

In (123)–(125) the nonnegative question can be expressed indirectly, but the corresponding negative question cannot, especially if Slifting applies, as in the (c) sentences. The related tag question is also odd:

(126) a. *??May I ask if those are real diamonds, aren't they?*
       b. *??I must ask if that's cannabis on your windowsill, isn't it?*
       c. *??Let me ask if you've lost weight recently, haven't you?*

These facts would imply some general restriction that prevents questions with the semantic properties of indirect speech acts described earlier in this chapter from also being questions about which the speaker has a strong assumption of what the answer is. The hearer is usually expected to confirm or deny this assumption. The painful or intrusive nature of the indirect question must, it appears, conflict with this expectation, perhaps for the same reason that entirely sincere and straightforward speech acts are the only kind that may be expressed indirectly.

NONRESTRICTIVE RELATIVE CLAUSES

Speech acts of various sorts occur in nonrestrictive relative clauses that are embedded, at least in surface structure, in another speech act. Examples are given in (127):

(127) a. *Theatre of Blood, which I promise not to reveal the ending of, was slightly too gory for me.*
   b. *I talked to the Old Field police, who I warn you are not very reasonable.*
   c. *Were your friends disturbed by the old guy who panhandles outside, who I beg you not to turn in to the cops.*
   d. *Trouble was averted by Inspector Clouseau, who I hereby thank for his help.*

The speech acts in the nonrestrictive clause can be expressed indirectly but not directly if imperative subject deletion or other rules operating in questions have applied.

In the examples that follow, the (a) sentence, containing an overt performative, is well-formed, while the corresponding (b) sentence is not:

(128) a. *I gave the message to Peter and Laurie, who I suggest you invite to the party.*

   b. **I gave the message to Peter and Laurie, who invite to the party.*

(129) a. *The answer, which I hereby ask to have returned, was in my desk last night.*
   b. **The answer, which return, was in my desk last night.*

(130) a. *This outrage, which I demand to know the perpetrator of, has upset everybody.*
   b. **This outrage, which who was it perpetrated by, has upset everybody.*

Indirect speech acts may be found in nonrestrictive relative clauses, expressing questions and requests as well as statements. They may have the otherwise forbidden subjectless or inverted form, and yet they are well-formed:

(131) a. *John, who let me tell you is a sterling fellow, has*
           just been elected dog catcher.
       b. *I just talked with the Old Field police, who may I*
           say are a little overzealous.
       c. *That cat, which I must say I don't like much, just*
           walked in and made itself at home.

The statements in the relative clauses in (131) have the form of an
imperative and a question, as well as a statement. Examples of questions and requests in relative clauses are given in (132) and (133):

(132) a. *The commissioner, who I have to ask if you ever*
           knew personally, was just indicted.[24]
       b. *That man, whose name could I ask you again, looks*
           exactly like my uncle.
       c. *That man over there, who let me ask if you've ever*
           seen before, is our chief suspect.

(133) a. *This is my cat, which I'd like to ask you to feed this*
           weekend.
       b. *This book, which may I ask you to return for me,*
           would be very helpful if it weren't written in Es-
           peranto.
       c. *Please hold my paycheck, which could I request you*
           also to send to this address in two weeks?
       d. *I am going to see that movie, which let me ask you*
           not to tell me the ending of.

The restriction on ordinary direct speech acts, forbidding the operation of subject deletion, and inversion in relative clauses, must be
suspended in order to produce the inversion in (133a), the subject
deletion in (133d), and the *wh*-fronting in nonstandard but possible
(134):

(134)   *?There's that man again, who I'd like*
           to know $\begin{cases} \textit{what was the name of.} \\ \textit{what's his name.} \end{cases}$

In other words, the restriction must be phrased so as to distinguish
between real questions and imperatives, and surface questions and
imperatives.

---

[24] The questions that are possible in nonrestrictive relative clauses are certainly
much more restricted than statements and requests. Certain speakers may not accept
these sentences. Even so, the fact remains that indirect speech acts having the force of
statements and requests are possible with imperative and interrogative surface form.

CONCLUSION

The preceding sections have defined some of the difficult tasks involved in constructing a single, satisfactory analysis of indirect speech acts, assuming that indirect speech acts form a single definable class. Few of the discussions of indirect speech acts include the same types of sentences. Gordon and Lakoff assume that all speech acts that can imply another speech act in some circumstances belong to the same class, to be accounted for in the same way. For example, they note that (135a) and (136a) imply (135b) and (136b), respectively:

(135) a. *It's cold in here.*
           [Gordon and Lakoff, 1971:63]
       b. *Shut the window.*

(136) a. *Can you take out the garbage?*
           [Gordon and Lakoff, 1971:64, (2b)]
       b. *Take out the garbage.*

The reason clause test I have proposed will differentiate between (135a) and (136a), in that the latter, but not the former, allows a reason clause appropriate to requests:

(137) a. *Shut the window, please, as it's my turn to move in the chess game.*
       b. **It's cold in here, as it's my turn to move in the chess game.*

(138) a. *Take out the garbage, please, since my hands are full.*
       b. *Can you take out the garbage, please, since my hands are full.*

The connection between the sentences of (136) seems to me much closer than those of (135). It is quite true that the conditions under which (135a) implies (135b) do not always hold (that the hearer is attentive to the wishes and comfort of the speaker), and yet if Gordon and Lakoff are correct in calling (135a) an indirect speech act, it is odd that (137b) is not possible when the conditions for implicature do hold. It would be easier to discuss the relative merits of proposed structures if it were clear what types of sentences were to be described in an explanatory way. I have tried to define a fairly uniform class by surface structure and various tests, such as reason clauses, replies, descriptions, and ability to undergo certain syntactic rules.

The ideal analysis will account for the semantic facts that indirect speech acts are always sincere, are used in conventional or real cases of conflict of interest, and resemble the act conveyed in most ways, though they are hardly at all like the act suggested by the surface structure. The analysis must account also for the generally destressed nature of the modals and other predicates in the surface structure (as in *I mŭst sây tʰat S*), for the elusive qualities of being transparent and of expressing attitudes, and, finally, for the fact that the illocutionary force suggested by the surface structure is in some way subordinate to the actual, conveyed illocutionary force of the speech act. The proposed remote structure or set of structures must make it possible to state, without adding greatly to the grammar, that many but not all of the constraints applying to direct speech acts apply also to the indirect speech acts corresponding in actual force.

As Sadock points out (Sadock, 1970), the relationship between the illocutionary force of the surface structure and the actual force cannot be expressed as normal syntactic subordination. If a whimperative like (136a) is both a question and an imperative, as he assumes, it is surely not a command to ask a question or a question about an imperative, which would be the two possible results of allowing one to dominate the other syntactically.

Linear sequence also expresses some sort of subordination; this is the case for antecedent and identical constituent that undergo reduction, and it is usually the case that if A precedes B in constituents of a certain size, then A dominates B.[25] Sadock (1970) uses linear sequence in the first attempt to account for whimperatives, requests

[25] Sadock (1970:235) proposes the following as the structure of:

(1)   *Will you give me a drink?*

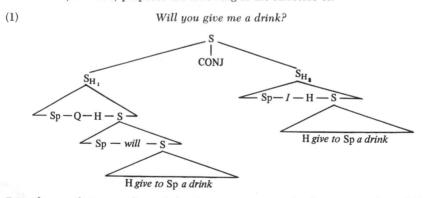

Precedence relations, order and dominance, enter into the description of restrictions on the crossing of quantifiers and negatives (McCawley, lectures on syntax and semantics, 1969).

with the form of questions, and without an overt verb of requesting. The imperative constituent is conjoined with a question, but it follows the question. The last constituent is the one that is combined with *please* and other things appropriate to requests. In the course of the derivation, the imperative verb and its complement are deleted, the latter by identity with the complement of the question. Sadock's analysis, then, manages quite elegantly both semantic cooccurences and surface structures. The whole structure containing conjoined performative verbs with redundantly alike complements does not provide a very good paraphrase of a whimperative, but as I have tried to show in the first section, the special meaning of indirect speech acts as a whole is rather complex and hard to paraphrase in a simple way.

Sadock claims, however, that whimperatives are simultaneously questions and imperatives. His structure does not indicate very explicitly that the request part is really primary semantically, as the request is second and in the normally subordinate position. It is not clear from his structure why nothing can be combined with the question part—a reason clause, for instance. It is also not clear why the modal and other predicates are destressed in the surface form, as this is the surface manifestation of the question conjunct, which is in antecedent position. Finally, the structure does not indicate any special semantic properties, even of politeness or deference, that set indirect speech acts apart from others.

Green (1970) considers a wider range of imperatives, ranging in vehemence from suggestions to commands:

(139)   a.   *Why don't you have another cookie?*
               b.   *Will you shut up?*

The structure she proposes uses both order and dominance relations to express properties of whimperatives. It has a highest and left-most performative verb, SUGGEST, REQUEST, or COMMAND, and so on, which dominates a conjoined structure. The first conjunct contains the act requested, and the second contains the verb TELL with the complement *that/why you won't S*, where S expresses the action requested. This structure gets the dominance relations right, defining the act as primarily a request or other imperative. The question part consists of the imperative component and *tell*, though unfortunately there is no easy way of combining them into one constiuent. Green's structure does predict the correct replies, and provides a more plausible paraphrase of a whimperative. It is not as general as Sadock's structure, which can be used for other speech acts with other surface forms. Green's could not be used to account for requests with the form of imperatives (*Allow me to request*, and so on), nor for indirect acts like statements, without major alterations.

Both Sadock and Green include in the remote structure of indirect speech acts some component representing the actual illocutionary force. Gordon and Lakoff start from the surface form of the speech act. In their analysis, the remote structure of (136a) as a request is the same as the remote structure of the sentence that is a question about ability. The question implies a request because it is a question about a hearer-based sincerity condition on requesting; the speaker must believe that the hearer is capable of carrying out the requested action. Assertion of a speaker-based condition on the sincere performance of a speech act also implies that speech act, in their analysis, as in (140) and (141):

(140) a. *I want you to shut the door.*
     [= Gordon and Lakoff, 1971:64, (2b)]
   b. *Shut the door.*
   c. *as it's freezing in here.*
   d. *Since you're the closest.*

(141) a. *I bĕliĕve it's time to go home.*
     [= Gordon and Lakoff, 1971:64, (2b)]
   b. *It's time to go home.*
   c. *as they've stopped serving drinks and*
     have taken away the chairs.

The (a) sentences, which I am assuming have relatively unstressed beginnings, imply the (b) sentences; the reason clauses could well be combined with either. Many indirect speech acts are given an attractive explanation for their surface form in this analysis.

But it will not do for all speech acts one would want to call indirect. Part of the great value of the paper is the clear discussion of the problems entailed by the analysis—for instance, the fact that it does not explain why statements of obligation and questions of permission convey a speech act, but questions of obligation and statements of permission do not; compare *I must offer* with *Must I offer?*.[26] Permission and obligation are not involved in the sincerity or other con-

---

[26] I have found counterexamples such as:

(1) *What about drinks? I may say that I found a good many empty gin and*
   whisky bottles in the cabin. [Farrers, 1955:246]

I find the following plausible indirect statements:

ditions on requests, statements, offers, and so on. In such indirect speech acts, which have been extensively discussed in this chapter, obligation and permission are involved in the speaker's acknowledgment of intrusion. Requests for permission expressed as imperatives (*allow me,* and so forth) are very much like the questions about permission, but the imperative form is not general, outside of these cases, and does not fit into the Gordon and Lakoff analysis.

Gordon and Lakoff note that there must be some specific context, which they represent with the cover symbol *, in which the rules of conversational implicature relate one speech act to another. This context (of beliefs and social situation, I would imagine) is not always present, so that speech acts that can convey another act have their literal meaning in some cases. The context in which indirect speech acts are not taken literally is the same one, as far as I can see from personal observation, that demands an indirect speech act as acknowledgment of intrusion, real or conventional. The idiomatic nature of many indirect speech acts, particularly whimperatives, cannot be ignored. They often express nothing more than conventional politeness, which requires the speaker to act as if his speech act is some sort of intrusion, though actually it would be nothing of the sort. The Gordon and Lakoff analysis might explain the origin of the usage, rather than describe a productive process.

Gordon and Lakoff note also that the conversational implicature analysis does not explain why some but not all speech acts can be expressed by others, since all speech acts have some sort of sincerity conditions, which could be asserted, if speaker-based, or questioned, if hearer-based. But this is not the case with accusing and promising (1971:78–79). At least part of the explanation should come from the fact that indirect speech acts express acknowledgment of conflict, as I proposed in the first section of this chapter. It follows from the nature of some speech acts that the situation of conflict between the speaker and the hearer does not arise and need not be apologized for. Real accusations (the ones that stick) are made by duly constituted authority, and promises, as I have tried to show, are not unsolicited acts.

A possible benefit accruing from the Gordon and Lakoff analysis is in the statement of conditions on rules that apply in structures to

---

(2) *I may tell you that John is about to resign.*

(3) *Need I say that we are behind you 1000%?*

(4) *Must I say that I find you repellent?* (a statement if one is trying to convey something without expressing it in the most extreme form possible)

which another speech act is related by conversational implicature. The related derivation can serve as a condition in the rule for its application, particularly if the rule normally applies in the related derivation. The example given in Gordon and Lakoff (1971) concerns a deletion rule applying only in the implicating structure.[27] I will consider here how the constraints on rules and the restrictions on combinations noted earlier in this chapter could or should be stated. I will suggest that they do not have to be transderivational constraints; at most, they could be stated in terms of nonadjacent stages of a single derivation [Lakoff's global constraints (Lakoff, 1970), which allow reference to stages of derivation other than the immediately preceding one, unlike ordinary transformational rules].

The restrictions suspended in nonrestrictive relative clauses look like paradigm cases of transderivational constraints. Inversion and subject deletion may not apply in nonrestrictive relative clauses, unless structures where they would apply conversationally imply some other speech act. Alternatively, these rules might not apply in such an environment unless some overt performative verb is included in the relative clause. There is some support for this being the crucial factor, as whimperatives are not allowed and whimperatives contain no overt performative verb:

(142) a. *That book, which may I ask you to hand me, has an interesting history.*

b. ??*That book, which* $\left\{ \begin{array}{l} \textit{would you} \\ \textit{will you} \\ \textit{won't you} \\ \textit{could you} \\ \textit{why don't you} \end{array} \right\}$ *hand me, has an interesting history.*

In the case of negative questions and tag questions, the restrictions could be stated as applying to sentences that imply yes–no questions. If indirect speech acts are analyzed semantically, as I proposed earlier, the negative and tag might be ruled out because of the as-

---

[27] The example concerns negative suggestions implied by questions [Gordon and Lakoff, 1971:72, (11) and (12)]:

(1)   *Why do you paint your house purple?*

(2)   *Why paint your house purple?*

(3)   . . . *you should not paint your house purple.*

If (1) implies the negative suggestion (3), the reduction rule operates on (1) to produce (2).

sumption of probability that is associated with both of them, and provides some explanation for why both are excluded from indirect questions. All of the restrictions that hold for both the direct speech act and the indirect speech act conveying the same illocutionary act could be stated transderivationally, but they could equally well be stated in terms of earlier stages of derivation at which a performative verb defining the actual illocutionary force would still be present.

I do not propose to discuss transderivational constraints exhaustively here, as the whole question is complex and it is not clear how much power they ought to have. I have suggested here that the restrictions discussed earlier do not have to be stated transderivationally, and that not stating them in this fashion might lead to the discovery of more precise or specific explanations for them. I would now like to consider whether a structure implying another speech act is automatically subject to all the restrictions applying to that related speech act.

An obvious case is that of the rules normally applying to questions and imperatives. These do not necessarily apply to structures that are conversationally related to imperatives or questions. For instance, in *Will you shut the door*, inversion gets there first, although the sentence implies a request and meets the structural description for subject deletion, at least in its lexical contents.[28]

Another case involves a rule (or several rules of the same type) that topicalize NPs in statements, as in (143), and questions and requests, as in (144) and (145):

(143) a. *John, I just can't seem to like, even if he is your best friend.*

 b. **John,* $\begin{Bmatrix} let\ me\ tell\ you \\ can\ I\ say \\ I\ have\ to\ say \end{Bmatrix}$ *I don't like (him), even if he is your best friend.*

(144) a. *That movie, who's in it?*

 b. *??That movie,* $\begin{Bmatrix} let\ me\ ask\ you\ who's\ in\ it. \\ I\ have\ to\ ask\ you\ who's\ in\ it. \\ can\ I\ ask\ you\ who's\ in\ it. \end{Bmatrix}$

---

[28] The presence of a performative verb of the wrong sort might serve to block the operation of these rules. This is not the case in the example in note 27, in which the presence of a question performative in (1) does not block the operation of a rule operating in the context of a suggestion. The rule of deletion in (2) is not general enough, however, to be clearly a parallel case.

(145) a.   *That movie, you should go see.*

b.   *??That movie,* $\left\{\begin{array}{l} I \text{ want you to shut up about.} \\ would \text{ you shut up about.} \\ can \text{ } I \text{ ask you not to tell me plot of.} \\ I \text{ have to ask you to shut up about.} \end{array}\right\}$

The versions containing direct speech acts sound to me far better than the ones with indirect speech acts. The latter would conversationally imply the derivations to which the topicalizing rules could apply. But the implication does not allow the properties of the implied act to carry over to the implying act automatically. This fact would mean that some if not all restrictions would have to be specifically stated as applying or not applying to related speech acts, a consequence that complicates the grammar without providing some gains that could be accomplished in no other way.

As I said at the outset, I do not have a perfect structure to propose for indirect speech acts either, though I think the facts presented here suggest a more complex structure for indirect speech acts than for direct speech acts. I would advance a structure combining the structure of an illocutionary with a structure expressing emotional attitudes of the speaker toward the act, but not with much confidence until transparent predicates and clauses are better understood. At present, there are few if any viable suggestions for combining the elements of such a complex structure, unless one resorts to crude idiomatic substitution.

ACKNOWLEDGMENTS

I am grateful to Beatrice and R. M. R. Hall and to Peter Reimold for criticisms and suggestions for the improvement of earlier drafts of this paper. Failure to do so, and other shortcomings and errors, are, of course, my responsibility. Susan Robbins gave considerable assistance as an informed informant. I am especially grateful to Elizabeth Wehr and Thomas Wehr, M.D., for their clear and perceptive descriptions of the meanings of indirect speech acts, which helped me considerably to clarify my own intuitions and attempts at description.

REFERENCES

Anderson, S. Pro-sentential forms and their implications for English sentence structure. Mimeo. Indiana University Linguistics Club, Bloomington, 1972.

Bell, Q. *Virginia Woolf.* Vol. 2. London: Hogarth Press, 1972.

Bouton, L. Identity constraints on the *Do–so* rule. *Papers in Linguistics,* 1969, 1(2), 231–247.

Davison, A. Performatives, felicity conditions and adverbs. Unpublished dissertation, University of Chicago, 1973. (a)

Davison, A. Words for things people do with words. In F. Corum, T. C. Smith–Stark, and A Weiser (Eds.), *Papers from the ninth regional meeting of the Chicago Linguistic Society*. Chicago: University of Chicago Department of Linguistics, 1973, 114–122. (b)

Farrers, K. *The Cretan counterfeit*. London: Penguin Books, 1955.

Gordon, D. and Lakoff, G. Conversational postulates. In D. Adams, M. A. Cambell, V. Cohen, J. Lovins, E. Maxwell, C. Nygren, and J. Reighard (Eds.), *Papers from the seventh regional meeting of the Chicago Linguistic Society*. Chicago: University of Chicago Department of Linguistics, 1971, 63–84.

Green, G. Whimperatives: Schizophrenic speech acts. Unpublished paper. Ann Arbor, Michigan, 1970.

Heringer, J. *Some grammatical correlates of felicity conditions and presuppositions. Working papers in linguistics, no. 11*. Columbus: The Ohio State University, Department of Linguistics, 1972, 1–110.

Lakoff, G. Global rules.*Language*, 1970, 46, 627–639.

Lakoff, R. The logic of politeness; or, Minding your p's and q's. In C. Corum, T. C. Smith–Stark, and A Weiser (Eds.), *Papers from the ninth regional meeting of the Chicago Linguistic Society*. Chicago: University of Chicago Department of Linguistics, 1973, 292–305.

Liberman, M. Some observations on semantic scope. M. A. thesis, MIT, Cambridge, Mass., 1973.

Ross, J. R. Embedded force rules. Paper delivered at the University of Texas conference on performatives, conversational implicature, and presuppositions, March 22–24, 1973. (a)

Ross, J. R. Slifting. In M. Gross, M. Halle, and M.-P. Schützenberger (Eds.), *The formal analysis of natural languages*. The Hague: Mouton, 1973, 133–169. (b)

Ross, J. R. Niching. In preparation.

Sadock, J. M. Whimperatives. In J. Sadock and A. Vanek (Eds.), *Studies presented to Robert B. Lees*. Edmonton, Alberta, and Champaign, Ill.: Linguistic Research, Inc., 1970, 223–238.

Searle, J. *Speech acts*. New York and London: Cambridge University Press, 1969.

HEDGED PERFORMATIVES

BRUCE FRASER
Boston University

INTRODUCTION

The focus of the investigation will be sentences like those in (1), which I will refer to as HEDGED PERFORMATIVES:

(1) a. *I can **promise** you that we will be there
        on time.*
     b. *I must **advise** you to remain quiet.*
     c. *I have to **admit** that you have a point.*
     d. *I wish to **invite** you to my party.*
     e. *I will henceforth **stipulate** that x = 4.5.*
     f. *I might **suggest** that you ask again.*

Each example sentence has the general form of a performative sentence, and each may count as the performance of the illocutionary act denoted by the performative verb (in bold type). However, each differs from the corresponding performative sentence in that it contains a modal or a semimodal. In addition, the sentence meaning of these examples is not identical to the corresponding performative sentence: *I must advise you to leave* is, literally, the statement that the speaker has the obligation to advise the hearer to leave, not, literally, that the speaker is, at the moment of speaking, advising the hearer to leave.[1]

For the purposes of this chapter, we will refer to examples like those in (1) as STRONGLY PERFORMATIVE in that they are easily seen as counting as the act denoted by the performative verb in the sentence. We will distinguish these from examples like those in (2), which we will call WEAKLY PERFORMATIVE, since their performative use is quite dubious and, in some cases, their grammaticality is open to question on the performative reading:

(2)   a. *I can claim that Henry VI is still alive.*
     b. *I must authorize you to leave now.*
     c. *I have to promise you that we will be there on time.*
     d. *I wish to permit you to try that.*
     e. *I might order you to stand up immediately.*
     f. *I could warn you that the bull is about to charge.*

The purpose of this chapter is to provide an account of why certain sentences are strongly performative, why others are only weakly performative. My approach will be to offer an account in terms of the literal sentence meaning in conjunction with certain principles of conversation, following the sense of Grice (this volume).

The chapter is divided into three parts. In the first, I present a summary of a previous analysis of illocutionary acts into eight

---

[1] There is no inherent theoretical significance to the set of sentences I have selected. They are bound, primarily, by the presence of the performative verb, the declarative sentence form, and a modal or semimodal. In the conclusion, I mention several other possible sentence types that might have been considered but were not, for reasons of time and space.

For purposes of exposition, I will adopt a variety of simplifying conventions. For example, I will speak of a sentence having a particular force, rather than saying the utterance of this sentence under the appropriate conditions may count as the performance of this particular illocutionary act having the associated illocutionary force, or something similar. I trust no confusion will result.

Finally, I should point out that, contrary to many current writers, I do not take the notion of a performative sentence to be a syntactic sentence type as are, for example, declarative, interrogative, and imperative sentences. Rather, a performative sentence exists because of a set of syntactic and semantic properties, analogous to the existence of a referring expression. The literature abounds with futile attempts to provide a set of syntactic criteria and, if that is not convincing, we need only observe that the following syntactic variations of performative sentences all result in a performative sentence in function, if not in form:

(i)   a. *You are (hereby) authorized to leave.*
           b. *I will be there, I promise you.*
           c. *I was, I admit, a little late.*
           d. *Those were remarks for which I hereby apologize.*

classes, a taxonomy that will prove useful in the subsequent discussion. In the second, I present the co-occurrence data for the various preverbal modifiers I have examined and an explanation for the performative strength. The third section presents some concluding remarks and suggestions for additional research.

A TAXONOMY OF ILLOCUTIONARY ACTS

In an earlier paper (Fraser, 1974a), I argued that the primary factor differentiating illocutionary acts was the intent of the speaker in performing the act; the speaker's intent (very similar to Searle's Essential Condition) is, in general, to create in the hearer an understanding of the speaker's position toward the proposition expressed in the sentence uttered.[2] If, for example, the speaker indicates that his position toward the proposition 'You will come early' is that it is to count as a response to the hearer's utterance, we can say that the speaker intended to perform the act of answering; if it is to count as an indication of a state of affairs that the speaker wishes the hearer to bring about by virtue of the speaker's position of authority, we can say that the speaker intended to perform the act of ordering; and if it is to count as the undertaking by the speaker of an obligation to bring about the state of affairs specified in the proposition, we can say that the speaker intended to perform the act of promising. And, of course, the speaker's position might be some complex combination of simple positions: One can and often does perform several illocutionary acts with a single utterance.

I claimed in that paper that there are basically eight positions a speaker might hold toward a proposition, and classified a large number of vernacular performative verbs into one or more of these eight types.[3] I include that classification here, both as a way of

---

[2] I am following Searle (1969) in using the term PROPOSITION EXPRESSED. Searle distinguishes between the propositional content of a sentence and its illocutionary-force-indicating device(s). For example, for the sentence *I promise that I will be there*, the proposition expressed in the sentence is 'I will be there' and the illocutionary-force-indicating device is the verb *promise* used performatively, thereby indicating that the speaker intends that the force of the utterance be that of a promise.

Although I will usually speak of the 'proposition expressed in the utterance,' it is often the case that the proposition in question is understood by both the speaker and the hearer and, therefore, not stated; the speaker's utterance might consist, then, of only the indication of what position the speaker holds toward this proposition.

[3] I use the term VERNACULAR in reference to performative verbs to refer to those denoting acts of a general, everyday variety, such as promising, admitting, defining,

(*Continued on page 190*)

providing the reader with a variety of performative verbs on which to test his intuitions concerning hedged performative sentences, and because the analysis that follows corresponds nicely, in some cases, with this taxonomy:

a. ACTS OF ASSERTING: *the speaker's assessment of how the proposition expressed fits into the conversation, and the speaker's strength of conviction in the truth of the proposition expressed*[4]

accuse	comment	inform	remark
acknowledge	concede	maintain	remind
add	conclude	mention	repeat
admit	concur	note	reply
advocate	confess	notify	report
affirm	confirm	observe	respond
agree	conjecture	point out	retort
allege	declare	postulate	say
announce	deduce	predict	state
apprise	denounce	proclaim	submit
argue	deny	profess	suggest
assent	disagree	prophesy	swear
assert	dispute	protest	tell
attest	emphasize	reaffirm	verify
aver	grant	recognize	warn
claim	hold	refuse	

---

requesting, and so forth. The term CEREMONIAL PERFORMATIVE is used to refer to those verbs denoting acts which rely for their successful performance on the existence of some codified legal, religious, business, government, sport, or similar activity. Such acts are nearly always performed by the use of the performative sentence (e.g., *I hereby pronounce you man and wife*) and, as Strawson (1964) has pointed out, whatever the possible locutions for pulling off these acts, they are very limited and conventionalized. The following list suggests some of these cases.

LEGAL: *acquit, adjourn, award, award a settlement, charge, convict, call to order, condemn, deputize, enter a plea, fine, levy a fine, move, nominate, overrule an objection, pronounce man and wife, sentence, sustain an objection, testify, vote*
RELIGIOUS: *annul, absolve, baptize, christen, consecrate, excommunicate, ordain*
BUSINESS: *demote, fire, hire, reinstate, resign*
GOVERNMENT: *abdicate, decree, dedicate, enact, proclaim, pronounce, repeal, veto*
SPORTS: *double* (at bridge), *bid, raise, call, declare safe, call out, checkmate*

[4] Within each of these eight classes of illocutionary acts, various subclasses can be motivated in terms of subsidiary, cross-classifying criteria such as the status of the speaker to the hearer. Most relevant to our present investigation, however, is the class

b. ACTS OF EVALUATING: *the speaker's assessment of the truth
of the proposition expressed, and the basis for this judgment*

adjudge	*conjecture*	*hold*	*postulate*
analyze	*date*	*hypothesize*	*put*
appraise	*declare*	*identify*	*rank*
assess	*describe*	*insist*	*read*
calculate	*diagnose*	*interpret*	*reckon*
call	*estimate*	*judge*	*regard*
certify	*figure*	*locate*	*rule*
characterize	*formulate*	*make it*	*speculate*
choose	*evaluate*	*measure*	*take*
cite	*find*	*picture*	*theorize*
classify	*grade*	*place*	*value*
conclude	*guess*	*portray*	

---

of asserting acts that divides neatly into two groups:

(i)   a. ASSERTING I: *add, announce, comment, declare, inform, notify, point out,
mention, remark, remind, reply, report, say, state, tell, . . .*

        b. ASSERTING II: *accuse, acknowledge, admit, advocate, affirm, agree, argue,
allege, assent, assert, attest, aver, claim, concede, conclude,
concur, confess, confirm, disclaim, grant, maintain, object,
predict, retract, . . .*

The first group has the property of requiring few, if any, conditions on the successful
performance of the associated illocutionary act. The other verbs of asserting place certain restrictions on successful performance of the act. *Accuse*, for example, entails that
the act specified has some pejorative sense associated with it; *concede* entails that the
speaker previously refused to assert the proposition; *maintain* entails that the speaker
has already once asserted the proposition; and *retract*, that the speaker has once asserted the proposition but now wishes to reverse his position. But because of the
nature of Class I, by using the performative verb grammatically in a wide range of
contexts, the illocutionary verb is necessarily performed, even in cases in which such
intent is explicitly denied. For example:

(ii)   a. *I will not* point out *to you that your face is dirty.*
            b. *I'm not going to* add *that we are now late.*
            c. *I can* mention *that we are lost.*
            d. *I might* remind *you that this book is overdue.*
            e. *I must* tell *you that they are coming immediately.*
            f. *I shall* state *that we must get out.*
            g. *I will* declare *that this wouldn't have happened
if John had been here.*
            h. *I would* comment *that this is uncalled for.*

Only Class II will be considered in further discussion.

c. ACTS OF REFLECTING SPEAKER ATTITUDE: *the speaker's assessment of the appropriateness of the state of affairs resulting from some prior act expressed by the proposition*

accept	commend	deplore	question
(apology)	commiserate	disagree	recognize
acclaim	complain	endorse	regret
admonish	compliment	excuse	salute
agree	congratulate	favor	sympathize
apologize	condemn	object to	thank
applaud	credit	oppose	toast
approve of	curse	praise	wish
blame	denounce	protest	

d. ACTS OF STIPULATING: *the speaker's desire for the acceptance of the naming convention expressed by the proposition*

abbreviate	classify	designate	recast
begin	code	distinguish	rule
call	declare	dub	select
characterize	describe	identify	specify
choose	define	nominate	stipulate
class	denote	parse	term

e. ACTS OF REQUESTING: *the speaker's desire for the hearer to bring about the state of affairs expressed in the proposition*

appeal	demand	inquire	pray
ask	direct	instruct	prohibit
beg	enjoin	invite	restrict
bid	forbid	order	request
call on	implore	petition	require
command	insist	plead	solicit

f. ACTS OF SUGGESTING: *the speaker's desire for the hearer to consider the merits of the action expressed in the proposition*

admonish	advocate	exhort	suggest
advance	caution	propose	urge
advise	counsel	recommend	warn

g. ACTS OF EXERCISING AUTHORITY: *the speaker's proposal to create a new state of affairs by exercising certain rights or powers*

abolish	*condemn*	*exonerate*	*repudiate*
abrogate	*consent*	*fine*	*rescind*
accept	*countermand*	*forbid*	*reject*
adopt	*credit*	*forgive*	*resign*
agree to	*declare*	*grant*	*restore*
allow	*decree*	*greet*	*retract*
apply for	*demur to*	*invoke*	*restrict*
appoint	*deny*	*nullify*	*revoke*
approve	*dismiss*	*permit*	*rule*
authorize	*disown*	*present*	*surrender*
bless	*dissolve*	*prohibit*	*take back*
cancel	*downgrade*	*recognize*	*tender*
choose	*excuse*	*relinquish*	*withdraw*
close	*exempt*	*renounce*	

h. ACTS OF COMMITTING: *the speaker's proposal to place himself under an obligation to bring about the state of affairs expressed in the proposition*

accept	*commit*	*guarantee*	*promise*
assume	*(oneself)*	*obligate*	*undertake*
assure	*dedicate*	*(oneself)*	*swear*
bind oneself	*(oneself)*	*offer*	*volunteer*
	give one's word	*pledge*	*vow*

AN EXPLANATION OF HEDGED PERFORMATIVES

Having presented a classification of illocutionary acts against which to examine the occurrence of certain preverbal modifiers, I now turn to the facts of co-occurrence. Predictably, not every preverbal modifier cooccurs equally well with each performative verb class, nor with each member of a given class. In some cases I can provide an explanation; in others I cannot.

Under the term MODALS, I include all of the standard modals (*can, could, may, might, must, shall, should, will,* and *would*), their periphrastic versions (*can/be able, must/have to, will/intend to*), and the forms *want to, would like to,* and *wish to,* which appear to function like the modals.

Must

The modal that cooccurs in a strongly performative manner most often and with the largest number of verbs is *must*. The following examples are illustrative:

(4)   a. *I must conclude that you are not interested.*
         b. *I must classify that job as inadequate.*
         c. *I must condemn you for saying that to him.*
         d. *I must stipulate that no one be allowed inside.*
         e. *I must request that you sit down immediately.*
         f. *I must suggest that you take it easy.*
         g. *I must forbid you from saying that.*

We begin to account for these observations by positing a general principle of rational behavior:

(5)   PRINCIPLE OF OBLIGATION FULFILLMENT: *Given nothing to suggest the contrary, whenever someone has an obligation to perform some action one can infer that he will perform that action.*[5]

For both examples in (6), for example, we can infer, according to (5), that John will fulfill his obligation and request Harry to leave:

(6)   a. *Tomorrow, John must request that Harry leave promptly.*
         b. *John must request that Harry leave promptly.*

In the first, the time of requesting is specified, while in the second, the time is left open. But I wish to suggest that the time is not quite so vague as one might imagine, and that in normal conversation we utilize what we can call a principle of unspecified time:

(7)   PRINCIPLE OF UNSPECIFIED TIME: *Given nothing to suggest the contrary, whenever the time of an action is left unspecified one can infer that the agent is expected to perform the action at the earliest chance.*

Of course, the time might be understood from the context of utterance. For example, in the utterance of the sentence *I'm going to ignore that last remark*, we understand the speaker to be referring to (at least) the present conversation; or, when the speaker has indicated previously that all orders should be carried out at the stroke of midnight and then utters *You must push the bell*, we understand the time to be midnight. In addition, there are numerous situations

---

[5] Throughout all this discussion, I will use the expression ONE CAN INFER to mean that it seems reasonable on the basis of what we know about how conversations operate that this inference could, though need not, be drawn.

I am well aware of the need to tighten and refine each of the principles I am suggesting; I trust the reader will take them as suggestive, not definitive proposals.

in which courtesy, if not convention, dictates the understood time. For example, one cannot usually utter *I'll dry the dishes* and then plead *But I didn't say when I'd do them* two hours later when confronted and accused of irresponsibility by the dishwasher. Nor can one reply to the request *Remind me to take out the garbage* with an immediate *Take out the garbage.*

Armed with (5) and (7), the hearer of any of the examples in (4) can legitimately infer that the speaker has an obligation that he will carry out (for example, to admit, to classify, and so on) and that he will do this at his very first opportunity. To move from this position to the inference that what the speaker intends in uttering (4e), for example, is indeed a request requires a third principle:

(8)   PRINCIPLE OF EFFICIENCY: *Given nothing to suggest the contrary, whenever a further utterance would be redundant one can infer that the speaker need not make the utterance but that he will operate as if he had made it and will expect the hearer to operate similarly.*

It is clear from (4e) that what might be uttered subsequently is a performative sentence of the sort *I request that you sit down immediately.* But, following (8), this sentence need not be uttered, and both the speaker and hearer are free, given nothing to the contrary, to operate as if it had been. Of course, if (4e) had been only (4e'):

(4e')   *I must request something of you.*

the content of the request would not be known and an explicit performative request would not have been redundant. With principles (5), (7), and (8), we are able to account for why sentences like those in (4) are strongly performative.

It is important to make clear at this point in the discussion that the interpretation of the strongly performative *must* sentences in (4) (as well as many of the other examples we will consider subsequently) receive the performative force not directly from the literal meaning of the sentence but through an interpretation of the speaker's intent in uttering the sentence, this interpretation based on the interaction of the sentence meaning and certain conversational principles of the sort we are suggesting. Note that the speaker can deny the performative force of these hedged performative sentences, but not true performatives, as the following examples illustrate:

(9)   a.   *I must request that you leave immediately . . . but I'll be damned if I'm going to make such a request.*

> b. *I must conclude you are not interested . . . unless, of course, you can provide me with some counterevidence.*

In addition, the hearer of the hedged performative with *must* can exercise the option of denying the implied force by responding with a *Don't bother, Please don't do that, You don't have to do that at all, do you?*, or something similar.

But we must push further to see the total interaction of the modal *must* with performative verbs. Use of *must* implies a sense of helplessness with respect to what it is that the sentence subject is obliged to do. For example:

(10)   a. *Johnny must go inside now to eat dinner.*
       b. *Mary had to report the infraction.*
       c. *Mike must come early, even though he wants to.*

Sentence (10a) might be uttered to Johnny's playmate by his mother as a way of indicating that poor Johnny does not have any say in the matter. Sentence (10b) implies that Mary probably did not really want to report the infraction and that the speaker sympathizes with her. And (10c) appears ungrammatical, presumably because of the conflict between *must* and the meaning of the second clause. In short, *must* can be used to relieve the speaker agent of some of the responsibility for the consequences of whatever he is obliged to do: It is a way of getting off the hook. Thus, when the speaker utters a sentence like those in (4), he is predicating the obligation to perform the particular act and, at the same time, implying that he would like to be relieved of at least some of the onus of the consequences.

We need not go into a detailed discussion of why a speaker might wish to avoid responsibility for the various types of illocutionary speech acts. It is clear, for example, that the speaker might not want to announce a conclusion that was counter to the hearer's views and thereby antagonize him, or classify a job as inadequate, or indicate that he condemns another's actions, or ask another to carry out some action that possibly would inconvenience him. When we examine the nature of the acts of exercising authority (3g) and of committing (3h), we find that nearly all of them entail a sense of positive orientation for the hearer concerning the state of affairs that the speaker is obliging himself to bring about. One does not make a promise to you to cut off your arm, guarantee you that the car will fall apart at the end of a month, volunteer to help you contract tuberculosis (unless you want it), and so forth. Consequently, sentences like those in (11) are weakly performative because a conflict arises between the use of *must,* implying an effort to avoid responsibility, and those verbs which denote acts in which the hearer specifically benefits and for which it is extremely difficult to determine why the speaker would want to avoid the consequences:

(11)   a. *I must promise you that I will marry*
              you tomorrow.
         b. *I must offer to help you out of that ditch.*
         c. *I must volunteer to assist your committee.*
         d. *I must grant you my entire fortune.*

Of course, we do find acts associated with the classes of exercising authority and committing for which the hearer effect is left unclear or is definitely negative. For these, strongly performative sentences result:

(12)   a. *I must refuse to carry out that request.*
         b. *I must assure you that you will be severely*
              punished.
         c. *I must deny you access to that building.*
         d. *I must cancel your promotion.*
         e. *I must restrict your movements to the*
              immediate vicinity.

A rather interesting partitioning appears to occur with the class of requesting verbs (3e), not in terms of how the hearer will be affected but in terms of the power position of the speaker with respect to the hearer:

(13)   a. *appeal, beg, bid, implore, invite, petition,*
              plead, solicit
         b. *ask, call on, forbid, insist, inquire, prohibit,*
              request, require
         c. *command, demand, direct, enjoin, instruct,*
              order, require, restrict

The acts in (13a), share the inherent property that the speaker is 'requesting' from a position of powerlessness, relative to the hearer. I do not beg you help me out of a ditch if I can easily do it myself; nor do I if I am quite aware you cannot help me. Those in (13b) seem inherently relatively neutral, from the standpoint of power. And those in (13c) share the property that the speaker wields some power vis-à-vis the hearer, perhaps assumed, perhaps institutionalized.

When we examine the hedged performative sentences with *must* and the verbs of requesting, we find the following breakdown: The speaker-powerless and speaker-powerful positions are weakly performative; the speaker-neutral cases are strongly performative:

(14) a. Powerless: *I must beg you help me out of here.*
      b. Power-neutral; *I must request you help me out of here.*
      c. Powerful: *I must order you to help me out of here.*

This is explainable in terms of our three principles if we assume (1) that a speaker requesting from a powerless position would not seek to avoid responsibility for the act or its consequences, since people are expected to aid one another; (2) that a speaker requesting from a powerful position would not seek to avoid responsibility, since the intent of the act is to get the hearer to do something by virtue of the power position; and (3) that the speaker requesting from a neutral position might wish to beg off owing to the inconvenience to the hearer, the confrontation, and so forth.

Finally, within a strongly performative combination there appears to be a relative 'strength,' depending on how one perceives the speaker's interest in avoiding the onus for the consequence of the act. In the following examples, the earlier examples appear more strongly performative than the later ones:

(15) a. *I must request that you* $\begin{cases} \textit{resign immediately from your} \\ \quad \textit{post.} \\ \textit{join me in a delicious dinner.} \end{cases}$

      b. *I must forbid you from* $\begin{cases} \textit{taking this medicine that} \\ \quad \textit{would help you.} \\ \textit{eating regularly.} \\ \textit{walking on that thin ice.} \\ \textit{cutting off your right arm.} \end{cases}$

In my account of the sentences in (4) I assumed that it is the sentence meaning in combination with the conversational principles that explain the strongly performative nature of the sentence. Accordingly, we should expect the various periphrastic versions of the modal *must* to provide us with the same degree of performative strength with a given performative verb. And indeed, this appears to be the case, as the following examples illustrate, although there appears to be a weakening from (16a) to (16d):

(16) a. *I must request that*
     b. *I have to request that*
     c. *I have the obligation to request that* — *you sit down immediately.*
     d. *It is necessary for me me to request that*
     e. *It is my obligation to request that*

Each example is strongly performative, which is exactly what we would predict if, in fact, it is sentence meaning that is playing the crucial role, and not sentence form. It does appear, however, that the performative verb must be present rather than some paraphrase of its meaning since, in the following examples, all are weakly performative:

(17) a. *I must indicate to you my desire that you sit down.*
      b. *I must form a final judgment that you are not interested.*
      c. *I must specify the condition that no one is allowed inside.*
      d. *I must offer up for your consideration the idea that you take it easy.*

Thus, the presence of the performative verb does play a crucial role in hedged performatives.

Can

Occurring with nearly as many performative verbs (all classes except that of requesting) is the modal *can*. However, *can* does not usually occur alone in what would otherwise be a simple performative sentence; rather, it must be accompanied by some adverbial, such as *now, finally, at last,* and so on. The following examples, which contain such an adverbial, are all strongly performative; without them, the examples are weakly performative:

(18) a. *I can now admit that it was I who sent that telegram.*
      b. *I finally can classify those birds as a new species.*
      c. *I can finally thank you for finding my cat.*
      d. *I can now define x = y + z.*
      e. *At last I can suggest that you ask Harry for the news.*
      f. *I can now authorize you to leave on vacation.*
      g. *I can now give you my word that he is safe.*

In all these cases, the speaker is not simply indicating that certain actions are available to him at the moment of speaking but is, in addition, implying that these were not available to him in the past. This implication is systematically associated with statements of ability when qualified by a time adverbial; we might formalize it as:

(19)   PRINCIPLE OF TIME-QUALIFIED ABILITY: *Given nothing to suggest the contrary, whenever the assertion of ability is qualified by some time adverbial referring to the movement of speaking, one can infer that such ability did not exist or was in some way restricted prior to that time.*

This principle applies not only to the examples in (18) above but also to the following examples:

(20)   a.   *I am now able to sit up straight.*
         b.   *I finally have the ability to argue with Max.*
         c.   *Can you now draw a straight line with your injured hand?*
         d.   *Are you finally able to see clearly?*

Now, using the mode of argument suggested by Grice (this volume), the hearer, upon hearing (18a), for example, could reason as follows:

(21)   a.   *The speaker has indicated that he suddenly has an ability to perform the illocutionary act of admitting, whereas he previously was restricted.*
        b.   *The speaker wouldn't have told me this unless he intended to use this new ability.*
        c.   *Thus, I can conclude that the speaker will perform the act of admitting.*
        d.   *But, by the principle of efficiency (8), there is no need to actually utter the redundant sentence I (hereby) admit that . . . , and we both can operate as if it had been uttered.*
        e.   *Thus, I can take (18a) to convey an admission to me.*

Indeed, the most questionable step in this reasoning is (21b), in which the hearer must move from being told about a new-found ability to the belief that the speaker intends to make use of this ability. This step might be formalized into the following conversational principle:

(22)   PRINCIPLE OF EXPRESSED ABILITY: *Given nothing to suggest the contrary, whenever someone indicates that he has a new ability to act one can infer that he intends to exercise this ability.*

This principle applies not only to the examples in (18) but also to (20a) and (20b). It would follow that someone uttering (20a), for example, intends to sit up straight, and someone uttering (20b) intends henceforth to argue with Max. In fact, if (22) is correct, we might expect the speaker of either (20a) or (20b) to explicitly add something like . . . *but I don't intend to* if he did not want to permit the implication following from (22) to be taken. I must admit that I am not very happy with (22) as the way to move from the inference that the speaker of (18a), for example, now has an ability that did not exist before, to the conclusion that the speaker intends to actually use this ability.

We find two classes of sentences in which the *can* co-occurs with a performative verb without a facilitating adverbial such as *now*. The first group, illustrated in (23), consists of the verbs from the committing class (3h), all of which involve the speaker's undertaking some obligation with the implication that he can, in fact, carry it out:

(23)   a.   *I can assure you that he is not at home.*
       b.   *I can give you my word that we are not in Berlin.*
       c.   *I can guarantee you that this will last three weeks.*
       d.   *I can offer you my best silverware for your party.*
       e.   *I can promise you that I will not squeal.*
       f.   *I can swear that no one saw me enter that building.*

But in these examples, unlike the others I have been discussing, if the *can* is replaced by any periphrastic version (for example, *be able, have the ability*), the sentences cease being strongly performative. In addition, the stress on *can* is usually reduced when these sentences are actually used performatively. My conclusion from these observations is that *can* is used in these cases simply to reinforce what is only conversationally implied, namely, the speaker's ability to perform. If the speaker were to stress the *can,* or use a periphrastic version and thereby call attention to the assertion of ability, it might provide the implication that there is some reason to doubt the speaker's ability.

The second group of *can* sentences (suggested by R. Posner, personal communication) is illustrated in (24), in which the verbs are drawn from the suggesting class (3f):

(24)   a. *I can recommend the Star Hotel.*
                      b. *I can suggest an aspirin.*
                      c. *I can advise bed rest.*
                      d. *I can propose the bus.*

Each of these sentences appears to be limited to being the answer to a request of the sort: *What can you recommend (suggest, . . .)?* and is spoken with a rising final intonation.

We discussed in the last section how the use of *must* not only enables the speaker to avoid total responsibility for the consequences of the particular illocutionary act but also permits the hearer to deny the implied force of the utterance. The use of *can* with *now* similarly implies that only at the moment of speaking is the speaker able to perform the act, thereby relieving him of the responsibility of not having performed it earlier; also, it is a useful device to give the hearer an option. For example, the hearer of (18a) can respond with *Oh, please don't do that; I don't want to talk about the matter any more.* To (21c), the hearer can respond, *Don't bother; it bit me, and I would like to sue you at this point!*

Want to/Wish to/Would Like to

I will treat the three formatives in the heading as if they are modals, and synonymous, and will consider an account of their occurrence in strongly performative sentences like those in (25):

(25)   a. *I want to concede that you were correct.*
                      b. *I would like to thank you for assisting
                          me there.*
                      c. *I want to ask you to sit down.*
                      d. *I would like to suggest that you try
                          another university.*

Let us begin by considering the use of *want to* in the following sentences:

(26)   a. *I want to bother you for a moment.*
                      b. *I want to ask you a question.*
                      c. *I want to tell you something.*
                      d. *I want to try this one.*
                      e. *I want John to go with you.*

In each example, the expression of speaker desire to perform some act is interpretable as a request for permission from the hearer to perform the act. Appropriate hearer responses to (26) might be *Sure, go ahead, Why not?, Be my guest, Please do,* all of which indicate that the hearer inferred a request for permission. We might formalize this as:

(27)   PRINCIPLE OF EXPRESSION OF DESIRE: *Given nothing to suggest the contrary, whenever a speaker expresses his desire for some state of affairs to come about, one can infer that the speaker is seeking the hearer's permission for this state of affairs.*

According to (27), the speaker of (25a) is indirectly asking permission to concede; in (25b), permission to thank; and so forth.

Just as I argued that, given nothing to suggest the contrary, it was reasonable to infer that someone with an obligation would carry it out, so I want to argue here that someone seeking permission will exercise the option to act, once the permission is given — for why else would he have asked? We can formalize this as:

(28)   PRINCIPLE OF PERMISSION SEEKING: *Given   nothing to suggest the contrary, whenever a speaker requests permission to act, one can infer that he will act, once given the permission.*

Armed with (27) and (28) as well as (8), the hearer of (25a), for example, can determine that unless he voices some opposition, the speaker will assume he has the permission to concede and will go about doing so; but, following (8), there is no need for the speaker to actually utter the sentence both speaker and hearer assume will be forthcoming. Thus, both can operate as if *I (hereby) claim that Henry is mentally defective* had actually been uttered, and (25a) will have conveyed the force of a claim.

There are several restrictions on the operation of (27) that limit the co-occurrence of *want to* with various performative verbs. Basically, it must be reasonable for the speaker to ask permission of the hearer. For example, none of the following sentences are strongly performative:

(29)   a.   (scientist speaking to a society matron)   *I want to classify this animal as octopus vulgaris.*
       b.   *I want to promise you that I will marry Helen.*
       c.   *I want to forbid you to leave.*
       d.   *I want to authorize you to take more vacation.*
       e.   *I want to order you to leave.*

In (29a), the speaker is seeking permission for a naming convention that, presumably, has little relevance to the society matron. It is, thus, irrelevant to seek such permission and unlikely that it will be interpreted as a permission-seeking utterance. In (29b), the speaker is indicating a desire to seek permission to do something that is necessarily beneficial to the hearer; it is highly unlikely that the speaker would need permission to do this, and rather redundant to ask for it. In (29c), on the other hand, the speaker is indicating a desire to perform an act that, presumably, is viewed unfavorably by the hearer. As such, it would presumably not be given, and it would seem absurd that anyone would even bother to ask. And in (29d) and (29e), the speaker is indicating that he wishes to authorize or order, neither of which he needs permission to do. To summarize, it is not reasonable to ask permission when the act does not involve the hearer, when the answer to the request is obvious (either positive or negative), and when no permission is necessary. In these cases, the hearer would not infer that permission is actually being requested and would, therefore, not find the sentences strongly performative.

As in the cases of *must* and *can*, the use of *want to* provides the hearer with the option of rejecting the implied force. He can, as before, respond to sentences like those in (29) with *Please don't, It won't do you any good to try*, and the like, as a way of indicating to the speaker that he is not agreeable to the request for permission and the consequences of the implied illocutionary act. However, unlike the first two cases, the use of *want to* does not indicate a desire to avoid responsibility for not doing the act or not having done it earlier. But, then again, such avoidance is inconsistent with requesting permission, an integral part of this interpretive process.[6]

---

[6] The following examples illustrate that a direct request for permission using *may I* results in the same distribution of performative verbs occurring in strongly and weakly performative sentences as presented in (25) and (29):

(i)   STRONGLY PERFORMATIVE (25):
                May I concede that you were correct.
                May I thank you for assisting me there.
                May I ask you to sit down.
                May I suggest that you try another university.

(ii)   WEAKLY PERFORMATIVE (29):
                May I classify this animal as octopus vulgaris.
                May I promise you that I will marry Helen.
                May I forbid you to leave.
                May I authorize you to take more vacation.
                May I order you to leave.

Will/Shall/Be Going to/Intend to

The fourth type of hedged performative to be considered contains the modals *will* and *be going to* and *intend to* (and sometimes *shall*, which I shall consider synonymous and not deal with here), as illustrated in the following strongly performative sentences:

(30)   a. *I will acknowledge that you have the biggest car.*
        b. *I'm going to propose that we stay overnight.*
        c. *I will classify this as outdated, if there is no objection.*
        d. *I'm going to ask you to stay a while after the others leave.*

In each of these examples, the speaker is indicating his intent to perform a particular illocutionary act at some point in the future. (This is, of course, different from the examples in (4), in which the speaker, by using *must,* was permitting the hearer to infer that he would subsequently perform the act.) But, from the statement of intent, we can reasonably infer that the speaker will carry out the intended action. We might formalize this as:

(31)   PRINCIPLE OF ASSERTED INTENTION: *Given nothing to suggest the contrary, whenever a speaker asserts his intent to perform some act one can infer that he will actually perform the act.*

Given (31) and our principle of efficiency (8), the interpretation of the examples in (30) as strongly performative is assured. There is no need in (30b), for example, for the speaker to actually state the proposal directly, since the hearer knows the content of what is to be proposed and can infer that the proposal will be made subsequently. Note that, because of the futurity associated with *will,* the principle of unspecified time (97) is not applicable.

A second group of *will* sentences follow a pattern like that of the *can* cases discussed earlier, in that an adverbial such as *now,* or *finally,* is present:

(32)   a. *I will now admit that you were correct.*
        b. *I am now going to hypothesize that this room is bugged.*
        c. *I am finally going to instruct you to enter a guilty plea.*
        d. *I will now suggest to you that you should take a rest.*

    e.   *I will now guarantee your safe passage out of here.*
    f.   *I am now going to allow you to say a few words.*

The account of why the examples in (32) are strongly performative is analogous to that of the *can* examples in (18). When the speaker of (32a), for example, indicates that he intends to immediately admit something, the hearer, following (31), can infer that he will in fact do it. But by the principle of efficiency, there is no need for him to actually utter this mutually understood sentence, for the hearer can operate as if it had been uttered. Thus, (32a) has the conveyed force of an admission.

For the *will* cases, the speaker can neutralize the implied performative force of the sentence by adding a disclaimer such as *unless you don't want me to, unless I hear some objection, if you agree with me on this,* or the like. Similarly, the hearer can deny the conveyed force of the sentences by responding with a *Don't bother,* and so on.

And, just as in the first three types of hedged performatives, not all performative verbs co-occur with *will* strongly. The examples in (33) illustrate several types of weakly performative sentences containing *will/be going to:*

(33)   a.   *I will congratulate you for helping me yesterday.*
        b.   *I will suggest that you eat an apple.*
        c.   *I will allow you to leave immediately.*
        d.   *I will promise you that we will not be late.*
        e.   *I will forbid you to go.*
        f.   *I will order you to sit down.*
        g.   *I will ask you to help me immediately.*
        h.   *I will beg you to pull me out of this ditch.*

Examples (33a–d) each involve an act that is inherently beneficial to the hearer. Seen this way by both the speaker and the hearer, the hearer of (33a), for example, will recognize that the speaker should have no interest in hedging on the performance of the act, nor should the hearer want to reject the force of congratulations. The hearer, thus, will have to conclude that the speaker is not, at present, offering his congratulations for some reason and will, as indicated, offer them in the future. In these cases, there is some reason to suggest the contrary, and principle (8) is not applicable. In (33e), on the other hand, the act intended by the speaker is clearly not beneficial to the hearer and, thus, the hearer can surely infer that the speaker, knowing this, will not expect the hearer to agree to the application of (18). That is, the hearer will not allow (33e) to convey

something he is opposed to and will either act as if (8) did not apply
or explicitly reject the implied force. In (33g), the speaker is indicating an intent to ask in the future for something he wants done
immediately, and any attempt to interpret it along the lines of the example in (30) will result in a conflict between the speaker's statement of intent, which he permits the hearer to consider (and, of
course, reject if appropriate), and the speaker's desire for immediate
performance of the same act. In (33h), the implied force of begging is
denied by what must be true at the time of utterance. If, on the one
hand, the speaker is in the ditch, one of two cases exists: Either he
wishes to get out or he wishes to remain. If the former, then the
hearer can infer that (33h) is not intended to count as an act of begging, since a more direct approach would have been used. If the
latter, the speaker intends the sentence to be taken literally, and the
hearer can wait for the future request (whether it could be thought of
as an act of begging is open to question). If, on the other hand, the
speaker is not in the ditch, then there is something very strange
about trying to beg for assistance when it is not needed. Thus, (33h)
is only weakly performative.

Would/Might/Should/Could

The final type of hedged performative I will consider involves the
modals *would, might, should,* and *could.* Of the four, I find *would*
co-occurring most freely, with *might* and *could* behind, and *should* a
distant fourth. I will discuss only examples with *would,* as illustrated
in (34):

(34)　　　a.　*I would claim that this is defective.*
　　　　　b.　*I would define this as ancient.*
　　　　　c.　*I would hypothesize that the revolution is over.*
　　　　　d.　*I would suggest that you take a stiff*
　　　　　　　drink of milk.

The explanation for the strongly performative interpretation of these
examples rests, I believe, with the claim that these sentences are not
grammatically well-formed unless they are viewed as elliptical versions of a condition sentence, along the lines of (35):

(35)　　　$\begin{cases} \textit{If you were to ask my opinion,} \\ \textit{Since you have asked my opinion,} \end{cases}$ *I would*
　　　　　claim/define/ . . .

That the sentences in (34) are ungrammatical in the present-tense sense (though, of course, not in the habitual sense) seems clear. That the antecedent of the conditional should be that (or equivalent to that) in (35) seems correct, since sentences that are only weakly performative with *would* are, at best, marginally acceptable in the full conditional form. The examples in (36) illustrate this:

(36)   *If you were to ask my opinion,/Since you have*
            asked me my opinion,
        a. *I would request you to sit down immediately.*
        b. *I would thank you for helping me out.*
        c. *I would permit you to leave.*
        d. *I would promise you to never say that.*

Thus, the strongly performative sentences in (34) are appropriate under circumstances when the speaker feels that it would be reasonable to offer his opinion, with or without being asked. But if this is correct, there is no need for any conversational principles to interpret these examples: The *would* is present because of requirements of modal forms in conditionals, and the sentences can be interpreted as if the *would* were absent. In fact, the speaker cannot deny the performative force of the sentences in (34), nor can the hearer reject any putatively conveyed force. It would seem, then, that the *would* cases are very different from the other hedged performatives.

CONCLUSIONS

Whatever the validity of the observations and analyses proposed earlier, it should be clear that the topic of hedged performatives is only the tip of the iceberg. For example, we might have included other types of declarative sentences with performative verbs that are strongly performative, such as those in (37):

(37)   a. *I am happy to **inform** you that we are here.*
        b. *I am sorry to have to **fire** you at this time.*
        c. *I regret to have to **admit** that you were right.*
        d. *I am **telling** you that you are lost.*
        e. *I am **promising** you that I will go.*
        f. *I raise the **objection** that we are financially broke.*
        g. *I must make the **claim** that Henry is a fine scholar.*
        h. *I hasten to **add** that Suzie might have seen that*
            also.

In addition, we did not consider cases of sequencing of modals, such as those in (38), which are strongly performative, or those in (39), which are weakly performative:

(38) a. *I will have to request that you leave at once.*
      b. *I would intend to suggest that an aspirin would help.*
      c. *I should now be able to assure you that this will work.*

(39) a. *I can have to request that you sit down.*
      b. *I might be able to promise you that we will arrive on time.*
      c. *I want to have to apologize for stepping on you.*

Nor did we consider the embedding of hedged performatives, as in the examples in (40):

(40) a. *Archie told Edith that he had to request that she leave.*
      b. *Mary reported to John that she could now assure him of victory.*
      c. *I mentioned to Harry that I would suggest he sit down.*

I do think, however, that this work represents a good start in defining the sorts of conversational principles that will ultimately play a role in an adequate theory of conversation. Whereas Grice's (this volume) work provides us with some general maxims to which serious conversational interaction adheres, I have attempted to present more explicit, particular principles to account for the hedged performative cases and, hopefully, others as well. I fully expect that the particular principles presented herein will be further refined and, in some cases, either combined with others or replaced by more adequate formulations. When that occurs, this paper will have served its purpose, and we can go about improving on the improved cases.

ACKNOWLEDGMENTS

I would like to thank R. M. Harnish, J. J. Katz, and John Ross for their valuable discussion and criticisms of earlier versions of this work. Accordingly, I do not hereby relieve them of all responsibility for the views presented herein.

The research reported on here was supported in part by USOE Grant No. OEG-0-72-4056-603 to the Department of Special Education, Boston University.

REFERENCES

Fraser, B. A partial analysis of vernacular performative verbs. In R. Shuy and C.-J. Bailey (Eds.), *Toward tomorrow's linguistics*. Georgetown University Press, 1974. (a)

Fraser, B. Review of *Speech acts* by John Searle. In W. Abraham, M. Halle, P. Hartmann, K. Kunjumni Raja, B. Mates, J. F. Staal, P. Verburg, and J. Wm. Verhoar (Eds.), *Foundations of language*. Dordrecht, Holland, and Boston, Massachusetts: D. Reidel Publishing, 1974. (b)

Searle, J. *Speech acts*. New York and London: Cambridge University Press, 1969.

Strawson, P. Intention and convention in speech acts. *The Philosophical Review,* 1964, **LXXIII** (4).

ASYMMETRIC CONJUNCTION AND RULES OF CONVERSATION

SUSAN F. SCHMERLING
The University of Texas at Austin

I

Linguists and philosophers have long noted the existence of English sentences containing *and* that differ from conjunction in standard propositional calculus in not exhibiting the property of symmetry. Thus, while sentences (1a) and (1b) are understood equivalently, thus exhibiting a linguistic property analogous to the equivalence stated in (2), the examples in (3)–(8) fail to exhibit symmetry and are, for this reason, generally referred to as examples of ASYMMETRIC CONJUNCTION:

(1)   a. *Paris is the capital of France, and Rome is the capital of Italy.*
         b. *Rome is the capital of Italy, and Paris is the capital of France.*

(2) $p \cdot q \equiv q \cdot p$

(3)   a. *Harry stood up and objected to the proposal.*
         b. *Harry objected to the proposal and stood up.*

(4)   a. *Smile and the world smiles with you.*
         b. **The world smiles with you and smile.*

(5)   a. *Roy called a secret meeting and offended Bob and*
           Jeff.
       b. *Roy offended Bob and Jeff and called a secret meet-*
           ing.

(6)   a. *I had suspected that the solution would turn out to*
           be elusive, and I was right.
       b. *I was right, and I had suspected that the solution*
           would turn out to be elusive.

(7)   a. *Joan sings ballads and accompanies herself on*
           the guitar.
       b. *??Joan accompanies herself on the guitar and sings*
           ballads.

(8)   a. *The discovery of such a case would be a blow to*
           me and the entire linguistics profession.
       b. *?*The discovery of such a case would be a blow to*
           the entire linguistics profession and me.

Sentences of this sort have received little serious attention, and it is
not hard to see why this should be the case. Under assumptions held
by generative grammarians until relatively recently, cases of asymmetric conjunction must be analyzed differently from cases of symmetric conjunction — and, furthermore, different cases of asymmetric
conjunction must be analyzed differently from each other. Yet the
correct analysis of these different cases is not at all obvious. Moreover, a transformational treatment of these sentences whereby many
different sources for sentences with *and* are posited would fail to
answer a very important question: Is it just an accident that we have
so many cases of 'conjunction' that seem so similar on the surface?
Given these problems, it is not hard to find a great deal of appeal in
suggestions by linguists, such as R. Lakoff (1971), that symmetric and
asymmetric conjunction are fundamentally the same phenomenon.
    Further support for the suggestion that 'conjunction' in English
(and, presumably, in natural language in general) is a unitary phenomenon comes from the pioneering work of Grice on 'conversational implicature' (Grice, this volume). Considering sentences like
(3a), in which we understand not only that two events transpired but
that they occurred in a particular temporal sequence [thus explaining why (3a) and (3b) are not understood as equivalent], Grice
suggested that the hearer of such a sentence may infer such a temporal sequence on the basis of a principle of conversation to the effect that we talk about events in the order in which they occurred

and, thus, that there is no need to set up a special 'and then' *and* for English. Grice's suggestion appears to receive support from the observation that the notion of temporal sequence can be canceled in such an example, as is the case with his 'implicatures' generally. Thus, while (9a) will normally be understood as conveying the information in (9b), on the basis of the 'conversational maxim' given in (10) (Grice's second maxim of Quantity), it need not be, as shown by (11):

(9)   a. *John has three children.*
       b. *John has only three children.*

(10)   *Do not make your contribution more informative than is required.*

(11)   *John has three children — in fact, he may have more.*

Material that is presupposed or asserted, on the other hand, may not be so canceled, as shown by (12) and (13):

(12)   **Sam doesn't know that John is telling the truth — in fact, he may not be.*

(13)   **John is telling the truth — in fact, he may not be.*

And, as (14) shows, the notion of temporal sequence may indeed be canceled in such a sentence:

(14)   *I got up and went to campus and wrote some letters and worked on a paper I'm writing and taught a couple of classes and met with some students — not necessarily in that order.*

If Grice is correct in the analysis he suggests for sentences like these, his approach has profound implications for linguistic theory. The problems alluded to earlier — finding a principled account of how various 'asymmetric' logical structures are related to surface 'conjoined' structures and explaining how there happen to be so many 'different' uses of *and* — simply disappear. For if Grice is right, there IS no difference in the logical representations of these seemingly different kinds of sentences with *and*. The various special relationships between the conjuncts in such sentences are 'implicated' by the speaker and inferred by the hearer on the basis of very general principles of conversation, which, on Grice's account, follow from principles governing human interaction in general. If Grice's analysis should turn out to be unworkable, however, this, too, will have profound implications for students of human language, for we will be left with the problems alluded to before and, in addition, the uncomfortable knowledge that a plausible and attractive explanation is wrong. It should be obvious, then, that the viability of Grice's suggestion has much greater significance than simply providing a specific explanation for an isolated phenomenon in English.

This chapter considers a number of sentences that exhibit asymmetric conjunction, under the defining criterion given earlier, and concludes that it is not a unitary phenomenon. We shall see that, while Grice's approach appears to be valid for a number of such cases, other cases provide a number of problems for such a treatment.

As a preparation for discussion of specific cases, it should be pointed out that a certain commonly held assumption concerning asymmetric conjunction is false, namely, the assumption, implicit in all discussions of the phenomenon that I have seen, that all such cases involve AT LEAST a temporal relationship between the conjuncts. Thus, it seems to be assumed generally that examples like (3a) illustrate the typical case, and that, in addition to temporal sequence, something extra, such as causation in (5a), may be involved.[1] The following examples are all cases that meet the defining criterion for asymmetric conjunction yet imply no temporal sequence between the conjuncts:

(15)   *The lights were off and I couldn't see.*

(16)   *What's he gone and done this time?*

(17)   *Joan sings ballads and accompanies herself on the guitar.*

(18)   *I had suspected that the solution would turn out to be elusive, and I was right.*

(19)   *John was being clever and taking the files with him.*

---

[1] This is claimed explicitly in Ruhl (1972). In an account of conjunction that may not be incompatible with Grice's approach, Ruhl states, 'I will claim that there is a graded strategy of invited inference [the term is due to Geis and Zwicky, 1971] used by both speakers and hearers which tends to make a coordinate structure as semantically complex as possible — or rather, as coherent as possible. The strategy is:

> If a structure A-and-B can be analyzed as a temporal sequence, it will be. If it can further be analyzed that A is a precondition for B, it will be. And, if A can be analyzed as a decisive condition — that is, a cause — of B, it will be. Only if the first stage — the temporal sequence — is not reached, will the coordinate structure be analyzed as symmetric . . . .'

(20) *That's what Bill says, and we all know how reliable he is.*

(21) *The coffee's nice and hot now.*

Such examples do not, of course, argue against the sort of approach proposed by Grice, but they do show quite clearly that the variety of sentences exhibiting asymmetric conjunction has not generally been appreciated.[2] A Gricean approach to asymmetric conjunction will clearly involve many more principles than Grice supposed.

II

In this section, a number of sentences will be discussed that present serious difficulties for a Gricean account. These cases all involve sentences that exhibit what appear to be conjoined verb phrases. While no alternative analyses will be proposed, it will be argued that many of the properties of the utterances that present problems for a Gricean analysis are automatically explained by any analysis that does not treat them as cases of logical conjunction. In discussing these cases, I will be assuming that such sentences would be treated under a Gricean analysis as involving some form of conjunction reduction.[3]

---

[2] It should also be noted that the general assumption that asymmetric cases that do involve temporal sequence can be paraphrased with *and then* in place of *and* [stated explicitly by Lakoff and Peters (1966), who also failed to note the existence of asymmetric cases in which temporal sequence was not involved] is also false. While (ia) and (ib) seem to be synonymous, this is not true of the remaining pairs of examples in the following set:

(i)   a.   *He grabbed his coat and left in a huff.*
        b.   *He grabbed his coat and then left in a huff.*

(ii)   a.   *He drove off and was never seen again.*
        b.   ?*He drove off and then was never seen again.*

(iii)   a.   *We investigated a number of cases and discovered that the problem was far more complex than had previously been supposed.*
        b.   *We investigated a number of cases and then discovered that the problem was far more complex than had previously been supposed.*

(iv)   a.   *The police came in and everyone swallowed their cigarettes.* [*from R. Lakoff, 1971*]
        b.   *The police came in and then everyone swallowed their cigarettes.*

The implications of this state of affairs are discussed later.

[3] That is, I will be assuming that the generally held assumption that a sentence like (i) is related to a logical structure like that schematized in (ii) is correct:

(i)   *John writes novels and criticizes poetry.*

(*Continued on page 216*)

Several of the cases to be discussed in this section were first pointed out to linguists by Ross (1967a), who noted that they appeared to provide counterexamples to his Coordinate Structure Constraint, stated in (22):

(22)   *In a coordinate structure, no conjunct may be moved,
          nor may any element contained in a conjunct be moved
          out of that conjunct* [p. 89, (4–84)].

Ross's examples are given in (23)–(26); that they are not subject to

---

(ii)

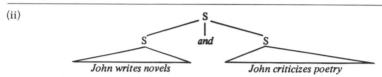

Ross (1967a) sketches an analysis of conjunction done by himself and G. Lakoff which is generally assumed to be correct, in its basic outline, for all cases of conjunction not involving conjoined noun phrases in sentences with symmetric predicates, as in (iii), or involving jointly performed actions, as in (iv):

(iii)   *John and Bill are similar.*
(iv)   *John and Bill killed Harry.*

This analysis assumes underlying conjoined structures conforming to the schema shown in (v):

(v)

In Ross and Lakoff's analysis, structures of this sort are converted into structures like the one shown in (vi) by a rule of Conjunction Copying, which Chomsky-adjoins a copy of the conjunction to each S:

(vi)

Such structures may then be reduced to structures with conjoined noun phrases, verb phrases, and so on, such that identical material in the different conjuncts appears only once on the surface. Under this analysis, then, if the leftmost *and* ends up in a coordinate structure that is not a full sentence, it may be optionally replaced by *both* or deleted, deletion being obligatory in the case of surface conjoined sentences. An additional rule will optionally delete all but the rightmost occurrence of *and*. While this sketch is incomplete in a number of important ways, I assume that its basic outline is one that is accepted by linguists and philosophers generally.

this constraint is shown by (27)–(30) (Ross, 1967a:93–94):

(23)   *I went to the store and bought some whisky. [(4-100a)]*

(24)   *She's gone and ruined her dress now. [(4-107a)]*

(25)   *I've got to try and find that screw. [(4-107b)]*

(26)   *Aunt Hattie wants you to be nice and kiss your granny.*
       [(4-107c)]

(27)   *Here's the whisky which I went to the store and bought.*
       [(4-101a)]

(28)   *Which dress has she gone and ruined now? [(4-108a)]*

(29)   *The screw which I've got to try and find holds the*
       frammis to the myolator. [(4-108b)]

(30)   *Which granny does Aunt Hattie want me to be nice and*
       kiss? [(4-108c)]

To these examples can be added examples (31) and (32):

(31)   *Lizzie Borden took an axe and gave her*
              mother forty whacks.

(32)   *Roy called a secret meeting and offended*
              Bob and Jeff.

These sentences also provide an embarrassment for the proposed
constraint:

(33)   *Who did Lizzie take an axe and whack to death?*

(34)   *?When was that meeting that Roy called and offended*
       Bob and Jeff?

In his brief discussion of such cases, Ross suggested that, despite the
presence of *and* in these sentences, they were not coordinate structures at the point where the rules in question applied, if ever, and
hence were not true counterexamples to his constraint. What is
noteworthy for the present discussion is that all of these apparent
counterexamples can be plausibly argued, by non-Griceans, not to involve logical conjunction.

Before proceeding to discussion of the implications of this set of
facts, I would like to discuss some of the aspects of meaning that are
conveyed by some of these examples. While all of these are cases of
'asymmetric conjunction,' as the reader can easily verify for himself,

it should become clear that they are not a unified class in terms of the 'extra' information they convey. First, only (23) is unquestionably an example of temporal sequence being conveyed. Sentence (24), which does not necessarily convey any notion of movement at all, despite the presence of *go*, is clearly not a sentence describing a sequence of events; in fact, it expresses something very remote indeed from logical conjunction. What such a sentence does convey is, rather, a mild sense of condemnation on the part of the speaker with respect to the act expressed in the second 'conjunct'; one senses that the speaker is trying to convey the notion, 'It was her fault'. Sentences (26) and (32) likewise turn out not to involve temporal sequence on close examination. The adjective in the first conjunct of a sentence like (26) is predicated not of the subject of the sentence but of the act expressed in the second conjunct. Thus, such a sentence might be paraphrased as in (35) or (36):

(35)   *It would be nice of you to kiss your granny.*

(36)   *Kissing your granny would be a nice thing*
             (for you) to do.

Similarly, a sentence like (32) may be paraphrased as in (37) or (38):

(37)   *Roy called a secret meeting and in so doing offended*
        Bob and Jeff.

(38)   *Roy's calling a secret meeting was offensive to Bob and*
        Jeff.

Temporal sequence thus does not seem to be involved in these cases at all. The remaining examples here — (25) and (31) — are more problematical. One might want to argue that (25) does involve such a sequence, since one must first go through certain motions in attempting something before one can succeed in the endeavor. Note, however, that *try* without a following complement is decidedly elliptical. Thus, consider a sentence like (39):

(39)   *I tried.*

While this sentence is perfectly grammatical, a complement must be recoverable from the context in which it is uttered. We seem, then, to be dealing with a so-called null anaphor here. But null anaphors generally obey the well-known constraints on backward pronominalization (cf., for example, Langacker, 1960; Ross, 1967b); thus, we get (40a) and (40b), but not (40c):

(40)   a.   *I don't think I can get it open, but I'll try.*
         b.   *Although I tried, I just couldn't get it open.*
         c.   **I'll try, but I don't think I can get it open.*
               (where *I'll try* = *I'll try to get it open*)[4]

This would seem to suggest that *try* in such a case is followed not by a null anaphor but by an actual complement—that *and find that screw* IS the complement. This is, of course, what the synonymy between (25) and (41) would suggest:

(41)   *I've got to try to find that screw.*

Notice, further, that *and* can appear in such a sentence only if *try* appears in an uninflected form:

(42)   **I tried and find that screw.*

Such a restriction on the appearance of *and* is not paralleled in any of the other cases.

A somewhat more plausible case for sequence of events being involved can be made for (31), on the basis of the fact that one must first take hold of an instrument before one can use it. However, as we shall see, it is probably wrong to identify the first 'conjunct' of this sentence with sentence (43):

(43)   *Lizzie Borden took an axe.*

In sum, the conveying of temporal sequence is in no way a common property of these utterances.

The second observation to be made concerning what is conveyed in these examples, which should already be obvious from the preceding discussion, is that the 'extra' material involved is quite different in the different cases. Sentence (23) involves, in addition to a sequence of actions, a locative expression in the first conjunct that is understood as included in the second as well. Sentences (24) and (26) are cases in which the first conjunct is, in a sense, a comment on

---

[4] There ARE sentences with *but* that do permit backward pronominalization:

(i)   *I tried and tried but I just couldn't*
                 open the door.

(ii)   *He$_i$'s a fool but I like John$_i$ anyway.*

These sentences point up a non-obvious difference between *and* and *but* and suggest strongly that the 'well-known' constraints on backward pronominalization are far from being thoroughly understood.

the second. Sentence (25) appears to be a case in which the second 'conjunct' is in fact the complement of the verb in the first. In (31) the first conjunct is an instrumental expression of some sort, while in (32) the event expressed in the first conjunct is understood as being the cause of the event expressed in the second. It seems clear that we are not dealing with a semantically unitary phenomenon.

We are thus faced with a state of affairs in which a set of sentences that appear to exhibit conjoined verb phrases have in common the facts that they are not understood as cases of logical conjunction and that they fail to be subject to a grammatical constraint that appears to be well-motivated for sentences exhibiting what is unquestionably logical conjunction. The implications of this state of affairs should be clear. Either these sentences are not to be analyzed as cases of true conjunction, or Ross's Coordinate Structure Constraint is a constraint of a different nature from the one he supposed. Thus, while these examples cannot be taken as decisive evidence against a Gricean treatment of all cases of 'conjunction,' they show clearly that an approach such as his has serious hurdles to face.

There are, however, a number of additional properties shared by the sentences presented in this section which cast serious doubt on the claim that they are to be considered cases of logical conjunction and which therefore suggest that Ross was correct in supposing that they were in fact not cases of logical conjunction. Recall first that, if these sentences ARE instances of logical conjunction, then we should expect that they are reduced forms of underlying structures in which two full sentences are conjoined. Consequently, we should expect to find related sentences in which this reduction does not occur. Consider, however, examples (44)–(49):

(44)   I went to the store and I bought some whisky.

(45)   ?She's gone and she's ruined her dress now.

(46)   I've got to try and I've got to find that screw.

(47)   Aunt Hattie wants you to be nice and she wants you to kiss your granny.

(48)   Lizzie Borden took an axe and she gave her mother forty whacks.

(49)   Roy called a secret meeting and he offended Bob and Jeff.

What is interesting about these sentences is that none of them can be understood as being equivalent to the 'reduced' versions given earlier. While temporal sequence may indeed be inferred in some of these cases, the 'extra' information conveyed in the 'reduced' versions simply is not present here. In (44) I need not have bought the whisky at the store. Sentence (45) is relating two separate events, as (24) is not. Sentence (46) IS understood as having a null anaphor following *try* that cannot be *I find that screw*. In (47) Aunt Hattie is asking two things of you. Sentence (48), likewise, involves two separate actions on Lizzie's part; while this sentence could be used to describe a situation in which Lizzie used the axe in doing the whacking, it is not necessary that she have used the axe. Finally, (49) is describing two actions on Roy's part. This sentence cannot be understood as meaning that it was his calling the meeting that caused Bob and Jeff to feel offended.[5]

A proponent of a Gricean account of these cases of asymmetric conjunction must therefore argue that a speaker who intends to convey the 'extra' information conveyed by the 'reduced' versions of these sentences MUST in fact utter such sentences in a reduced form. Thus, in addition to having to find various principles of conversation that can explain how the hearer of such a sentence can infer this information, he must also find an explanation for the obligatoriness of conjunction reduction in these cases. Notice, however, that the facts presented here follow automatically from an analysis in which sentences (23)–(26), (31), and (32) are not treated as instances of logical conjunction. In such an analysis conjunction reduction is not involved in the derivations of such sentences, and hence, the fact that the 'reduced' and 'unreduced' versions are not equivalent is a nonproblem.

---

[5] In addition to the fact that none of the 'extra' information conveyed in the 'reduced' versions is conveyed in the full versions, the Coordinate Structure Constraint holds for the latter:

(i) *This is the whisky which I went to the store and I bought.

(ii) *This is the dress which she's gone and she's ruined now.

(iii) *The screw which I've got to try and I've got to find holds the frammis to the myolator.

(iv) *Which granny does Aunt Hattie want me to be nice and want me to kiss?

(v) *Who did Lizzie take an axe and she whack to death?

(vi) *When was that meeting that Roy called and he offended Bob and Jeff?

This, then, is further evidence, if such was needed, that the correlation between the applicability of the Coordinate Structure Constraint and the way sentences with *and* are understood is not a spurious one.

Another characteristic of sentences like these that we should expect to find if they are indeed instances of logical conjunction is the ability to take *both* preceding the first of the 'conjoined' verb phrases. That is, we should expect that the paraphrase relation obtaining between (50a) and (50b):

(50)   a. *John writes novels and criticizes poetry.*
                  b. *John both writes novels and criticizes poetry.*

will be one that obtains in the cases under discussion as well. Contrary to this expectation, however, it does not; sentences (51)–(56) cannot be understood as equivalent to the types of sentences under discussion here:

(51)   *I both went to the store and bought some whisky.*

(52)   *?She's both gone and ruined her dress now.*

(53)   *I've got to both try and find that screw.*

(54)   *Aunt Hattie wants you to both be nice and kiss your granny.*

(55)   *Lizzie Borden both took an axe and gave her mother forty whacks.*

(56)   *Roy both called a secret meeting and offended Bob and Jeff.*

These sentences are understood, rather, as being equivalent to the 'unreduced' versions in (44)–(49). The proponent of a Gricean treatment of such sentences will thus have to argue that a special strategy is involved in the use of *both*, to the effect that *both* has the function of canceling certain implicatures. It is not at all obvious, however, what the explanatory value of such a claim would be. On the other hand, the impossibility of using *both* in the sentences under discussion would again follow automatically from any analysis that did not treat such sentences as instances of logical conjunction. The reason should be clear: If such sentences are not instances of underlying conjoined sentences, a rule like Ross and Lakoff's Conjunction Copying could never apply in the derivation of such sentences, since the input structures for such a rule would not exist in these cases, and thus, there would be no source for *both*.

There is a third formal property of sentences exhibiting true conjoined verb phrases that fails to appear in the cases under discussion.

This is the alternation between *and* and *or* which appears in cases like (57):

(57)   a.   *John doesn't write novels, and he doesn't criticize poetry.*
       b.   *John doesn't write novels or criticize poetry.*

This alternation appears to be the English counterpart of one of DeMorgan's Laws:

(58) $\sim p \cdot \sim q \equiv \sim (p \lor q)$

If the sorts of sentences we are discussing here are instances of logical conjunction, then, we should expect negative versions of them to show *or* instead of *and*. This is not the case, however; the (a) versions of (59)–(64) can only be interpreted as not conveying any of the 'special' information with which we are concerned. The (b) versions, which are understood as the negative counterparts of the sentences under discussion, continue to show *and*:

(59)   a.   *I didn't go to the store or buy the whisky.*
       b.   *I didn't go to the store and buy the whisky.*

(60)   a.   *For once she didn't go or ruin her dress.*
       b.   *For once she didn't go and ruin her dress.*

(61)   a.   *I didn't try or find that screw.*
       b.   *I didn't try and find that screw.*

(62)   a.   *Don't be mean or tease Aunt Hattie.*
       b.   *Don't be mean and tease Aunt Hattie.*

(63)   a.   *Lizzie Borden did not take an axe or give her mother forty whacks.*
       b.   *Lizzie Borden did not take an axe and give her mother forty whacks.*

(64)   a.   *Things would be much simpler if Roy hadn't called a secret meeting or offended Bob and Jeff.*
       b.   *Things would be much simpler if Roy hadn't called a secret meeting and offended Bob and Jeff.*

I can see no way in which the proponent of a Gricean treatment of these sentences can explain the absence of the *and/or* alternation in these cases. Once again, however, the absence of this alternation follows automatically from any analysis in which these sentences are not treated as instances of logical conjunction.

What is particularly striking about all the formal properties of these mysterious sentences I have discussed in this section is that they are embarrassments for a Gricean treatment in exactly the same way. While these sentences are very different from each other in terms of what the speaker of such sentences is trying to convey, they agree in failing to show properties that one would, a priori, expect to find in sentences exhibiting logical conjunction. Otherwise similar sentences that do show these properties are invariably interpreted as not conveying the 'special' information in question. To put it another way, the rules of English grammar do not treat these sentences as if they were instances of logical conjunction.

There is an additional problem presented by many of the sentences here for the sort of analysis that Grice seems to envision for asymmetric conjunction. His approach would seem to imply that sentences of the sort we have been discussing are interpreted as instances of logical conjunction plus something extra. Yet, in several of these cases, the 'conjuncts' in isolation cannot be understood in the same way they are understood in the 'conjoined' versions. This should be clear, from previous discussion, in the case of (24), in which no idea of motion is conveyed in the 'conjoined' version, despite the presence of *go,* and (25), in which *try* is not interpreted in the 'conjoined' sentence as being followed by a null anaphor. Similar observations can be made for other examples. Thus, consider (26):

(26)   *Aunt Hattie wants you to be nice and kiss*
             your granny.

As suggested earlier, *nice* in such a sentence is understood as a predication, not on *you* but on the proposition *you kiss your granny.* To see this, consider what would happen if the addressee replied to such a request with (65):

(65)   *I'll be nice, but I won't kiss my granny.*

Such a reply would probably earn the speaker a spanking. On the other hand, a reply like (67) to (66):

(66)   *Make your bed and put away your clothes.*

(67)   *I'll make my bed, but I won't put away*
             my clothes.

might be taken as an indication that the speaker of (67) was obstinate, but not that he was a smart aleck. Thus, the first 'conjunct' in such an example is understood quite differently from the way an identical sentence in isolation is understood, and the 'conjoined' sentence is not understood as simply conveying the sum of the two 'conjuncts' plus something extra.

A sentence like:

(31)   *Lizzie Borden took an axe and give her*
                 mother forty whacks.

shows the same sort of problem even more clearly. Notice that:

(68)   ·   *Lizzie Borden took an axe.*

is elliptical. A nonelliptical sentence with *take* must contain an explicit source, as in (69), or goal, as in (70):

(69)   *Lizzie took an axe from the woodshed.*
(70)   *Lizzie took an axe to the bonfire.*

Thus, while a sentence like (68) is certainly possible, some source or goal must be recoverable from the context in which it is uttered. This is not true of sentence (31), however. The first 'conjunct' is not understood elliptically; no source or goal need be mentioned at any point in the discourse. This strongly suggests, then, that in this and in other cases, it is wrong to identify one of the 'conjuncts' with an independently occurring sentence that is identical in (surface) form.

To sum up this section, then, we see that there are a number of English sentence types which exhibit what appear to be conjoined verb phrases and which display a variety of 'special' meanings. This variety cannot be explained on the basis of any one general principle. These sentences have a number of negative characteristics in common which seem to indicate that they are not instances of logical conjunction; furthermore, many of the 'conjuncts' in such sentences do not seem to contribute to the utterance as a whole a meaning that they have in isolation. These facts would seem to suggest very strongly, then, that the English word *and* frequently does not correspond to logical conjunction.

III

The sentences discussed in the preceding section of this chapter argue against the position that ALL instances of use of the English word *and* can be considered instances of logical conjunction — and, hence, they argue against the viability of an approach that tries to explain all the special properties of such sentences in terms of principles of human interaction. They do not, however, provide any evidence against the claim that such principles exist. In this section, I

shall discuss a number of sentences that suggest that a very general
rule of conversation IS involved in our use of sentences exhibiting
asymmetric conjunction.

Consider the following sentences:

(71)   *I started to type and the power went off.*

(72)   *I left the door open and the cat got in.*

(73)   *We investigated a number of cases and we discovered
         that the problem was far more complex than had
         previously been supposed.*

(74)   *Jackie announced her intention to marry Ari and the
         rumors started flying.*

(75)   *The lights were off and I couldn't see.*

Each of these sentences can be understood as conveying 'extra' information beyond what is overtly expressed in the two conjuncts. In
(71), the extra information is temporal sequence; we understand that
I started to type before the power went off. Temporal sequence also
seems to be involved in (72) through (74), but in these cases additional information is conveyed as well. Sentence (72) implies that the
cat got in as a result of my leaving the door open. Sentence (73)
implies that we discovered the complexity of the problem in the
course of investigating a number of cases and, furthermore, that it
was the investigating that was the cause of the discovery. Sentence
(74) implies that Jackie's announcement was the direct cause of
rumors. Sentence (75) does not involve temporal sequence—it relates two concurrent states—but the situation expressed in the first
conjunct is understood as the reason for the state expressed in the
second. Thus, like the cases of what appear to be verb phrase conjunction discussed earlier, extra information is involved.

The question to be asked at this point, of course, is whether or not
we are dealing with the same sort of situation in this section, and I
shall argue that we are not. Note, first of all, that the arguments based
on formal properties in the cases of what appeared to be conjoined
verb phrases are not applicable in these cases. We are not dealing
with what appear to be sentences that have undergone conjunction
reduction; these look like clear cases of conjoined sentences in
which no reduction has taken place. The argument based on *both* is
inapplicable because *both* can never appear before a full sentence—that is, we find *both* only in cases of conjunction reduction.
The evidence from negation is hard to interpret, since the only kind
of test case that can be found involves external negation, as in (76):

(76)   *It's not the case that I started to type*
         and the power went off.

Since external negation is relatively poorly understood, it is hard to see what conclusions could be drawn from such an example.

An important difference between the sentences considered here and those considered in the previous section involves the semantic integrity of the various conjuncts. In many of the latter cases, as we have seen, the 'conjuncts' are not understood in the full sentences in the same manner as they are in isolation, and I used this fact to argue that such cases could not be considered to involve logical conjunction plus something 'extra.' In all of the cases under consideration in this section, however, the conjuncts in isolation are understood in exactly the same way as they are in the full sentences. Thus, it does seem to be the case here that we are dealing, in some sense, with conjunction plus something else, as we were not in the preceding section.

Another very important difference between the sentences in the two sections involves the classification of the 'extra' information conveyed. In the preceding section, it was easy to classify the various examples into different types. Given an additional example of apparent conjoined verb phrases such as:

(77)   *John was being sneaky and taking the*
         files with him.

we have no trouble seeing where it fits on our list: It goes with (26). This is not the case with the examples in this section, however. While (71) seems to be a clear case of simple temporal sequence, and (74) seems to be a clear case of causation, the other cases are fuzzier. Given an additional sentence like:

(78)   *My wallet was stolen and I had to get*
         a new driver's license.

we cannot say, 'Ah, that's just like (72)' or 'That's just like (74).' Our reaction is more like, 'Well, that's sort of like (72).' These sentences, then, do not seem to differ from each other, in terms of what type of 'extra' information is conveyed, in a discrete fashion.

This fact becomes all the more clear when we try to paraphrase the various examples involved in such a way that everything conveyed by the examples is made explicit in the paraphrase. As indicated in footnote 2, not everything that seems to involve temporal sequence can be paraphrased with *and then*. Several of the cases of the sort discussed here can be paraphrased more or less adequately with *and thus, and therefore,* or *and thereby,* but in many cases one is hard put to decide which is the most appropriate. Thus, consider various attempts at paraphrases of (73):

(79)   a.   *We investigated a number of cases and we thus discovered that the problem was far more complex than had previously been supposed.*

         b.   *We investigated a number of cases and we therefore discovered that the problem was far more complex than had previously been supposed.*

         c.   *We investigated a number of cases and we thereby discovered that the problem was far more complex than had previously been supposed.*

These 'paraphrases' seem equally unsatisfactory. What is wrong with all of them is that they are too precise: Each seems to express a relationship between the conjuncts which is more narrow and clearly defined than the relationship conveyed in (73).

We are thus left with a situation in which it is hard to pinpoint precisely the differences between the various examples given. On the other hand, it is easy to see what they have in common. In each case the first conjunct has some sort of priority over the second. In many cases, it is temporal priority, as in (71), and frequently it is more than that. Thus, consider (72), in which more than temporal priority is conveyed. We understand that the cat got in as a result of my leaving the door open. Yet it would be wrong to say that the relationship between the two conjuncts in this case was one of causation: The cat was able to get in because I left the door open, but she went in because she wanted to. Thus, my leaving the door open was a necessary but not a sufficient condition for the cat to get in. In some cases, of course, a necessary condition will also be a sufficient condition for some event to occur or some situation to obtain, as in (74) and (75), and it is in such situations that we are likely to interpret the sentence as conveying a notion of causation.

The priority involved here need not be a necessary condition, however. Thus, consider (73) again. We could have learned about the complexity of the problem not through our own investigations but from hearing about the work of someone else. And in (71), my starting to type was neither a necessary nor a sufficient condition for the power to go off (unless one is a staunch believer in Murphy's Law). I thus deliberately use the vague term PRIORITY to refer to the relationships between the two conjuncts in these cases—the relationship does, indeed, seem to be a vague one.

We have seen, then, that sentences like these have in common the fact that the first conjunct has some sort of priority over the second. In many cases, the meanings of the specific conjuncts involved and our knowledge of the world will enable us to infer a more precise relationship such as causation, but it is not possible to catalogue a small number of distinct 'special meanings' such sentences can have. The fundamentally different character of the types of sentences treated in the previous section from that of those treated in this section suggests very strongly that a rule of conversation is responsible for the asymmetry of the latter: In conversation, we first lay a groundwork for what we are going to say next. This is, of course, a very general principle, and, like Grice's other principles, it is not limited to conversation.

The rule that we lay a groundwork is not a binding one; as with Grice's other rules, the 'implicatures' involved in these cases may be canceled. The possibility of cancelation provides another very interesting and important difference between the two types of cases discussed in this chapter. Thus, consider the difference between the cancelations of causation attempted in the two kinds of examples:

(80)   *Roy called a secret meeting and offended Bob and Jeff—though I don't want to say it was his calling the meeting that offended them.*

(81)   *We went out to a Chinese restaurant last night and this morning I was sick—though that's probably just a coincidence.*

Sentence (80) has a very suspicious ring to it: It sounds at best like a legalistic play on words. Sentence (81), on the other hand, is a perfectly natural utterance.

We have, thus, seen that a number of considerations lead to the conclusion that many sentences that appear to exhibit conjoined verb phrases are in fact not instances of logical conjunction. The same sorts of considerations that led to that conclusion, however, support the contention that other instances of asymmetric conjunction probably should be treated as instances of logical conjunction and that they owe their asymmetry to a very general principle of human behavior.

IV

I have not attempted in this chapter to provide a thorough discussion of asymmetric conjunction, and I have specifically omitted any discussion of conjoined noun phrases, the difficulties in the analysis of which are well-known (see, for example, Gleitman, 1965; Lakoff and Peters, 1966; Quang, 1971). I have, instead, attempted to establish the following points: (1) Asymmetric conjunction is exhibited in a wide variety of sentences, a variety that has not previously been appreciated; (2) it is wrong to identify 'logical conjunction' with 'symmetric conjunction'; and (3) 'conjunction' in English is not a unitary phenomenon.

The general approach taken by Grice would appear to receive support from the considerations that I, as a linguist, have brought to bear on the issue of asymmetric conjunction. These same considerations, however, suggest that his proposals do not offer linguists the hope of an explanation for all cases of asymmetric conjunction that his approach promised. We are still faced with the existence of a number of different types of sentences involving *and* which current theory must treat as unrelated. The answer to the question of whether or not there is an explanation for this widespread use of *and* must await further research.

ACKNOWLEDGMENTS

I am grateful to Arlene Berman for making comments on an earlier draft of this paper that led to several improvements. The material covered in this paper overlaps to some extent material included in Schmerling (1972), and I would like to thank several linguists at the University of Illinois for many thought-provoking comments on that earlier paper. Responsibility for errors is mine alone.

REFERENCES

Geis, M. L., and Zwicky, A. M. On invited inferences. *Linguistic Inquiry*, 1971, **2** (4).

Gleitman, L. R. Coordinating conjunctions in English. *Language*, 1965, 41, 260–293. Reprinted in D. A. Reibel and S. A. Schane, *Modern studies in English*. Englewood Cliffs, N. J.: Prentice-Hall, 1969.

Lakoff, G., and Peters, S. Phrasal conjunction and symmetric predicates. In *Mathematical linguistics and automatic translation, Harvard Computation Laboratory, Report No. NSF-17*, 1966. Reprinted in D. A. Reibel and S. A. Schane, *Modern studies in English*. Englewood Cliffs, N. J.: Prentice-Hall, 1969.

Lakoff, R. If's, and's, and but's about conjunction. In C. J. Fillmore and D. T. Langendoen (Eds.), *Studies in linguistic semantics*. New York: Holt, Rinehart & Winston, 1971.

Langacker, R. W. On pronominalization and the chain of command. In D. A. Reibel and S. A. Schane, *Modern studies in English*. Englewood Cliffs, N. J.: Prentice-Hall, 1969.

Quang Phuc Dong. A note on conjoined noun phrases. In A. M. Zwicky *et al.* (Eds.), *Studies out in left field*. Edmonton, Alta.: Linguistic Research, Inc., 1971.

Ross, J. R. Constraints on variables in syntax. Unpublished Ph.D. dissertation, MIT, Cambridge, Mass., 1967. (a)

Ross, J. R. On the cyclic nature of English pronominalization. In *To Honor Roman Jakobson II*. The Hague: Mouton, 1967. [Reprinted in D. A. Reibel and S. A. Schane, *Modern studies in English*. Englewood Cliffs, N.J.: Prentice-Hall, 1969.] (b)

Ruhl, C. Why the exceptions to Ross' Coordinate Structure Constraint aren't exceptions. Paper presented at the 1972 Summer Meeting of the Linguistic Society of America, Chapel Hill, North Carolina, 1972.

Schmerling, S. F. Apparent counterexamples to the Coordinate Structure Constraint: A canonical conspiracy. *Studies in the Linguistic Sciences*, 1972, 2 (I).

WHERE TO DO THINGS WITH WORDS*

JOHN ROBERT ROSS
Massachusetts Institute of Technology and Brown University

Austin (1962) uses the term MASQUERADE to point up a crucial distinction between such sentences as (1a) and (1b):

(1)   a.   *I move the piano.*
             b.   *I move the question.*

While the speaker of (1a) makes an assertion, which can be said to be true or false, (1b) has a quite different status. Depending on quite complicated conditions (such as whether a meeting is in progress, whether the speaker has been recognized by the chair, and whether, in fact, a motion calling for a vote is at present on the floor), a particular utterance of (1b) will be said to be FELICITOUS (to use a term proposed by Austin) if all of the FELICITY CONDITIONS just mentioned (as well as some others), have been met, and INFELICITOUS if some of them have not been met.

Thus, despite the harmless SVO superficial form of (1b), which would lead us to expect it to be an assertion, an utterance of this sentence is a horse of another color. Depending on such felicity conditions as those cited earlier, it will either 'make it' as a motion or not: It is, to use another term invented by Austin, a PERFORMATIVE utterance. The study of the different kinds of felicity conditions on the use of verbs that can appear as the main verbs of performative utter-

*©John Robert Ross

ances — verbs like *sentence, ask, vow, guarantee, request, excommunicate, absolve, promise, confess, bet,* and *bequeath,* to give a random and fractional list [fuller treatments are to be found in Fraser (1974) and McCawley (to appear)] — and of the complex interactions between such felicity conditions, has occupied a number of researchers since Austin's pioneering work called attention to the existence of this interesting and important area in the philosophy of language.

I would like to borrow Austin's metaphor of the masquerade to discuss an area of recent research that is a descendant of the original work on performatives. Thus note that though the sentences in (3) have the same superficial form as the performative utterances in (2), they only masquerade as a promise and a question, respectively:

(2) a. *I promise you my continuing support, if you decide to run again.*
   b. *I ask you where you were on the night of the 14th.*

(3) a. *I promise you a good spanking if you pour any more sugar into my gas tank.*
   b. *I ask you how any decent citizen can give his vote again to Governor Schamlos.*

Typically, while (2a) would be used to make a promise — a commitment to perform an act in the future which the speaker believes is desired by his interlocutor — (3a) would be used to issue a warning to the interlocutor, that is, to describe a future event that the speaker believes is NOT desired by his interlocutor. And while (2b) could be used by a prosecutor trying to elicit information from a witness, (3b) can, for me, be used only as a rhetorical question (the *any* in the embedded subject forces this interpretation). That is, (3b) is only masquerading as a question: Really, it is closer in its ILLOCUTIONARY FORCE (another term of Austin's) to being a negative assertion like (4):

(4)   *No decent citizen can give his vote again to Governor Schamlos.*

What interests researchers who try to 'see through' such masquerades is questions like the following: Why is it that sentences that look like promises on the surface, like (3a), can be used as warnings, while sentences that look like warnings, like (5), do not have the potential to be taken as promises?

(5)   *I warn you that I will read your manuscript carefully.*

And why is it that sentences that look like requests for information, like (6a), can be used as rough paraphrases of declaratives like (4), while recommendations like (6b) cannot be?

(6)   a.   *I ask that you tell me how any decent citizen can give his vote again to Governor Schamlos.*

        b.   *I recommend that you tell me how any decent citizen can give his vote again to Governor Schamlos.*

Among the speech acts that a sentence can be used to perform are the illocutionary acts of the sentences. We will say that the BASIC illocutionary force of such sentences as (2a) is that of a promise, but that under a speaker assumption that giving support to the hearer will not be desired by the hearer, (2a) can also have a DERIVED force: the force of a warning. Thus, one task of the semantactician/philosopher of language is to specify that while promises can acquire, via a DERIVED FORCE RULE, the forces of warnings, warnings cannot acquire the forces of promises. Naturally, the researcher will not be content to merely state that this curious asymmetry exists, but will also attempt to explain it.[1]

In this chapter, I will be concerned, in part, with specifying the conditions under which one such derived force rule (or possibly a family of similar rules) can operate. This is the rule that specifies that

---

[1] In the case at hand, the explanation will probably be found to lie in the more general asymmetry which specifies that the positive member of a pair of polar opposites is the unmarked member, as has often been noted. Thus, contrast the grammaticality of the question–answer sequence in (i) with the ungrammaticality of the mixed sequence in (ii):

(i)   Q: *How wide is it?*

                               A: *Quite* $\begin{Bmatrix} wide \\ narrow \end{Bmatrix}$.

(ii)   Q: *How narrow is it?*

                               A: *Quite* $\begin{Bmatrix} {}^{*}wide \\ narrow \end{Bmatrix}$.

Note also such contrasts as (iii)–(*iv), which were first pointed out by Paul Chapin (cf. Chapin, 1965):

(iii)   *To say that a tree is* $\begin{Bmatrix} thick \\ thin \end{Bmatrix}$ *is to say something about its thickness.*

(iv)   *To say that a tree is* $\begin{Bmatrix} {}^{*}thick \\ thin \end{Bmatrix}$ *is to say something about its thinness.*

such sentences as those in (7) can be taken to be requests on the part
of the speaker for action on the part of the hearer:

(7)   a.   *I want you to hand over your valuables.*
                  b.   *Could you hand over your valuables?*

The basic force of (7a) is that of a declarative, as can be seen by the
fact that, as a direct quote, it can be followed by such appositives as
those in (8):

(8)   *Knucks McGonagle said, 'I want you to hand over your*
          valuables,' $\begin{Bmatrix} which\ was\ a\ lie \\ which\ was\ obviously\ true \\ which\ must\ have\ been\ false \end{Bmatrix}$.

To the best of my knowledge, only true declaratives can antecede
such appositives, as is shown by the ungrammaticalities of such close
semantic pairs as those in (9)–(11):

(9)   a.   *Bill said, 'England is over there,' which was a lie.*
       b.   *??Bill said, 'There's England over there,' which was*
            a lie.

(10)   a.   *Mme. Post said, 'Nobody could help gagging on*
            a quiche like that,' which was probably true.
       b.   *??Mme. Post said, 'Who could help gagging on a*
            quiche like that?,' which was probably true.

(11)   a.   *?Tex said, 'She never saw him at all, I gather,'*
            which was a lie.
       b.   *??Tex said, 'I gather (?*that) she never saw him at*
            all,' which was a lie.

Here, apparently, the deictics, rhetorical questions, and 'pulled
punch assertions'[2] in the (b) examples are not close enough to quint-
essential declaratives to allow the type of appositives we see in (8).

And the basic illocutionary force of (7b) is that of a question, as we
see from the fact that it can be followed by such appositives as those
in (12). These are possible only after true information-seeking questions, as the oddnesses in (13) show:

(12)   *Knucks said, 'Could you hand over your valuables?,'*
          $\begin{Bmatrix} which\ was\ not\ obvious \\ which\ no\ one\ knows\ to\ this\ day \\ which\ I\ had\ been\ wondering\ about\ myself \end{Bmatrix}$.

----

[2] 'Hedged' assertions would probably be a better term. For an important beginning
on the incredibly difficult semantic problems posed by hedges of various sorts, cf. G.
Lakoff (1972a).

(13)   *Mme. Post said, 'Who could help gagging on a quiche
         like that?,'*
$$\left\{\begin{array}{l} \text{?*which was not obvious} \\ \text{?*which no one knows to this day} \\ \text{??which I had been wondering about myself} \end{array}\right\}.$$

However, though the basic forces of (7a) and (7b) are those of a declarative and a request for information, respectively, they can also be used as a request to the hearer to hand over the valuables, as the sentences in (14) indicate.

(14)   *Knucks said to Mme. Post,* $\left\{\begin{array}{l} \text{'I want you to hand over} \\ \text{Could you hand over} \end{array}\right.$

         your valuables?' $\Big\}$*, and she complied.*
         your valuables?'

As Robin Lakoff has pointed out to me, the verb *comply* can be used anaphorically, as it is in (14), only when the clause to which it refers is taken to have the force of a request.[3] Some examples of the types of ungrammaticalities that result when this condition is not met can be seen in:

(15)   **Knucks said to Mme. Post,*
         $\left\{\begin{array}{l} \text{'Sure is nice out.'} \\ \text{'Might the Redlegs have won?'} \\ \text{'How scrawny these ruffians are!'} \end{array}\right\}$ *and she complied.*

It is possible to force the request-for-action interpretation of the sentences in (7) by inserting the morpheme[4] *please* preverbally, as in:

(16)   a.   *I want you to please hand over your valuables.*
         b.   *Could you please hand over your valuables?*

That these sentences can only be interpreted as requests can be seen by the impossibility of following them with the types of typically declarative appositive clauses used in (8), or with the types of infor-mation-seeking question appositive clauses shown in (12). Both of

---

[3] This is only a necessary, not a sufficient, condition, as the following sentence in-dicates:

(i)   **The Duke said to Bottomley, 'It's cold in
                 here,' and Bottomley complied.*

The point is that though statements can also have the derived forces of requests, such requests cannot be referred to anaphorically with *comply*.

[4] Or morphemes? Cf. the noun *plea*.

the sentences in (17) are ungrammatical:

(17)   a.   *Knucks said to Mme. Post, 'I want you to please
            hand over your valuables,' which was a lie.
       b.   *Knucks said to Mme. Post, 'Could you please hand
            over your valuables?,' which was not obvious.

This preverbal *please* is a litmus for requests, and much of the remainder of this chapter will concentrate on how the generalizations concerning its distribution are to be stated.[5]

In Gordon and Lakoff (1971), a general procedure is described for formally deriving some of the nonbasic illocutionary forces of a sentence by making reference to some of the felicity conditions on the forces in question. Thus, since requests have the felicity conditions shown in (18), among others:

(18)   a.   *The act requested is subsequent to the time of
            requesting.*

---

[5] It is important to distinguish the behaviors of preverbal *please*, sentence-final *please*, and sentence-initial *please*. Thus, note the contrast between (i) and (ii), which points up the first distinction:

(i)   ??*Are you able to please call back later?*
(ii)   *Are you able to call back later, please?*

and that between (iii) and (iv), which points up the second one:

(iii)   *It's cold in here, please.
(iv)   Please—it's cold in here.*

As far as I know, the following general law holds:

(v)   Preverbal please ⊃ *sentence-final* please ⊃
                             sentence-initial please

That is, the set of all sentences that can add a preverbal *please* is a subset of the set of all sentences that can add a final *please*, and this last is a subset of all sentences that can add an initial *please*. Incidentally, such sentences as *(vi), which were pointed out to me by George Lakoff, show that it is not possible to maintain that just any sentence can add an initial *please:*

(vi)   *Please—away ran the troopers.*

Naturally, it is not sufficient to merely state such implicational laws as (v)—one must seek explanations not only for the existence of positionally conditional differences but also for the direction of the implication.

Unfortunately, however, I have nothing to suggest at present. I have pointed out these distinctions merely to call the reader's attention to the fact that the generalizations that I formulate in the text are not intended to describe the syntax of all three types of *please*, but merely to serve as first steps in describing the distribution of the most restricted *please*—the preverbal one.

b. *The speaker wants the act requested to be performed.*
c. *The speaker believes that the hearer has the ability to carry out the act.*
d. *The speaker believes that the hearer is willing to carry out the act.*

such sentences as those in (19), which violate these conditions in various ways, are infelicitous to varying degrees:[6]

(19)   a.   **Yesterday, I asked him to return the day before.*
       b.   *?Please write me a check, though I don't want you to.*
       c.   *?*You can't, but please start the car.*
       d.   *?*Repaper the ceiling, though I know you don't want to.*

What Gordon and Lakoff suggest is the following general law for deriving nonbasic illocutionary forces:

(20)   *A sentence that states a speaker-based felicity condition for a speech act of some kind will have that kind of speech act as a derived force, and a sentence that asks a yes–no question about a hearer-based felicity condition for some kind of speech act will have that kind of speech act as a derived illocutionary force.*

Thus, since (18b) and (18c) are speaker-based and hearer-based felicity conditions on requests, (7a) and (7b) can have, as (20) predicts, the derived forces of requests.

And if we say that preverbal *please* can appear only in sentences whose basic or derived illocutionary force is that of a request, we can explain the deviance of the sentences in (17): The *please* forces the request interpretation, which is incompatible with the appositive clauses.

The basic idea of (20) seems correct to me, but we should not conclude that the problem of derived illocutionary force resides in semantics alone, as is implicit in such formulations as (20). Rather, the way a particular semantic entity finds expression is of crucial importance.

---

[6] In order to limit the scope of this chapter, I will not take up the important problem of drawing distinctions between the different types of felicity conditions, and the different types of violations that result from violating these different types of restrictions. Cf. Searle (1970) for some discussion.

Thus, note that while (21a) and (21b) are exactly synonymous, on a reading, with the other sentences in (21) also being quite close to (21a) in meaning, only (21a) is fully natural with preverbal *please*, as the sentences of (22) indicate:

(21)   a.   *Can you lift your boots?*
       b.   *Are you able to lift your boots?*
       c.   *Would you be able to lift your boots?*
       d.   *Would it be possible for you to lift your boots?*
       e.   *Is it possible for you to lift your boots?*

       f.   *Do you have the* $\begin{Bmatrix} ability \\ capacity \\ power \end{Bmatrix}$ *to lift your boots?*

(22)   a.   *Can you please lift your boots?*
       b.   ?*Are you able to please lift your boots?*
       c.   ?*Would you be able to please lift your boots?*
       d.   ?*Would it be possible for you to please lift your boots?*
       e.   ??*Would it be possible for you to please lift your boots?*

       f.   *Do you have the* $\begin{Bmatrix} ability \\ capacity \\ power \end{Bmatrix}$ *to please lift your boots?*

Similarly, while the sentences without *please* in (23) are all in the same semantic ballpark, we find that only some of them have viable derived request forces and can tolerate preverbal *please:*

(23)   a.   *I* $\begin{Bmatrix} want \\ would\ like \end{Bmatrix}$ *you to (please) sign here.*
       b.   *I would like it if you'd (?please) sign here.*
       c.   *I would appreciate it if you'd (??please) sign here.*
       d.   *I would be* $\begin{Bmatrix} glad \\ grateful \end{Bmatrix}$ *if you'd (?please) sign here.*
       e.   *I would be* $\begin{Bmatrix} happy \\ appreciative \end{Bmatrix}$ *if you'd (??please) sign here.*
       f.   *I'd be ecstatic if you'd (*please) sign here.*[7]

---

[7] While I cannot digress into the fascinating problems that would arise in seeking a detailed explanation of such contrasts as those in (21)–(23), I might point out in pass-

What this indicates is that transderivational rules like (20) cannot be conceived of as relations between one logical structure and another one but rather must be thought of as relationships between one logical structure (the request interpretation) and part or all of another derivation.

Nonetheless, my major concern in this chapter will not be in documenting further the need for this relatively trivial departure from (20), which embodies that spirit of the Gordon–Lakoff proposal, but, rather, in arguing for a different kind of extension. To this end, consider the syntactic process of SLIFTING, which converts such sentences as those in (24) into such sentences as those in (25):[8]

(24)   a. *I take it that you are a Plutonian.*
         b. *Remember that I am slower than you.*
(25)   a. *You are a Plutonian, I take it.*
         b. *I am slower than you, remember.*

In particular, let us investigate the following problem: When can

---

ing that the difference between (22a) and (22b) is not accidental. Sentences containing modals typically have more derived forces than synonymous sentences without modals, as Bruce Fraser has pointed out to me. Thus, note the contrasts in:

(i)   *Will you (please) leave?*
(ii)   *Are you going to (?°please) leave?*
(iii)   *May I (please) have those spurs?*
(iv)   *Am I permitted to (°please) have those spurs?*

Since parallel contrasts appear to exist in other languages, such as German and French [cf. (v) and (vi)]:

(v)   a. *Können Sie (bitte) Ihren Hut abnehmen?*
             can   you please your hat take off
             'Can you (please) take off your hat?'
         b. *Sind Sie imstande (°bitte) Ihren Hut abzunehmen?*
             are you able   please your hat to take off
(vi)   a. *Pouvez-vous enlever vôtre chapeau, s'il vous plaît?*
             can   you take off your hat   please
         b. *??Etes-vous capable d'enlever vôtre chapeau, s'il vous plaît?*
             are you able   of to take off your hat   please

the conclusion that naturally suggests itself is that one of the relevant parts of a language-universal definition of the concept MODAL VERB is precisely this 'force shiftiness.'

[8] Cf. Ross (1973c) for arguments that parentheticals such as those in (25) derive from such sources as (24).

question clauses be slifted? The conversion of (26)–(27) shows some instances in which SLIFTING can operate,[9] and the impossibility of converting (28) into (*29) shows some instances in which it cannot:

(26)   a.   *I want you to tell me when dinner will be ready.*
        b.   *Tell me where you were staying.*
        c.   *I wonder how long he has been floating near me.*
        d.   *Can you tell me who Sam is pitching to next?*

(27)   a.   *When will dinner be ready, I want you to tell me.*
        b.   *Where were you staying, tell me.*
        c.   *How long has he been floating near me, I wonder.*
        d.   *Who is Sam pitching to next, can you tell me?*

(28)   a.   *I (don't) want Fat Albert to tell me when dinner will be ready.*
        b.   *(Never) tell Ed where you were staying.*
        c.   *They may have wondered how long he has been floating near me.*
        d.   *Are you able to tell me who Sam is pitching to next?*

(29)   a.   **When will dinner be ready, I (don't) want Fat Albert to tell me.*
        b.   **Where were you staying, (never) tell Ed.*
        c.   **How long has he been floating near me, they may have wondered.*[10]
        d.   **Who is Sam pitching to next, are you able to tell me?*[11]

---

[9] One argument that SLIFTING, or some rule functionally equivalent to it, is involved in the production of such sentences as (27)—that is, that (27) cannot be a remote structure—will be developed in footnote 16 in connection with examples like (35b).

[10] Since *wonder* is a verb that can take direct quotes, (29c) might be interpretable as a slifted form of something like:

(i)   *(Each$_i$ of) them may have wondered 'How long has he been floating near me$_i$?'*

where the first-person pronoun *me* refers, as is mandatory in direct quotes, to the subject of the quote-taking verb, not to the utterer of the sentence. If *me* in (29c) is taken to refer to a suppressed *each*, as in (i), then (29c) might be grammatical for some speakers. But if the question is forced to be an indirect quote, by taking this *me* to refer to the utterer, then (29c) is impossible, and this is the reading on which I have starred it.

[11] This string of words is grammatical if read as a sequence of two sentences, each of which is a question, but it is out if read with the kind of single-sentence intonation that (27d) can be given. The contrast emerges even more clearly if the parentheticals

The first hypothesis that suggests itself is given in:

(30)   GENERALIZATION I: *Embedded questions can be*
       slifted only if the sentences in which they appear have
       the (basic or derived) illocutionary force of a request
       on the part of the speaker for the hearer to provide the
       relevant information about the wh-ed parts of the ques-
       tion that is to be slifted.

This generalization, coupled with the independently necessary
statement to the effect that questions based on *can* (and other
modals) can convey requests for action, while questions based on *be*
able to (and other periphrastic constructions) cannot [cf. the contrast
between (22a) and the other sentences of (22)], would explain the
contrast between (27d) and *(29d). Similarly, since *I want you to X*
has the derived force of a request to X, whereas neither *I want Fat*
Albert to X nor *I don't want Fat Albert to X* can have such a force,
(27a) would be allowed by (30), but not *(29a). And since other
meaning postulates must account for the rough equivalences
shown in:

(31)   a.   *X wants Y to tell X Z* $\cong$

                 X wants to $\begin{Bmatrix} hear \\ know \end{Bmatrix}$ *Z from Y*[12]

            b.   *I want to know Z from you* $\cong$ *I wonder*
                 (about) Z

Generalization I can also account for the contrast between (27c) and
*(29c).

The full range of data which (30) can provide explanations for, in
ways that I will not spell out in detail here, is suggested by the
complex array of facts shown in:

---

in (27d) and in (29d) are inserted, by a rule I refer to as NICHING [cf. Ross (in preparation) for details], into their respective main clauses, as (i) shows:

(i)   *Who,* $\begin{Bmatrix} ?can\ you \\ *are\ you\ able\ to \end{Bmatrix}$ *tell me, is Sam*

                       pitching to next?

   [12] Of course, this rough equivalence should be reduced to the more basic one shown
in (i):

(i)   *Y tell Z to X* $\cong$ *Y* $\begin{Bmatrix} hear \\ know \end{Bmatrix}$ *Z from Y*

(32)

a. $\left\{\begin{array}{l} \left[\begin{array}{l} \left\{\begin{array}{l} I \\ They \end{array}\right\}\left\{\begin{array}{l} want \\ expect \end{array}\right\}\begin{array}{l} \left\{\begin{array}{l} you \\ Jan \end{array}\right\} to\ tell\ \left\{\begin{array}{l} me \\ Bob \end{array}\right\} \\ (Sam)\ to\ \left\{\begin{array}{l} know\ from \\ remember \end{array}\right\}\left\{\begin{array}{l} you \\ Jan \end{array}\right\} \end{array} \\ \\ \left\{\begin{array}{l} Could \\ Can \end{array}\right\}\left\{\begin{array}{l} you \\ Jan \end{array}\right\}\ tell\ \left\{\begin{array}{l} me \\ Bob \end{array}\right\} \\ \\ Will\ \left\{\begin{array}{l} you \\ Jan \end{array}\right\}\left\{\begin{array}{l} know \\ tell \end{array}\right\}\left\{\begin{array}{l} me \\ Bob \end{array}\right\} \\ \\ \begin{array}{l} Would\ \left\{\begin{array}{l} you \\ Jan \end{array}\right\}\ be \\ \left\{\begin{array}{l} Are\ you \\ Is\ Jan \end{array}\right\} \end{array}\ willing\ to\ tell\ \left\{\begin{array}{l} me \\ Bob \end{array}\right\} \\ \\ Do\ you\ think\ \left\{\begin{array}{l} you \\ they \end{array}\right\}\left\{\begin{array}{l} could \\ can \\ would\ be\ willing\ to \end{array}\right\}\ tell\ \left\{\begin{array}{l} me \\ Bob \end{array}\right\} \end{array}\right]\right.$ when dinner will be?

⇓ (SLIFTING)

b. When will dinner be,

$\left[\begin{array}{l} \left\{\begin{array}{l} I \\ *they \end{array}\right\}\left\{\begin{array}{l} want \\ *expect \end{array}\right\}\begin{array}{l} \left\{\begin{array}{l} you \\ *Jan \end{array}\right\} to\ tell\ \left\{\begin{array}{l} me \\ *Bob \end{array}\right\}.^{13} \\ (*Sam)\ to\ \left\{\begin{array}{l} ?know\ from \\ *remember \end{array}\right\}\left\{\begin{array}{l} you \\ *Jan \end{array}\right\}. \end{array} \\ \\ \left\{\begin{array}{l} could \\ can \end{array}\right\}\left\{\begin{array}{l} you \\ *Jan \end{array}\right\}\ tell\ \left\{\begin{array}{l} me \\ *Bob \end{array}\right\}? \\ \\ will\ \left\{\begin{array}{l} you \\ *Jan \end{array}\right\}\left\{\begin{array}{l} *know \\ tell \end{array}\right\}\left\{\begin{array}{l} me \\ *Bob \end{array}\right\}? \\ \\ \begin{array}{l} would\ \left\{\begin{array}{l} ??you \\ *Jan \end{array}\right\}\ be \\ *are\ you \\ *is\ Jan \end{array}\ willing\ to\ tell\ \left\{\begin{array}{l} me \\ *Bob \end{array}\right\}? \\ \\ ?do\ you\ think\ \left\{\begin{array}{l} you \\ *they \end{array}\right\}\left\{\begin{array}{l} could \\ can \\ ?*would\ be\ willing\ to \end{array}\right\}\ tell\ \left\{\begin{array}{l} me \\ *Bob \end{array}\right\}? \end{array}\right]$

[13] I am aware that many of the asterisks in (32b) (and in corresponding sentences later on) are too uncharitable, particularly with respect to the NP occurring where *you* occurs. Thus, the tag in:

In the bracketed expressions in (32), only those sequences of words that can convey requests for information are in bold type. The important parts of these underlined sequences are repeated in (33) and (34):

(33)   a. *I want you to (please) X.*

         b. $\begin{Bmatrix} Could \\ Can \end{Bmatrix}$ *you (please) X?*

         c. *Will you (please) X?*

(34)   a. *I want to (?please) know X from you.*

         b. *Would you be willing to (??please) X?*

         c. *Do you think you could (?please) X?*

As I have already pointed out in connection with (21)–(23), sentences starting with such sequences as those in (33a) and (33b) can convey requests. The Gordon–Lakoff rule stated in (20) accounts for this, and Gordon and Lakoff also explain, along similar lines, how sentences starting with *will you* can convey requests. Thus, all of these sentences can exhibit a preverbal *please*.

The introductory subsequences in (34) are not as good in conveying requests, as the prefixes before the inserted *please*'s in these examples indicate. While we need not inquire in detail as to what the conditions are under which it is less than completely possible to achieve the derived force of a request, the mere fact that 'quasi-requests' like those in (34) exist is of considerable interest, for it suggests that no discrete treatment of the problem of derived illocutionary force is likely to be viable. To account for such quasi-requests as these,[14] it will eventually be necessary to construct

---

(i)   *. . . , I want Jan to tell me.*

is interpretable in a context in which the speaker is addressing a group containing Jan, or in a context in which the speaker is requesting the person(s) addressed to get Jan to answer his question. The same obtains for the tags in:

(ii)   a. *. . . , could Jan tell me?*
                b. *. . . , will Jan tell me?*

Also, when *Bob* replaces *me* in such tags, interpretations are usually possible under which the questioner is one of a group including Bob, and so on. But for the purposes of providing a simplified look at a complex situation, I have ruthlessly given asterisks to these 'further out' interpretations. In any case, they do not materially affect the main point, which is that a parallel exists between (32) and (35), for the asterisks in this latter example should also be taken to be under the same caveat.

[14] Other examples of quasi-requests are the strings in (22) and (23) that are less than fully grammatical.

formal rules that will assign DEGREES of requesthood, declarativeness, hortatoriness, and so on.[15]

At any rate, the fact that the sliftability of the embedded question
of (32a) varies directly with the extent to which the sentence in
which it occurs can convey a request for information provides some support for the correctness of Generalization I.

Nonetheless, it is necessary to reformulate this generalization, for
we also find that questions can be slifted out of declarative sentences
that REPORT requests. It is clear that the conversion of (35a) into
(35b) closely parallels that of (32a) into (32b):[16]

(35)

a. Archie_i $\left\{ \begin{array}{l} \text{told Edith}_j \text{ that} \left\{ \begin{array}{l} he_i \\ they \end{array} \right\} \left\{ \begin{array}{l} wanted \\ expected \end{array} \right\} \left\{ \begin{array}{l} \left\{ \begin{array}{l} her_j \\ Jan \end{array} \right\} \text{to tell} \left\{ \begin{array}{l} him_i \\ Bob \end{array} \right\} \\ (Sam) \text{ to} \left\{ \begin{array}{l} know\ from \\ remember \end{array} \right\} \left\{ \begin{array}{l} her_j \\ Bob \end{array} \right\} \end{array} \right\} \\[4ex] \begin{array}{l} asked\ \text{Edith}_j \left\{ \begin{array}{l} she_j \\ Jan \end{array} \right\} \\ whether \end{array} \left\{ \begin{array}{l} could\ tell \left\{ \begin{array}{l} him_i \\ Bob \end{array} \right\} \\ would \left\{ \begin{array}{l} know \\ tell \end{array} \left\{ \begin{array}{l} him_i \\ Bob \end{array} \right\} \right\} \\ \left\{ \begin{array}{l} would\ be \\ was \end{array} \right\} willing\ to\ tell \left\{ \begin{array}{l} him_i \\ Bob \end{array} \right\} \\ thought \left\{ \begin{array}{l} she_j \\ they \end{array} \right\} \left\{ \begin{array}{l} could \\ would\ be \\ willing\ to \end{array} \right\} tell \left\{ \begin{array}{l} him_i \\ Bob \end{array} \right\} \end{array} \right\} \end{array} \right\}$

when dinner would be.

---

[15] I have argued for the postulation of SQUISHES — matrices representing the interactions of nondiscretely varying parameters — in a number of recent articles (cf. Ross,
1972, 1973b, 1973d). The semigrammaticalities of (22), (23), and (34) make it seem
likely that the area of derived illocutionary force will present many similarities to the
problems these articles take up.

[16] One argument that sentences like those in (35b) have been produced by SLIFTING
stems from the fact that the rule accounting for sequence-of-tense facts has operated to
produce the *would* in the question clause. If (35b) were not derived from (35a), but
was, rather, basic, then in order to produce the *would* of the question clause of (35b),
any sequence-of-tense process that would proceed from the past tense of *told* or *asked*
to introduce the past-tense morpheme on *would* would not proceed down the tree but
would, instead, go backward into a noncommanded clause — the question clause of
(35b). In Ross (1973c), I argue that a general constraint on rules should be imposed
which would preclude any such case.

On the other hand, if (35a) underlies (35b), the sequence-of-tense rule will be able
to proceed down the tree, from *told* or *asked* to *would,* before SLIFTING, in conformity
with the constraint just mentioned.

 (SLIFTING)

b. *When would dinner be,*

$$
Archie_i
\begin{cases}
\begin{cases}
told\ Edith_j\ that
\begin{Bmatrix} he_i \\ {}^*they \end{Bmatrix}
\begin{Bmatrix} wanted \\ {}^*expected \end{Bmatrix}
\begin{cases}
\begin{Bmatrix} her_j \\ {}^*Jan \end{Bmatrix} to\ tell \begin{Bmatrix} ??him_i \\ {}^*Bob \end{Bmatrix} \\
({}^*Sam)\ to \begin{Bmatrix} know\ from \\ {}^*remember \end{Bmatrix} \begin{Bmatrix} ??her_j \\ {}^*Bob \end{Bmatrix}
\end{cases}
\\[2em]
\begin{cases}
asked\ Edith_j \\ whether
\end{cases}
\begin{Bmatrix} she_j \\ {}^*Jan \end{Bmatrix}
\begin{cases}
could\ tell \begin{Bmatrix} him_i \\ {}^*Bob \end{Bmatrix} \\
would \begin{Bmatrix} {}^*know \\ tell \begin{Bmatrix} ??him_i \\ {}^*Bob \end{Bmatrix} \end{Bmatrix} \\
\begin{Bmatrix} would\ be \\ {}^*was \end{Bmatrix} willing\ to\ tell \begin{Bmatrix} ?{}^*him_i \\ {}^*Bob \end{Bmatrix} \\
{}^*thought \begin{Bmatrix} she_j \\ they \end{Bmatrix} \begin{Bmatrix} could \\ would\ be \\ willing\ to \end{Bmatrix} tell \begin{Bmatrix} him_i \\ Bob \end{Bmatrix}
\end{cases}
\end{cases}
\end{cases}.
$$

Similarly, the conversion of (37a) into (37b) is possible only under conditions closely parallel to those under which (36a) can be converted into (36b):

(36)   a.   *I ask you (to tell me) when dinner will be.*

⇓ (SLIFTING)

       b.   *When will dinner be, I ask you (?to tell me)?*

(37)   a.   *Archie_i asked Edith_j (to tell him_j) when dinner would be.*

⇓ (SLIFTING)

       b.   *When would dinner be, Archie_i asked Edith_j (??to tell him_i).*

I have described these parallels only as 'close,' not as 'exact,' because it is obvious that there is an asymmetry here:

(38)   *Whenever it is possible to slift a question out of a reported request, it is possible to slift it in a corresponding sentence that is a request, or has the force of one, but not conversely.*

In other words, whenever a construction in (35b) or (37b) is possible, the corresponding construction is possible in (32b) or (36b), but not conversely. This is one reflection of a quite general phenomenon, which I have stated here in a rough form:

(39)   THE PENTHOUSE PRINCIPLE: *Any rule that can operate in embedded contexts can also operate in unembedded ones, but not conversely.*[17]

Therefore, since it appears that the asymmetry noted in (38) can be made to follow from the Penthouse Principle, I will not attempt here a detailed account of the differences between (32) and (36), on the one hand, and (35) and (37), on the other, and will instead assume in what follows that a single characterization should be given for both types of sentences.[18]

The rule stated in (40) can serve as a first approximation to such a characterization:

(40)   GENERALIZATION II: *Embedded questions can be slifted only if the agent of the next-highest verb of saying is being requested by the indirect object of this verb to provide the relevant information about the wh-ed parts of the question that is to be slifted.*

While there are several inadequacies in (40),[19] I doubt that the three conclusions that I will draw from it would be affected in any

---

[17] This principle is explained and argued for in detail in Ross (1973a).

[18] The following is a brief sketch of what I would hope would turn out to be the structure of a more detailed account. In line with my comments on the differences between (33) and (34), I assume that the rules that assign derived illocutionary forces will give graded outputs, and will say, for instance, that a sentence like (34c) can only partially attain the force of a request. Let us say that these squishy derived force rules assign strings some index of requesthood, x, where $0 \leqslant x \leqslant 1$. For the sake of discussion, let us say that, in isolation, (34c) would be assigned the value [0.43 Request]. The effect of the Penthouse Principle on such derived force rules would be to lower, in embedded contexts, all values of x produced in isolation, possibly, but not necessarily, by some constant amount. Thus, though strings like (34c) would receive the value of 0.43 in isolation, when they appear as the object of *Archie asked Edith*, as in (35b), the embedding decrement might bring x down to 0.13, say, which would be below the '*' threshold, as far as requests were concerned.

While this sketch is brief and programmatic in the extreme, I think the approach that I would attempt to implement should be sufficiently clear.

[19] One obvious defect is the fact that (40) will not account for the grammaticality of (27c) or the corresponding embedded case in:

(i)   *When would dinner be, Archie wondered.*

major way by any reformulations that would be necessary to arrive at a more adequate rule.

CONCLUSION 1

Though I have not stated in detail the formal rules that assign requesthood, it seems clear to me that it will only be possible to cast these rules in a maximally general way if the performative analysis of declaratives is assumed. That is, we want the conversion of (41a) to (41b) to be possible under precisely the same conditions as the conversion of (26a) to (27a) is possible. But this identity of conditions is apparent only if the latter two sentences are reanalyzed, in accordance with the performative analysis, as deriving from remote structures that include a highest performative, as in (42a) and (42b):

Assuming the performative analysis for declaratives (cf. Ross, 1970 for details), the source of (i) would be (ii), approximately:

(ii)   *I tell you that Archie wondered when dinner would be.*

Here, the first verb of saying above the question is *tell*, and it is not its subject that is requesting information. The only way to retain (40) in its present form would be to show that independent justification existed for decomposing *wondered* into something on the order of *said–want–tell*, as in:

(iii)   *I tell you that Archie$_i$ said to X that he$_i$ wanted X to tell him$_i$ when dinner would be.*

While I know of no difficulty in principle with such a decomposition, at present it would be ad hoc.

It might appear that the version of (37b) that does not contain the verb of saying *tell* would also cause problems for (40), but in fact, as Postal has pointed out (cf. Postal, 1970), there exists independent evidence for a rule deleting *tell* under the conditions suggested in:

(iv) X *ask* Y [(Y) ⌐ tell X ⌐ Q]$_s$

                        Equi ∅ ⇓   ⇓ **Tell** DELETION
                                   ∅

First of all, this rule regularizes the distribution of *ask*, for it allows one to simply specify that *ask* is an equi-subject predicate (cf. Perlmutter, 1971 for a definition of this term), instead of making it necessary to call it EITHER an equi-subject predicate OR a question-taking predicate. Second, it resolves an apparent irregularity in the control problem. In (v), the indirect object of *ask* deletes the subject of *buy*, while in (vi), the subject of *ask* does so:

(v)   *I asked Josh to buy a leech.*
(vi)   *I asked Josh when to buy a leech.*

(*Continued on page 250*)

(41)   a.   *Archie$_i$ told Edith$_j$ that he$_i$ wanted her$_j$ to tell him$_i$*
            when dinner would be.

$$\Downarrow \quad \text{(SLIFTING)}$$

       b.   *When would dinner be, Archie$_i$ told Edith$_j$ that he$_i$*
            wanted her$_j$ to tell him$_i$.

(42)   a.   *I tell you that I want you to tell me when dinner*
            will be.

$$\Downarrow \quad \text{(SLIFTING)}$$

       b.   *When will dinner be, I tell you that I want you to*
            tell me.

There exist many other parallels between apparently unembedded cases like (32) and obviously embedded cases like (35). All of these provide further support for the performative analysis.

Under the **Tell** DELETION analysis, however, the controller of the deleted subject of *buy* in (vi) is really the indirect object of the deleted *tell*, as is shown in:

(vii)   *I asked Josh [he tell me [when I should buy a leech]].*

Thus, the short version of (37b) does not cause any problems for (40).

But there is a second problem with (40), which was pointed out to me by Jim Mc-Cawley. Namely, as (40) is formulated at present, it will allow all of the sentences in (viii) to undergo SLIFTING, yielding the corresponding sentences in (ix). However, not all of these are grammatical:

(viii) a.   *I think that Archie asked Edith when dinner would be.*
        b.   *I doubt that Archie asked Edith when dinner would be.*
        c.   *Archie tried to ask Edith when dinner would be.*
        d.   *Archie failed to ask Edith when dinner would be.*
        e.   *Archie could not have failed to ask Edith when dinner would be.*

(ix)   a.   ?*When would dinner be, I think that Archie asked Edith.*
        b.   *When would dinner be, I doubt that Archie asked Edith.*
        c.   *When would dinner be, Archie tried to ask Edith.*
        d.   *When would dinner be, Archie failed to ask Edith.*
        e.   ??*When would dinner be, Archie could not have failed to ask Edith.*

The complexity of the conditions that seem to be involved here suggests that a great deal of research may be necessary to repair the deficiency of (40) that McCawley pointed out.

Conclusion 2

The basic idea of Gordon and Lakoff was to account for derived illocutionary forces by transderivational rules that would relate one logical structure [one expressing a declarative, like (42a), say] to a different logical structure [one expressing a request, like (43)]:

(43)   *I ask you to tell me when dinner will be.*

But the preceding discussion has shown, in effect, that the type of rules that Gordon and Lakoff postulate must be assumed to be able to apply also in embedded contexts, WITHOUT CHANGING THE FORCE OF THE STRUCTURE IN WHICH THEY APPLY.

An example may make this point clearer. The basic illocutionary force of (41a) is that of a declarative. Since the derived force rules will specify that it is an assertion to the effect that Archie has requested Edith to answer the embedded question, Generalization II will allow this question to be slifted. The result, (41b), SEEMS TO RETAIN ITS DECLARATIVE FORCE.[20]

---

[20] Dick Oehrle has pointed out to me that there may be some change of force involved in changing (41a) to (41b). In particular, while the former could be followed by such appositives as *which was a lie* [cf. (i)], which I argued, in connection with (8)–(11), to be restricted to declaratives:

(i)   *You said, 'Archie told Edith that he wanted her to tell him when dinner would be,' which was a lie.*

the latter is somewhat odd when such tags are appended to it:

(ii)   ??*You said, 'When would dinner be, Archie told Edith that he wanted her to tell him,' which was a lie.*

A shorter example of the same type, (iii), seems better:

(iii)   ?*You said, 'When would dinner be, Archie asked Edith,' which was a lie.*

The '?' prefix on (iii) shows that the rule assigning declarativeness will not give it a 1.0 rating, but it certainly cannot be regarded as having the force of a question, either, as (*iv) shows:

(iv)   *You said, '[[When would dinner be], Archie*
$\quad$ $_{S_1}$
            asked Edith],'
$\quad\quad$ $_{S_2}$

$\begin{Bmatrix} ?which_1 \\ {}^\circ which_2 \end{Bmatrix}$ *was not obvious.*

It is weakly possible to follow (iv) with a question-requiring appositive, but only if the *which* refers to Archie's question, not to the whole direct quote.

Thus, while such sentences as (41b) seem not to be perfect as declaratives, they seem to come closer to having this force than to having any other. I conclude, then,

(Continued on page 252)

Conclusion 3

Assuming, for the sake of discussion, the correctness of Conclusion 2 (though bearing in mind the caveat of footnote 20), we see that derived force rules must be integrated into the grammar much more tightly than has sometimes been held to be necessary. In particular, they must be able to apply in embedded contexts, IN SUCH A WAY THAT A SYNTACTIC TRANSFORMATION—the rule of SLIFTING—CAN APPLY TO THEIR OUTPUT. In other words, if derived force rules are taken to be rules of pragmatics, and I believe this conception to be quite a traditional one, then it is not possible to relegate syntactic and pragmatic processes to different components of a grammar. Rather than it being possible for the 'work' of linking surface structures to the sets of contexts in which these structures can be appropriately used to be dichotomized into a set of pragmatic rules and a set of semantactic rules, it seems to be necessary to postulate that this work is to be accomplished by one unified component, in which rules concerned with such pragmatic matters as illocutionary force, speaker location, and so on, and rules concerned with such semantic matters as synonymy, metaphoric extension of senses, and so on, and rules concerned with such syntactic matters as the distribution of meaningless morphemes,[21] the choice of prepositional versus postpositional languages, and so on, are interspersed in various ways.[22] Following a recent practice of Fillmore, we might term the study of such mixed components PRAGMANTAX.

Note that accepting the conclusion that there is a pragmantactic component does not necessarily entail abandoning the distinction between pragmatic, semantic, and syntactic aspects of linguistic structure. Conceptually, at least, it does seem possible to draw these traditional distinctions, and it may even sometime be possible to

---

that applying derived force rules in embedded contexts does not change the force of the superordinate structure. It is obvious, however, that this whole area will require intensive study in the future. In particular, what are the theoretical implications of another of Oehrle's observations—namely, that such sentences as (35b) and (41b) occur only in narration? These are deep waters, and I must leave the many questions that denizen them unanswered.

[21] If such there be.

[22] Surely, it will in the course of time be possible and necessary to isolate possible from impossible types of interspersions and admixtures of these various (and other various) types of rules, but at present, in my opinion, not enough mixed cases have been studied to allow any such constraints to be formulated with an adequate empirical basis.

show that pragmatic violations (like including a first-person pronoun in a newspaper article that has no byline), semantic violations (like asserting that something fell upward), and syntactic violations (like keeping the first occurrence of *and*, rather than the last, in a coordinate structure [*winter, and spring, summer, fall* instead of *winter, spring, summer, and fall*]) all produce psychologically different reactions. At present, however, there are no known psychological correlates of this tripartite distinction. If future research should uncover empirical support for these conceptual distinctions, it would still be perfectly possible to maintain the hypothesis that there is a pragmantactic component, in which rules of psychologically distinct types were intermixed. For to claim that there is a pragmantactic component is merely to claim that rules of the three types interact in a way that would preclude their being studied in isolation from each other.

How could this conclusion—that pragmatic rules like Generalization II must apply before syntactic transformations like SLIFTING—be avoided? It is worthwhile examining in some detail a hypothetical reanalysis of the type of facts I have been dealing with, for there might be some who would see in such a reanalysis a serious alternative to accepting the postulation of a pragmantactic component.

Supposing, for instance, that one were to say that there is no 'syntactic' difference between (44a) and (44b)—that the syntactic component, operating in total isolation from any pragmatic inputs such as those in Generalization II, specifies both of the strings in (44) as being 'syntactically well-formed':

(44)   a. *When did Tom leave, I want to know.*
         b. *When did Tom leave, I don't want to know.*

After the syntactic component had applied, an independently operating pragmatic component, which would contain the equivalent of Generalization II, would specify that certain syntactically well-formed strings, like (44b), were 'pragmatically deviant.'

Under such a conception, which would shrink the traditional domain of syntax by removing from the syntactic component the work of specifying the distribution of so-called 'empty *do*' in English, as well as the work of specifying the conditions under which tensed auxiliaries precede the subjects of their clauses, my claim—that it is necessary to intersperse pragmatic and syntactic rules—would have been avoided. But at what cost?

The cost, it seems to me, would be that of abandoning a rather traditional definition of the term SYNTAX—namely, that syntax is the field that specifies the set of possible construction types of a language, and the distribution of the grammatical, nonlexical, morphemes of the language in these constructions. Grammatical morphemes have usually been taken to be the morphemes that indicate case, mood, and tense; often the complementizers and other subordinators of a language; and various morphemes involved in particular constructions (like the -er of comparison, the expletives *there* and *it*, etc.). Some scholars would also include under syntax the laws governing the distribution of certain lexical items (like *remind*), but this is a disputed area.

To say that (44b) is syntactically well-formed is to imply that the laws governing the distribution of empty *do* and the laws specifying the conditions under which auxiliaries precede subjects are not syntactic, a conclusion that would be at variance not only with the previous literature in generative grammar but with traditional usage as well.

But what's in a name, we may ask. After all, the term SYNTAX is a theoretical term, one having sense only within the theory in which it is embedded. Just as we are free to devise new theories of linguistic organization, so we must be free to change the meanings of the theoretical terms that figure in each of these new theories.

To a certain extent, this is true. The meanings of such terms as PHONEME, MORPHEME, DIALECT, and so on, vary widely if surveyed across various structuralist and transformational theories of language. On the other hand, after particularly radical theoretical changes, older theoretical terms simply have no counterparts in later theories. For instance, it would be hard to find anything that corresponds to PHLOGISTON or HUMOR in modern-day thermodynamics or medicine.

In one sense, then, we are free to reapply such traditional linguistic terms as SYNTACTIC and SEMANTIC to rules that differ, in that they have odd and even numbers of terms in their structural descriptions, respectively, or to rules whose names begin with vowels and consonants, respectively, or to rules whose discoverers were born in leap and non-leap years, respectively, or to any other conceivable difference between rules.

However, if someone were to propose to apply the syntax–semantics distinction in any of the cases of the last paragraph, it would surely be objected that he had adopted a confusing terminology. One would want to know why traditional terms had been retained instead of new terms being fashioned.

With regard to such contrasts as those in (44), it seems to me that the situation is essentially the same. That is, to claim that (44b) is syntactically well-formed would be to use SYNTACTIC in such a novel way as to extend its meaning beyond recognition, and one would have to inquire as to the utility of such an extension. That is, what would be gained by partitioning the set of all strings into two sets — 'syntactically well-formed' strings (let us refer to this set more neutrally as Set A) and its complement, Set B? How would Sets A and B be connected to empirically observable facts?

Unless such facts can be brought to light, Conclusion 3 — that linguistic systems relating contexts and surface structures do not admit of the traditional partitioning into pragmatic, semantic, and syntactic components, but are describable only by mixed components of the type that I have been referring to as 'pragmantactic' — must stand. It is a far from novel observation — much recent work of Fillmore (1971), G. Lakoff (1969, 1972b, 1974), and R. Lakoff (1972a, b; 1973a, b, c) has had the exploration of such mixed systems as its goal — but since it is that consequence of the sets of facts that I have examined in this paper that is most at variance with previously held conceptions of the relationship between language use and linguistic structure, it is the consequence that should be subjected to the closest theoretical scrutiny in future research.

ACKNOWLEDGMENTS

This work was supported in part by a grant from the National Institute of Mental Health (Grant Number 5P01 MH13390-06), for which I am grateful. I also wish to thank several friends whose comments have greatly influenced my thinking. So, Karin Demarest, Bruce Fraser, Susumu Kuno, George Lakoff, Jim McCawley, and Dick Oehrle, I want you to tell me whether you think you could (°please) accept my thanks — especially Bruce, who read a draft, purging the most salient errors therefrom.

REFERENCES

Austin, J. L. *How to do things with words.* Cambridge, Mass.: Harvard University Press, 1962.

Chapin, P. G. Some lexical features of English adjectives. Unpublished paper, MIT, Cambridge, Mass., 1965.

Fillmore, C. J. Toward a theory of deixis. *University of Hawaii Working Papers in Linguistics,* 1971, 3(4).

Fraser, J. B. An analysis of vernacular performative verbs. In C.-J. N. Bailey and R. Shuy (Eds.), *Toward tomorrow's linguistics.* Washington, D. C.: Georgetown University Press, 1974.

Gordon, D. and Lakoff, G. Conversational postulates. In D. Adams, M. A. Cambell, V. Cohen, J. Lovins, E. Maxwell, C. Nygren, and J. Reighard (Eds.), *Papers from the seventh regional meeting of the Chicago Linguistic Society.* Chicago: Chicago Linguistic Society, University of Chicago, 1971, 63–84.

Lakoff G. Presuppositions and relative grammaticality. In W. Todd (Ed.), *Studies in philosophical linguistics: Series One.* Evanston, Ill.: Great Expectations Press, 1969, 103–116.

Lakoff, G. Hedges: A study in meaning criteria and the logic of fuzzy concepts. In P. M. Peranteau, J. M. Levi, and G. C. Phares (Eds.), *Papers from the eighth regional meeting of The Chicago Linguistic Society*. Chicago: Chicago Linguistic Society, University of Chicago, 1972, 183–228. (a)

Lakoff, G. Linguistics and natural logic. In D. Davidson and G. Harman (Eds.), *Semantics of natural language*. Dordrecht, Holland: D. Reidel, 1972, 545–665. (b)

Lakoff, G. Fuzzy grammar and the performance/competence terminology game. In C. Corum, T. C. Smith–Stark, and A. Weiser (Eds.), *Papers from the ninth regional meeting of the Chicago Linguistic Society*. Chicago: Chicago Linguistic Society, University of Chicago, 1973, 271–291.

Lakoff, G. Pragmatics in natural logic. In E. Keenan (Ed.), *Proceedings of the formal semantics colloquium*. New York and London: Cambridge University Press, 1974.

Lakoff, R. The pragmatics of modality. In P. M. Peranteau, J. N. Levi, and G. C. Phares (Eds.), *Papers from the eighth regional meeting of the Chicago Linguistic Society*. Chicago: Chicago Linguistic Society, University of Chicago, 1972. (a)

Lakoff, R. Language in context. *Language*, 1972, 48(4), 907–927. (b)

Lakoff, R. Language and woman's place. *Language and Society*, 1973, 1(2). (a)

Lakoff, R. The logic of politeness; or, minding your P's and Q's. In C. Corum, T. C. Smith–Stark, and A. Weiser (Eds.), *Papers from the ninth regional meeting of the Chicago Linguistic Society*. Chicago: Chicago Linguistic Society, University of Chicago, 1973, 292–305. (b)

Lakoff, R. Questionable answers and answerable questions. In Braj Kachru *et. al.*, *Festschrift for Henry and Renée Kahane*. Urbana: University of Illinois Press, 1973. (c)

McCawley, J. D. Remarks on the lexicography of performative verbs. In A. Rogers, R. Wall, and J. Murphy (Eds.), untitled anthology to be published by the Center for Applied Linguistics, Washington, D. C.

Perlmutter, D. M. *Deep and surface structure constraints in syntax*. New York: Holt, Rinehart & Winston, 1971.

Postal, P. M. On coreferential complement subject deletion. *Linguistic Inquiry*, 1970, 1(4), 439–500.

Ross, J. R. Niching. Manuscript in preparation.

Ross, J. R. On declarative sentences. In R. A. Jacobs and P. S. Rosenbaum (Eds.), *Readings in English transformational grammar*. Waltham, Mass.: Ginn, 1970, 222–272.

Ross, J. R. Endstation Hauptwort: The category squish. In P. M. Peranteau, J. N. Levi, and C. G. Phares (Eds.), *Papers from the eighth regional meeting of the Chicago Linguistic Society*. Chicago: Chicago Linguistic Society, University of Chicago, 1972, 316–328.

Ross, J. R. The penthouse principle and the order of constituents. In C. Corum, T. C. Smith–Stark, and A. Weiser (Eds.), *Papers from the ninth regional meeting of the Chicago Linguistic Society*. Chicago: Chicago Linguistic Society, University of Chicago, 1973, 397–422. (a)

Ross, J. R. A fake NP squish. In C.–J. N. Bailey and R. Shuy (Eds.), *New ways of analyzing variation in English*. Washington, D. C.: Georgetown University Press, 1973. (b)

Ross, J. R. Slifting. In M. Gross, M. Halle, and M.–P. Schützenberger (Eds.), *The formal analysis of natural languages*. The Hague: Mouton, 1973, 133–172. (c)

Ross, J. R. Nouniness. In O. Fujimura (Ed.), *Three dimensions of linguistic theory*. Tokyo: TEC Corp., 1973. (d)

Searle, J. R. *Speech acts*. New York and London: Cambridge University Press, 1970.

THE SYNCHRONIC AND DIACHRONIC STATUS OF CONVERSATIONAL IMPLICATURE

PETER COLE
University of Illinois, Urbana

I. INTRODUCTION

An important and controversial problem in contemporary linguistics is to determine the theoretical implications of the notion of conversational implicature, proposed by Grice (chapter 2 of this volume). Grice argues that there are aspects of what a speaker intends to communicate by a sentence that are conversationally implied by the sentence but are not part of the logical structure of the sentence.[1] For instance, Pamela, upon being asked (1), might reply (2):

(1)   *How are you doing in your new position at*
           San Andreas Fault University?

(2)   *Well, I haven't been fired yet.*

---

[1] As I shall use the term, LOGICAL STRUCTURE is assumed to refer to a single linguistically significant level, which is both the input to the rules of grammar mapping underlying structure onto surface structure, and is the input to the interpretive rules of a model theoretic formal semantics. I do not assume that the logical structure of a sentence is the standard translation of a natural language sentence into the notation of first-order predicate calculus. I leave open the question of whether first-order predicate calculus (or, in fact, any extant logical system) is adequate for the representation of natural language. In addition, I follow in the footsteps of earlier generative grammarians in not assuming any great degree of similarity between underlying, logical structure and the surface structure of a sentence.

(*Continued on page 258*)

257

Although the logical structure of (2) is roughly that of the proposition that Pamela has not yet lost her job, more than that is implied. Either seriously or jokingly, Pamela is suggesting that being fired is a distinct possibility for her.

The idea that Pamela may be on the verge of being fired is conversationally implied by (2) on the basis of the logical structure of (2) and an inferential system, possibly based on Grice's Cooperative Principle, that requires, inter alia, that answers to questions be relevant to the question asked. When an answer is not directly relevant, as is the case in (2), the person to whom the answer is directed asks himself what conditions must obtain for the answer to be relevant. By hypothesizing what these conditions might be, he may deduce what the answerer intended to communicate by means of his answer. The deduction is based on the literal meaning of the answer and on the hypothesized state of affairs that would make the answer relevant to the question. Thus, Pamela's interlocutor must understand the literal sense of (2) in order to infer that Pamela is not doing well.

A version of Grice's proposal has been adopted by Gordon and Lakoff (chapter 4 of this volume), who have argued that there are 'rules of grammar, rules governing the distribution of morphemes in a sentence, that depend upon [conversational] principles.' According to Gordon and Lakoff, there are syntactically relevant aspects of meaning that are properly represented as conversational implicatures of the logical structure of sentences. In this chapter, I shall examine a class of sentences that are apparently excellent candidates for analysis in terms of Gordon and Lakoff's hypothesis. I shall argue, however, that such an analysis is incorrect in this case, and shall contend that the failure of Gordon and Lakoff's hypothesis for sentences of the sort I will discuss can be generalized in a way that suggests that Gordon and Lakoff's approach is incorrect.[2]

In taking these positions, this chapter may well constitute a departure from the assumptions about the logical structure of natural language sentences that led Grice to develop the notion of conversational implicature. I should like to make clear from the outset that my intention is not to write an exegesis of Grice's work but, rather, to develop a notion first suggested by Grice, which, I believe, is of relevance to semantic investigations conducted within the framework of generative grammar.

It should also be noted that I employ the adjective *Gricean* as though Grice's work were limited to his theory of conversational implicature. Readers familiar with the totality of Grice's work should take care to maintain this fiction while reading this chapter.

[2] Gordon and Lakoff do not discuss the construction that I shall examine. Thus, my criticisms are not criticisms of their linguistic analysis of this construction — since they have not proposed one — but, rather, criticisms based on predictions that follow from their general hypothesis.

II. USES OF *LET'S*

There are a number of ways in which *let's* is used in impositives. (The term IMPOSITIVE, coined by Green (this volume), refers to orders and requests.) Compare (3a–b) and (4a–c):

(3) a. *Let's wash our hands. We've gotten filthy. I've got grease on mine.*
  b. *Let's think about this for a few days. Maybe we can come up with something better. I'll try to write my ideas up.*

(4) a. *Let's wash our little handsy-wandsies before we eat our chicki-chicky.*
  b. *Now let's all think before we raise our hands.*
  c. *Let's have our medicine now. It doesn't taste bad at all.*

The sentences of (3) are what I shall call 'literal' *let's* sentences. The speaker of such sentences proposes a course of action in which he himself plans to participate. This is not true for the sentences of (4). Sentence (4a) might be spoken by a nursemaid who wants to induce her charge to wash, but who does not plan to wash herself. Sentence (4b) is appropriate for a teacher who has just asked his first-grade class how much two plus two equal. Sentence (4c) is felicitous for a nurse to state before giving a patient his nightly cod-liver oil. What the sentences of (4) have in common is that a person in authority makes use of a form normally reserved for action in which the speaker and the addressee will both participate without having any intention of participating in the action.

The issue is how the logical structure of (4) should be represented. The conveyed meaning of (4) is similar to that of:

(5) a. *Wash your hands before you eat your chicken.*
  b. *Now think before you raise your hands.*
  c. *Have your medicine now. It doesn't taste bad at all.*

Are the logical structures of (4) similar to those of (5) or to those of (3)? That is, are the sentences of (4) cases in which a Gricean approach is called for? If so, nonliteral *let's* sentences like those of (4) are related to literal *let's* sentences by conversational principles.

In the sections that follow, I shall argue that although (4a–c) are apparently related to (5a–c) by rules of conversation, sentences similar to those of (4), in which the conveyed meaning of *let's* as second person is reflected syntactically, are not related to (5) by rules of conversation. I shall argue that structures similar to those underlying (5) are not the conversational implicatures of the logical structures of *let's* sentences with second-person syntactic properties but, rather, ARE the logical structures of these sentences.

III. A CLEAR CASE OF CONVERSATIONAL IMPLICATURE

A short digression is necessary at this point. Perhaps there are cases for which the Gricean approach is clearly correct. From such cases the essential features of conversationally implied meaning may be apparent. Consider an example adapted from Gordon and Lakoff. A duke addresses his butler:

(6)   *Duke: It's cold in here.*

(7)   *Butler: I'll close the window, sir.*

It is clear that the butler has understood the duke's meanderings on meteorology as an impositive. Hence his reply in (7). It would be counterintuitive, however, to claim that the logical structure of (6) is that underlying (8):

(8)   *Close the window.*

Gordon and Lakoff are surely correct in analyzing (6) as having a DERIVED impositive force similar to (8): (8) is the result of a deduction, or inference, from (6). The fact that the structure underlying (8) is not the logical structure of (6) is indicated in Gordon and Lakoff's analysis by the Gricean derivation of (8) from (6).

In order to bring out the reason for the intuitive correctness of a Gricean treatment in this case, it is useful to reconstruct what may have gone on in the butler's mind on hearing (6). The butler realizes that his occupational goal is to cater to his master's wants. Upon hearing and understanding the literal sense of (6), the butler asks himself why the duke is telling him about the temperature. Dismissing as improbable that the duke is merely commenting on the end of summer, the butler concludes that the duke is uncomfortable and that he, the butler, had better correct this state of affairs. Thus, he replies as in (7).

IV. CRITERIA FOR CONVERSATIONAL IMPLICATURE

Three facts about the way (6) is understood lead us to believe that (8) must be the result of an inference. First, (6) has two levels of meaning in context: the literal sense of (6) (that it is cold), and a fact that may be inferred from the literal sense (that the butler had better do something about the cold). The inferred meaning of (6) is dependent on the literal meaning. Both are psychologically real levels of meaning.

Second, one can trace the chain of inference from the literal meaning to the meaning in context on the basis of reasonable assumptions about the world and people's interaction in the world (e.g., on the basis of Grice's conversational maxims). A plausible chain of inference leading from a literal understanding of (6) to what the butler understands in this situation was outlined in the previous section.

Third, facts about the world determine whether a deduction is to take place. For example, assume that the duke and the butler are members of a network of spies. The butler is the duke's controller. They are alone and the butler has started explaining to the duke what the latter must accomplish during the coming week. The duke shivers and utters (6). For the butler to reply as in (7) would be infelicitous under the circumstances. This is because there is no reasonable chain of deduction from the literal sense of (6) to an implied meaning similar to (8). In any case in which a sentence has a Gricean overlay of conversational implication in addition to its logical structure, it should be possible to reconstruct the chain of deductions leading from the logical structure to the contextual meaning. I believe that the three properties just noted are characteristic of Gricean deduction.

V. SOME ADDITIONAL EXAMPLES OF NONLITERAL *LET'S*

With these three characteristics of sentences that demand a Gricean analysis in mind, it should now be possible to determine if sentences with nonliteral *let's* require a Gricean analysis. In addition to the sentences cited previously, consider:

(9)   *Listen, Sam. Let's get that work out before*

     we lose the client, $\begin{cases} will\ you? \\ why\ don't\ you? \end{cases}$

I shall discuss (9) with regard to the three properties of conversational implicatures noted in the previous section. Are there two psychologically real levels of meaning in (9)? Can we trace a chain of inference from the literal meaning to the meaning in context? Is the applicability of the deduction determined by facts about the world? In order to answer these questions, it is helpful to paraphrase the putative literal meaning and the contextual meaning of the sentence under consideration.

I shall assume that (9) is spoken by a boss to an employee. The boss does not plan to help get the work out. Sentence (10) is a rough paraphrase of the putative literal sense of (9), and (11) is a paraphrase of the meaning understood in context:

(10)   *I propose that we get the work out before*
             we lose the clients, $\begin{Bmatrix} * \ will\ you? \\ * \ why\ don't\ you? \end{Bmatrix}$

(11)   *Listen, Sam. Get that work out before*
             we lose the client, $\begin{Bmatrix} will\ you? \\ why\ don't\ you? \end{Bmatrix}$

In (10), *let's* is paraphrased as first-person plural, while in (11), *let's* is paraphrased as second person.[3] In (10), the *you* of *will you* and *why don't you* must have a different referent from that of *let's* (and hence, the tags are ungrammatical). In (11), however, they are represented as having the same referent.

The first question to be considered is whether a speaker must have (10) in mind in order to understand (11) from (9). The answer would seem to be negative.

The second question is whether there is a reasonable line of deduction from (10) to (11). If the connection is Gricean, it should follow from principles of cooperation in discourse that upon hearing (10), one would infer (11) in the context I have provided. Such a deduction does in fact appear plausible in this context. This shows that the relationship between (9) and (11) constitutes an appropriate CANDIDATE for conversational implicature, while the relationship between (12) and (13), for example, does not:

(12)   *You're full of shit.*

(13)   *You're completely wrong.*

The fact that (11) could be conversationally derived from (10) is a necessary rather than a sufficient condition for (11) to be a conversational implicature of (9). It must still be shown that it is the putative literal meaning of (9) [i.e., (10)] that leads the hearer to understand (11) from (9), and that (9) is not idiomatically associated with (11) just as (12) **is** idiomatically associated with (13).

---

[3] More precisely, the subject of the caluse immediately below the performative clause in logical structure is represented as first-person plural in (10) and as second person in (11).

The third question is whether facts about the world as perceived by the hearer determine the applicability of the inference. The importance of facts about the world for conversational implicature is that they constitute assumptions that allow the deduction of the correct conversational implicature. I showed in Section IV that, if the (perceived) context changes, so does the set of conversational implicatures. The literal meaning of a sentence, however, is not determined by context. Thus, context cannot alter the fact that (12) may be understood as something like (13).[4] The question to be asked regarding (9) is whether the fact that (9) is understood as (11) is dependent on the context or independent of context: That is, is the relationship between (9) and (11) like that of (6) and (8), or like that of (12) and (13)? I have not been able to construct a context in which (9) is not understood as (11). Unless this is due to a failure of imagination on my part, this indicates that a Gricean treatment of (9) is in error.

VI. SYNTACTIC EVIDENCE

I have argued that the fact that certain nonliteral *let's* sentences [e.g., (9)] are understood as imperatives does not mean that these sentences should be analyzed as instances of conversational implicature. I shall now turn to the syntactic properties of nonliteral *let's* sentences.

A striking fact about nonliteral *let's* sentences is that these sentences pattern syntactically as though *let's* were second person. I shall examine the syntactic properties of nonliteral *let's* sentences in some detail because, I believe, the syntax of these sentences reveals their semantic properties. Most syntactic investigation within the framework of semantically based generative grammar has been founded on the implicit assumption that behavior with respect to syntactic rules and cooccurrence restrictions is indicative of underlying (or derived) syntactic and semantic structure. If this assumption is correct, which I shall argue is the case, three syntactic rules can be used as diagnostics of the underlying representation of

---

[4] Though context does not affect literal meaning, it can, of course, rule out certain readings of ambiguous surface structures. Thus, for example, the inherently ambiguous surface structure (i) would be understood unambiguously as (ii) in the context of an answer to (iii).

(i)   *Next year we're visiting professors.*
(ii)   *Next year we will be employed as visiting professors.*
(iii)   *Are you teaching at Illinois next year?*

nonliteral *let's* sentences: tag question formation, reflexivization, and equi-noun-phrase deletion. In addition, nonliteral *let's* shares the cooccurrence restrictions peculiar to the second person.[5]

Consider (14), which is similar to (9):

(14)   *Tommy! Let's finish that oatmeal,* $\begin{cases} will\ you? \\ why\ don't\ you? \end{cases}$
           It's already after 8:30.

For many speakers, nonliteral *let's* sentences may take a second-person tag ending, as in (14). In general, tag endings cannot be employed unless the subject of the appropriate clause (usually the highest clause) of the matrix sentence is also second person. Compare (15) and (16):

(15)   *You'll finish by three o'clock, won't you?*
(16)   **We'll finish by three o'clock, won't you?*

In addition to obeying the general restrictions on second-person tag endings, *will you* and *why don't you* are limited to imperatives. *Will you* and *why don't you* are grammatical tags for (17), an imperative, but not for (18), an admonition (see Green, chapter 5 of this volume, for a detailed discussion):

(17)   *Finish that by tomorrow,* $\begin{cases} will\ you? \\ why\ don't\ you? \end{cases}$

(18)   ** You should finish that by tomorrow,*
                 $\begin{cases} will\ you? \\ why\ don't\ you? \end{cases}$

The ungrammaticality of (18), in contrast to (14) and (17), is of considerable importance. This is because (19a) may, in the proper contexts, conversationally imply (19b):

(19)   a. *You should finish that by tomorrow.*
                  b. *Finish that by tomorrow.*

If tag question formation were sensitive to the conversational implicatures of sentences, then (18) would be grammatical. The fact that (18) is ungrammatical, therefore, is very strong evidence that *let's*

---

[5] It could, perhaps, be claimed that these are all really arguments based on coocurrence restrictions rather than on the applicability of a particular rule. That is, there may be cooccurrence restrictions between the matrix sentence and the tag question, between the subject of a sentence and pronominal objects of the verb, and between the subject of a sentence and the pronominal object of an infinitival construction. An argument to this effect would not vitiate my claim that nonliteral *let's* has the syntactic properties of a second-person subject.

sentences with *will you* and *why don't you* tag endings are underlyingly second-person imperatives.

Since Lees and Klima (1963), grammarians have taken the appearance of a second-person reflexive pronoun to constitute evidence for an underlying (i.e., sometimes covert) second-person subject. Lees and Klima argue that the absence of non-second-person reflexives in imperatives is evidence that an underlying second-person subject has been deleted, as in:

$$(20) \qquad \text{Protect} \begin{Bmatrix} *myself \\ yourself \\ *himself \\ *herself \\ *ourselves \\ yourselves \\ *themselves \end{Bmatrix} now.$$

Nonliteral *let's* sentences manifest a pattern of grammaticality isomorphic to (20):

$$(21) \qquad \text{Let's protect} \begin{Bmatrix} *myself \\ yourself \\ *himself \\ *herself \\ *itself \\ *ourselves^6 \\ yourselves \\ *themselves \end{Bmatrix} now.$$

Thus, there is strong reason to believe that nonliteral *let's* sentences have underlying second-person subjects.

The evidence based on equi-noun-phrase deletion presupposes the correctness of Lees and Klima's reflexivization argument in favor of the hypothesis that imperatives have underlying second-person subjects. Consider:

(22)   *Let's try to wash yourself quickly.*

[6] *Let's protect ourselves now* is, of course, grammatical as an instance of literal *let's*. As was shown with regard to (4), literal *let's* may conversationally imply an impositive.

Another part of Lees and Klima's argument is that sentences like (i) are ungrammatical:

(i)   *Protect you.*

The same pattern is found with *let's* sentences. Sentence (ii), in contrast to (iii), can be understood only as an instance of literal *let's*:

(ii)   *Let's try to protect you.*
(iii)   *Let's try to protect yourself.*

The presence of the reflexive pronoun *yourself* is assumed to be evidence that *you* is the underlying subject of *wash*. Subjects deleted by equi-noun-phrase deletion must be identical to the noun phrase controlling the deletion. Thus, *let's,* the only possible controller, and the underlying subject of *wash* must be identical.

Perlmutter's (1968) Like Subject Constraint provides additional reason to believe that the *let's* of (22) is underlyingly second person. Perlmutter argues that the subject of the complement of *try* must be identical to the subject of *try*. Assuming, again, that *yourself* shows that *you* must be the subject of *wash*, the subject of *try* (that is, *let's*) must also be second person.[7]

A further syntactic argument that *let's* is underlyingly second person is based on cooccurrence restrictions associated with *own*, first noted by Lees and Klima (1963). In indicative sentences, intensive *own* can be used with all possessives, as illustrated by:

(23)   a. *I love my own puppy.*
         b. *You love your own puppy.*
         c. *John loves his own puppy.*
         d. *Mary loves her own puppy.*
         e. *We love our own puppy.*
         f. *You* (plural) *love your own puppies.*
         g. *John and Mary love their own puppies.*

The sentences of (24) show that the possessive pronoun and the subject noun phrase must agree in person and number for intensive *own* to be used:

(24)

a.   *I love* $\begin{Bmatrix} your \text{ (singular)} \\ his \\ her \\ our \\ your \text{ (plural)} \\ their \end{Bmatrix}$ *own puppy.*

b.   *You* (singular) *love* $\begin{Bmatrix} my \\ his \\ her \\ our \\ your \text{ (plural)} \\ their \end{Bmatrix}$ *own puppy.*

[7] This argument was suggested to me by Jerry Morgan.

c. *John loves $\left\{\begin{array}{l}my \\ your \text{ (singular)} \\ her \\ our \\ your \text{ (plural)} \\ their\end{array}\right\}$ own puppy.

d. *Mary loves $\left\{\begin{array}{l}my \\ your \text{ (singular)} \\ his \\ our \\ your \text{ (plural)} \\ their\end{array}\right\}$ own puppy.

e. *We love $\left\{\begin{array}{l}my \\ your \text{ (singular)} \\ his \\ her \\ your \text{ (plural)} \\ their\end{array}\right\}$ own puppy.

f. *You (plural) love $\left\{\begin{array}{l}my \\ your \text{ (singular)} \\ his \\ her \\ our \\ their\end{array}\right\}$ own puppy.

g. *John and Mary love $\left\{\begin{array}{l}my \\ your \text{ (singular)} \\ his \\ her \\ our \\ your \text{ (plural)}\end{array}\right\}$ own puppy.

Sentence (25) shows that the possessive and the subject noun phrase must be coreferential:

(25)   *John$_i$ loves his$_j$ own puppy.

Lees and Klima noted that the intensive reflexive *own* can be used only in imperatives with second-person possessives. Compare (26) and (27):

(26)   a. *Use my pencil.*
                        b. *Use your pencil.*

        c.   *Use his pencil.*
        d.   *Use her pencil.*
        e.   *Use our pencil.*
        f.   *Use their pencil.*

(27)   a.   **Use my own pencil.*
        b.   *Use your own pencil.*
        c.   **Use his own pencil.*
        d.   **Use her own pencil.*
        e.   **Use our own pencil.*
        f.   **Use their own pencil.*

The pattern of grammaticality manifested in (27) can be analyzed as a special instance of the principles governing (24) if imperatives are assumed to have underlying second-person subjects. Without this assumption, (27) must be considered an arbitrary fact about English, unrelated to (24).

An argument similar to that of Lees and Klima can be constructed for nonliteral *let's* sentences. Compare (27) and (28):

(28)   a.   **Let's wash my own hands.*
        b.   *Let's wash your own hands.*
        c.   **Let's wash his own hands.*
        d.   **Let's wash her own hands.*
        e.   **Let's wash our own hands.*[8]
        f.   **Let's wash their own hands.*

The same pattern is manifested in (27) and (28). Thus, if Lees and Klima's argument that imperatives have second-person subjects is sound, the same argument shows that nonliteral *let's* sentences have second-person subjects.

In Section V, I showed that nonliteral *let's* sentences are understood without the mediation of inference from the literal meaning, while genuine instances of conversational implicature rely on inference from the literal meaning to the import in context. In this section, I have adduced a number of arguments showing that if classic examples of abstract syntactic argumentation (e.g., Lees and Klima, 1963) are sound, nonliteral *let's* sentences have underlyingly second-person subjects.

The assumptions on which abstract syntactic argumentation are based have been presented succinctly by Lakoff (1971:289):[9]

---

[8] *Let's wash our own hands* is, of course, grammatical as a literal *let's* sentence.

[9] I have generalized Lakoff's claim by substituting the term LINGUISTIC ELEMENTS where VERBS appears in the original text.

> If the syntactic phenomena that occur in sentences with certain overt [linguistic elements] occur in sentences without those [linguistic elements], and if those sentences are understood as though those [linguistic elements] were there, then we conclude (1) a rule has to be stated in the cases where the real [linguistic elements] occur; (2) since the same phenomenon occurs with the corresponding understood [linguistic elements], then there should be a single rule to cover both cases; (3) since we know what the rule looks like in the case of real [linguistic elements], and since the same rule must apply, then the sentences with understood [linguistic elements] must have a structure sufficiently like those with the overt [linguistic elements] so that the same general rule can apply to both.

It necessarily follows from the assumptions of abstract syntax that the nonliteral *let's* sentences cited in this section have second-person subjects. The rejection of this conclusion necessitates the rejection of paradigmatic examples of abstract syntactic argumentation. A single example should suffice to show why this is so. Consider again Lees and Klima's argument that imperatives have underlying second-person subjects: see, e.g., example (20). Lees and Klima conclude that the absence of non-second-person reflexive pronouns in imperative sentences indicates that imperatives have underlying second-person subjects. Such a conclusion is justified if it is assumed that syntactic rules may refer only to elements overtly present in the phrase marker at some stage in the derivation.[10] If, however, it is possible for rules to refer to the conversational implicatures of the logical structure of the sentences in question, the syntactic evidence adduced by Lees and Klima might indicate either that a second-person subject is present in underlying structure or that a second-person subject is conversationally implied by the sentences in question. No principled way is provided by Gordon and Lakoff to determine which source is the correct one. Thus, Gordon and Lakoff's hypothesis casts doubt on the validity of all arguments of the form of Lees and Klima's: for example, the arguments for abstract performative verbs proposed by R. Lakoff (1968), Ross (1970), and Sadock (1969), inter alia.[11]

[10] The reader should note that I am reformulating Lees and Klima's claims in terms of the current model.

[11] This point was made previously by Green (chapter 5 of this volume).

It is logically possible that conversationally implied structure always determines the application of syntactic rules and that logical structure is irrelevant for that purpose. Such a claim, which I do not attribute to Gordon and Lakoff or to any other author, would be subject to attack on empirical grounds. It would predict that sentences like (18) are grammatical, since (19a) can conversationally imply (19b). The ungrammaticality of (18) contradicts this prediction.

(*Continued on page 270*)

It may be useful to compare nonliteral *let's* sentences with sentences having similar import in context but lacking the syntactic manifestations of second-person imperatives, for example:

(29)   *Listen, Sam. We should get that work out*
              before we lose the client, shouldn't we?

I suggested that (29) can be understood in context as having an import similar to that of (9). Sam knows that his boss will not help him get the work out. Thus, he concludes that he is expected to do the work himself. Sam's conclusion follows from a literal understanding of (29) and from facts about the world that are susceptible to change. For example, Sam's previous boss may have helped out when the work was heavy. If Sam's previous boss had uttered (29), Sam could reasonably have expected some help. This would not have been true had he said (9). On the basis of the criteria argued for in Section IV, (29) and (11) are related by rules of conversational implicature. As I showed previously, the same claim cannot be upheld for (9) and (11).

If syntactic rules may refer to the conversational implicatures of sentences, it would be expected that sentences like (29) would have the same syntactic properties as sentences like (9). In fact, sentences like (29) lack the syntactic properties of second-person imperatives. Note the ungrammaticality of second-person tag questions in (30), second-person reflexive pronouns in (31), equi-noun-phrase deletion in (32), and second-person possessives with intensive *own* in (33):

(30)   **Listen, Sam. We should get that work out before*
              we lose the client, $\begin{cases} \textit{shouldn't you?} \\ \textit{will you?} \\ \textit{won't you?} \end{cases}$

(31)   **We should wash yourself, dear. It's almost*
              time for supper.

(32)   **We should try to wash yourself quickly,*
              dear. Supper's on the table.

(33)   **We should wash your own hands.*

Despite the fact that conversationally (29) may imply (11), the syntactic behavior of (9) and (29) is quite different. Gordon and Lakoff's

---

I understand Gordon and Lakoff's position to be that syntactic rules are sometimes, but not always, sensitive to the conversational implicatures of logical structure. It is this position that I am discussing here.

theory of conversational implicature would not predict such differences.

VII. THE STATUS OF SYNTACTIC EVIDENCE

Two sets of facts have been observed: (1) Nonliteral *let's* sentences are not amenable to a Gricean analysis because no deduction from the literal to the nonliteral meaning can be shown. (2) Nonliteral *let's* sentences have syntactic properties typical of sentences with second-person subjects. There is, I believe, a causal relationship between these two sets of facts. Nonliteral *let's* sentences are not understood as involving an inference from the putative literal meaning to the meaning in context because the syntactic properties of these sentences are evidence for the speaker (as well as for the linguist using the methodology of abstract syntax) that these sentences are to be understood unambiguously as second-person imperatives.

This fact about *let's* sentences can be generalized to all cases in which it might be claimed that syntactic processes must refer to the conversational entailments of logical structure. In order to do so, it is necessary to examine the circumstances in which a linguist holding the position advocated by Gordon and Lakoff would propose that a rule might refer to the conversational entailments of logical structure. This has not been done by Gordon and Lakoff and other advocates of their view. It is, however, fairly clear from Gordon and Lakoff's examples which conditions would constitute prima facie motivation for a rule making reference to conversational implicature. Three conditions would have to be fulfilled for such a rule to have at least apparent motivation:[12] (1) What the sentence to which the rule applies is understood to mean is different from the literal meaning conveyed by the words making up the sentence; (2) there exists a plausible chain of inference from the putative literal meaning of the sentence to the conveyed meaning; and (3) the application of the syntactic rule (or of cooccurrence restrictions) is consistent only with the conveyed meaning of the sentence and not with the putative literal sense of the sentence.

The first and second criteria are intended to guarantee that the pair consisting of a sentence and a conveyed meaning might reasonably be related by conversational implicature. The first crite-

---

[12] The adoption of these criteria might eliminate the uncertainty noted previously with respect to certain cases of abstract syntactic structures. It is noteworthy that the status of argumentation for abstract performative verbs would remain in doubt.

rion would eliminate the possibility of claiming that the meaning 'John eats fried rice on Tuesday' is conversationally implied by the sentence *John eats fried rice on Tuesday*.[13] The second criterion would prevent us from considering the relationship between *John kicked the bucket* and *John died* as one of conversational implicature. The third criterion differentiates between pairs of sentences like (6) and (8), in which there are no putative syntactic manifestations of conversational implicature, and pairs of sentences like (9) and (11), in which the contextual meaning is reflected in the syntactic properties of the construction.

The third criterion, while appearing to justify the claim that syntactic rules may make reference to conversational implicature, is in fact incompatible with the notion that the meanings in question are the result of conversational implicature, or of inference of any kind. Note that the application of a syntactic rule sensitive to conversational implicature can take place only if the sentence is interpreted as having the appropriate contextual import. There is, however, no inference possible in such cases, because the application of the rule allows only one reading of the sentence. To claim that these cases involve inference is equivalent to claiming that upon seeing Fred driving his red jeep I have inferred that Fred is driving his red jeep. If cases in which there is an immediate perception of meaning are grouped with cases in which a deduction has taken place, the distinction that motivated Grice's use of conversational principles in the first place will be lost. Thus, the conditions under which there is prima facie motivation for a syntactic rule that makes reference to conversational inference are just those conditions under which inference (in any nontrivial sense) is impossible.

I claim, then, that the relationship between syntax, logical structure, and conversational implicature is:

(34)   *A rule of grammar (transformation, derivational constraint, level constraint, and so forth) may refer to stages in the derivation of a sentence from logical structure to surface structure. A rule of grammar, however, has no access to the conversational entailments of logical structure.*

---

[13] Alternatively, it could be claimed that the literal sense of a sentence is a trivial case of conversational implicature, on a par with the rule of logic that every proposition entails itself. This alternative would seem unacceptable because it results in the loss of the distinction between inference and the immediate perception of meaning. This distinction provides the basis for the concept of conversational implicature in Grice's work. I shall discuss the need for this distinction in another context later.

Compare (34) with (35), which is intended to represent the position taken by Gordon and Lakoff:

(35)   *A rule of grammar may refer to stages in the derivation of a sentence from logical structure to surface structure. It may also refer to the conversational entailments of logical structure.*

I have shown that a serious attempt to provide criteria for the application of (35) in grammatical analysis leads to a contradiction.[14]

VIII. CONVERSATIONAL IMPLICATURE AND LANGUAGE CHANGE

I have shown that the syntactic properties of a construction reveal the underlying semantic structure of sentences that are instances of that construction, and that these properties do not reveal the conversational implicatures of the semantic structure. Synchronically, the relationship between (9) and (11) is not one of conversational implicature. Rather, it is similar to the relationship between (12) and (13): the relationship between an idiom and its meaning.[15] Diachronically, however, conversational implicature is almost certainly involved in the derivation of (9). What appears to have taken place is that the conversational implicatures of the literal *let's* construction have, by convention, been assimilated to the literal meaning of the lexical item. I shall refer to the process by which conversational meaning becomes literal meaning as the lexicalization of conversational meaning. This process would take place as a result of the frequent use of a construction to convey meanings not inherent in the logical structure of the sentences employing the construction. Speakers would tend to associate the sentences so used with the conversa-

[14] There is an additional reason to prefer (34) to (35). Evidence for the two being equal, a stronger hypothesis is of greater interest than a weaker one. This is because strong hypotheses are more readily falsifiable than weak ones. Hypothesis (34) is a stronger one than (35) because (34) supplies a decision procedure for determining when an aspect of the meaning of a sentence cannot have a conversational derivation: If an aspect of meaning is reflected in the syntactic properties of a sentence, then that meaning must be represented as part of the logical structure of the sentence. Hypothesis (35) provides no decision procedure. In order to falsify (34) is is necessary to find a case for which there is strong independent evidence favoring a Gricean analysis of a sentence, the relevant logical properties of which correlate with syntactic properties. I would claim that careful examination will show that there are not true counterexamples to (34).

[15] This was argued for earlier by Sadock (1972).

tionally implied meaning rather than with the literal meaning. In cases in which there is no syntactic evidence to the contrary, children would tend to reanalyze the logical form of these sentences in such a way as to eliminate the conflict between the conveyed meaning and the literal meaning of the sentences. Thus, the existence of a syntactic reflection of meaning would constitute evidence that lexicalization has taken place. So viewed, Gordon and Lakoff's position [i.e., (35)], though in error as synchronic analysis, is seen to reflect a previously unnoted principle of language change. Conversational implicature provides a historical explanation for the fact that certain sentences do not mean what a literal interpretation of the sentences would suggest. The syntactic properties of the sentences reveal that a change in underlying meaning has taken place. The error in Gordon and Lakoff's formulation is that it confuses synchrony and diachrony.

Besides having the virtue of providing a plausible explanation for the facts observed in Section VII, there is some additional evidence that lexicalized nonliteral *let's* sentences are derived historically from the conversational implicatures of literal *let's* sentences. In presenting data on nonliteral *let's*, I have ignored variation among speakers' responses. These differences, however, may indicate the nature of linguistic change. Labov (1963), inter alia, has shown that a linguistic change in process will often reveal itself in variation among speakers' responses. While I have not engaged in a rigorous variationalist study, the variation found in the responses of my informants suggests that, as I hypothesized earlier, a process of lexicalization is taking place with respect to nonliteral *let's*.

In a sample of about twelve informants I found three idiolectal groupings. Group I accepted such sentences as (36) as instances of nonliteral *let's*, but not (37) and (38). Group II accepted (36) and (37), but not (38). Group III accepted (36), (37), and (38):[16]

(36)   *Children, let's (try to) dress ourselves.*
           It's time to go out.

(37)   *Let's (try to) wash your own hands, boys.*

(38)   *Children, let's (try to) dress yourselves.*
           It's time to go out.

These responses may be summarized as follows:

---

[16] It may be of some interest that Group III was considerably larger than Group I or Group II.

(39)

	First-Person Reflexive	Second-Person Possessives + Own	Second-Person Reflexives
Group I	yes	no	no
Group II	yes	yes	no
Group III	yes	yes	yes

Group I would appear to be composed of speakers for whom lexicalization of nonliteral *let's* has not yet taken place. Group II would seem to be a transitional grouping, while in Group III nonliteral *let's* is apparently fully lexicalized.

In addition to the idiolectal variation just presented, there is another reason to believe that the lexicalization of nonliteral *let's* constitutes a historical change from the previous situation. Lexical splits are frequently characterized by a semantic differentiation between the two descendants of a single lexical unit. This appears to have taken place with respect to nonliteral *let's* in English. Informants who accept lexicalized nonliteral *let's* sentences [e.g., (9)] note a difference in the situations in which lexicalized nonliteral *let's* and unlexicalized nonliteral *let's* are appropriate. Sentence (36), an instance of unlexicalized nonliteral *let's*, was felt to be associated with parents, teachers, and nurses. The employment of the first-person plural by such speakers was taken as an indication of the patronizing relationship of these speakers to their addressees. Informants suggested that (4b), for example, provokes resentment on the part of the addressee because the speaker is pretending to share the situation of the addressee while in fact he does not.

In contrast to (36) and (4b), (37) and (38) were not felt to be patronizing on the part of the speaker.[17] This is predictable from the hypothesis that (37) and (38) have undergone lexicalization and, hence, are not the result of conversational implicature. The direct understanding of (37) and (38) does not require the pretense that the speaker shares the addressee's situation.

I have proposed that conversational implicature tends to become lexicalized as literal meaning, except when syntactic evidence conflicts with the results of conversational implicature. I argued that nonliteral *let's* is in the process of lexicalization. Individual variation exhibiting the stages of lexicalization was summarized in (39). In ad-

---

[17] This is not to suggest that the contexts for (37) and (38) are unmarked. These sentences seem particularly appropriate when the speaker is exasperated with the addressee.

dition, lexicalized nonliteral *let's* has lost the connotative properties associated with the conversational implicature necessary to relate literal *let's* sentences like (4b) and (36) and their meanings in context.

The process of lexicalization would seem to involve a number of stages. Prior to lexicalization, a sentence would be associated with a literal meaning, which, by means of principles of conversation, might be associated with a variety of contextual meanings.[18] During this period, the meaning of the whole sentence is a function of the meaning of the component parts (the lexical items) and of their hierarchical organization.

In the second stage, one of incipient lexicalization, although the speaker would remain aware of the literal import of the sentence (that is, the meaning of the whole as a function of its parts), a meaning different from the literal meaning would be associated with the sentence. The new, idiomatic meaning might at first be similar to the original literal meaning, but as time passed it might become more and more disassociated from the original, literal import. Typical of the second stage of lexicalization are lexicalized nonliteral *let's* sentences like (9) and idioms like (12).

In the final stage of lexicalization, there would be no consciousness of the original components of the sentence in question: in other words, the original literal meaning would be lost. Typical of the final phase of lexicalization are phrases like *good-bye*, which most speakers do not associate with its etymological meaning of:

(40)   *God be with you.*

It would appear probable that *good-bye* was derived from (40) by the process of lexicalization of conversational implicature just described.

IX. FACTORS LEADING TO THE LEXICALIZATION OF CONTEXTUAL MEANING

In the previous section, I sketched a theory of conversational implicature and linguistic change. My discussion was speculative, but, I believe, it provides the basis for an understanding of the role of conversational implicature in language. I would like to turn now to the question of why some contextual meanings are more likely to be lexicalized than others. My hypothesis is that there is a general

[18] That is, every surface structure is associated with a semantic structure, which, in turn, is associated by various inferential principles with a number of other logical structures.

tendency for language learners to assume that the conveyed meaning of a sentence reflects the logical structure of the sentence rather than the conversational entailments of logical structure. Such an assumption is falsified if the syntactic properties of a sentence clash with the hypothesized logical structure. In such a case, speakers retreat to the second possibility: that the meaning of the sentence in context is derived from the literal meaning by means of inferential principles such as Grice's Cooperative Principle. Hence, if a speaker, upon being exposed to sentences like (29), were to hypothesize a logical structure like that underlying (11), the fact that (29) behaves syntactically like a sentence with a first-person subject [see (30)–(33)] would falsify the hypothesis. The overt evidence for a first-person subject in literal *let's* sentences, however, is much weaker than in sentences like (29). For example, for many speakers of English (41) and (42) are grammatical but (43) is ungrammatical:

(41)   *Let's you and me go to the show tonight.*

(42)   a.   *Let's us go to the show tonight.*
        b.   *Let us consider the following possibilities.*

(43)   a.   **Let's you wash the dishes and me dry them.*
        b.   **Let us us consider the following possibilities.*

Literal *let's*, which means something like *I propose that S*, requires that the embedded sentence take a first-person plural subject. The fact that (41) and (42a) [in comparison to (43b)] are not felt to be redundant shows that *'s* no longer has the full force of the pronoun *us*.

Lexicalized nonliteral *let's* sentences provide confirmation that speakers do not consider the lexical item *let's* to be first-person plural. Although (9) is grammatical for many speakers with a second-person tag ending, (44) is not:

(44)   **Let's* $\begin{Bmatrix} us \\ you\ and\ me \end{Bmatrix}$ *get that work out before we lose*

        the client, $\begin{Bmatrix} will\ you? \\ why\ don't\ you? \end{Bmatrix}$

When an indication of first-person plurality occurs overtly in *let's* sentences, only literal *let's* may be understood. Therefore, my hypothesis predicts that the conveyed meaning of *let's* is highly susceptible to lexicalization and reanalysis, but the conveyed meaning of sentences like (29) is not.

X. A CROSS-LINGUISTIC PREDICTION

The hypothesis that conveyed meaning tends to be lexicalized except when there is strong syntactic counterevidence available to the language learner entails predictions about the extent to which constructions parallel to nonliteral *let's* are lexicalized in languages other than English. If there is overt evidence of first-person plurality, my hypothesis predicts that it is improbable that the contextual meaning will be lexicalized. I have compared *let's* constructions in English and Hebrew, and have found the relevant data to be consistent with my claim.

In modern Hebrew, the equivalent of literal *let's* has been extended to a range of situations similar to that of (4). There is no evidence, however, that this construction has undergone lexicalization. In Hebrew the literal meaning of *let's* is expressed by the imperative *bo* 'come,' followed by a verb in the first-person plural of the future. Thus, (45) would be expressed as (46):

(45)   *Let's eat, gang.*

(46)   *Bo nuxal xevre.*
              Come we will eat gang.

In a manner similar to English, *bo + first person plural future* can be extended to situations in which the speaker wishes the addressee to perform the action. Thus, a mother might coax her child to pick up his toys by saying:

(47)   *Bo naasof et hacacuim.*
              Come we will gather acc. def. part. the toys

Sentence (47) is perfectly felicitous if Mommy is in the kitchen washing the floor and she wants her child to have picked up the toys in the living room by the time she finishes in the kitchen. It is not necessary for the speaker to participate in picking up the toys.

There are a number of differences, however, between Hebrew and English. With the exception of tag question formation, the syntactic tests applied to English sentences in Section VI may be applied to Hebrew sentences. Consider the restrictions on reflexive pronouns. The sentences of (48) illustrate the fact that reflexive pronouns must agree with the subject of the clause:

(48)

a.   *Ani roxec et*
$$\left\{\begin{array}{l} acmi.^{19} \\ {}^{*}acmexa. \\ {}^{*}acmex. \\ {}^{*}acmo. \\ {}^{*}acma. \\ {}^{*}acmeno. \\ {}^{*}acmexem. \\ {}^{*}acmam. \end{array}\right\}$$

I wash acc. def. part.
$$\left\{\begin{array}{l} \text{myself} \\ {}^{*}\text{yourself (masc.)} \\ {}^{*}\text{yourself (fem.)} \\ {}^{*}\text{himself} \\ {}^{*}\text{herself} \\ {}^{*}\text{yourselves} \\ {}^{*}\text{themselves} \end{array}\right\}$$

b.   *ata roxec et*
$$\left\{\begin{array}{l} {}^{*}acmi. \\ acmexa. \\ {}^{*}acmex. \\ {}^{*}acmo. \\ {}^{*}acma. \\ {}^{*}acmenu. \\ {}^{*}acmexem. \\ {}^{*}acmam. \end{array}\right\}$$

you (masc. sing.) wash acc. def. part.
$$\left\{\begin{array}{l} {}^{*}\text{myself} \\ \text{yourself (masc.)} \\ {}^{*}\text{yourself (fem.)} \\ {}^{*}\text{himself} \\ {}^{*}\text{herself} \\ {}^{*}\text{ourselves} \\ {}^{*}\text{yourselves} \\ {}^{*}\text{themselves} \end{array}\right\}$$

c.   *At roxecet et*
$$\left\{\begin{array}{l} {}^{*}acmi. \\ {}^{*}acmexa. \\ acmex. \\ {}^{*}acmo. \\ {}^{*}acma. \\ {}^{*}acmenu. \\ {}^{*}acmexem. \\ {}^{*}acmam. \end{array}\right\}$$

[19] I shall ignore the pronominal forms *acmexen* 'yourselves (feminine)' and *acman* 'themselves (feminine)' and similar forms, the usage of which is declining.

$$\text{You wash acc. def. part.} \begin{cases} \text{*myself} \\ \text{*yourself (masc.)} \\ \text{yourself (fem.)} \\ \text{*himself} \\ \text{*ourselves} \\ \text{*yourselves} \\ \text{*themselves} \end{cases}$$

Examples of agreement between third-person masculine subjects and *acmo* 'himself,' third-person feminine subjects and *acma* 'herself,' first-person plural subjects and *acmenu* 'ourselves,' second-person plural subjects and *acmexem* 'yourselves,' and third-person plural subjects with *acmam* 'themselves' are omitted for the sake of brevity. The same pattern of agreement is found for all subjects and reflexive pronouns.

As in English, imperative sentences require a second-person reflexive pronoun. This is illustrated by:[20]

(49)
$$\begin{Bmatrix} \textit{Tirxac} \\ \textit{Rxac} \end{Bmatrix} \textit{et} \begin{cases} \textit{*acmi,} \\ \textit{acmexa,} \\ \textit{*acmex,} \\ \textit{*acmo,} \\ \textit{*acma,} \\ \textit{*acmenu,} \\ \textit{*acmexem,} \\ \textit{*acmam,} \end{cases} \textit{Yonatan.}$$

$$\begin{Bmatrix} \text{You (masc. sing.)} \\ \text{will wash} \\ \text{Wash} \end{Bmatrix} \text{acc. def. part.} \begin{cases} \text{*myself} \\ \text{yourself (masc.)} \\ \text{*yourself (fem.)} \\ \text{*himself} \\ \text{*herself} \\ \text{*ourselves} \\ \text{*yourselves} \\ \text{*themselves} \end{cases} \text{Jonathan}$$

'Wash yourself, Jonathan.'

In Hebrew, however, the sentence analogous to (21) is ungrammatical:

(50)   *Bo nirxac et acmexa, Yonatan.*
        Come we will wash acc. def. part. yourself Jonathan
        'Let's wash yourself, Jonathan.'

---

[20] The feminine singular of the imperative requires *acmex* 'yourself (feminine singular),' and the plural imperative requires *acmexem* 'yourselves,' as would be expected.

The same pattern is found in infinitival constructions parallel to (22). Although (51) is grammatical, (52) is not:

(51)   *Tenase lirxoc et acmexa, Yonatan.*
              you will try to wash acc. def. part. yourself
              (masc.) Jonathan
              'Try to wash yourself, Jonathan.'

(52)   *Bo nenase lirxoc et acmexa, Yonatan.*
              come we will try to wash acc. def. part.
              yourself (masc.) Jonathan
              'Let's try to wash yourself, Jonathan.'

Sentences (48)–(52), unlike the analogous English sentences, provide no evidence for the lexicalization of (the Hebrew equivalent of) nonliteral *let's* sentences.

The Hebrew reflexive pronoun is also employed in a fashion similar to English intensive *own*.[21] Compare (53) and (54):

(53)

$$\textit{Ani osef et hacacuim} \begin{cases} \textit{šeli} \\ \textit{šelxa} \\ \textit{šelax} \\ \textit{šelo} \\ \textit{šela} \\ \textit{šelanu} \\ \textit{šelaxem} \\ \textit{šelahem} \end{cases} \textit{bilvad.}^{22}$$

$$\text{I gather acc. def. part. the toys} \begin{cases} \text{of me} \\ \text{of you (masc. sing.)} \\ \text{of you (fem. sing.)} \\ \text{of him} \\ \text{of us} \\ \text{of you (pl.)} \\ \text{of them} \end{cases}$$

---

[21] The use of the reflexive pronoun in intensive possessive constructions like (54) is not accepted by all speakers of Hebrew. This 'error,' however, is heard with some frequency in the unaffected conversation of native speakers. Even those speakers who reject the construction (on normative grounds, I believe) agree that the sentences of (54) with asterisks are much less acceptable than those in which agreement takes place. For many speakers, these sentences are more acceptable when they are read with contrastive stress on the intensive possessive.

[22] Similar examples showing the compatibility of other subject pronouns with the full set of possessive pronouns have been omitted in order to conserve space.

'I pick up
$\begin{Bmatrix} \text{my} \\ \text{your (masc. sing.)} \\ \text{your (fem. sing.)} \\ \text{his} \\ \text{her} \\ \text{our} \\ \text{your (pl.)} \\ \text{their} \end{Bmatrix}$
toys.'

(54)

Ani osef et hacacuim šel
$\begin{Bmatrix} acmi \\ *acmexa \\ *acmex \\ *acmo \\ *acma \\ *acmenu \\ *acmexem \\ *acmam \end{Bmatrix}$
bilvad.[23]

I gather acc. def. part. the toys of
$\begin{Bmatrix} \text{myself} \\ *\text{yourself (masc.)} \\ *\text{yourself (fem.)} \\ *\text{himself} \\ *\text{herself} \\ *\text{ourselves} \\ *\text{yourselves} \\ *\text{themselves} \end{Bmatrix}$

'I pick up
$\begin{Bmatrix} \text{my} \\ *\text{your (masc.)} \\ *\text{your (fem.)} \\ *\text{his} \\ *\text{her} \\ *\text{our} \\ *\text{your (pl.)} \\ *\text{their} \end{Bmatrix}$
own toys.'

In the imperative, sentences with intensive *ecem* (the uninflected form of the intensive possessive) require second-person subjects. Compare (55) and (56):

[23] Similar examples showing the incompatibility of the intensive possessive with other subject pronouns with which it is not coreferential are omitted for brevity's sake.

(55)

$$\left\{\begin{array}{l} Taasof \\ Esof \end{array}\right\} \text{ et hacacuim} \left\{\begin{array}{l} šeli \\ šelxa \\ šelax \\ šelo \\ šela \\ šelanu \\ šelaxem \\ šelahem \end{array}\right\} \text{ bilvad, Eli.}$$

$$\left\{\begin{array}{l} \text{You will gather} \\ \text{Gather} \end{array}\right\} \begin{array}{l} \text{acc. def. part.} \\ \text{the toys} \end{array} \left\{\begin{array}{l} \text{of me} \\ \text{of you (masc. sing.)} \\ \text{of you (fem. sing.)} \\ \text{of him} \\ \text{of her} \\ \text{of us} \\ \text{of you (pl.)} \\ \text{of them} \end{array}\right\} \text{only, Eli}$$

$$\text{'Pick up only} \left\{\begin{array}{l} \text{my} \\ \text{your (masc. sing.)} \\ \text{your (fem. sing.)} \\ \text{his} \\ \text{her} \\ \text{our} \\ \text{your (pl.)} \\ \text{their} \end{array}\right\} \text{toys, Eli.'}$$

(56)

$$\left\{\begin{array}{l} Taasof \\ Esof \end{array}\right\} \text{ et hacacuim sel} \left\{\begin{array}{l} {}^*acmi \\ acmexa \\ {}^*acmex \\ {}^*acmo \\ {}^*acma \\ {}^*acmenu \\ {}^*acmexem \\ {}^*acmam \end{array}\right\} \text{ bilvad, Eli.}$$

$$\left\{\begin{array}{l} \text{You will gather} \\ \text{Gather} \end{array}\right\} \begin{array}{l} \text{acc. def. part.} \\ \text{the toys of} \end{array} \left\{\begin{array}{l} {}^*\text{myself,} \\ \text{yourself (masc.),} \\ {}^*\text{yourself (fem.),} \\ {}^*\text{himself (fem.),} \\ {}^*\text{herself,} \\ {}^*\text{ourselves,} \\ {}^*\text{yourselves,} \\ {}^*\text{themselves,} \end{array}\right\} \text{only, Eli}$$

$$
\text{'Pick up only} \left\{ \begin{array}{l} {}^{*}\text{my} \\ \text{your (masc.)} \\ {}^{*}\text{your (fem.)} \\ {}^{*}\text{his} \\ {}^{*}\text{her} \\ {}^{*}\text{our} \\ {}^{*}\text{your (pl.)} \\ {}^{*}\text{their} \end{array} \right\} \text{own toys, Eli.'}
$$

The equivalent of (55) may be conveyed by (57):

(57)   *Bo naasof et hacacuim šelxa, Eli.*
            Come we will gather acc. def. part. the toys
               of you Eli
            'Let's pick up your toys, Eli.'

But sentence (58), unlike such similar English sentences as (28b), is ungrammatical:

(58)   **Bo naasof et hacacuim šel acmexa, Eli.*
            Come we will gather acc. def. part. the toys
               of yourself Eli.
            'Let's pick up your own toys, Eli.'

The Hebrew data just presented contrast with the English data found in Section VI. Although *let's* constructions can be interpreted as imperatives in both languages, the Hebrew equivalent of nonliteral *let's* does not show the syntactic characteristics of imperatives. Thus, there is no reason to believe that *bo + first-person plural future* has been lexicalized.

Since *let's* sentences in Hebrew have none of the syntactic properties of sentences with second-person subjects, it might be supposed that the import of these sentences in context is the result of conversational implicature. That is, the literal and implied meanings of these sentences should be related by a process of deduction, as is the case with regard to (6) and (8). But this does not appear to be so. Sentences with *bo + first-person plural* do not satisfy the first of the three criteria for conversational implicature discussed in Section IV: They fail to manifest two levels of meaning in context.

This raises the question of whether the nonliteral import of a construction can become conventionalized without the lexicalization of the structure. It is of interest to note that the use of nonliteral *let's* sentences in Hebrew has been restricted to a limited number of contexts. The construction is found with particular frequency in the speech of kindergarten teachers and nurses. When used in appropriate contexts, the import of nonliteral *let's* sentences is immediately apprehended and is not, apparently, mediated by a chain of deduction. Thus, it would seem that the structure has undergone a process of cultural conventionalization without having undergone linguistic conventionalization (that is, lexicalization). It is notable that in Hebrew there is no attenuation of the first-person plurality of *bo + first-person plural future* similar to the phonological attenuation of *us* in English *let's*. The Hebrew first-person plural future is indicated morphologically by the prefix *n-*. This supports the hypothesis proposed in Section IX, that the lexicalization of contextual meaning tends to be blocked by overt reflections of the literal meaning. In Hebrew the overt presence of the first-person plural future morpheme appears to have prevented lexicalization, despite the fact that cultural conventionalization of conversational implicature seems to have taken place.

XI. SUMMARY OF CONCLUSIONS

The Gricean hypothesis that there are aspects of the meaning of sentences that are inferred by speakers from the logical structure of the sentences and the contexts in which the sentences are uttered explains a large body of problematic linguistic data. If principles of conversational implicature are to explain the body of data for which they were originally intended [e.g., (2)], however, they cannot be extended to sentences like (9), in which the meaning in context of a construction is reflected in the syntactic properties of the construction. This is because the presence of syntactic correlates of contextual meaning destroys the psychological reality of the literal, or context-free, meaning.

I have hypothesized that language learners assume the conveyed meaning of a sentence to be the logical structure of the sentence except when there is syntactic or morphological evidence to the contrary. In the case of English *let's* constructions, there is independent reason to believe that *'s* has lost the force of the pronoun *us* in indicating first-person plurality. This has allowed speakers to associate the morphological entity *let's* with a logical structure similar to *I propose that you*, in addition to the more usual association with a logical structure *I propose that we*. Sentences with *we should* in English, and the construction equivalent to *let's* in Hebrew, differ from English *let's* in that there is ample syntactic evidence against an underlying structure like *I propose that you*. As a result, only English *let's*, and not the equivalent construction in Hebrew, has been reanalyzed as second-person plural in logical structure, a fact that is now reflected in the syntax of sentences like (9).

XII. Appendix

It might be supposed that the principles governing conversational implicature are instances of universal principles governing human interaction, or, at least, are universal principles of linguistic discourse. It would follow from this supposition that the set of possible (unlexicalized) conversational implicatures for a given construction would not vary from language to language. This does not appear to be true. Although Yiddish and Swahili have constructions equivalent to literal *let's*, these constructions cannot be used with the illocutionary force of imperatives. Consider the following data from Swahili:

(59)   *Twende nyumbani.*
                     'Let's go home.'
(60)   *Nenda nyumbani.*
                     'Go home.'
(61)   *Uende nyumbani.*
                     'You go home.'

Sentence (59) is appropriate only if the action of going home is to be participated in by both the speaker and the addressee. Thus, (59) could not be used by a parent who wishes his child to go home but does not plan to go home himself. Rather, (60) or (61) must be employed. But, as I showed previously, the English sentence (62) could be used without implying the speaker's participation. Sentence (62) might be used by a school janitor to persuade diligent members of an athletic team to leave the gymnasium and thereby allow him to clean it:

(62)   *Come on. Let's go home already, kids. I have to stay
         and clean this place up for the game tomorrow.*

Such a use of the equivalent to *let's* is not possible in Swahili. Similarly, (63) is a possible sentence of Swahili only if the literal meaning is intended:

(63)   *Tule mtoto mzumi.*
                     'Let's be a good boy.'

Sentence (63) can only be taken as a proposal that the speaker and the addressee jointly be a good boy (e.g., as part of a game that they are playing). It cannot be used as an admonition by the speaker that the addressee be a good boy.

In Yiddish there are a variety of nonliteral uses of forms of the first-person plural. Sentences (64) and (65) can have the force of admonitions. The most natural way to render these sentences in English would seem to be (66) and (67), rather than (68) and (69):

(64)   *Az mir wel ə rebe zayen, məz mir lernen.*
        if we will a rabbi be must we learn

(65)   *Mir məz hant in moyl ništ arayn legen.*
        we must hand in mouth not into place

(66)   *If* $\begin{Bmatrix} you\ want \\ one\ wants \end{Bmatrix}$ *to be a rabbi,* $\begin{Bmatrix} you\ have \\ one\ has \end{Bmatrix}$ *to study.*

(67) $\begin{Bmatrix} You \\ One \end{Bmatrix}$ *mustn't put* $\begin{Bmatrix} your \\ one's \end{Bmatrix}$ *hand in* $\begin{Bmatrix} your \\ one's \end{Bmatrix}$ *mouth.*

(68)   *If we want to be a rabbi, we have to study.*

(69)   *We mustn't put our hand in our mouth.*

The use of *mir* 'we' in (64) and (65) seems to correspond to the generic *you* of:

(70)   *Speaker A: If you spend too much time at*
                         Treno's you'll get brain rot.
            Speaker B: You sure will.

Thus, Yiddish allows the use of the first-person plural in a nonliteral sense. However, a *let's* construction cannot be used as an imperative. Compare (71), (72), and (73):

(71)   *Let's quit fooling around.*

(72)   *Fatik mit də špilin.*
                finished with the playing

(73)   *Ləz mir zayn fatik mit də špilin.*
                let us be finished with the playing

Sentence (73) cannot be understood as:

(74)   *Let's quit fooling around, will you?*

Only literal *let's* can be intended. However, (75) is fully grammatical and is equivalent to (76):

(75)   *Ləz mir gayn špatsiren.*
                    let us go strolling

(76)   *Let's go for a stroll.*

I have shown that in both Swahili and Yiddish constructions analogous to those with nonliteral *let's* in English are ungrammatical. It would appear from these data that the principles governing conversational implicature are culture specific.

ACKNOWLEDGMENTS

I should like to thank Bruce Fraser, Georgia Green, Malcah Jaeger, Stephanie Kaylin, Charles W. Kisseberth, George Lakoff, Jerry Morgan, Jerry Sadock, Susan Schmerling, and Richard Wright for their comments on various earlier versions of this chapter. I also appreciate the patience and acumen of my informants: Rina Gal-Shapira, Chanah Gorzynski, Vered Nachson, Avraham Ziv, and Yael Ziv (Hebrew); Raphael Nyiti (Swahili); and Pauline Kaylin and Samuel O. Kaylin (Yiddish). The reader should note that the Yiddish data, although an accurate report of my informants' speech, may not be typical of Yiddish in general, since my informants were raised in the United States. This would have no effect on the theoretical claims I have made.

This chapter is the linear descendant of an earlier paper (Cole, 1974). Although I have made free use of certain sections of that work, little has been adopted unchanged. Many of the theoretical claims made in the earlier paper have been modified radically here. Of particular importance is the clarification of the diachronic and synchronic status of conversational implicature, which is the theme of the present work.

This research was funded in part by grants from the National Endowment for the Humanities and the University of Illinois Research Board. Their help is gratefully acknowledged.

REFERENCES

Cole, P. Conversational implicature and syntactic rules. In *Towards tomorrow's linguistics.* Washington, D. C.: Georgetown University Press, 1974.

Labov, W. The social motivation of a sound change. *Word,* 1963, **19,** 273–309.

Lakoff, G. On generative semantics. In *Semantics: An interdisciplinary reader in philosophy, linguistics and psychology.* New York and London: Cambridge University Press, 1971.

Lakoff, R. *Abstract syntax and Latin complementation.* Cambridge, Mass.: MIT Press, 1968.

Lees, R. B., and Klima, E. S. Rules for English pronominalization. *Language,* 1963, **39,** 17–28.

Perlmutter, D. M. *Deep and surface constraints in syntax.* Ph.D. dissertation, MIT, Cambridge, Mass., 1968.

Ross, J. R. On declarative sentences. In *Readings in English transformational grammar.* Waltham, Mass.: Ginn, 1970.

Sadock, J. M. Hypersentences. *Papers in Linguistics,* 1969, **1,** 283–370.

Sadock, J. M. Speech act idioms. In P. M. Peranteau, J. M. Levi, and C. G. Phares (Eds.), *Papers from the eighth regional meeting of the Chicago Linguistic Society.* Chicago: University of Chicago Department of Linguistics, 1972.

SOME INTERACTIONS OF SYNTAX AND PRAGMATICS

J. L. MORGAN
University of Illinois

Suppose that among those factors that make up competence at language one can isolate two distinct subsystems: a syntacticosemantic component, as in the work of Chomsky and others,[1] and a pragmatic component[2] of the sort discussed by Grice (chapter 2 of this volume) and work inspired by Grice's observations — Gordon and Lakoff (chapter 4 of this volume), for example. Then we might say that the former has to do with the relation between meaning[3] and (syntactic) form of sentences, and the latter with how to use a language — how to get things done by verbal means. More specifically, we might conceive of a syntacticosemantic derivation as a mapping between a logical structure and a surface structure, in the usual sense of these terms, the syntacticosemantic component then consisting of principles that define the set of well-formed derivations for the language at hand. And we might conceive of the pragmatic component as some set of principles or strategies for arriving at inferences about the in-

---

[1] The question of whether this component involves a discrete intermediate level of 'deep structure' or not — the interpretive versus generative semantics controversy — has no bearing on what I have to say, as far as I can see.

[2] By using the phrase 'pragmatic component,' I do not mean to take the position that pragmatic 'competence' is a purely linguistic matter.

[3] In this chapter, I will use the word *meaning* in the somewhat restricted sense of 'logical structure' as this notion is defined in the works of the so-called generative semanticists.

289

tentions one's interlocutor has in saying what he says, or, put the other way round, for selecting what one says in a way such that one can feel fairly confident that the interlocutor will recognize one's intentions, these principles or strategies perhaps being, as Grice proposes, particular manifestations of more general principles of cooperation.

Now I think that what I have sketched is not an entirely unreasonable view of things; or, at least, it is not an entirely uncommon view.

Then, following common sense, one is plausibly led to two subsidiary conclusions. The first of these is that these two components — the syntacticosemantic and the pragmatic — are relatively free of interaction. Viewed from the pragmatics side, this amounts to saying that principles of pragmatics have to do with the content ('logical structure,' 'semantic representation,' and so forth) of sentences, and are independent of the form ('surface structure,' 'grammatical structure,' and so forth) of sentences, except where form itself becomes an issue in the conversation, as it does in Grice's hypothetical circumlocution for the verb *sing*, his discussion of the exploitation of ambiguity, and so forth. So I think it is a priori perfectly reasonable to expect that matters bearing on what we might call the 'applicability' of pragmatic principles will be traceable to some aspect or aspects of logical structure and context, and not, say, to the number of syllables in the main verb, or to whether or not the rule of particle movement has applied in the derivation of the sentence, or to structural properties of the superficial form of the sentence, like constituency, command, islandhood, and so forth. We might without too much trepidation consider this sort of pragmatics to be 'grammar free.'

The second plausible conclusion common sense might lead to, at least as common sense occurs among linguists, is that the syntacticosemantic component is regular in such a way that it might be described as 'pragmatically transparent,' that is, that the principles involved in the derivation — the mapping between logical structure and surface structure — do not have the effect of obscuring properties having crucial pragmatic consequences — for example, that derivational principles do not have the effect of neutralizing regular correspondences between grammatical form and illocutionary force. Let me give some examples of what I mean by neutralization in order to make matters clearer. It is a fact that sentences having superficial grammatical properties usually associated with genuine questions can often be used with the pragmatic effect of negative assertions. In saying (1), I might well have in mind to convey what (2) conveys; or in saying (3), it might be my intention to convey what (4) conveys:

(1)   *Would I lie to you?*
(2)   *I wouldn't lie to you.*
(3)   *Who can make any sense of what the*
                          President does?
(4)   *Nobody can make any sense of what*
                          the President does.

There is nothing I know of that would IN PRINCIPLE prevent one from claiming that this is a case of neutralization, that is, that the logical structure of (1) is in fact identical to that of (2); that the logical structure of (3) is the same as that of (4); and that there are rules in the grammar of English that have the effect of assigning a superficial structure usually associated with questions to a logical structure not that of a question, thus neutralizing the difference in grammatical form that corresponds to the difference between a question and an assertion.

One can see a similar case in sentences like (5), which might be used with roughly the import of (6) or of (7):

(5)   *Doctor Jones thinks water is carcinogenic.*
(6)   *Water is carcinogenic, or at least that is*
                          Doctor Jones' opinion.
(7)   *Among the things Doctor Jones thinks is*
                          that water is carcinogenic.

Thus, in context, one might use (5) in the sense of (6) as a reply to (8), or in the sense of (7) as a reply to (9):

(8)   *Tell me something that's carcinogenic.*
(9)   *Why do you think Doctor Jones is a quack?*

One might hypothesize for this case, as for the previous one, a neutralization analysis, wherein (5) is claimed to be ambiguous, so that the rules of the syntacticosemantic component associate with the surface structure of (5) two distinct logical structures, to capture the two senses of (6) and (7). But I think many linguists, perhaps most, would be tempted to reject out of hand analyses of the sort I have sketched, on the grounds that they have no initial plausibility, that language just does not work in such a devious fashion, or at least ought not to be considered to work in such a fashion except in the face of overwhelming evidence. Taking this position seems especially reasonable, since for the cases I have discussed one can see the outlines of a treatment in pragmatic terms, as an alternative to the neutralization analyses. The latter strike one as somehow ugly and implausible; the possibility of an intuitive and natural pragmatic solution is doubly appealing insofar as it eliminates the ugliness of the neutralization analyses. One might then take this general stance to its extreme, and adopt the position that there are in fact no genuine cases of neutralization of the correspondence between illocutionary force and grammatical form—that grammar is in fact 'pragmatically transparent.'

Let me sum up: I have sketched a plausible approach to studying language as a communication system, in which approach one can isolate two distinct systems—a pragmatic component and a syntacticosemantic component. Further, I have pointed out two accompanying assumptions one might reasonably want to make: first, that the pragmatic component has to do with what we mean, and what we mean to imply, when we converse, and as such is 'grammar free' in that none of the principles involved depends on (or is sensitive to) the operation of syntactic rules or matters of superficial grammatical form; second, that the syntacticosemantic component is 'pragmatically transparent' in that grammatical principles that define syntactic derivations do not operate to systematically neutralize regular correspondences between superficial form and illocutionary force.

Now, I am sure that there are many linguists who subscribe to at least one of these assumptions. No doubt there are some who hold both; at any rate, it seems to me not unreasonable in any obvious way to hold both. But my purpose, what I intend to do in the rest of this chapter, is to show that the facts of English are such that one cannot simultaneously maintain both of these assumptions—one of them must go. Either grammar—the principles that relate logical structure and superficial form—is not pragmatically transparent, or the principles of the pragmatic component are not grammar-free. I propose to demonstrate my point by presenting cases that, so far as I can see, can be accounted for only by abandoning one of the two assumptions. In particular, I shall present cases in which one is forced to choose between a derivational treatment that is not pragmatically transparent, and a pragmatic treatment that is not grammar-free.

There has been a considerable amount of research on formal syntactic properties. Among the most important is John Ross's monumental work *Constraints on variables in syntax*. Ross shows that there are certain types of structural configurations ('islands'), defined in terms of category labels and tree shape, which have important properties relative to certain grammatical rules: 'chopping rules.' Roughly, no constituent can be removed from an island by any rule containing an essential variable in its structural description. Islandhood is defined, in part, by the following (simplified) conditions, with the relevant element in the illustrations set in bold type.

A. THE COORDINATE STRUCTURE CONSTRAINT: *No element may be chopped from a conjoined constituent:*

(10)   a.   *John likes ice cream and cake.*
          b.   **What does John like ice cream and?*
          c.   **This is the cake which John likes ice cream and.*

B. THE COMPLEX NP CONSTRAINT. *No element may be chopped from a relative clause:*

(11)   a.   *The man who shot the plumber may be an agent.*
          b.   **Who may the man who shot be an agent?*
          c.   **This is the plumber who the man who shot may be an agent.*

C. THE SENTENTIAL SUBJECT CONSTRAINT: *No element may be chopped from a sentence that is itself in subject position in a higher sentence:*

(12)   a.   *That the plumber ate the tadpoles annoyed Harry.*
          b.   **What did that the plumber ate annoy Harry?*
          c.   **These are the tadpoles which that the plumber ate annoyed Harry.*

Notice that if the sentential subject is moved out of subject position by the optional rule of extraposition, the sentence corresponding to the (b) and (c) versions of (12) are well-formed:

(13)   a.   *It annoyed Harry that the plumber ate the tadpoles.*
          b.   *What did it annoy Harry that the plumber ate?*
          c.   *These are the tadpoles which it annoyed Harry that the plumber ate.*

There is more to Ross's work than this, but this much will suffice for my purposes. At the risk of belaboring the obvious, let me point out that these constraints are seen as purely formal constraints on the operation of syntactic rules.

Now I will take up some cases in which Ross constraints play a role counter to one's expectations and counter to Ross's formulation of them as constraints on chopping rules. What is important about these cases is that they lead to the dilemma I described, wherein one is faced with a choice between a derivational analysis that is not pragmatically transparent and a pragmatic analysis that is sensitive to superficial grammatical properties.

There are three cases in which Ross constraints show up in surprising ways: sentence fragments, interjections, and certain non-direct replies.

The case with fragments is this: Not all syntactically well-formed utterances are sentences. Some replies are single words, as in (15), (17), and (19):

(14)   *What does Trick eat for breakfast?*
(15)   *Bananas.*
(16)   *Did Nixon go to Florida?*
(17)   *No, China.*
(18)   *Henry just left with somebody.*
(19)   *Who?   (that is, who did he leave with?)*

These obviously have the conversational import of sentences. But what is their underlying structure? One is tempted here to appeal to a pragmatic analysis, claiming that the logical structure of *bananas* in example (15) is just 'bananas,' since it is obvious that the import of any given utterance of (15) will depend on the context in which it is uttered, and matters depending crucially on context for interpretation seem natural candidates for pragmatic treatments. Moreover, the problem of defining what constitutes a possible reply is one that seems to deserve an account in terms of rules of conversation. But, quite unexpectedly, Ross constraints bear on this problem. One can reply to an utterance U either with a full sentence like (20) or with a fragment like (15):

(20)   *He eats bananas for breakfast.*

But (15) cannot be used as a reply if the corresponding sequence in U is in an island; in such cases, only a larger construction can be used. This is illustrated in the following examples, where the single-word (b) replies are ill-formed as replies to the respective (a) sentences; that is, the (b) fragments are not interchangeable with the full-sentence (c) versions:[4]

---

[4] Mysteriously, acceptability increases if the corresponding sequence in U is near the end of the sentence. Thus, (v) as a reply to (iv) is better than (ii) as a reply to (i), where these replies are to be understood in the sense of the full sentences that follow them [(iii) and (vi), respectively]:

(i)   *Did the man leave town who Tricia fired?*
(ii)   ?*No, Thelma.*
(iii)   *No, the man left town who Thelma fired.*
(iv)   *Did the man leave town who fired Tricia?*
(v)   ?*No, Thelma.*
(vi)   *No, the man left town who fired Thelma.*

Notice that both are more acceptable than (24b) as a reply to (24a). For a fuller treatment of fragments, see Morgan (1973).

(21) a. *John and somebody were dancing a moment ago.*
      b. **Who?*
      c. *Who was he dancing with?*

(22) a. *A man who shot somebody just ran out the door.*
      b. **Who?*
      c. *Who did he shoot?*

(23) a. *Did Harry's talking to Martha annoy Harriet?*
      b. **No, Thelma.*
      c. *No, his talking to Thelma annoyed Harriet.*

(24) a. *Did the man who Tricia fired leave town?*
      b. **No, Thelma.*
      c. *No, the man who Thelma fired (left town).*

Then either the attempt at a pragmatic account of these cases must be given up, or rules of conversation must somehow be sensitive to Ross constraints, which supposedly have to do with purely formal properties of syntactic rules or derivations.[5]

A second case involving Ross constraints, discussed first by James (1972), has to do with interjections of surprise, like *ah* in (25), in which the speaker is expressing his surprise at the content of the accompanying sentence:

(25)   *Ah, Kissinger is a vegetarian.*

But James points out that cases like (26) are ambiguous:

(26)   *Ah, it's been announced in the Times that*
                Kissinger is a vegetarian.

That is, one can use (26) either to express surprise that Kissinger is a vegetarian, when the speaker is not necessarily surprised that that fact appeared in the *Times,* or to express surprise that the fact was announced in the *Times,* when the speaker may already have known Kissinger's dietary habits. The problem here is this: How is the

---

[5] There is another possibility, of course. This is that matters of islandhood are not in fact purely formal properties of syntactic rules and/or derivations, but are pragmatic in origin. For example, it is possible that an understanding of the communicative function of relative clauses and of chopping rules will show that questioning an element in a relative clause is pragmatically incoherent. An illustrative analogue: Given that the function of restrictive relatives is to describe a referent so that one's interlocutor is able to isolate in his mind just who it is one is talking about, then it makes no practical sense to attempt such a description by asking a question about the referent. Accordingly, we need not give a syntactic account for the fact that questions cannot occur as restrictive relatives, as in:

(i)   **The man who where was he born called today.*

apparent ambiguity of (26) to be captured? Shall we claim that (26) has two distinct logical structures, and that the rules of English neutralize this difference, or shall we say that (26) has just one logical structure, with rules of conversation accounting for the fact that (26) can be used for either of two quite different conversational intents? Again one is, I think, tempted to choose a pragmatic approach. But again formal syntactic properties are apparently crucial, for, as James points out, this sort of construction cannot be used to express surprise at a sequence that is in an island. Thus, (27) and (28) are unambiguous and cannot be used, as (26) can, to express surprise at the idea that Kissinger is a vegetarian.

(27)   *Ah, a man who says that Kissinger is a vegetarian just came in the door.*

(28)   *Ah, that Kissinger is a vegetarian has been announced in the Times.*

Similarly, (29) can be used only to express surprise at BOTH conjuncts, not just one of them:

(29)   *Ah, Nixon is in Moscow and Kissinger is a vegetarian.*

Compare this with the fact that, as Ross points out, constituents can be chopped out of conjoined structures if they are chopped out of both conjuncts (not just one):[6]

(30)   a.   *This is the house that John built and Harry bought.*
       b. * *This is the house that John built and Harry died.*

There is also a class of exceptions to the Coordinate Structure Constraint discussed by Ross. An example of this class is (31), in which it is understood that the two acts described are somehow closely connected; in this sense, (32) is well-formed, even though the constituent *the ouzo* had been in a conjunct:

(31)   *I went to the store and bought some ouzo.*

(32)   *This is the ouzo which I went to the store and bought.*

---

[6] Furthermore, as in the case of fragments, the effects of violating Ross constraints are mitigated if the constituent in question is near the end of the sentence; the following sentence is more likely than (27) to be used to express surprise at Kissinger's diet (cf. footnote 4):

(i)   * *Ah, a man just came in the door who says that Kissinger is a vegetarian.*

Just so, in such cases one can express surprise at a single conjunct; thus, (33) can be used to express surprise at John's buying ouzo, even though the speaker is aware that John's going to the store is a common occurrence:

(33)   *Ah, John went to the store and bought some ouzo.*

The choice is either to abandon the pragmatic analysis in favor of a derivational one, assigning sentences like (26) two logical structures and hoping to find a way of accounting for the effects of Ross constraints in terms of chopping rules, or to attempt a pragmatic analysis, with rules of conversation sensitive not only to meaning per se but also to structural properties of superficial sentence form.

There are similar data, probably related to the phenomena James discusses, in certain kinds of nondirect replies, exemplified in (35) and (37a):

(34)   *When is it going to rain?*

(35)   *It says in the Times that it's going to*
          rain on Thursday.

(36)   *Why was Angela arrested?*

(37)   a.   *It says in the Times that she bought*
                some guns.
          b.   *≠ Because it says in the Times that she*
                bought some guns.
          c.   *≠ It says in the Times that she was arrested*
                because she bought some guns.

Notice that example (35) could be a reply either to (34) or to (38):

(38)   *What does it say in the Times?*

Notice, also, that (37a) can be asserted as a reply to (36), even if (37b) and (37c) are both false. I take this as evidence that (37a) is truly a nondirect reply, rather than an elliptical version of (37b) or (37c). The conversational import of, for example, (35) as a reply to (34) seems to be roughly as follows:

(39)   *I don't know the answer to your question, but you*
          might consider the fact that the Times says it will
          rain on Thursday, and consider concluding from that
          fact that it will indeed rain on Thursday.

In the same way, the import of (37a) as a reply to (36) seems to be as follows:

(40)   *I don't know the answer to your question, but you might consider the fact that the Times says that she bought some guns, consider concluding from that fact that she bought some guns, and consider concluding that that was the reason she was arrested.*

These cases are obvious candidates for a pragmatic analysis. But again Ross constraints show up. The (a) examples of (41)–(43) differ from their (b) counterparts in that the former are much more likely than the latter to be used as replies to (36) with the import of, mutatis mutandis, (40). If the (b) examples are at all acceptable as replies, they are several degrees more indirect than the respective (a) examples:

(41)   a.   *It was reported in the Times that she bought some guns.*
       b.   *That she bought some guns was reported in the Times.*

(42)   a.   *The man who lives next door thinks she bought some guns.*
       b.   *The man who thinks she bought some guns lives next door.*

(43)   a.   *The Times says she bought some guns.*
       b.   *The Times says she bought some guns and that it's going to rain.*

And just as constituents can be chopped from both conjuncts of a coordinate structure but not, generally, from just one, (44) is an acceptable reply if what is intended is that one should consider both conjuncts (separately or jointly) as leading to a possible explanation for Angela's arrest:

(44)   *The Times says she bought some guns and Newsweek says she's a communist.*

Finally, just as conjoined structures like (31) are exceptions to the Coordinate Structure Constraint in that a constituent can be chopped from a single conjunct, so (45) can be understood to suggest that the mere purchase of guns led to Angela's arrest; going to a store is not yet a criminal offense:

(45)   *The Times says she went to a store and*
                 bought some guns.

Again the same choice: to attempt a derivational solution — claiming
that (37a), for example, has two distinct logical structures, one when
it is a direct reply, the other when it is a nondirect reply — or to go for
a pragmatic account, with rules of conversation somehow sensitive to
syntactic islandhood.

A final case involving Ross constraints: There is a class of conjoined structures alluded to earlier, pointed out by Ross and studied
in greater detail by Schmerling (chapter 8 of this volume) that are exceptions to the Coordinate Structure Constraint. The cases have a
common property: Although they contain only the word *and*, more is
conveyed than merely that both conjuncts are true. In most cases, it
is at least temporal order, but often there is more than that. In (46),
only order seems to be involved. In (47), there is also the connection
that it was at Gino's that I bought the raki. In (48), Spiro told a joke
and *thereby* infuriated Paul:

(46)   *John got up and tripped over a skate.*
(47)   *I went to Gino's and bought some raki.*
(48)   *Spiro told a joke and infuriated Paul.*

Each of these sentences can be used in two ways: when all that is intended is that both conjuncts are true, or when what is intended is
that both are true and that there are some connections between the
conjuncts. Thus, (47) could be used to convey a report of two separate things I did, or it could be used to report two connected acts.

Then one might propose that the logical structure for both senses
is the same, with the conveyed connections not part of logical structure but inferred in context by rules of conversation. But Ross constraints distinguish the two senses. When no connection is intended,
the Coordinate Structure Constraint holds; when the connections are
intended, the Coordinate Structure Constraint can be violated with
impunity. Thus, (49)–(51) can be understood only in their respective
connected senses:

(49)   *This is the skate that John got up and tripped over.*
(50)   *Where's the raki I went to Gino's and bought?*
(51)   *That's the joke Spiro told and infuriated Paul.*

In all these cases we find roughly the same situation: a choice
between a derivational solution and a pragmatic solution. In each

case we must give up either the assumption that rules of conversation are grammar free or the assumption that grammar is pragmatically transparent in the way I outlined earlier.

Ross constraints are not the only area in which formal syntactic properties appear to interact with pragmatic ones. The application of apparently optional syntactic rules can have pragmatic consequences. A case of this can be found in certain uses of comparatives and similes in English. In these constructions the second occurrence of a verb may optionally be replaced by the pro-verb *do*, or deleted:

(52)   a. *John is taller than Bill is.*
        b. *John is taller than Bill.*

(53)   a. *John has more money than Bill has.*
        b. *John has more money than Bill does.*
        c. *John has more money than Bill.*

(54)   a. *John runs faster than Bill runs.*
        b. *John runs faster than Bill does.*
        c. *John runs faster than Bill.*

(55)   a. *John talks as much as Martha talks.*
        b. *John talks as much as Martha does.*
        c. *John talks as much as Martha.*

(56)   a. *John walks like his father walks.*
        b. *John walks like his father does.*
        c. *John walks like his father.*

But comparative and similes have, in addition to their literal sense, a use as conventionalized hyperbole, in which the speaker is understood not as lying but as merely making a transparent exaggeration, as in the following:

(57)   *Mary is bigger than a house.*
(58)   *Wilt is as tall as the Empire State Building.*
(59)   *Harry has more money than the Bank of America.*
(60)   *Ralph is as old as Methuselah.*
(61)   *John runs as fast as a deer.*
(62)   *Royal drinks like a fish.*
(63)   *Hans leaps like a gazelle.*

Notice, though, that in these cases the second occurrence of the verb cannot remain; (64)–(70) can be understood only as literal statements, not as exaggerations:

(64)	*Mary is bigger than a house is.*
(65)	*Wilt is as big as the Empire State* *Building is.*
(66)	*Harry has more money than the Bank* *of America has.*
(67)	*Ralph is as old as Methuselah is/was.*
(68)	*John runs as fast as a deer runs.*
(69)	*Royal drinks like a fish drinks.*
(70)	*Hans leaps like a gazelle leaps.*

Again, there are two directions for an explanation. We can take a pragmatic approach, and claim that exaggeration and literal comparatives like (57) and (64) have the same logical structure. The conversational rule determining the hyperbolic interpretation is then sensitive to the application of the syntactic rule of comparative reduction. Or we can take a derivational approach, in which literal and exaggeration comparatives differ in logical structure and, thus, in derivational properties, but the underlying differences are neutralized by the operation of (unknown) syntactic rules.

A similar case arises in regard to a syntactic truncation rule found in colloquial speech, as discussed by Schmerling (1973) and Thrasher (1973). This is the rule that deletes certain left-most elements of sentences, as in (72) as a variant of (71):

| (71) | *Have you seen John lately?* |
| (72) | *Seen John lately?* |

In some constructions, the verb *have* can be deleted as well, as in (74) as a variant of (73):

| (73) | *Do you have any idea where the bathroom is?* |
| (74) | *Any idea where the bathroom is?* |

But there is a pragmatic effect to this rule beyond the obvious difference in style it carries. Notice that the full version of a sentence like (75) can be used in two distinct ways: It could be used in the sense of (76a), (76b), or (76c):

(75)   *Do you have any idea how much that vase*
       was worth?

(76)   a. *Is it the case that you have knowledge of*
        the value of that vase?
    b. *Please tell me how much that vase was worth.*
    c. *You have no idea how much that vase was worth.*

This last sense is clearly present when Mrs. Portnoy says to young Portnoy:

(77)   *Do you have any idea how much I've
                   sacrificed for you?*

Now, notice that the application of the truncation rule distinguishes among these senses. Mrs. Portnoy would not say (78) as a reproach, but only as a question; and (79) is interpretable only as a question, not as a prediction:

(78)   *Any idea how much I've sacrificed for you?*

(79)   *Any idea how bad things will be if he's
                   reelected?*

Then if we say that it is through a rule of conversation that we can understand a sentence like (77) as a sort of assertion (I do not mean that it is an assertion in the strict sense, but only that it has the effect of one), then we must also say that that rule of conversation is in some way conditioned by the application of the truncation rule. On the other hand, if we say that (77) is indeed derivationally ambiguous—that it is associated with two or more distinct logical structures that converge on the same surface structure, then we must acknowledge that grammar need not be pragmatically transparent—that regular correspondences between illocutionary force and grammatical form can be neutralized by syntactic rules.

Hopefully, by now I have established my point, that one of the two assumptions must be given up. Unfortunately, I can say nothing about which of them has to be abandoned, especially in view of the sorry state of affairs discussed by Sadock (chapter 14 of this volume) in regard to what counts as evidence in linguistic studies of such matters. The line between semantics and syntax, on the one hand, and pragmatics, on the other, needs closer scrutiny than it has yet been given. The apparent interactions are especially disturbing in that apparently optional syntactic rules turn out to have pragmatic consequences in quite unexpected ways, counter to the common expectation that many of these rules (truncation, comparative reduction, extraposition, and so forth) will eventually be shown to have origin in matters of perceptual strategies and sentence processing. There is more here than meets the eye.

REFERENCES

James, D. Some aspects of the syntax and semantics of interjections. In P. M. Peranteau, J. M. Levi, and G. C. Phares (Eds.), *Papers from the eighth regional meeting of the Chicago Linguistic Society.* Chicago: University of Chicago Department of Linguistics, 1972.

Morgan, J. L. Sentence fragments and the notion sentence. In B. B. Kachru *et al.* (Eds.), Issues in linguistics: Papers in linguistics in honor of Henry and Renée Kahane. Urbana: University of Illinois Press, 1973.

Ross, J. R. Constraints on variables in syntax. Ph.D. dissertation, MIT, Cambridge, Mass., 1967.

Schmerling, S. Subjectless sentences and the notion of surface structure. In C. Corum, T. C. Smith–Stark, and A. Weiser (Eds.), *Papers from the ninth regional meeting of the Chicago Linguistic Society.* Chicago: University of Chicago Department of Linguistics, 1973.

Thrasher, R. A conspiracy on the far left. *University of Michigan Papers in Linguistics,* 1973, 1 (2).

'MEANING'

RICHARD T. GARNER
The Ohio State University

THE REJECTION OF MEANINGS

Many philosophers interested in language have come to hold in common the belief that expressions like:

(1)   *the meaning of a word*
           the meaning of the word 'muggy'
           what a word means
           what the word 'muggy' means

do not function as referring expressions. According to Alston (1963b:84), "phrases of the form 'the meaning of E' do not have the function of referring to anything at all, or, to put the point in a perhaps misleading way, . . . there are, in point of logic, no such things as meanings." (Cf. also Austin, 1940; Wittgenstein, 1958; Ayer, 1940, especially pp. 92 ff.; Ryle, 1931–32, 1957, 1961; and Quine, 1948, 1951.) The standard argument goes like this: If there were such things as meanings, we could refer to them by using expressions like 'the meaning of E'. In that case, whenever we uttered a sentence like:

(2)   *The meaning of 'procrastinate' is the same*
          as the meaning of 'put things off'.

305

we would be saying that the thing that is the meaning of 'procrastinate' is identical with the thing that is the meaning of 'put things off',
i.e.:

(3)   *The meaning of 'procrastinate' = the meaning*
             of 'put things off'.

Then, by a commonly accepted principle of logic, it would follow
that anything said about the meaning of 'procrastinate' could also be
said about the meaning of 'put things off', and vice versa, without a
change in truth value.[1] But:

(4)   *John taught Yoko the meaning of 'put things off'.*

could be true and yet:

(5)   *John taught Yoko the meaning of 'procrastinate'.*

could easily be false.

Often meaning theorists attempt to identify the meaning of an
expression with what that expression refers to, with a concept or an
idea, or with some set of activities. The standard example involves a
theorist who is imagined to hold something like:

(6)   *The meaning of 'look out' is a set of*
             activities like ducking and fending.

It would follow from such a view that whatever is true of the
meaning of 'look out' is also true of that set of activities identified as
the meaning of 'look out'. But, as Alston (1964a:20) points out:

> Although it is true that I sometimes engage in such activities, it can hardly be
> true that I sometimes engage in the meaning of 'look out'.[2]

So far, the argument has been directed against the claim that the
subject expressions in sentences like:

---

[1] The law is called the substitutivity of identity and is formulated by logicians as:

$$(x)\,(y)\,[x = y] \supset (F_x \supset F_y)]$$

(cf. Cartwright, 1971; Kripke, 1971).

[2] Cf. Austin (1950:119) for a similar argument deployed against treating propositions as meanings of sentences. He argues that, while we say that a proposition is true
or false, we do not say that the meaning of a sentence is true or false. Cf. also Strawson
(1950a:172), who says, "If I talk about my handkerchief, I can, perhaps, produce the
object I am referring to out of my pocket. I can't produce the meaning of the expression 'my handkerchief' out of my pocket."

(7)   *The meaning of the word W is* _____.

function as referring expressions. But it is also held that sentences of
that form as well as sentences of the form:

(8)   *(The word) W means* _____.

are not completed by expressions that designate objects or entities of
any sort. The general form of the argument is formulated by Alston
(1964a:20) in the following words:

> No matter what sort of entity we try to identify meanings with, we find many
> things that we would be prepared to say about an entity of that sort but would
> not be prepared to say about a meaning, and vice versa. Since many things are
> true of one but not true of the other, they cannot be identical.[3]

SYNTACTIC CONSIDERATIONS AGAINST MEANINGS

Stampe (1968) exploits syntactic arguments to establish the hypothesis that the complements of 'mean' as well as expressions like
'the meaning of x' do not have a referring function, and he suggests
that this hypothesis accounts for a number of syntactic peculiarities
of the verb 'mean'. He classifies 'mean' as a "middle verb" in virtue
of the facts that:

(F1)   *'Mean' does not have a true passive.*

and:

(F2)   *'Mean' does not take manner adverbs.*

He also classifies 'mean' as a "factive–agentive" (FA) verb. An FA
verb is distinguished by the fact that it can take as subjects both
expressions referring to persons or agents and expressions referring
to occurrences or facts. A subclass of FA verb take 'that' clauses as
complements in both agentive environments:

---

[3] The considerations philosophers have brought to bear on the status of meanings
have often been closely linked to ontological considerations. For example, philosophers in the tradition of Russell, who held that the meaning of an expression was
whatever the expression referred to, were faced with the embarrassing problem of
trying to say what words like 'if', 'fast', and 'tomorrow' referred to. The problem was
embarrassing because these philosophers usually also subscribed to the view that
whatever can be referred to exists. The result was usually a bloated ontology, and
always an implausible one. The preceding argument, however, is designed to show
that even theories that attempt to identify meanings with entities that have a
quasiplausible ontological status face highly counterintuitive consequences.

(9)   *John meant (proved, indicated) that p.*

and factive environments:

(10)   *That he was late meant (proved, indicated) that p.*

Stampe calls these verbs FA-t verbs. The third syntactic fact of note about 'mean' is that:

(F3)   *'Mean' is the only FA-t verb (with the possible excep-*
       tion of 'imply') that does not freely take a direct object.

For example, we have:

(11)   *X indicated (proved, suggested) to so-and-so*
                   that p.

(12)   *X showed John that p.*

but not:

(13)   **X meant to so-and so that p.*

   Stampe argues that if we limit our attention to sentences of the form:

(A)   *Agent-mean$_{nn}$-NP.*[4]

the preceding three facts, as well as the facts that:

(F4)   *In sentences of form (A), action nominalizations (*His*
       meaning that p was rude) are deviant.

and:

(F5)   *There are no imperatives (*Mean that p) corresponding*
       to sentences of form (A).

are explained by the fact that:

> to say that someone meant something by such-and-such is not to say what he *did,* is not to answer the question, What did so-and-so do? [1968:142]

But while he thinks that this semantic fact explains the behavior of 'mean' in constructions like (A), he notes that:

> it is of little worth in the case of mean$_{nn}$, or in the case of constructions such as *'Feu* means$_{nn}$ fire', where an expression-denoting term serves as the subject of mean$_{nn}$ [1968:142].

---

[4] I use 'mean$_n$' and 'mean$_{nn}$' in the sense introduced in Grice (1957) (cf. also pp. 325 ff).

These facts, as well as the fact that:

(F6) *The complements of 'mean' cannot stand in apposition
to some categorizing expression.*

can be explained only by the further fact that the complements of the
verb in sentences like:

(14) *Smoke means$_n$ fire.*
 'Feu' means$_{nn}$ fire.
 Pierre means$_{nn}$ fire.
 'Masticate' means$_{nn}$ chew.

are syntactically incapable of being used to make reference
(1968:144). According to Stampe, 'chew' in:

(15) *'Masticate' means chew.*

cannot be used to refer because it is not a nominal expression. But he
also argues that even when the complement of 'mean' is a nominal
expression, as it is in:

(16) *'Feu' means fire.*

it cannot be used to refer to anything. In support of this he argues
that:

> if the complement of a verb in a given sentential context is a referring expres-
> sion, it will be possible to substitute for that expression some more general or
> more specific expression "categorizing" what is referred to, producing a sen-
> tence (in which the verb retains its original sense) which is grammatical, and
> which does not necessarily say anything inconsistent with what the original
> sentence said [1968:145].[5]

[5] Stampe (1968: sec. VII) offers an argument designed to show that expressions like:

(i) *what 'masticate' means*
 what John means
 the meaning of 'masticate'

even when occurring as subjects of sentences, are not functioning there as referring
expressions. He argues that:

(ii) *The meaning of the passage was clear.*

and:

(iii) *What he meant was obscure.*

are transformationally related to interrogative nominals, and hence their subjects are
not functioning as referring expressions. By contrast, sentences like:

(iv) *His proof of the claim was convincing.*

(*Continued on page 310*)

In a discussion of Stampe's article, Davis (1970) argues that Stampe has committed the fallacy of ambiguity. He says that the form of Stampe's argument is:

(17)   *'Feu' mean fire.*
(18)   *Fire is a form of oxidation.*
(19)   *∴'Feu' means a form of oxidation.*

and that Stampe:

> has assumed that the two instances of 'fire' in the two premises are not homonyms. But 'fire' in the first premise is the meaning of 'feu' and the meaning of 'feu' is not a form of oxidation. Hence 'a form of oxidation' cannot be substituted for 'fire'. This can be brought out more clearly when we consider that 'fire' in the second sentence refers to instances of combustion, whereas 'fire' in the first premise, if it refers to anything, does not refer to instances of combustion. Those who claim that it is a referring expression, such as Frege, Church, and Katz, hold that it refers to a sense or a concept. Instances of combustion are neither of these [1970:69].

This is somewhat misleading, though. What Stampe is saying is that if the complement of (17) is a referring expression that refers to fire, then, since (18) is true, there will be another sentence (19) formed by replacing 'fire' in (17) with an expression that specifies the category to which the referent of 'fire' [in (17)] belongs, which is grammatical and uses the verb in its original sense, and which is not inconsistent with the original sentence (17). Thus, we should be able to say:

(20)   *Max likes Olga.*
(21)   *Olga is a left-handed Russian checker player.*
(22)   *∴Max likes a left-handed Russian checker player.*

---

or:

(v)   *What he suggested was obscene.*

are related to relative nominals, and so the phrases 'his proof of the claim' and 'what he suggested' may serve as referring expressions. However, the proof is inconclusive, and Stampe himself does not seem to think it shows that phrases like:

(vi)   *the meaning of the passage*

never act like relative nominals. He says that:

(vii)   *The meaning that the passage has is clear.*

is not an intolerable paraphrase of:

(viii)   *The meaning of the passage is clear.*

Still, he denies that 'the meaning of the passage' functions as a referring expression in (viii). In order to establish this, he constructs a fairly plausible regress argument.

The new sentence, (19), should stand to (17) in just the way that (22) stands to (20), but in fact either (19) contradicts (17) or 'means' must be understood as 'refers to', in which case the verb is being used in another sense. Therefore, the complement of (17) is not a referring expression that refers to fire.

Davis does not think that 'fire' in (17) MUST refer to fire, although he allows that it might refer to something. But what could it refer to if not to fire? The only possibility seems to be to say that it refers to the meaning of 'fire'. But this is no improvement, for suppose that 'fire' in (17) does refer to the meaning of 'fire'. In that case, we can categorize the meaning of 'fire' as:

(23)   *a meaning*
                        a concept
                        an idea

and construct a parallel argument. If the complement of (17) is a referring expression that refers to $\begin{Bmatrix} a\ meaning \\ a\ concept \\ an\ idea \end{Bmatrix}$, then there will be another sentence:

(24)   *'Feu' means* $\begin{Bmatrix} a\ meaning \\ a\ concept \\ an\ idea \end{Bmatrix}$.

formed by replacing 'fire' in (17) with an expression that specifies the category to which the referent of 'fire' in (17) belongs, which is grammatical and which is not inconsistent with the original sentence (17). This new sentence, (24), should stand to (17) in just the way that (22) stands to (20). But in fact, either (24) does contradict (17) or 'means' must be understood as 'refers to', in which case the verb is being used in another sense. If 'feu' means fire, as (17) says, then it is false that 'feu' means a meaning, because 'fire' and 'a meaning' certainly do not mean the same thing.

Davis' claim is that 'fire' in (17) and 'fire' in (18) are homonyms. Presumably, this means that they have different meanings (the charge of "ambiguity"). But by itself this claim is quite implausible, for if 'fire' did not have its standard meaning in (17)—there is, presumably, no question but that it has its standard meaning in (18)—then nobody could use (17) to tell anybody what 'feu' means.

Note that Davis says that (*a*) 'fire' in the first premise is the meaning of 'feu' and that (*b*) 'Fire' in the second premise refers to instances of combustion. However, to say that 'fire' is the meaning of 'feu', as Davis does, is to say that the meaning of a French word is an English word. The meaning of 'feu' is neither 'fire' nor what 'fire' refers to when it does refer. Fire burns, but the meaning of 'feu' does not. Fire starts with a match and 'fire' starts with an 'f', but the meaning of 'feu' does not start with anything. That Davis' literal claim (*a*) is false is shown by the ungrammaticality or the falsity (take your pick) of:

(25)   *The meaning of 'feu' is the word fire.

and the falsity of:

(26)   The meaning of 'feu' is the word 'fire'.

Davis also concludes that 'chew' in:

(15)   'Masticate' means chew.
(27)   What 'masticate' means is chew.
(28)   Chew is what is meant by 'masticate'.
(29)   Chew is what 'masticate' means.

is a nominal expression, but this seems only to mean that it should be assigned to a node labeled NP. He does not categorically reject Stampe's claim that 'chew' in these sentences is not used to refer, but only his syntactic arguments for this claim and, accordingly, his explanation of the facts based on that hypothesis. What Davis allows is that it is possible that expressions like:

(30)   what John means
                  what 'masticate' means
                  the meaning of 'masticate'

function as referring expressions and serve to refer to meanings (1970:70). I think this claim needs to be rejected. If both 'chew' and 'the meaning of 'masticate'' function as referring expressions in a sentence like:

(31)   The meaning of 'masticate' is chew.

then (31) would function like the identity statement:

(32)   The meaning of 'masticate' = chew.

This would allow us to take the truth expressed by (15) and, by substituting a coreferential expression for 'chew', arrive at the falsehood:

(33)   'Masticate' means the meaning of 'masticate'.

A SEMANTICAL TREATMENT OF 'MEAN'

Dissatisfaction with some of Stampe's arguments led Davis to reject his attempt to explain the behavior of 'mean' by looking at the

complements of the verb and to offer an account of his own that
focused not on the complements of 'mean' but on the verb itself and
its status as a "stative" verb. The distinction between stative verbs
and active verbs is a semantic distinction which appeals to the fact
that active verbs indicate that something was done and stative verbs
do not. But, as Davis was aware, the classification of 'mean' as a stative verb does not, by itself, explain the facts in question. The examples of stative verbs Davis gives are:

(34)
mean	*have*
believe	*resemble*
know	*want*
regret	*lack*
expect	*like*
hope	

He mentions two conditions that are sufficient for a verb to be stative:

(S1) *It cannot occur in the imperative:*
          *Mean that you want a sandwich.
          *Resemble a duck.
(S2) *It cannot take manner adverbials:*
          *Mean that you want a sandwich enthusiastically.
          *Resemble a duck enthusiastically.

and one necessary condition:

(N)   *If a verb is stative it cannot take an*
              indirect object:
                  *Mean to Mary that you want a duck.
                  *Resemble a duck to Mary.

He also gives a different test, which operates, apparently, as a sufficient condition:

(S3) *A verb is stative if it cannot occur in the*
          following frames:
              What he did was _____.
              He is careful in (at) _____.
              I saw him _____.
              He _____ instead of _____.
              I order him to _____.
              He kept on _____.
          and if it cannot cooccur with instrumental
          'with', 'locatives', 'do so', 'for someone's
          sake' and 'progressive'.

As it stands, (S1) and (S2) qualify 'mean' for stative status, but then the claim that 'mean' is stative can hardly be used to EXPLAIN why that verb cannot be used in the imperative (F5) or take manner adverbials (F2). 'Mean' meets all of the additional tests, but only 'know' and 'resemble' are like 'mean' in this respect:

(35)   *He kept on believing it in spite of the evidence.*
(36)   *He kept on regretting his decision.*
(37)   *He kept on expecting to be appointed.*
(38)   *He kept on hoping that she would call him.*
(39)   *He kept on wanting to be emperor.*
(40)   *He kept on liking her in spite of her behavior.*
(41)   *I was expecting her to explode at any moment.*
(42)   *I was hoping she wouldn't notice.*
(43)   *I was having a fit (bowl of turnip soup,*
             insight).   (But *I was having a car.)*
(44)   *I was wanting to leave.*
(45)   *I was lacking the means to achieve my goal.*

What is worse, many of the verbs on the list do have a passive (F1):

(46)   *It was believed by many that there were no statives.*
(47)   *It was known only by a few that 'mean' is the only*
             stative.
(48)   *It was expected that I bring my panda.*
(49)   *It was hoped that the room would be large enough.*

and some appear in imperative constructions (F5):

(50)   *Believe me.*
(51)   *Expect (hope for) the best.*
(52)   *Have a good time.*

Also, some can have complements that stand in apposition to a categorizing expression:

(53)   *I believe the proposition that all men are*
                 created equal.
(54)   *I regret the fact that I work so hard.*
(55)   *I expect the boy George to finish.*
(56)   *I resemble the dog Lassie.*
(57)   *I like the category miscellaneous.*

Thus, the status of 'mean' as a stative cannot by itself be used to explain (F1)–(F6). Consequently, Davis suggests:

a refinement of this classification. I think we will find that there is a class of
verbs, exemplified by 'mean', which meets all the tests I have given above for
stative, and in addition do not take the passive. There will be another class,
which can be passivized, and yet another, exemplified by 'expect', which can
take passive and progressive [1970:74].

What we have just seen, however, is that the only statives Davis lists
that meet ALL the tests he gives are *mean, know,* and *resemble.* Of
these, 'know' takes the passive, and the complements of 'resemble'
can stand in apposition to some categorizing expression. So, while
there is a class that meets all the tests Davis gives, only 'mean' and
'resemble' meet all the tests and in addition do not take the passive;
and only 'mean' meets all the tests and exhibits the full range of syntactic characteristics that were to be explained. Therefore, it would
be pointless to attempt to explain (F1)–(F6) by noting that 'mean'
belongs to a special subclass of statives, since, for all we now know,
that subclass contains just one member — the verb 'mean'. This
amounts to saying that the membership of 'mean' in the unit class
that contains 'mean' explains why 'mean' behaves as it does. It
behaves as it does because it belongs to a class of which it is the only
member, where membership is determined by the facts about its
behavior.

Davis speculates that there is no sharp division between active
and stative verbs and that expecting that p is "more action-like" than
knowing that p, and that knowing that p is "more action-like" than
meaning that p. Apparently, meaning that p is the least action-like of
all. In defense of this he argues:

> Some things we do, such as running a race, stretch over a period of time
> while other things we do occur at particular times, such as scoring a goal.
> Meaning something neither occupies a stretch of time nor occurs at a particu-
> lar time. Hence it is not an action, nor does it share any features of actions.
> This in turn explains the facts given by Stampe [1970:74].

But why does meaning something not occur at a particular time? I
could utter the sentence:

(58)   *Mary took Bill's pants off.*

at 3 o'clock and again at 4 o'clock. At 3 o'clock I might mean that
Mary took Bill's pants off Bill (to put them on herself), and then at 4
o'clock I might mean that she took them off herself (to put them back
on Bill). Did I not mean something different at the two times, and so
does it not follow that I meant something at each time?

I fear that Davis has failed to provide an explanation of the syntactical behavior of 'mean', but even if 'mean' could be shown in some way not to be the sole member of the relevant class, a great deal would have to be said about the concept of an "action" before it became possible to make very much sense out of the claim that meaning something is less of an action than knowing, or that believing, liking, hoping, and wanting are equally action-like, but less so than knowing. Finally, if any verb on Davis' list is not used to describe an action it is 'know', but 'know' does take a passive construction. This does not seem explainable by saying that knowing something is just a little more action-like than meaning something.

These considerations lead me to conclude that even if the complements of 'mean' are incapable of being used to make reference, and even if meaning something is not an action, we still need to know both how the complements of 'mean' function and what, if anything, is being said about a person, fact, or linguistic expression when someone uses sentences like the following:

(59)   *Sam means that he is likely to be helping the grass to grow.*
(60)   *The fact that she is eager means that she will be easy to please.*
(61)   *'Procrastinate' means put things off.*

In the next section, I want to make a start at answering some of these questions.

THEORIES OF MEANING AS ATTEMPTS TO CHANGE THE SUBJECT

I began by pointing out that many philosophers have come to reject the view that the meaning of a word or expression can be identified with that object to which the word or expression refers. A great many articles by philosophers have been devoted to making this point, and I think we cannot really understand why this is so unless we realize that, at least at first, there was a strong bias toward the opposite opinion. Owing to the efforts of Austin, Wittgenstein, Ryle, Quine, and those influenced by them, the idea that 'the meaning of the word or expression x' referred to any sort of entity became a dead dogma, more often attacked than held as the years progressed. The argument we considered in the first section, and arguments based on the syntactical behavior of the words 'mean' and 'meaning', take as their starting point the things speakers of the language actually say ABOUT meaning, and things they say WITH 'meaning' and 'mean'. That is, the arguments are based on the way these words are actually used and understood by those who use and understand them from day to day.

Ryle (1931–1932) remarks that:

> the ordinary man does not pretend to himself or anyone else that when he makes statements containing such expressions as 'the meaning of "x",' he is referring to a queer new object: it does not cross his mind that his phrase might be misconstrued as a referentially used descriptive phrase [p. 97].

The same point is made, with a bit more style, by Austin (1940):

> Supposing a plain man puzzled were to ask me 'What-is-the-meaning-of (the word) "muggy"?', and I were to answer, 'The idea or concept of "mugginess"' or 'The class of sensa of which it is correct to say "This is muggy"': the man would stare at me as at an imbecile. And that is sufficiently unusual for me to conclude that that was not at all the sort of answer he expected: nor, in plain English, *can* that question *ever* require that sort of answer [p. 59].[6]

To see what someone is asking for when he asks a question like:

(62)   *What does 'muggy' mean?*

we may compare (62) with:

(63)   *What does Tom mean?*

and:

(64)   *What does Tom see?*

In contrast with (62) or (63), (64) calls for an identification of a visible object. One who uses (64) presupposes that there is something that Tom sees. There must BE something that Tom sees if he sees anything, but even though Tom might mean something, there need BE nothing that he means. We can explain what Tom means and we can point to what he sees, but we can neither explain nor point to what

---

[6] For an understanding of Austin's use of hyphens and the distinction between:

(i)   *What-is-the-meaning-of (the word) 'muggy'?*

which Austin classifies as a "specimen of sense," and:

(ii)   *°What is the-meaning-of-(the-word)-'muggy'?*

see Austin (1940).

'muggy' means. Sentence (63) calls for information about Tom's intentions, but what (62) calls for is help in gaining an understanding of how to use the word 'muggy'. One who asks (62) is standardly asking for instruction in the use of the word 'muggy'. Austin (1940) says:

> If I am asked 'What is the meaning of the word *racy*?' I may
>   (a) reply in words, describing, giving examples of sentences in which one should and should not use the word
>   (b) try to get the questioner to imagine or actually experience situations which we should describe by using sentences containing *racy* and related words [p. 57. Cf. also the opening paragraphs of Wittgenstein (1958), Alston (1963b:83ff.), and Ayer (1940:92ff.)].

Since philosophers who ask (62) are not attempting to learn how to use the word 'muggy' they would hardly be satisfied if we attempted to take them somewhere where they could get a proper experience of the sort of situation appropriately described as being muggy. What DID satisfy some philosophers were answers based on the assumption that the meaning of a word is a concept or an idea. But such theories already go hand in hand with the view that the phrase 'the meaning of the word W' functions as a referring phrase and the subsequent search for the objects or kinds of objects it refers to.[7]

The only way to get away with treating the phrase 'the meaning of W' as a referring phrase is to STIPULATE that meanings shall be treated as things of this or that kind. Bloomfield (1933), for example, remarks:

> We have defined the meaning of a linguistic form as the situation in which the speaker utters it and the response which it calls forth in the hearer [p. 139].

This may or may not be a covert attempt to change the subject, but more explicit attempts are readily available.[8] While there may be ample reason for changing the subject, we ought to recognize that that is what is happening. But what was the original subject? The expected answer, 'meaning' is not a great deal of help, because usually

---

[7] For a similar view about the nonreferring status of certain other singular substantives, see Strawson (1950b:191).

[8] Perhaps the most explicit, as well as the best-known, attempt to change the subject is found in the notorious slogan of the early "ordinary language" philosophers: "Don't ask for the meaning, ask for the use."

the subject is changed in an effort to introduce some question to replace the question, "What are meanings?" And the reason people have been so anxious to replace that question is that there seems to be no satisfactory way to answer it. One way to change the subject that is not quite so drastic as suggesting, for example, that the meaning of a sentence is the method of its verification is to turn from questions like, "What is the meaning of a word?" to the question, "What is an explanation of the meaning of a word?" (cf. Wittgenstein, 1958:1). Another, which may be equivalent, is to examine the way we go about answering our PARTICULAR questions about the meaning of particular words and then to interpret our GENERAL questions about meaning as Austin (1940) did, asking:

What-is-the-meaning-of (the phrase) 'what-is-the-meaning-of (the word) "x"?'? [p. 60].

In general, it seems that "theories" of meaning are attempts to change the subject—sometimes overt and sometimes not, perhaps sometimes not even recognized by their propounders as such. The new subject deals with some of the old questions but introduces new questions of its own. More recent disputes are not theoretical ones about what meanings are, or even about whether there are meanings, but, rather, practical ones about what sorts of things one who is interested in language should be studying. Should we talk about the way language is used, about the intentions of speakers or about the truth conditions of sentences? The question suggests that we are faced with a choice among three exclusive alternative ways to replace the old paradigm of looking for the right kind of entities to identify as meanings. Sometimes it is suggested that the three mentioned theories are not exclusive alternatives but each necessary at a certain level (Harman, 1968). This may or may not be a way of getting opposing theorists off our backs so that we can get on with a study of what (we believe) needs to be studied.

Both Wittgenstein's and Austin's suggestions flow from the insight that our talk about meaning should at least start with the things speakers of our language (not just philosophers and linguists) say about meaning. These things, for better or worse, are based on the understanding of 'meaning' that everybody holds in common. This understanding is the one integrated into our conceptual scheme and reflected in our ability to use and understand expressions containing words like 'mean' and 'meaning'. Once we begin to look at the actual behavior of 'mean' and 'meaning', theories of meaning designed to tell us what sort of things meanings are lose most of their plausibility and importance. In the next section, I shall indicate the type of meaning formula on which I propose to concentrate — I call it the "basic" meaning formula. Then, I shall attempt to discover how three "theories of meaning" attempt to deal with problems connected with the basic meaning formula without thereby adopting the view that THERE ARE, in any important sense, meanings.

THE "BASIC" MEANING FORMULA

There is a class of expressions that might appropriately be uttered in response to a question about the meaning of some word or expression. Since such questions are often asked about words of some language other than the one in which the question is asked, and since an answer to such a question might often contain a word of a language different from the one in which that answer is phrased, it is at least possible that the response contain words of three different languages.[9] So far, I have contented myself with writing the formula I shall call the BASIC MEANING FORMULA like this:

(65)   *'Feu' means fire.*

Stampe writes it:

(66)   **Feu means fire.**

but the bold type is simply an alternative device to the single quotes, so I shall employ my convention here. (I shall discuss single quotes later.[10]) Even so, we are still left with three different ways to write the basic meaning formula, each of which represents the complement of 'mean' in a different way:

(67)   *'Small' means little.*[11]

[9] Moore (1962:303ff.), for example, spends some time discussing the case of telling somebody that 'mensa' means '$\tau\rho\acute{\alpha}\pi\epsilon\zeta\alpha$'.

[10] There is an advantage to single quotes over italics, for it allows one to talk about a word, or about a word surrounded by single quotes. To talk about the word 'dog,' we can place single quotes around it, writing ''dog''. There is, unfortunately, no way to italicize italics, though I have noticed something like the law of double negation occasionally working: to italicize an italic, return the expression to its unitalicized form. This method has its limitations, but it is neater. The use of bolder type is also limited, and far from perspicuous.

[11] For an actual example of (67), see Searle (1969:10):

(i)   *'Oculist' means eye doctor.*

(68)   *'Small' means 'little'.*
(69)   *'Small' means little.*

Perhaps it will be thought that these are insignificant notational variations, and in a sense they are, since they all could be employed to represent the same spoken utterance, depending on the notational predilections of the writer. Yet as written formulations they exercise a certain control over their interpretation. Sentence (67) lends itself to ambiguity more easily than (68) or (69). Sentence (68) may give some unwarranted plausibility to the mistaken view that the word 'little' does not appear after the verb, but that its name ' 'little' ' does. Generally, I will follow Alston's example in using (69) and at this stage only note that he explains his use of italics (or bold type) as intended to "indicate that there is something special about the occurrence of this expression." (1963a:407).

TREATMENTS OF THE BASIC MEANING FORMULA

One way to deal with word meaning is to suggest that sentence meaning be defined in terms of truth conditions and that the meaning of a word he explained as the contribution it makes to the truth conditions of the sentences in which it occurs (cf. Davidson, 1967, and Wiggins, 1971). This suggestion relates to the conception of truth given by Tarski (1944):

> Consider the sentence *"snow is white."* We ask the question under what conditions this sentence is true or false. It seems clear that if we base ourselves on the classical conception of truth, we shall say that the sentence is true if snow is white, and that it is false if snow is not white. Thus, if the definition of truth is to conform to our conception, it must imply the following equivalence:
>> *The sentence "snow is white" is true if, and only if, snow is white*
> [p. 15].

He proposed to use *true* in such a way that all equivalences of the

---

or Moore (1962:310):

(ii)   *'Lexicon' means dictionary.*

For an example of (68) see Moore (1962:311):

(iii)   *'Lexicon' means 'dictionary'.*

For an example of (69), see Alston (1963a:411):

(iv)   *'Procrastinate' means **put things off**.*

form:

X is true if, and only if, **p**.

can be asserted, where '*p*' is replaced by any sentence in the language "to which the word 'true' refers" and '*X*' is "replaced by a name of this sentence." [1944:16]. He listed a rigorous set of conditions under which the structure of a language can be regarded as exactly specified and then noted that:

> At the present time the only languages with a specified structure are the formalized languages of the various systems of deductive logic, possibly enriched by the introduction of non-logical terms.

> *The problem of the definition of truth obtains a precise meaning and can be solved in a rigorous way only for those languages whose structure has been exactly specified.* For other languages — thus, for all natural, "spoken" languages — the meaning of the problem is more or less vague, and its solution can have only an approximate character [1944:19].

Davidson (1967) is aware of Tarski's remarks, but he seems to think that there are ways around them that warrant "an optimistic and programmatic view of the possibilities for a formal characterization of a truth predicate for a natural language" [p. 465]. His suggestions, however, seem to involve an essential limitation of scope and a necessary incompleteness. In one place he seems hesitant to tolerate the use of nonextensional operators like 'let it be the case that' and 'it ought to be the case that'. He remarks:

> When we depart from the idioms we can accommodate in a truth definition, we lapse into (or create) language for which we have no coherent semantical account — that is, no account at all of how such talk can be integrated into the language as a whole [1967:462].

Perhaps I misunderstand this, but it seems to me to be saying that the intractability of an idiom is good grounds for its rejection, no matter what the facts of language. This amounts to saying that the truth definition works in just those areas of language in which it works. But if a truth definition cannot deal with certain expressions that are actually used by speakers of a language, then it is not the expressions that should be questioned, but the truth definition. Just about any theory of meaning you can think of would be correct if it were possible to select the "right" (i.e., the tractable) utterances as data.

As Davidson admits:

> a staggering list of difficulties and conundrums remains. To name a few we do not know the logical form of counterfactual or subjunctive sentences; nor of sentences about probabilities and about causal relations; we have no good idea what the logical role of adverbs is, nor the role of attributive adjectives; we have no theory for mass terms like 'fire', 'water' and 'snow', nor for sentences about belief, perception and intention, nor for verbs of action that imply purpose. And finally, there are all the sentences that seem not to have truth values at all: the imperatives, optatives, interrogatives, and a host more [1967:465].

Staggering as these difficulties are, I would like to suggest an elaboration of one of them pertaining to mass terms. Wiggins (1971) argues that:

> To know the sense of an indicative sentence s ['Snow is white.'] it is necessary to know some condition p which is true if and only if s is true and which is the designated condition for s [p. 22].

Presumably, the designated condition for the truth of s would be the condition that snow is white. Thus:

'Snow is white' is true iff snow is white.

But as a matter of fact, snow in New York City is either brown or grey. It will not do to say that s only means that (i.e., is true iff) SOME snow is white, because this would result in the false view that it is also true that:

(s')   *Snow is brown.*

and:

(s'')   *Snow is grey.*

Yet, if I say s, I have said something true, and if I say s' or s'' I have said something false. How can this be?

I believe that this can be explained only by appealing to the fact that something other than the color of snow bears on the truth of s. Austin (1950) and (1962) holds that this is something about the circumstances in which s was uttered, the audience it was intended for, and the purposes for which it was intended. Wiggins alludes to Austin's distinctions (1962) between the locutionary, illocutionary, and perlocutionary acts, and suggests that if we "unpack the speech act layer by layer" we will find at the first level (that of the locution) what is strictly said. It is this, he says, that we must isolate "before we can explain how circumstances, conventions, and whatever else add implicatures, forces, or illocutions; and how these in their turn secure perlocutionary effects." [p. 21].

Now it might seem that Wiggins could exploit this notion of what is strictly said to explain the puzzle about the truth of s — i.e., that he could say that we need concern ourselves only with what is strictly said by s when we are seeking its truth conditions. I would argue that such an attempt would fail, because while the factors Austin mentioned do bear on the truth of s (i.e., on the correctness of saying of s that it is true), nothing bears on the truth of what is strictly said by s because what is strictly said is a LOCUTION, and 'true' and 'false' are not applicable to locutions but only to illocutionary acts of the constative sort, and not always even to them.[12]

Nor could the difficulty be avoided by adapting a solution suggested by Davidson (1967) to deal with sentences containing ambiguous terms. He says that:

> as long as ambiguity does not affect grammatical form, and can be translated, ambiguity for ambiguity, into the metalanguage, a truth definition will not tell us any lies [p. 461].

One might try to argue that even though it is sometimes right to say s and sometimes not, this will go over, circumstance for circumstance, into the metalanguage so that:

'Snow is white' is true if, and only if, snow is white.

tells us no lies. But this will not work, because ordinarily the context determines how we are to interpret and evaluate an assertive utterance of s, but 'snow is white' as it appears on the right-hand side of the preceding formula is not asserted and, consequently, has no context or, alternatively, always has the same context.

Both Davidson and Wiggins are concerned at the first level with the meaning (truth conditions) of sentences, and while Wiggins does hold that the meaning of a word can be explained in terms of the contribution it makes to the meaning (truth conditions) of the sentences in which it occurs, nothing much that he says helps us understand the actual way 'means' functions in the basic meaning formula. Add to this the self-acknowledged difficulties facing "meaning is truth conditions" theorists and their apparent lack of concern for details of ordinary use, and it becomes clear that help in answering

---

[12] I take this to be Austin's view, but the matter is controversial. For a discussion of the issue, cf. Garner (1972).

questions about the basic meaning formula is more likely to be found in other quarters.

An alternate approach treats sentence meaning in terms of "illocutionary act potential" and then relates the meaning of a word to the contribution it makes to the illocutionary act potential of the sentences in which it occurs. Alston (1964a) proposes such an account, based on the following specifications for sentence meaning (S) and word meaning (W):

S_1 means $S_2 =_{df} S_1$ and S_2 have the same illocutionary act potential.

W_1 means $W_2 =_{df} W_1$ and W_2 can be substituted for each other in a wide range of sentences without altering the illocutionary act potentials of these sentences [pp. 36–37].

Alston has much more to say about these definitions (and other related ones) in both (1964a) and (1964b). One of the most important and most difficult tasks facing anyone hoping to provide this sort of an account of word meaning is the task of making the notion of an illocutionary act clear enough to underwrite an approach of this sort. Alston (1964b) and Searle (1969) have done work in this area, but much more needs to be done. For our purposes, however, the account is suggestive in that it relates the basic meaning formula to the idea of providing a warrant for making substitutions. We shall return to this idea later, but now let us examine one more approach to the meaning formula that does not rely on the notion that expressions like 'the meaning of x' serve to make reference.

Grice (1957) distinguishes a use of the words 'mean' and 'meaning' in the "natural sense" (meaning$_n$) from a use of them in the "non-natural sense" (meaning$_{nn}$). The sentence:

(70) *Those spots mean measles.*

is a paradigm of the use of 'mean' in the natural sense, and the sentence:

(71) *Those three rings on the bell mean that the*
bus is full.

is a paradigm of the use of 'mean' in the nonnatural sense. He attempts to provide an analysis of:

(72) *A meant$_{nn}$ something by x (on a particular*
occasion).

and of:

(73)   A meant$_{nn}$ by x that so-and-so (on a
                 particular occasion).

in terms of a complex set of conditions involving essential reference
to speakers' intentions. He also suggests that:

(74)   x means$_{nn}$ (timeless) that so-and-so.

might "as a first shot be equated with some statement or disjunction
of statements about what 'people' (vague) intend . . . to effect by x."
(1957:58). The nearest thing to the basic meaning formula Grice discusses in (1957) is (74), but in (1969) we find that talk about expressions of the form of (74) has been replaced by talk about expressions
that look like:

(75)   '_____' means ' . . . '.

This change allows Grice to distinguish between *a specification of a
timeless meaning of a complete utterance type:*

(76)   S$_1$ means S$_2$.

(where 'S$_1$' and 'S$_2$' stand for sentences) and *a specification of a timeless meaning of an incomplete utterance type:*

(77)   W$_1$ means W$_2$.

(where 'W$_1$' and 'W$_2$' stand for words or phrases). He then points out
that "since a complete utterance-type x may have more than one
timeless meaning, we need to be able to connect with a particular
utterance of x just one of the timeless meanings of x to the exclusion
of the others." (1969:148). One who did this would be giving *a specification of the applied timeless meaning of a complete utterance
type.* This takes the form of:

(78)   S$_1$ meant here S$_2$.

and is distinguished from *a specification of the applied timeless
meaning of an incomplete utterance type*, which takes the form of:

(79)   W$_1$ meant here W$_2$.

Let 'S' stand for the sentence:

(80)   If I shall then be helping the grass to grow,
                 I shall have no time for reading.

Grice points out that it might be true to say of a particular utterer (U)
of S that when U uttered S he meant by S (by the words of S):

(81)   *If I am then dead, I shan't know what is*
         going on in the world.

One who makes such a specification is providing what Grice calls *a specification of the occasion meaning of an utterance type*. The general form of such a specification is:

(82)   *U meant by (the words of) S_1, S_2.*

The final type of meaning specification Grice mentions is the only one involving indirect discourse, and it takes the following form:

(83)   *U meant by uttering S that p.*

A specifications of this sort is called *a specification of an utterer's occasion meaning*.

One of the most important changes between (1957) and (1969) is that (73) in the earlier article was replaced by (82) and (83). The distinction (73) misses is that between a speaker's meaning something by *x* and a speaker's meaning something by uttering *x* (cf. Ziff, 1967). In (1969) Grice pays very little attention to specifications like (82) and concentrates primarily on ones like (83). We may summarize what has just been said by pointing out that, according to Grice, a formula like:

(75)   '_____' *means* ' . . .'.

is used in giving:

(A)   specifications of timeless meaning for an utterance type
(B)   specifications of applied timeless meaning for an utterance type
(C)   specifications of utterance type occasion meaning[13]

and that a formula like:

(83)   *U meant by uttering S that p.*

is used in giving:

(D)   specifications of an utterer's occasion meaning.

For our purposes, we can note that if we are specifying the timeless meaning of an utterance type (A), we may offer a formulation like

---

[13] Note that (A), (B), and (C) are all presented by Grice in the form of:

(1)   'Small' *means* 'little'.

(76) or one like (77). In the latter case, we confront something that looks very close to our basic meaning formula, since (77) is instantiated by specifications like:

(84)   'Grass' means 'lawn material'.

and:

(85)   'Grass' means 'marijuana'.

Grice's general strategy is to attempt to explain (D) in terms of utterers' intentions and then to explain (A), (B), and (C) in terms of (D). In (1969) he attempts the first task, and in (1968) he considers the relations between (A), (B), and (D).

The difficulties with Grice's account, and especially with the explication of (D) in terms of speakers' intentions, are well-known. There is the disturbing possibility of an infinite regress of intentions discussed by MacKay (1972), Garner (1974), and Schiffer (1972), as well as an insufficiently appreciated oddity infecting the very notion of an intention. What, after all, are intentions if we have to allow that people might have an infinite number of them for each utterance they produce, or that they regularly have intentions that they are not aware of or that are so complicated that they could not even understand them if they were looking at them written out before them? Wittgenstein (1967) raises serious questions about the notion of an intention, but Stampe (1968) says:

> The great gain of such an analysis as Grice's is that, whatever its difficulties, the concept of intention, unlike the concepts of an idea, a concept, semantic marker, semantic regularity, and so forth, at least does not swim in the same orbit of conceptual space as does "meaning" itself [p. 168].

We may have here another change of subject (do not ask for the meaning, ask for the intentions), but it is not obvious that once the change of subject (or orbit) has been made we are any closer to understanding meaning (or our basic meaning formula) than before. One might, of course, attempt to provide a behavioristic analysis of intentions, or one might attempt to regard them as "theoretical constructs." However, the former alternative turns Grice's theory into a winding detour on the way to a behavioristic analysis of meaning, and the latter does place intentions in the same conceptual space as semantic markers.

One of the most serious problems a theory like Grice's would have to face is that of explaining the timeless meaning of an incomplete utterance type in terms of more basic notions and, finally, in terms of speakers' intentions. If this could be accomplished, it might provide us with some understanding of the basic meaning formula. In (1968) Grice does make a stab at explicating timeless meaning in U's idiolect (cf. D.5 on p. 236), and he remarks that "an explication of timeless meaning in a language can, perhaps, be provided by adapting D.3.," but he adds: "I shall not attempt this task now" [p. 236].

In discussing possible transformational relations between various types of meaning locutions, Stampe (1968) suggests that:

(86)   *'Aggravate' means make some condition more serious.*

is transformationally related to:

(87)   *By 'aggravate' people, when speaking correctly,*
            mean make some condition more serious.

and to:

(88)   *By 'aggravate' one means make some condition*
            more serious.

Davis (1970:81) criticizes Stampe's transformations, but offers further arguments to establish a similar but more general thesis about FA verbs. He claims that sentences of the form:

(89)   *One Verb$_{fa}$ NP$_1$ by NP$_2$.*

are transformationally related to sentences of the form:

(90)   *NP$_2$ Verb$_{fa}$ NP$_1$.*

But he adds (p. 81) that all of the arguments showing that these sentences are related will also show that they are related to sentences of the form:

(91)   *One uses NP$_2$ to Verb$_{fa}$ NP$_1$.*

According to Stampe, something of the form of (89)—e.g., (88)—is 'basic'; and according to Davis, something of the form of (91) is.

What seems to be surfacing here is the dispute between an intentionalist theory of meaning and a use theory of meaning. But it would be wrong to assume that this is so without pursuing the matter further. A use theory of meaning is, as we have seen, one like Alston's, which persistently tries to show that we can use 'use'-talk to say whatever we need to say about meaning (i.e., to say whatever we had previously used 'meaning' talk to say). A theory like this eliminates a tendency to bloat one's ontology by reifying "meanings," and at the same time remains much closer to the subject (i.e., meaning) than any offered so far by those who abandon 'meaning' talk in favor of 'truth condition' talk. An intentionalist theory of meaning, like Grice's, attempts to achieve the same ends, only by replacing talk about meaning with talk about intentions rather than with talk about use. (I am here speaking very roughly.) One place this dispute really surfaces is in the area of questions about the relative importance of the role of intention and convention in language (cf. Strawson, 1964). Another place it surfaces is in disputes about how the references of proper names and definite descriptions get established. Use theorists often emphasize the role of convention in that they typically subscribe to some form of the "cluster theory" of proper names and standardly adopt a straightforward conventionalist treatment of definite descriptions used attributively. (Cf. Wittgenstein, 1953:§79; Searle, 1958; Strawson, 1959; and Jones, 1973.)

The tendency to treat only descriptions used attributively has been criticized by Donnellan (1966 and 1968), and the cluster theory of names by Donnellan (1970) and Kripke (1972). Donnellan offers an intentionalist account of the referential uses of definite descriptions in (1966 and 1968) and, as far as I can tell, something approaching an intentionalist account of the use of proper names in (1970). Interestingly enough, a third theory appears in Kripke (1972) that relates to the theory proposed by Davidson (1967) and Wiggins (1971), which was briefly discussed at the beginning of this section. Kripke rejects both the cluster theory of proper names and the intentionalist account of referential uses of definite descriptions proposed by Donnellan (1966). Or, rather, he claims that Donnellan's treatment of descriptions used referentially belongs to the theory of speech acts and that that theory needs to be kept separate from a theory of semantics or (is this the 'or' of identity?) truth conditions (1972:343, n.3).

It is in these areas that disputes between intentionalist and conventionalist theories emerge, but in the conflicting analyses of Stampe and Davis very little effort has been made to connect with issues of this sort. Stampe, for example, explicitly restricts himself to advancing "the cause of this analysis only within the limited terms of the grammatical analysis presented here," and proposes to say nothing "about the adequacy of Grice's analysis of "meaning something by an utterance," itself a seemingly inexhaustible topic" [1968:168]. Stampe does claim, however, that the transformation he proposes preserves meaning in the sense that, for every sentence of the form:

(92)   *by-x-Agent-Aux-mean-y-(adverbial phrase)*,

there is a sentence of the form:

(93)   *x-Aux-mean-y-(adverbial phrase)*

"which means the same thing, and conversely." And he says that "this would perhaps serve as a fair statement of Grice's proposal" [1968:170]. I want to note three things about this thesis. First, Stampe, accepting the view that transformations preserve meaning, makes a synonymy claim for his transformationally related formulas. What is interesting about this is that when Grice actually states his "explications" in (1957) he speaks of a "rough equivalence," and when he states them in (1969) he does so in the form:

'U meant by uttering x that _____' is true iff

_____.

This is not synonymy, but truth functional equivalence. It is not easy to see what is going on here, especially since the very concept under discussion is meaning. Second, the formula that Stampe takes to represent Grice's explication of utterer's meaning is actually one that Grice ended up discarding in (1969). Stampe works with:

(73)   *A meant$_{nn}$ by x that so-and-so.*

whereas the difficulties with (73) seem to necessitate something like:

(83)   *U meant by uttering S that p.*

instead. Finally, Stampe's transformational account is out of date. (Aren't they all!) This, of course, is an inherent problem in attempting to relate work done in philosophy of language very closely to work done by the transformational linguists. These three points seem to warrant some skepticism pertaining to Stampe's transformationalist hypothesis relating word meaning to utterer's meaning, his claim to have accurately characterized Grice's theory, and his explanations of the syntactical facts he lists.

Davis also fails to carry his analysis forward to the heart(s) of the matter. Rather than relating meaning to illocutionary act potential or conventional rules in the spirit of a use theorist, he terminates his analysis with the notion of using *x* to *mean* something. It is not altogether clear what it is to use *x* to mean something. What, for example, would it be to use 'masticate' to mean 'chew'? One answer might be that it is to use 'masticate' as 'chew' is used. But one who is doing this is operating on the assumption that 'masticate' means what 'chew' does, and this may threaten the analysis with circularity or at least cast some doubt on the assumption that his preferred formula (91) is more basic than (90).

In sum, both Stampe and Davis leave 'mean' and 'meaning' unexplained in their transformational enterprises. In a way, this should not be surprising, for developing a transformational account of the relation between the basic meaning formula and some of the more elaborate accounts of utterers' meaning that Grice proposes in (1968 and 1969) would almost certainly be impossible. We can see why this is so if we attempt the experiment of trying to update Stampe's suggestions. First, we must take as basic not (73), but:

(83)   *U meant by uttering S that p.*

Now, this seems to involve two basic elements:

(83)   a.   *U uttered S.*
                        b.   *U meant that p.*

and the idea that they are related in a certain way. If (83) is to be transformationally related to the basic meaning formula:

(75)   '_____' *means* '. . .'.

it will also have to be related transformationally to the ultimate ANALYSANS, which makes reference only to utterers' intentions. This suggests that what we need is a deep structure for the DEFINIENS Grice proposes for (83) that shows how (83a) and (83b) are related as well as how they are related to something of the form of (75). I have no idea how to begin to construct a tree to represent any of the more complex formulations Grice proposes in (1969), and even the task of constructing one for one admittedly inadequate definition given in (1969) is no simple matter. Possibly it would look something like (94), but I suggest this in part only to show how implausible it is to suppose that we are really going to be able to find rules to take us from anything like an adequate representation of some reasonably adequate DEFINIENS for (83) to (83) itself, and ultimately to some version of the basic meaning formula diagrammed on page 333.

This tree is aimed at providing a representation of the definiens of what Grice (1969:153) calls "Redefinition I," which reads:

'U meant something by uttering *x*' is true iff:
    (i) U intended, by uttering *x*, to induce a certain response in A.
    (ii) U intended A to recognize, at least in part from the utterance of *x*, that U intended to produce that response.

(94)

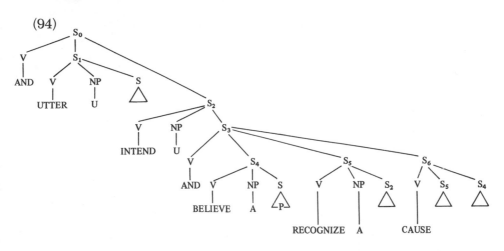

    (iii) U intended the fulfillment of the intention mentioned in (ii) to be at least in part A's reason for fulfilling the intention mentioned in (i).

I have represented *x* as a sentence (s), and I have made the intended response a belief response. This is controversial, but not clearly incorrect. However, the tree fails to capture the distinction Grice explicitly draws between reasons and causes, as well as one or two other subtleties. What has been captured, and made surprisingly explicit, is the infinite regress an account like Grice's invariably faces. (Cf. MacKay, 1972; Garner, 1974; and Schiffer, 1972.)

    I hold no brief for this tree, but at the very least it makes it clear that something far more complicated than the transformations Stampe and Davis discuss will have to be introduced to establish transformational relations among various statements about meaning, and between these and some statement about what speakers intend. Now, recall that we have for some time been wondering about the basic meaning formula. A transformational analysis will throw light on this formula only if the ultimate underlying source is reasonably well-understood and only if the rules that relate this underlying source to the basic meaning formula are at least conceivable. I suspect that neither is the case, and so I suggest that we look directly at the basic meaning formula and at what speakers who produce it are standardly attempting to do. That is, I propose to table the assumption that what is needed to understand formulas like:

(84)   *'Grass' means 'lawn material'.*

and:

(85)   *'Grass' means 'marijuana'.*

are transformational rules relating something like:

(89')   *One means NP_1 by NP_2.*

or:

(91')   *One uses NP_2 to mean NP_1.*

to something like:

(90')   *NP_2 means NP_1.*

   This is not to deny that what words mean is related to what speakers mean by them, or to what speakers mean by them when they are using them properly, but it is to question certain assumptions about the character and the content of the speech act being performed by anyone who, using a formulation like (90'), tells somebody what some word or expression means. I do not think it is impossible that the UTTERER'S meaning can be analyzed in terms of speaker's intentions, and I know that there is a causal relation between the intentions speakers who use a certain word have and what that word means — but I think the causality goes both ways. If we want to understand what goes on when somebody tells somebody else what some word or expression means, the causal account and any transformational account of the relationship between utterer's meaning and word meaning may turn out to be unhelpful. On the other hand, if one wants to give a causal account of the relationship between utterer's intentions and word meaning, or any kind of transformational account of the relations among different meaning specifications, it may be very important to see just what sort of speech act is being performed by people who use the basic meaning formula. In the next section, I shall begin by looking at some facts about the basic meaning formula and several variations on it, and I shall introduce one hypothesis that might throw some light on some of the problems we have encountered.

THE USE OF THE BASIC MEANING FORMULA

   If we want to understand the syntactical behavior of the basic meaning formula, or, indeed, of any expression containing the words 'mean' or 'meaning', it is advisable to become as clear as possible about how expressions containing those words are actually used. As Stampe notes, we understand why 'Smith meant that p', unlike 'Smith indicated that p', does not report what someone does when we realize that the former sentence "is used to *explicate* something Smith said or did," and so "implies, but does not say, that Smith did something" [1968:143]. If we could discover such a fact about the basic meaning formula, we would be well on our way to an understanding of much of its syntactical behavior. To this end, let us consider the basic meaning formula and several variations:

(95)   a.   *'Small' means little.*
            b.   *The word 'small' means little.*
            c.   *'Small' means the word little.*
            d.   *The word 'small' means the word 'little'.*

The same pattern will be found for:

(96)   a.   *The meaning of 'small' is little.*
        b.   *The meaning of the word 'small' is little.*
        c.   *The meaning of 'small' is the word little.*
        d.   *The meaning of the word 'small' is the word 'little'.*

(97)   a.   *Little is what 'small' means.*
        b.   *Little is what the word 'small' means.*
        c.   *The word little is what 'small' means.*
        d.   *The word 'little' is what the word 'small' means.*

(98)   a.   *What 'small' means is little.*
        b.   *What the word 'small' means is little.*
        c.   *What 'small' means is the word little.*
        d.   *What the word 'small' means is the word 'little'.*

Stampe would explain these patterns of grammaticality by pointing out that 'little' is syntactically incapable of being used to make reference in these sentences, and so any categorizing phrase is out of place. I think this points in the right direction, but that more can be said. Note that the pattern is different in the following cases:

(99)   a.   *The meaning of 'small' is the same as the meaning of 'little'.*
       b.   *The meaning of the word 'small' is the same as the meaning of 'little'.*
       c.   *The meaning of 'small' is the same as the meaning of the word 'little'.*

    d. *The meaning of the word 'small' is the same as the meaning of the word 'little'.*

(100) a. *'Small' means the same (thing) as 'little' does.*

      b. *The word 'small' means the same (thing) as 'little' does.*

      c. *'Small' means the same (thing) as the word 'little' does.*

      d. *The word 'small' means the same (thing) as the word 'little' does.*

In the formulas in (99) and (100), the appositive construction occurs freely, and a categorizing phrase can occur in front of ''little'' as well as in front of ''small''. It hardly seems possible to explain these patterns by appealing to the hypothesis that in (95)–(98) the word 'little' is "syntactically incapable of being used to make reference," while in (99) and (100) ''little'' is used to refer to the word 'little'. In the first place, this fails to explain the ungrammaticality of (97c) and (97d). More importantly, such an "explanation" gives us no clue as to how the word 'little' is being used in any of the formulas in (95)–(98). The hypothesis that in (95)–(98) we are not, while in (99)–(100) we are, talking about both words is far from satisfactory. Still, the understanding of ''little'' in (99) and (100) is no less clear than the understanding of the use of ''small'' in those sentences, and that is usually taken to be clear enough. This might suggest that we take the relatively intelligible (99) or (100) as "primary" and attempt to relate the basic meaning formula (95a) to one or the other of them.

To do this we would need first to decide whether to begin with (99) or with (100). I shall begin by looking at (99). I think it is a good idea to start with the (d) formulation because we can always get rid of the phrase 'the word' by a transformation I shall call CATEGORIZING PHRASE CONSUMPTION (CPC) – it is not so different from one Ross (1972) calls METALINGUISTIC NOUN DELETION. Thus, we begin with (99d) and by CPC we get (99a). Perhaps we could think up another transformation (OBJECTIONABLE PHRASE REMOVAL) to get rid of phrases like 'the meaning of', but in this case that would yield:

(101)   **'Small' is 'little'.*

which, if not ungrammatical, is certainly not true. But since neither (101) nor:

(102)   **'Small' is little.*

would serve our purposes, I am led to think that we might be better served by beginning with (100), which CPC would take into (100a).

'Thing' never had a firm status, so let us suppose we have found some way to eliminate it (or to omit putting it in in the first place). This yields:

(103)   'Small' means the same as 'little'.

Now if we could just treat 'means' as a variation on 'means the same as,' we would at least have arrived at:

(104)   'Small' means 'little'.

However, this was not the formulation of the basic meaning formula I earlier favored, namely:

(95a)   'Small' means little.

In (104) we seem to have represented 'small' and 'little' as operating in the same way (however expressions surrounded by single quotes operate), whereas in (95a) 'small' was surrounded by single quotes and 'little' was set in bold type. Of course, this results from starting with the (d) formulation, but I will not apologize for that now. If it turns out that "'small'" (not 'small') and "'little'" (not 'little') are in fact functioning in the same way in (104), it will not matter much how we represent them. What we want to know, and have all along, is how they are operating. If they are operating in the same way, we might be able to treat (95a) as some kind of identity statement (for now, call it an M identity, where 'M' stands for 'meaning').

We will examine identity statements in more detail later, but now let us note a few simple facts about them, and about their possible representation in tree notation. If we attempt to represent:

(105)   Cicero is Tully.

by some simple deep structure like:

(106)

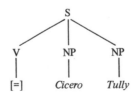

we will run afoul of a principle Postal notes in (1971:186) governing predicates that are logically reflexive or irreflexive and blocking such ungrammatical sentences as:

(107)   *Harry is related to himself.
(108)   *Harry is distinct from himself.
(109)   *Harry is identical to himself.

This is the principle that in "propositional representations" of the form:

(110)

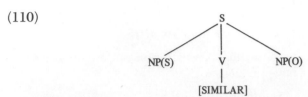

the NP(S) and the NP(O) cannot be coreferents. A violation of the principle occurs in (106) and would, if (106) were accepted as the "propositional representation" of (105), result in the ungrammatical:

(111)   *Cicero is himself.*

or perhaps:

(112)   *Cicero is identical $\begin{Bmatrix} to \\ with \end{Bmatrix}$ himself.*

An alternative candidate for a representation of (105) might be:

(113)

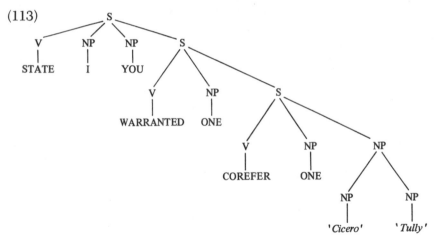

What (113) suggests is that an identity statement states that "one" is warranted in substituting 'Cicero' for 'Tully', in using either to refer. Apart from the misleading impression that ordinary proper names function like logically proper names, this does not seem too far off. However, it conflicts with the "standard" definition of identity given by logicians:

(114) $x = y \cdot =_{df} \cdot (P)(P_x \equiv P_y)$

This is Russell's definition, and both Wittgenstein (1961:5.302) and Ramsey (1931:31) object. Wittgenstein says:

> 5.302 Russell's definition of '=' is inadequate because according to it we cannot say that two objects have all their properties in common. (Even if this proposition is never correct, it still has *sense*.)

Wittgenstein's alternative was this:

> 4.241 When I use two signs with one and the same meaning, I express this by putting the sign '=' between them.
> So '$a = b$' means that the sign 'b' can be substituted for the sign 'a'.

We might try the following admittedly inaccurate representation of Wittgenstein's alternative:

(115)

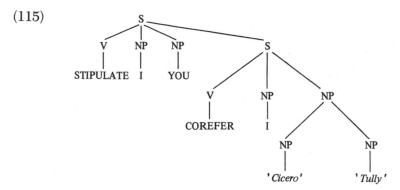

This representation would have the merit of giving us a way to distinguish between:

(105)   *Cicero is Tully.*

and

(116)   *Cicero$_i$ is Cicero$_i$.*

which I think is grammatical only for logicians. Just as I really cannot state that you are warranted in replacing 'Cicero' with 'Cicero', neither can I stipulate that I shall use 'Cicero' and 'Cicero' coreferentially.

Now what about:

(95a)   *'Small' means little.*

I suggest that this should not be represented as:

(117)

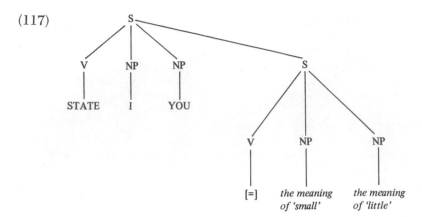

since this would result in the objectionable:

(118)   *The meaning of 'small' is itself.

What seems more promising is a tree like:

(119)

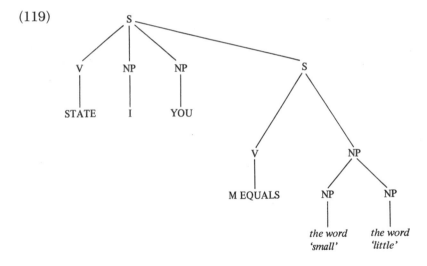

Of course, it is just the notion of "M identity" that needs further analysis. When two expressions are "said" to be M identical, one is IN SOME WAY indicating that they function in the same way, that a speaker could use either and his purpose would be served equally well. But it does not seem right to say that someone who utters the basic meaning formula is actually ASSERTING this, or that the whole, or even the basic, point of standard uses of the basic meaning formula is to somehow get this across. What, then, is going on when a speaker indicates that two expressions are M identical? What speech act, or what kind of speech act, is he performing? Taking a clue from Wittgenstein, and from some of the things that have already been said, we could say that he is providing his hearer with directions for using one of the words. But he will succeed in this only if the hearer already knows how to use the other word, and that he does know how to do this is something the speaker might be said to presuppose.

I would like to suggest that one who utters (95a) is not ordering or advising his hearer to use the word 'small' as he uses the word 'little', nor is he merely informing his hearer that the two words are used equivalently. He is, in fact, not making an assertion about either or both of the words in question and is not even using those words (or their names) to refer either to their meanings or to themselves. Least of all is he telling his audience that two THINGS (meanings) are really one thing. If we treat M identities on the model of Wittgenstein's treatment of identity statements in general, we might say that he is producing the words in question and employing the M identity "statement" form to instruct his hearer in the use of the word 'small'—he is literally presenting his audience with an alternative expression that can be used in place of 'small'. If we understand M identities like (95a) as operating like:

(120) *I state (to you) that one is warranted in using 'little' and 'small' in the same (or at least in a wide range of similar) contexts.*

and suppose that in some way (120), or something like it, makes explicit the way (95a), (103), and (104) are actually employed, we will find ourselves faced with some rather serious problems. These will emerge in some of the arguments given by Moore and discussed later. The problems Moore raises cannot be escaped by supposing that:

(103)   *'Small' means the same as 'little'.*

and:

(95a)   *'Small' means little.*

state different things. Rather, we need to reject the view that either equivalence formulas like (103) or sentences having the form of the basic meaning formula (95a) are standardly used in a statement-making role. The acceptance of this will, by the way, provide another reason for refusing to relate the basic meaning formula to statements about what one standardly means by 'small' or to statements about what 'small' is standardly used to mean, since it will involve the view that the basic meaning formula is not used in making statements at all.

It is often argued that equivalence formulas are not themselves "equivalent" to meaning formulas (even if the two sorts of formulas are truth-functionally equivalent). Commenting on the difference between:

(121)   *'Lexicon' means 'dictionary'.*

and:

(122)   *'Lexicon' has the same meaning as 'dictionary'.*

Moore (1962:310–311) says:

> Now a person who doesn't understand either 'lexicon' or 'dictionary' may quite well understand the sentence . . . " 'Lexicon' has the same meaning as 'dictionary'," since the proper meaning of this is " 'L' & 'D' " both mean something or other, & what they mean is the same." A person who has told you this has not told you what either means . . . .

He adds that (122):

> is like 'x has for father the man who is father of y'. A man who tells you that is not telling you who was the father of x; though if you happen to know who was father of y, you can infer who was father of x [p. 311].

In all, Moore seems to have three arguments for the radical difference between (121) and (122):

1. A person who understands neither 'lexicon' nor 'dictionary' may understand (122) but not (121).
2. A person who has told someone (122) has not told someone what 'lexicon' (or 'dictionary') means, but a person who has told someone (121) has told him what 'lexicon' means.
3. One who believes (121) is believing something about 'lexicon', but one who believes only (122) is not believing this about 'lexicon'.

1. 'UNDERSTAND'

A person who heard EITHER (121) or (122) but understood neither 'lexicon' nor 'dictionary' could only gather that the speaker was saying that the two words meant the same thing. Only one who supposes that the complex consisting of a word and two flanking single quotes is a name of the expression between the quotes, and also supposes that one can understand a sentence without understanding the names used in it, will find it plausible to say that one could understand (122) without understanding (121). The practical effect of (121) and (122) as they are used in explaining what words mean is the same. If one understands 'dictionary' either (121) or (122) can be used to give him the meaning of 'lexicon'. This is the important thing about both formulations, and the contrary belief is based on the implausible assumption that all language is, in some very simple way, descriptive.

2.   'TELL'

Here the operative word is 'tell' rather than 'understand'. If someone asks me what 'lexicon' means, I might respond by uttering either (121) or (122). If my hearer knows what 'dictionary' means, he will understand my answer in either case. So what is there to prevent me from saying that if he knows what 'dictionary' means I will, in either case, have told him what 'lexicon' means? Moore introduces another sentence into the discussion:

(123)   *A lexicon is a dictionary.*

and says that one who utters (123) will have told his audience what 'lexicon' means only if his audience understands 'dictionary' (and the rest of the sentence). I would add that a necessary condition for someone who utters (123) to be said to have told his audience what 'lexicon' means is that his audience recognize (or at least that he have grounds for supposing that his audience will recognize) that the situation was one in which the speaker was trying to "tell" him what 'lexicon' means. Sentence (123) is like:

(124)   *A lexicon is a book.*

From the form of the sentence alone, a person who does not know what 'lexicon' means will not be able to determine whether he is being told something about lexicons (124) or what 'lexicon' means (123). There is a sense, then, in which (123) is different from (121) and (122), for in the latter two the form of the sentence used makes it clear that the speaker is attempting to tell somebody what a word means. But there is another sense in which (123) is not in the least different from (121) and (122). In the context of a question like:

(125)   *What does 'lexicon' mean?*

the three are in the same boat. If a hearer understands that he is being told (given) the meaning of the word 'lexicon', any one of them would do the job.

There is an important disanalogy between being told:

(126)   X *has for a father the man who is father of y.*

and being told (122). It seems that when I am told something like (126) I DO have to figure out who the father of x is, and this lends some plausibility to the claim that someone who tells me (126) has not told me who x's father is. However, one who utters (122) has more of a right to suppose that his hearer (if he is a native speaker) knows what 'dictionary' means than speakers usually have to presuppose genealogical knowledge. Yet if the speaker of (126) knows for a fact that his hearer knows who y's father is, there seems to be no good reason for refraining from saying that in uttering (126) he did tell his hearer who x's father was.

3. 'BELIEVE'

It is difficult to say, just like that, what one who believes (121) is believing about 'lexicon'. He would assent to the question:

(127)   *Is a lexicon a dictionary?*

as readily as to the question:

(128)   *Does 'lexicon' mean the same thing as 'dictionary'?*

Would he, in assenting to those two questions, be expressing different beliefs? Moore thinks he would, but we should pause and think about what it means to believe ONLY (122). Presumably, if one believed (122) and understood EITHER 'lexicon' or 'dictionary,' he would also believe (121). But could one really believe (122) without understanding either 'lexicon' or 'dictionary'? Perhaps the difference between believing (121) and believing (122) is like the difference between believing of a particular animal that the word used to describe it is 'cow' and believing of a particular animal that it is a cow. But what is THAT difference?

I conclude that when the meaning formula is expressed in a given language and deals with words in that same language, there is no functional difference between (121) and (122). When we bring in different languages, however, matters become a little more complex. Moore (1962:304) says:

> "I told him that 'mensa' meant τράπεζα; but I didn't tell him what 'mensa' meant" is a perfectly sensible thing to say . . . It is certainly sensible to say: "I told him that 'mensa' meant τράπεζα, but he didn't know what τράπεζα

meant, so of course I wasn't answering his question—I didn't succeed in telling him what 'mensa' meant." This shows conclusively (?) that to make an assertion of the form " 'mensa' means the same as '_____' " is not the same thing as to tell a person what "mensa" means: you will not be telling him what "mensa" means unless he *understands* the word that takes the place of the dash.

I agree with the first half of this passage, but I do not think that it shows conclusively that to make an assertion (if it is an assertion) of the form:

(129)   *'Mensa' means the same as '____   _____'.*

is not the same thing as to tell someone what 'mensa' means. (The question mark following 'conclusively' is Moore's, not mine.) If the word filling the blank in (129) is in a different language from the rest of the sentence (excluding 'mensa'), it would make some sense to deny that the speaker told his hearer what 'mensa' means. But when the speaker knows that the hearer understands the foreign word filling the blank, it might be correct to say that he has told him what 'mensa' means. The point is that speakers of English are warranted in supposing that other speakers of English know what 'table' means but not, without some evidence, warranted in supposing that they know the word for 'table' in Greek. When both words are in English it is much more plausible to say that the speaker did tell his hearer what the first word meant.[14]

Stampe (1968:145) mentions the case of a French teacher telling a pupil, as a hint, that 'feu' means the same as (the German word) 'Feuer', and he says that in this case the teacher has not said what 'feu' means. Whether the French teacher has "said" what 'feu' means depends on what he is warranted in supposing the student knows about German. Suppose I ask you who took my copy of *Syntactic Structures*, and you reply:

(130)   *I can't say, but his name is spelled*
             b-i-l-l s-m-i-t-h.

Did you tell me or "say" who took it? If you gave away a secret you could hardly get off by saying that you did not.

In this section, I have been considering the possibility that sentences like:

(95a)   *'Small' means little.*

---

[14] Perhaps this needs qualification in virtue of Johnson's definition of 'net'. But then, Johnson was not attempting to tell someone how to use the word 'net'.

are best understood by relating them not to sentences making reference to the utterer's meaning but, rather, to sentences like:

(100d)   *The word 'small' means the same (thing) as*
              the word 'little' does.

I suggested that (95a) and (100d) are used to express what I called "M identities," that their function is the same, and that in the standard case one who produces either one of them is giving directions for using the word 'small'. In the latter part of the section, it emerged that if we persist in treating utterances like (95a), (100d), and

(121)   *'Lexicon' means 'dictionary'.*

as straightforward statements of fact, we will find it hard to meet arguments of the sort Moore has made. However, when we keep their actual function in language in mind and pay attention to the speech act one who uses any of them is standardly performing, we can find an easy way to circumvent Moore's arguments.

Wittgenstein's insight is that an identity "statement" is not a statement at all. He says:

> 5.5303 Roughly speaking, to say of *two* things that they are identical is non-
> sense, and to say of *one* thing that it is identical with itself is to say
> nothing at all.

If, as I propose, we take this very seriously, and apply it to M identities as well, we will discover a general objection to theories that argue that statements about what speakers mean can be related to truth-functionally equivalent "statements" about what words mean, since the latter, being directives, have no truth conditions. In the next section, I will explore a little further the hypothesis that M identities be given a non-truth-functional performative analysis.

THE "SYNTAX" OF THE BASIC MEANING FORMULA

Recall that Alston (1963a:407) explained writing the meaning formula as:

(131)   *'Procrastinate' means **put things off**.*

by saying that he set in boldface what followed 'means' in order "to indicate that there is something special about this occurrence of the expression." We are not, he says, using 'put things off' in the ordinary way, "nor are we referring to it in a way that would be marked by enclosing it in quotes." The occurrence is called "exhibiting." In this section, I propose to take this quite literally. It is compatible with Stampe's claim that the complements of the meaning formula are not suitable for making reference. They are, in fact, being offered up as words that, given the circumstances and our use of the meaning formula, help our hearer understand that word occurring as the subject.

In answer to the question:

(132)   *What does 'small' mean?*

we might say either:

(133)   *'Small' means little.*

or we might simply say

(134)   *'Little'.*

Morgan (this volume) discusses single-word replies to certain questions by considering dialogues like:

(135)   *What does Nixon eat for breakfast?*
(136)   *Bananas.*

His suggestion is that the underlying structure of (136) is just 'bananas', and that "its import is inferred by means of rules of conversation, since it is obvious that the import will vary with conversational context." Conversational assumptions are certainly at work in cases involving sentences like (132), (133), and (134), and so it might be tempting to suggest that when someone answers (132) by saying (134), the underlying structure of his utterance is just ''little'' (not 'little'). But in fact (as we shall see), answering (132) by saying (134) is more like answering question (135) by producing a banana. We would hardly ask what the underlying structure of a banana is, and by the same token, it may be unwise to ask what the underlying structure of the word produced in answer to (132) is.

Or again, consider entries in foreign language dictionaries:

kuumuus, heat
tosin, certainly.

Here, we are inclined to say that we simply have a pairing of words whose uses (jobs, roles, functions, etc.) in the two languages are equivalent. It is implausible to suggest that each such pairing is (or must be represented as) a disguised assertion of the form:

(137)   *'Kuumuus' means heat.*

(In fact, I have been suggesting that even (137) can be treated as a straightforward assertion only at the cost of considerable confusion.) When someone responds to (132) by producing (134), or when a writer compiles a dictionary of foreign words and phrases, his aim is not so much to provide information as it is to provide equivalent expressions. What he generally presupposes is that his audience will understand the equivalent expression he provides. I suggest that utterances like (137) and (133) be understood in the same way and that, standardly, one who issues an utterance like (133) is not asserting anything about 'small', because he is not making an assertion at all. 'Means *little*' is not a predicate in the way that 'means little' (i.e., 'has little meaning') is, or in any other way. It is only when wrested out of its standard place in language and put into philosophy books about meaning that the basic meaning formula seems to operate like a normal assertion. In real life, the phrase ''small' means' is almost always redundant, because usually the context is one in which someone is inquiring about the meaning of 'small'. The conversational or contextual circumstances make it clear what an answer like (134) would be an answer to. Sentence (134) would not always, by the way, be an answer to question (132), since it could be produced appropriately as a response to any of the following:

(138)   *What word would you use to describe her?*
(139)   *What word did Gulliver use to describe them?*
(140)   *What is a six-letter word indicating a*
           diminutive stature?

What, then, is the syntax of the basic meaning formula? It is not clear to me how much sense it makes to say that it has a syntax. More support will be found for this suggestion in the following sections.

THE UNIQUENESS OF 'MEAN'

In an earlier section, we saw how Davis' explanation of the syntactic facts (F1)−(F6) concerning 'mean' was based on a subclassification of statives that contained 'mean' as its only member. An examination of Stampe's classification of 'mean' as an FA-t verb and as a middle verb will help clarify the sense in which 'mean' is unique among verbs. When Stampe classifies 'mean' as an FA-t verb, it is on the grounds that it takes as subject expressions terms referring to persons or agents as well as terms referring to facts, and that it takes 'that' clauses as complements in either factive or agentive environments. First, consider the class of FA verbs (verbs that take factive or agentive subjects). In the basic meaning formula:

(141)   *'Small' means little.*

as well as in formulas like:

(142)   *'He is small' means he is little.*
(143)   *'Small' means the same thing that 'little' does.*

the subject expressions refer to neither facts nor agents. 'Mean,' as it occurs in (141)–(143), will count as an FA verb only if those sentences are related to other, more basic, sentences that do have (in this case, since we are dealing with 'meaning$_{nn}$') agents as subjects. Stampe attempts to provide transformations that do just this. The other FA verbs that Stampe mentions take manner adverbials and have true passive forms, but 'mean,' he says, "is the lone exception" [1968:140].

'Mean' is unique among FA verbs in another way, since there is no single sense of 'mean' that qualifies it for inclusion among FA verbs. Rather, 'mean$_n$' takes factive environments and 'mean$_{nn}$' takes agentive environments. As Stampe points out, all the other FA-t verbs take both kinds of subjects (the defining characteristic of an FA verb); but, unlike 'mean', they "do *not* have two senses, properly so-called, corresponding to a natural and a nonnatural interpretation" [1968:155–56].

The FA-t verbs Stampe lists are, in addition to 'mean':

indicate	reveal	tell
imply	demonstrate	inform
prove	show	remind
suggest	warn	

They are said to be FA-t verbs because they are all capable of taking 'that' clauses as complements. But 'mean' is also unique among FA-t verbs because, in addition to taking 'that' clauses as complements, it alone takes as complements words or expressions, as in (141), but not designations of words or expressions, as in:

(144)   **'Fire' means the word 'fire'.*
(145)   **'Fire' means the word one writes with 'f',*
         'i', 'r', and 'e', in that order.

In this respect, it is both like "manner of speaking" verbs and unlike them. We can say either:

(146)   *He shouted (said, whispered) 'fire'.*

or:

(147)   *He shouted (said, whispered) the word 'fire'.*

It is this peculiarity of 'mean', when it occurs in the nonnatural sense, that leads me to say that it is unique among verbs. In the long run, it may be more economical to recognize the lexical difference between 'mean' as it permits phonological complementation and other uses of the expression, even in the nonnatural sense. As we shall see in the following sections, considerations about identity statements and about quoted expressions provides further support for this hypothesis.

Just as 'mean' is unique among statives and FA-t verbs, so, it turns out, is it unique among middle verbs. The list Stampe provides of middle verbs is:

> mean   lack
> cost   weigh
> resemble

We can say either:

(148)   *x means y.*

or:

(149)   *x means the same as y.*

Whatever we think about the synonymy or lack of synonymy between (148) and (149), it must be granted that they can be used in a wide variety of circumstances to accomplish the same task. But now examine the other verbs on the list. While we say:

(150)   a. *x costs y.*
                    b. *x weighs y.*
                    c. *x lacks y.*
                    d. *x resembles y.*

there is a difference between (150d) and the rest. We cannot say:

(151)   **x resembles the same as y.*

But we can say:

(152)   a. *x costs the same as y.*

and:

                    b. *x weighs the same as y.*

and possibly:

(153)   ?*x lacks the same as y.*

Saying (152a), (152b), or (153) is saying that x and y cost, weigh, and possibly lack the same thing (amount), not what x (or y) costs, weighs, or lacks. (Curiously, we can say that x resembles the same thing as y as well as that x resembles y, but not, as in the other cases: *'X resembles the same as Y'.) When we say (150a) or (150b), we are explicitly giving the cost or weight of x; and when we say (148), we are explicitly giving the meaning of x — I am now dealing with cases in which both the subject and the complement of 'mean' are expressions. But while (149) standardly serves the same function as (148) — or so I have argued — (152a) or (152b) only serve the same function as (150a) or (150b) if a special presupposition is satisfied — namely, that the hearer knows how much y costs or weighs. This presupposition has to be renewed for each different use of a sentence like (152a) or (152b). What allows (148) and (149) to standardly serve the same function is that the presupposition that underwrites the speaker speaking to the listener in the first place (that they are speaking the same language) also underwrites using either (148) or (149) to tell someone what x means (that x and y are words of the language being spoken).

What we have seen is that 'mean' has been classified as a stative, as an FA-t verb, and as a middle verb, but that it is a very poorly behaved member of each of these classes. Stampe explains the behavior of 'mean' by providing transformational rules to link a number of constructions in which it occurs. An alternative treatment is to recognize the differences between 'mean' and the members of those classes of verbs, and that many (but not all) of the phenomena might be as readily explained by providing a separate treatment for that use of 'mean$_{nn}$' which occurs between two expressions in the meaning formula. The complements of 'mean' in the basic meaning formula are exhibited rather than used. In the preceding pages, they have been variously represented by italics (bold type in examples) and quotation marks, but what we will see in the next section is that a proper understanding of the function of single quotes (which does not consist in their forming names of names) leads to the view that the subjects of 'mean' in the basic meaning formula occur in the same way. This lends further support to the hypothesis considered in the previous two sections that:

(154)   *'Lexicon' means 'dictionary'.*

and:

(155)   *'Lexicon' has the same meaning as 'dictionary'.*

differ in no significant way, for in both sentences two words are
exhibited and brought together by some realization of 'mean' in an
act of directing someone in the use of a word.

QUOTATION

In recent years, philosophers have spent much effort and ingenuity
on problems connected with sentences of the following sort:

(156)   *'Tully was a Roman' is trochaic.*
(157)   *'Cicero' contains six letters.*

The examples are Quine's, as are the views that the grammatical subject of each of these sentences is a singular term, a name of the
expression between the quotes, and that in fact any expression can
be mentioned by using a name formed in this way. We read, "the
name of a name or other expression is commonly formed by putting
the named expression in single quotation marks." Being a singular
term, the quotation "figures as a single irreducible word" [Quine,
1958:23, 33], and what occurs inside "may be looked upon as an
orthographic accident, without logical status, like the occurrence of
'cat' in 'cattle' " [Quine, 1953:159]. These passages suggest a principle about how names of expressions are formed:

  (P1) We form the name of an expression *a* by enclosing it between single quotes,
       and the new expression *b* which is formed in this way is a definite singular
       term "whose parts count for no more than serifs or syllables" [Quine,
       1958:26].

An acceptance of (P1) seems to lie behind Quine's willingness to
say that:

(158)   *'Tully was a Roman.'*

is "the singular term, of quotational form, that is the grammatical
subject of (156)" [Quine, 1960:143]. But some additional principle
about the OCCURRENCE of expressions within other expressions is at
work when he claims that the personal name 'Tully' has nonreferen-
tial position in both (156) and its grammatical subject.

Commenting on (157), Quine remarks:

> An expression which consists of another expression between single quotes constitutes a name of that other expression; and it is clear that *the occurrence of that other expression* or a part of it, within the context of quotes, is not in general referential. In particular, the *occurrence of the personal name* within the context of quotes in [(157)] is not referential, not subject to the substitutivity principle. *The personal name occurs there* merely as a fragment of a longer name which contains, beside this fragment, the two quotation marks [Quine, 1961a:140]. [My italics]

Here the personal name 'Cicero' is said, in three different ways, to occur "within the context of quotes." These and other passages suggest that Quine subscribes to the following principle concerning the names of expressions:

(P2) When we form a new expression *b* by enclosing some expression *a* between single quotes, *a* "occurs in" *b*. If *a* is a sentence, then *b* "contains" that sentence; if *a* is a proper name, then *b* "contains" that name. Further, if *a* contains a proper name, then *b* also contains that name.

Principles (P1) and (P2) are incompatible, and not in any subtle or unobvious way, but plainly so. According to (P1), we form the name of:

(159)   *New York*

by writing:

(160)   '*New York*'

but if we take (P1) seriously and treat (160) as a "definite singular term," a single irreducible word, then we should no more expect to be told, as we are by (P2), that the name 'New York' is contained in it than we should expect to hear about the several pronouns, the definite article, and the adverb contained in the word 'helianthus'.

Principle (P1) provides one way, but not the only way, of referring to expressions. An alternative method, which Quine (1953:159) calls "spelling," would allow us to transcribe:

(161)   '9 > 5' *contains just three characters.*

as:

(162)   *n g f contains just three characters.*

Two further methods are mentioned in Quine (1958:26). Searle (1969:73–76) says that we could, if we wished, let 'John' be the name of 'Socrates', in which case:

(163)   *'Socrates' has eight letters.*

could be rewritten as:

(164)   *John has eight letters.*

Since (P1) and (P2) are incompatible, if we insist on accepting them both we will have a thoroughly inadequate understanding of the working of single quotes, and it will be easy to be stopped short by "ANALYSIS puzzles" of the sort raised in Anscombe (1956:121):

> It is impossible to be told anyone's name. For if I am told 'That man's name is "Smith",' his name is mentioned, not used, and I hear the name of his name but not his name.

The author of the one answer considered publishable held that there exists a "(tacit) convention that a name and its name are denoted by the same word, and so the name of a name 'tells' us the name" [Tajtelbaum, 1957:53]. Before long, both the puzzle and the winning answer were attacked by Whiteley (1957), who argued that the source of the paradox in the original problem is the assumption that when a word is mentioned in discourse, it is mentioned by name. This assumption, he argued, is a mistake, for when one who is asked a man's name replies by saying 'Smith', he has not given the name of the man's name, but has "produced the name itself." The word is not, Whiteley claimed, mentioned by name, "it is exhibited in person [pp. 119–120].[15]

[15] For another, similar treatment, see Christensen (1967), who holds that:

> It is not necessary, in general, to mention a linguistic expression in order to say something about it. On the contrary, in most cases where we manage to talk about linguistic expressions we do so by actually producing them [p. 358].

He compares sentences like:

(i)   *'Socrates' has eight letters.*

with what happens when, standing in front of a Studebaker, we point at it and say: "A Studebaker!" (p. 360). His main arguments are directed against (P1), and he attempts to show that since there is nothing "names of words" share with other proper names, it is quite unclear how (1) should be understood. He relates the ordinary use of an expression like 'Boston', its use in referring to a city, to the scholastic notion of suppositio formalis, and the use of 'Socrates' in (1) to suppositio materialis. He then introduces what he takes to be a third kind of suppositio and calls it suppositio semantica. This occurs, we are told, when we say things like "'Oculist' means the same as 'eye doctor'". Here we are said to be using 'eye doctor' as "a sound-and-letter complex *with* a definite meaning" [p. 364]. Quine makes a number of similar distinctions in (1958:24).

Perhaps the clearest formulation of this view is to be found in Searle (1969), who claims that "when we want to talk about a word it is almost always possible to produce the word itself" [p. 75]. Searle's view is that when we surround a word with single quotes we are indicating that this is an exhibition of the word rather than a more conventional use. He claims that the same word occurs at the beginning of both:

(165)   *'Socrates' has eight letters.*

and:

(166)   *Socrates was a philosopher.*

He characterizes (165) by saying that:

> the word itself is *presented* and then talked about, and that it is to be taken as presented and talked about rather than used conventionally to refer is indicated by the quotes. But the word is not referred to, nor does it refer to itself [1969:75–76].[16]

We may allow this passage to serve as the model for a statement of an alternative to (P1) and (P2):

> (P*) When an expression *b* is formed by surrounding an expression *a* with single quotes, then as long as *b* occurs in a sentence being used to talk about *a*, that very expression *a* can be said to have been presented and talked about rather than used conventionally to refer; and this is indicated by the quotes. There is no reference to *a*, and no referring done by *a* (or by *b*).

I believe that (P*) is an extremely plausible principle and that something very much like that is happening when someone gives somebody's name to another. Thus, if I am asked:

(167)   *What is his name?*

and I reply:

(168)   *John ('John')*

I have performed the same speech act as if I had replied:

(169)   *His name is 'John'.*

[16] Searle's formulation was in terms of words rather than expressions (where this latter word is taken to include words, phrases, and sentences). For an explicit adoption of this view to deal with sentences as well as words, cf. Rundle (1967–68), who flatly denies that we must use a name of an expression that can be formed by surrounding the expression with single quotes, and adds, "If I state 'His name is "John," ' then I simply give the person's name, not a name of it, and if I correctly report that James said 'man is mortal', then I cite rather than name his actual words" [p. 189].

Neglect of this fact creates trouble for philosophers and linguists alike and disguises the extent to which a spoken language is different from a logical calculus. Telling somebody a person's name is, in the right circumstances, uttering the name. If the circumstances are quite right, that is all we have to do—if they are not, we may need to make them right by prefacing the name with an appropriate lexical item. Is the completed project a sentence? Is it grammatical? Is 'bananas' or even a banana, when given in response to the question about Nixon's breakfast? And words produced to direct people in the use of other words in the basic meaning formula are in the same (banana) boat, for there, too, the speaker is producing or exhibiting expressions rather than using other expressions, or those very expressions, to refer.

It should not be surprising that this procedure meshes very poorly with syntax. As a result, we find linguists compelled to deal with such disturbing examples as:

(170)   *John, which is my brother's name*   (Bach, 1968)
(171)   *This's spelling is regular*   (Ross, 1972)
(172)   *We named our dog Him.*
         (*Him is our dog.*)

Either utterances like these have to be arbitrarily excluded from treatment or else an account must be provided that is comprehensive enough to deal with bananas as well as with 'bananas', with ''John'' as well as 'John,' and with ''meaning'' as well as 'meaning'.

Grice, at least, would classify U's holding up the banana as an utterance, and an utterance is something that is such that in issuing it, the utterer meant$_{nn}$ something. But neither a banana nor THAT banana meant$_{nn}$ anything. Yet if U meant something by holding up a banana, then what he meant might be either true or false. It would seem, then, that "a comprehensive theory of meaning for a natural language must cope successfully with each of these problems" [Davidson, 1967:465]. I do not know how a truth condition account of meaning would cope with utterances of this sort nor, for that matter, where such utterances as 'bananas' or U's holding up a banana fit into propositional representations or onto trees. Naturally, the point is not restricted to bananas, but applies to names and "meanings" as well. Now we know why, as Stampe said, 'little' is syntactically incapable of making reference in the basic meaning formula:

(173)   *'Small' means little.*

When this sentence is seriously uttered, neither 'small' nor 'little' is "used" at all—but this does not mean that it is, therefore, mentioned. Rather, it is exhibited. The point of its being exhibited is determined by the situation in which it is exhibited; and the standard situation in which it is exhibited is one in which a speaker is attempting to direct a hearer in the use of a word and does this by producing an expression he must be assumed to suppose that the hearer understands.

REMARKS ABOUT IDENTITY STATEMENTS

The points I have been making about exhibiting words and names, of course, affect our understanding of identify (and M identity) statements; but the theory proposed is capable of throwing light on some questions about identity that have always puzzled philosophers. In (1892) Frege employs an argument against the view that "what is intended to be said by $a = b$ seems to be that the signs or names 'a' and 'b' designate the same thing, so that the signs themselves would be under discussion" [p. 56]. He objects that if that were all there were to identity statements, then no "proper knowledge" (knowledge about the "subject matter") would be expressed by them, but only knowledge about its mode of designation. Frege had been convinced by the morning star–evening star example that genuine knowledge was expressed by an identity statement. The man who discovered that the morning star is the evening star made an important astronomical discovery, and his announcement of this discovery did not seem to be merely an announcement of a discovery about how things are designated.

Sometimes it is held that identity statements convey a minimum amount of information, so that if someone asserts '$a = b$', and 'a' and 'b' are names, all that is being asserted is the minimal claim that a person is self-identical. I want to say that even this minimal claim is too much and that there is no way to ASSERT that a person is self-identical. We (nonlogicians) find:

(174)   *Socrates is identical to himself.*

unacceptable, while:

(175)   ?*Socrates is identical with the teacher of Plato.*

is sometimes bothersome, and:

(176)   *The teacher of Plato is Socrates.*

is quite acceptable. I would say that in these cases we are not telling anybody anything about *Socrates* [unless we have chosen either (175) or (176) as an odd way of saying that Socrates taught Plato]. More generally, when we "tell" someone that $a = b$, we are not telling him anything about a, because if we were telling him anything about a, it could only be that a is identical with b, that is, with a—and to tell somebody this (whatever words we use) is to tell him nothing at all. Thus, identity statements are not statements about the individual whose designations they relate. They do sometimes provide us with information, however, so we do need to know how they do this.

My hypothesis is that identity statements are BELIEF-WORLD ADJUSTERS. When we hear that $a = b$, we look around our belief world and see if we have the name 'a' attached to one set of characteristics and the name 'b' to another. If we do, we know to combine these two sets of characteristics. This is why 'b' is a useful answer to the question, "Who is a?" and 'a' is not. It is why $a = b$ has a use and $a = a$ does not. There is no single fact that we find out by empirical investigation correspondence with which makes an identity statement true. We find out that there was only one person where previously we thought there were two. We do not discover that the writer is actually the denouncer, or that the denouncer is actually the writer. We find out that Cicero (Tully) did numerous things we had not thought he did.

Likewise, when we say:

(177)   '*Small*' means *little*.

or:

(178)   '*Small*' means the same as '*little*'.

we are not asserting anything about '*small*'. M identities are LANGUAGE-WORLD ADJUSTERS.

I have been suggesting that a fairly large number of phenomena can be understood in a similar way—but that to do this it is necessary to examine what people who use language are actually doing with it. Thus, in the case of giving someone a person's name, a word's meaning—and telling someone that x is identical with y—we find that phonological complementation is perhaps our only alternative to the traditional view that surrounding an expression with quotes forms the name of a name and that when one utters an expression in a sentential context he is always using it according to some standard grammatical notions, is always either referring or predicating. That is just not the way it works, and so there is really no reason to suppose that an analysis that assumes that it works that way is going to throw anything but darkness on the phenomenon. If I assume something that is false for methodological reasons, that is poor methodology.

REFERENCES

Alston, W. P. Meaning and use, 1963. In J. F. Rosenberg and C. Travis (Eds.), *Readings in the philosophy of language*. Englewood Cliffs, N. J.: Prentice-Hall, 1971, 403–419. (a)

Alston, W. P. The quest for meanings. *Mind*, 1963, **72**, 79–87. (b)

Alston, W. P. *Philosophy of language*. Englewood Cliffs, N. J.: Prentice-Hall, 1964. (a)

Alston, W. P. Linguistic Acts. *American Philosophical Quarterly*, 1964, 138–146. (b)

Anscombe, E. *Analysis* Competition — Tenth Problem. *Analysis*, 1956, **16**, 120.

Austin, J. L. The meaning of a word, 1940. In J. L. Austin, *Philosophical papers*. Oxford: Clarendon Press, 1970, 55–75.

Austin, J. L. Truth, 1950. In J. L. Austin, *Philosophical papers*. Oxford: Clarendon Press, 1970, 117–133.

Austin, J. L. *How to do things with words*. Cambridge, Mass: Harvard University Press, 1962.

Austin, J. L. *Philosophical papers*. Oxford: Clarendon Press, 1970.

Ayer, A. J. *The foundations of empirical knowledge*. London: Macmillan, 1940.

Bach, E. Nouns and noun phrases. In E. Bach and R. Harms (Eds.), *Universals in linguistic theory*. New York: Holt, Rinehart, & Winston, 1968, 91–122.

Bach, E., and Harms, R. (Eds.). *Universals in linguistic theory*. New York:, 1968.

Bloomfield, L. *Language*. New York: H. Holt, 1933.

Butler, R. J. (Ed.). *Analytical philosophy: Second series*. Oxford: Blackwell, 1965.

Cartwright, R. Identity and substitutivity. In M. K. Munitz (Ed.), *Identity and individuation*. New York: New York University Press, 1971, 119–133.

Caton, C. E. (Ed.). *Philosophy and ordinary language*. Urbana, Ill.: University of Illinois Press, 1963.

Christensen, N. E. The alleged distinction between use and mention. *Philosophical Review*, 1967, **76**, 358–367.

Davidson, D. Truth and meaning, 1967. In J. F. Rosenberg and C. Travis (Eds.), *Readings in the philosophy of language*. Englewood Cliffs, N. J.: Prentice-Hall, 1971, 450–465.

Davis, S. Meaning and the transformational stew. *Foundations of Language*, 1970, **6**, 67–88.

Donnellan, K. Reference and definite descriptions, 1966. In J. F. Rosenberg and C. Travis (Eds.), *Readings in the philosophy of language*. Englewood Cliffs, N. J.: Prentice-Hall, 1971, 195–211.

Donnellan, K. Putting Humpty Dumpty together again. *Philosophical Review*, 1968, **79**, 203–215.

Donnellan, K. Proper names and identifying descriptions. *Synthese*, 1970, **21**, 335–358.

Fillmore, C. J., and Langendoen, D. T. (Eds.). *Studies in linguistic semantics*. New York: Holt, Rhinehart, & Winston, 1971.

Frege, G. On sense and reference, 1892. In P. Geach and M. Black, *Translations from the philosophical writings of Gottlob Frege.* Oxford: Blackwell, 1952, 56–78.

Garner, R. On saying what is true. *Noûs*, 1972, 6, 201–224.

Garner, R. Grice and MacKay on meaning. *Mind*, 1974, 83, 417–421.

Geach, P., and Black, M. (Eds.). *Translations from the philosophical writings of Gottlob Frege.* Oxford: Blackwell, 1952.

Grice, H. P. Meaning, 1957. In D. D. Steinberg and L. A. Jakobovits, *Semantics.* Cambridge: University Press, 1971, 53–59.

Grice, H. P. Utterer's meaning, sentence-meaning and word-meaning. *Foundations of Language*, 1968, 4, 225–242.

Grice, H. P. Utterer's meaning and intention. *Philosophical Review*, 1969, **78**, 147–177.

Harman, G. Three levels of meaning, 1968. In D. D. Steinberg and L. A. Jakobovits, *Semantics.* Cambridge: University Press, 1971, 66–75.

Harman, G., and Davidson, D. (Eds.). *Semantics of natural language.* Dordrecht, Holland: Reidel, 1972.

Jones, M. T. Intentionalist and conventionalist solutions to problems of reference in the philosophy of language. Unpublished Ph.D. dissertation, 1973.

Kripke, S. Identity and necessity. In M. K. Munitz (Ed.), *Identity and individuation.* New York: New York University Press, 1971, 135–164.

Kripke, S. Naming and necessity. In G. Harman and D. Davidson (Eds.), *Semantics of natural language.* Dordrecht, Holland: Reidel, 1972, 253–355.

Linsky, L. *Semantics and the philosophy of language.* Urbana, Ill.: University of Illinois Press, 1952.

MacKay, A. Professor Grice's theory of meaning. *Mind*, 1972, **81**, 57–66.

McCawley, J. D. 1972, The role of semantics in a grammar. In E. Bach and R. Harms (Eds.), *Universals in linguistic theory.* New York: Holt, Rinehart, & Winston, 1968, 124–169.

Mace, C. A. (Ed.). *British philosophy in the mid-century.* London: Allen and Unwin, 1957.

Moore, G. E. *Commonplace book.* London: Allen and Unwin, 1962.

Munitz, M. K. (Ed.). *Identity and individuation.* New York: New York University Press, 1971.

Parkinson, G. H. R. (Ed.). *The theory of meaning.* London and New York: Oxford University Press, 1968.

Postal, P. M. On the surface verb 'remind'. In C. J. Fillmore and D. T. Langendoen (Eds.), *Studies in linguistic semantics.* New York: Holt, Rinehart, & Winston, 1971, 181–270.

Quine, W. V. O. On what there is, 1948. In W. V. O. Quine, *From a logical point of view.* Cambridge, Mass.: Harvard University Press, 1961, 1–19.

Quine, W. V. O. Two dogmas of empiricism, 1951. In W. V. O. Quine, *From a logical point of view.* Cambridge, Mass.: Harvard University Press, 1961, 20–46.

Quine, W. V. O. Three grades of modal involvement, 1953. In W. V. O. Quine, *Ways of paradox and other essays.* New York: Random House, 1966, 156–174.

Quine, W. V. O. *Mathematical logic.* New York: Harper and Row, 1962.

Quine, W. V. O. *Word and object.* Cambridge, Mass.: Cambridge Technology Press of MIT, 1960.

Quine, W. V. O. *Word and object.* Cambridge, Mass.: Cambridge Technology Press of MIT, 1960.

Quine, W. V. O. Reference and modality. In W. V. O. Quine, *From a logical point of view.* Cambridge, Mass.: Harvard University Press, 1961, 139–159.   (a)

Quine, W. V. O. *From a logical point of view.* Cambridge, Mass.: Harvard University Press, 1961. (b)

Quine, W. V. O. *Ways of paradox and other essays.* New York: Random House, 1966.

Ramsey, F. P. In R. B. Braithewaite (Ed.), *The foundations of mathematics.* London: Routledge and Kegan Paul, 1965.

Rosenberg, J. F. and Travis, C. (Eds.). *Readings in the philosophy of language.* Englewood Cliffs, N. J.: Prentice-Hall, 1971.

Ross, J. R. Doubl-ing. *Linguistic Inquiry,* 1972, 3, 61–86.

Rundle, B. Transitivity and indirect speech. *Proceedings of the Aristotelian Society,* 1967–68, **68,** 187–205.

Ryle, G. Systematically misleading expressions, 1931–1932. In M. Weitz (Ed.), *Twentieth-century philosophy: The analytic tradition.* New York: Free Press, 1966, 181–204.

Ryle, G. The theory of meaning. In C. A. Mace *British philosophy in the mid-century.* London: Allen and Unwin, 1957, 239–264.

Ryle, G. Use, usage and meaning, 1961. In G. H. R. Parkinson (Ed.), *The theory of meaning.* London and New York: Oxford University Press, 1968, 109–116.

Schiffer, S. R. *Meaning.* Oxford: Clarendon Press, 1972.

Searle, J. R. Proper names, 1958. Reprinted in C. E. Caton (Ed.), *Philosophy and ordinary language.* Urbana, Ill.: University of Illinois Press, 1963, 154–161.

Searle, J. R. *Speech acts.* Cambridge: University Press, 1969.

Stampe, D. Toward a grammar of meaning. *Philosophical Review,* 1968, **77,** 137–174.

Steinberg, D. D., and Jakobovits, L. A. *Semantics.* Cambridge: University Press, 1971.

Strawson, P. F. On referring, 1950. In C. E. Caton (Ed.), *Philosophy and ordinary language.* Urbana, Ill.: University of Illinois Press, 1963, 162–193.   (a)

Strawson, P. F. Truth, In P. F. Strawson, *Logico-linguistic papers.* London: Menthuen, 1971, 190–213.   (b)

Strawson, P. F. *Individuals.* London: Menthuen, 1959.

Strawson, P. F. Intention and convention in speech acts, 1964.

Strawson, P. F. *Logico-linguistic papers.* London: Menthuen, 1971.

Tajtelbaum, A. It is impossible to be told anyone's name. *Analysis,* 1957, **17,** 53.

Tarski, A. The semantic conception of truth, 1944. In L. Linsky, *Semantics and the philosophy of language.* Urbana, Ill.: University of Illinois Press, 1952, 13–47.

Weitz, M. (Ed.). *Twentieth-century philosophy: The analytic tradition.* New York: Free Press, 1966.

Whiteley, C. H. Names of words: a note on *Analysis* 'problem' no. 10. *Analysis,* 1957, **17,** 119–120.

Wiggins, D. Identity statements. In R. J. Butler (Ed.), *Analytical philosophy: Second series.* Oxford: Blackwell, 1965, 40–71.

Wiggins, D. On sentence-sense, word-sense and difference of word-sense. Towards a philosophical theory of dictionaries. In D. D. Steinberg and L. A. Jakobovits, *Semantics.* Cambridge: University Press, 1971, 14–34.

Wittgenstein, L. *Philosophical investigations.* Oxford: Blackwell, 1953.

Wittgenstein, L. *Preliminary studies for the "Philosophical investigations."* New York: Harper and Row, 1958.

Wittgenstein, L. *Tractatus logico-philosophicus.* London: Routledge and Kegan Paul, 1961.

Wittgenstein, L. *Zettel.* Berkeley: University of California Press, 1967.

Ziff, P. On H. P. Grice's account of meaning. *Analysis,* 1967, **28,** 1–8.

MEANING$_{nn}$ AND CONVERSATIONAL IMPLICATURE

RICHARD A. WRIGHT
Talladega College

If we are to deal fully and adequately with the notion of conversational implicature, we must soon ask a crucial question—What (if any) is the relation between the implicature of an utterance and the meaning of that utterance?[1] My effort here will be to sketch a possible answer to that question, based on an understanding of what meaning consists in for Grice.

I will key my work on Grice's (1957) paper, *Meaning*, because the distinction between 'natural' and 'nonnatural' meaning which is presented there is assumed in and integral to his later papers on meaning (1964 and 1968).[2] Further, his later papers do not substantially change the doctrine of (1957) but, instead, are attempts to fix up various problems in the intentional analysis which is a part of the

---

[1] I should emphasize *utterance* here in order to keep this question separate from the similar (and equally important) question, discussed by O'Hair (1969) about the relation between the meaning and implication of such WORDS as *know, believe,* and so on, that is, the 'propositional attitude' verbs. I shall consider only the broader question at this point in an effort (hopefully) to avoid some messy epistemological issues.

[2] He begins the (1964) study by saying that he will be talking about the word *mean* "in what I have [previously] called a non-natural sense of the word . . ." [p. 1], while in (1969) he says that he will "take as a starting-point [for this paper] the account of 'non-natural' meaning which [was] offered in [the] article 'Meaning,' [1957] . . ." [p. 150].

original theory.[3] In my discussion, I shall try to do several things: (1) briefly explicate Grice's fundamental position and show that his essential notion of an 'utterance' is both nonstandard and ambiguous; (2) argue that Grice's notion of 'meaning$_{nn}$' is confused and incorrect when applied to nonlinguistic communication acts, even though he argues for its applicability in those cases; (3) sketch how my analysis and the subsequently modified notion of 'meaning$_{nn}$' (a) indicates a class of communication acts that includes both linguistic and nonlinguistic acts and (b) suggests felicity conditions for such acts; and finally, (4) propose that conversational implicature is based on this revised notion of 'meaning$_{nn}$'.

I

Taken on a broad, long-range perspective, Grice may be seen as trying to discover what conditions must be satisfied if we are to correctly say that any utterance has meaning (or, alternately, has a meaning).[4] His approach to this broader question is to ask what must occur in any given utterance situation if the particular utterance in question is to be judged as meaningful. Basically,[5] he concludes that an utterance x has meaning when used by a speaker S if and only if, in using that utterance, S intends to produce an effect E in an addressee[6] A and, further, that S at the same time intends A to recog-

[3] There are other indications that the three works are supposed to be in the same mold, but these are nicely covered in MacKay (1972) so will not be pursued here.

[4] This problem is one of three that are traditionally dealt with by philosophers considering semantics. The other two are: What are the conditions (or criteria) that must be met if we are to say that two elements of language (words or sentences) mean the same thing, that is, are synonymous? What does it mean to say that something has a meaning and, if we say that something has meaning, what is it that IS its meaning? This second question admits of two different approaches; ontologically, the question becomes, 'What sort of THING is a meaning?' Is it an entity and, if so, what sort of entity is it? Epistemologically, the question is taken as a request for an explanation of the considerations that must be made in determining the meaning of a linguistic element, no matter what the meaning turns out to be, ontologically.

[5] For detailed explication and analysis of Grice's view, as well as full incorporation of criticism, see Schiffer (1972, esp. chaps. I and II).

[6] We are using the term ADDRESSEE throughout this chapter, rather than AUDIENCE or HEARER, to avoid the problem (for Grice) that, if an utterance is not intended for Y as 'audience', then Y, who may nonetheless 'hear' the utterance as part of the 'audience', should not be able to know what the utterance 'means'. This, in addition to other problems of accidental discourse participants, for example, the problems of shared speaker–hearer knowledge, are also avoided by specifying the analysis in terms of an 'addressee', that is, THE one to whom the utterance is directed by the

nize his (S's) first intention and produce the effect E at least partially on the basis of the recognition of S's intention that he, A, produce that effect. Grice carefully stipulates that the effect E must be something "which in some sense is within the control of the audience . . ." [1957:385]; but within this boundary any cognitive or affective attitude (disposition) or action may serve as the intended effect.

Although the form of the argument and the particulars of intention recognition are modified in subsequent papers (on the basis of received criticism), the elements just sketched are fundamental to all versions of the theory. But the formulation is not as simple as it might appear. The 'meaning' being discussed and explicated is what Grice calls 'nonnatural meaning', schematized as 'meaning$_{nn}$'; and 'meaning$_{nn}$' is explained through discussion of various sorts of 'utterance'. Since we want to understand and discuss 'meaning$_{nn}$', we need to first try to understand Grice's use of 'utterance'.

As commonly used by native speakers, the word *utterance* is applicable to linguistic acts (or entities) and, further, it is taken to apply ONLY to cases of linguistic acts (or entities) that count as speech production. Even in technical usage, for example, that of linguists, the term is applicable only to the performance (versus competence) aspects of language. This usage is reflected in the fact that (1) and (2) are not acceptable sentences of English, while (3)–(5) are acceptable:

(1)   *In his book on Africa he made the following utterance . . .
(2)   *Every utterance in his article was carefully checked for accuracy.
(3)   Every utterance at his trial was carefully recorded.
(4)   'He held us spellbound on his every utterance.'
(5)   His final utterance was lost in the crash of the springing trapdoor.

Grice does not want to be confined to the normal usage of the term *utterance,* however; instead, he says, he will "use 'utterance' as a neutral word to apply to any candidate for meaning$_{nn}$" [1957:380].

Such a 'definition' would be adequate were it not for two factors. First, 'meaning$_{nn}$' is what we are supposed to be explicating by analyzing 'utterances.' To thus define 'utterance' in terms of 'meaning$_{nn}$' leaves us with our fundamental concepts vacuously interdefined.

---

speaker. Further, this makes the matter at hand one of communication and helps to avoid such questions as, for example, those of meaning in private languages, or the like, as well as the Strawson, Ziff sorts of objections.

On the other hand, Grice may feel that his examples are sufficient to stipulate the scope of 'utterance' for his argument. But if we use the examples to set the scope of 'utterance', the term is seen to be far from 'neutral'. For his examples of 'utterances' are such things as an artist drawing a picture, a conductor ringing a bell, and a police officer waving to a driver,[7] which are surely not linguistic acts (or entities). They are nonlinguistic acts, and entities; noises, bodily movements, and so on, which while obviously being used in (at least attempted) communication, certainly do not belong to the class of things to which 'utterance' is normally taken to refer.[8]

This is not to argue that there is no category of phenomena such as those which Grice wishes to call 'utterances'. Rather, that without making clear to what the term applies he does nothing toward helping us to see what that class of phenomena consists of, and does nothing toward helping us to understand the intricacies of the class thus delineated. For Grice is clearly using 'utterance' in reference to ANY act or entity, linguistic or nonlinguistic, that may be used by an agent (the 'speaker') as a means for communicating; and this is certainly not a 'neutral' usage of the term 'utterance'.

Further, this nonstandard usage of 'utterance' is four ways ambiguous. For the act–object ambiguity (which Grice noted as being 'convenient') is present in both the linguistic and nonlinguistic cases of 'utterance'. We may be talking about the act of saying, what was said in saying (the noises made, the sentence vocalized, and so on), the act of doing, or what was done in the doing (the noises produced, the movement made, and so on). Recognition and accommodation of this ambiguity is of paramount importance if we are to be clear in our analysis. To accomplish clarity, one must distinguish between linguistic utterance and nonlinguistic utterance, as well as indicate when one is talking about the utterance object or utterance act in each case in which confusion might arise. However, since we will be talking only about nonlinguistic utterances, we may simply stipulate that 'utterance' is to be taken as meaning 'nonlinguistic utterance' in all occurrences. If other than nonlinguistic utterances are being discussed, they will be fully noted, that is, as 'linguistic utterances.'

[7] All examples, unless specifically noted, are Grice's own.

[8] The consideration of communication, that is, the role of 'utterance' in a speech act situation, does not become explicit in Grice until later papers, and then in response to criticisms such as those by Strawson (1964) and later by Ziff (1967). This reference to the communication sense of 'utterance' is then somewhat anachronistic, but nothing to which Grice could object.

II

Grice employs two different sorts of analysis in his attempt to draw the distinction between natural meaning, 'meaning', and nonnatural meaning, 'meaning$_{nn}$'. Initially, he elaborates a series of linguistic generalizations[9] based on occurrences of the word *mean* in sentences of English. This analysis is less than helpful, however, because the generalizations are formed on the basis of linguistic intuitions that are not shared, thus not corroborated.[10] Furthermore, it is not clear that determination of classes of usage for *mean* is of any value in telling us what meaning consists in.

More helpful is the examination of cases that have been classified as one or the other sort of meaning; this is Grice's second sort of analysis and the one on which I shall concentrate. As paradigms of 'meaning' we have, for example, the head of St. John being presented to Salome, the photograph that shows Mrs. X being familiar

[9] The things Grice (1957:377–378) uses are roughly as follows:

1. In the case of 'meaning', but not 'non-natural meaning' (hereafter 'meaning$_{nn}$') "x meant that p and x means that p entail p" [p. 377].

2. In the case of 'meaning$_{nn}$', but not 'meaning', we can argue from "x meant that p" to "what is (was) meant by x (is) (was) p" [p. 378].

3. In the case of 'meaning$_{nn}$', but not 'meaning', we can argue from "x means that p" to "A means p by x", where A is somebody or other (p. 378).

4. Any case of 'meaning$_{nn}$', but not 'meaning', may be restated as "x meant 'p' " [p. 378].

5. Any case of 'meaning', but not 'meaning$_{nn}$', may be paraphrased in a sentence of the form "The fact that . . ."

6. All cases of 'meaning$_{nn}$', but not 'meaning', are paraphrasable as 'A means something by x' or 'A means by x that . . .', while all cases of 'meaning' may be paraphrased by sentences "of the pattern 'A means (meant) *to do* so-and-so (by x)' " [p. 378].

[10] For example, most sources will not assent to (1) in footnote 9 unless it is stated what sense Grice attaches to 'entail'. Item (2) is unacceptable because for speakers of American English the paraphrases are quite acceptable, yet for speakers of British English they are not; for example, to go from 'Those spots mean that he has measles' to 'What is meant by those spots is that he has measles' seems quite normal. Item (5) is unacceptable on two counts: (a) 'The fact that . . .' DOES seem to paraphrase some cases, for example, the bellringing, although not all, and (b) Grice resorts to meaning as an explanation of meaning in saying that the 'the fact that . . .' paraphrase does 'not have, even approximately, the same meaning [as the original sentence]' [1957:378]. Finally, (6) is simply false, since later discussion (p. 379ff) shows that 'A meant *to do* so-and-so (by x)' is the paradigm for meaning$_{nn}$. In short, there is little agreement on these generalizations and, since they depend on such agreement for their usefulness, they should not be a crucial factor in understanding 'meaning$_{nn}$'.

with Mr. Y, the police officer stopping a car by standing in its path, and spots that show that a patient has measles. In some of these cases, for example, the spots, no agent (speaker) activity is involved; in others, agent activity is involved but the wishes or intentions the agent might have at the time of use are of no consequence in conveying the desired message.[11] As such, these nonlinguistic utterances tell the addressee exactly what he is to know, just as surely as smoke tells us there is fire.[12]

On the other hand, paradigmatic of 'meaning$_{nn}$' are a drawing that suggests that Mrs. X is being familmar with Mr. Y, a police officer stopping a car by waving at the driver, and a bus conductor indicating the bus' fullness by ringing a bell three times. In each case,

---

[11] Grice (1957) does not mention, and in fact seems to ignore, the fact that the objects of discussion, 'utterances' are elements of communication acts. But given Strawson's (1971) argument and Grice's subsequent changes (1964, 1969), there seems to be no reason to avoid talking about communication situations and messages.

[12] In the case of the photograph, the distinction Grice is attempting to draw is relatively clear. It is made even clearer if the case is modified. Imagine, for example, that I come upon the photograph and, knowing that Mr. X has a heart condition, I make an effort to keep from him the fact that Mrs. X has been familiar with Mr. Y. But purely by accident, for example, I am hiding the picture behind my back and drop it, with X retrieving it, X sees the picture and learns about his wife. My intention has clearly been that X NOT know about his wife, but the photograph has 'let him know' just that which I wanted to keep from him, contrary to my intentions in the matter. Thus, the photograph has 'meaning' in and of itself, just as measles spots have meaning in and of themselves. On an even further extreme, it is possible to imagine that Mr. X has been out taking pictures of a local park. From a distance he sees two lovers embracing. He thinks the setting idyllic and takes a picture. Unknown to him (for example, as the mirror on his SLR rises), the woman looks up and has her face photographed. When X develops the prints, he sees that one of the lovers is his wife. The photograph has told its tale, with no way AT ALL for consideration to be given to the intentions of anyone.

The point of exaggerating Grice's examples in this way is to try to emphasize what Grice takes to be an important point of difference between cases of meaning and cases of meaning$_{nn}$. In the former cases, the form of 'telling' that the utterance does is 'deliberately and openly letting someone know.' This is not the case in the latter, meaning$_{nn}$. Here the speaker must 'get the addressee to think' something, must get him to infer whatever it is that he wishes the addressee to know. Thus, Grice argues that a drawing (as opposed to a photo) of Mrs. X being familiar will not 'tell' in the strong sense but only 'tell' in the sense of getting Mr. X to think, but then only just in case Mr. X understands the artist as intending to get him to think something versus, for example, just drawing a picture. That is, the drawing cannot depict Mr. Y and Mrs. X unless the artist so intends his work (1957:383).

Granted, there would have to be different senses or sorts of natural meaning if this is to work, for these cases are different from, say, the measles case. But such different senses do not seem contrary to Grice's argument and, in fact, he suggests just this (p. 379) when he talks about "one or another natural sense of mean."

Grice tells us, the utterance constitutes an instance of 'meaning$_{nn}$' because of two factors. First, none of the utterances directly gives the addressee the message the speaker wishes to convey; rather, the addressee must do a certain amount of inference. [This sort of 'telling' he calls 'getting someone to think something', as opposed to 'directly and openly telling someone something'—the latter being the sort of 'telling' involved in 'meaning' (1957:380).] Second, and more important, the conveyance of the 'message' in each instance is a function of the speaker's intention, addressee recognition of the speaker's intention, and addressee response on the basis of that recognition of intention.

The viability of 'meaning$_{nn}$' as a classification of utterances than rests on his analysis of the role of intentions in the meaning situation. For this reason, a great deal of time and effort has been expended (see References) in trying to understand this role of intentions. In particular, the necessity of intention recognition has come under careful scrutiny. For if Grice is correct, every instance of what is normally considered to be communication will have to involve the intention-recognition pattern. Yet if the intention-recognition pattern is as complex as recent studies seem to indicate, it is difficult to understand how we manage to communicate. At the same time, it does not seem reasonable to assume that the intentions of the speaker play no role at all in the communication situation. The question, then, is not whether intentions have a role in communication situations but what that role might be. In terms of 'meaning' versus 'meaning$_{nn}$', it is a question with three parts: (1) Do intentions play a role in 'meaning$_{nn}$' but not in 'meaning', and (2) if intentions play a role in 'meaning$_{nn}$', is it as Grice describes, and (3) if not, does the difference alter the initial distinction between 'meaning' and 'meaning$_{nn}$'? Let us look at his examples of nonlinguistic utterances, then, to see how these questions might be answered.

Grice seems to place great emphasis on the case in which we are asked to compare a photograph with a drawing. The drawing is said to have 'meaning$_{nn}$' because the intention of the artist and the recognition of his intention by the addressee are crucial to the case. It is argued that the artist cannot be depicting Mrs. X and Mr. Y being familiar unless that is what he intends to depict. For the drawing must be made or composed; the figures must be somehow recognizable, and so on. Should the addressee, Mr. X, believe only that the artist is producing a work of art rather than trying to give him a message or get him to come to a conclusion, he will not have recognized the artist's intention and the drawing will not impart the meaning intended. In short, this is a case that exactly fits the requirements for 'meaning$_{nn}$'.

But closeness with the Gricean analysis does not appear in the other examples. Consider the case of the conductor and the three rings on the bell. We are told that the conductor rings the bell three times because he intends his addressee, on the basis of the addressee's recognition of that intention, to form the belief that the bus is full. The implausibility of this becomes obvious if we simply note that the conductor used three rings on the bell, not two or one or six. The conductor's utterance, "ding, ding, ding" (made by means of the bell)[13] will have been standardized (conventionalized) if the conductor is to have any hope of getting his message across without following up the bell rings with, for example, an announcement (in which case the bell rings 'mean$_{nn}$' not 'bus is full' but 'give me your attention').

In a similar way, we are told that the police officer would have to do no more than simply intend that his utterance "hand wave" (uttered by means of his hand) cause the addressee to stop the car on the basis of the addressee's recognition of that intention. This is as implausible as the bell-ring case, if not more so; unless the officer uses an utterance that will be readily recognized by the driver as one that 'means$_{nn}$' 'Stop your car' (as opposed to 'Make a left turn' or 'Hi!'), he will have little hope of getting the car stopped. He cannot use any old utterance; he cannot simply make up his utterances as he goes along. He must use a conventionalized hand signal, or at least one that is close enough to a conventionalized model so that the motorist will not become confused, misunderstand him, and so on. The utterance in question for the conductor, as well as the police officer, must be such that the addressee has some chance of recognizing it and understanding what he is supposed to do on the basis of that recognition. But note that it is the utterance that is initially recognized, NOT the speaker's intentions. At best, the intention recognition is secondary. The driver stops his car because he recognizes the utterance "upturned palm" as telling him that the officer intends him to do just that; the passengers stop trying to get on the bus because they recognize the conductor's utterance as telling them that he intends for them to do just that; and so on.

---

[13] There is an obvious difficulty here, since quotes are usually reserved for linguistic utterances. Further, what we must quote here are not the linguistic representations of bell rings but the actual bell rings. Since the latter is impossible, we will, by convention, use double quotes for 'utterances,' understanding by their use that the actual 'utterance' is considered as quoted, not just its representation.

In short, the intention of the speaker to elicit a response from the addressee is relevant to the utterance only in that the intention dictates which conventional utterance would best suit his purpose. To see the point here, and to see a further indication of the cooperative (versus exclusive) role of intentions, consider what happens when the speaker fails to achieve his goal in the communication situation. If Grice is correct, it simply means that he has not intended hard enough, or correctly. But if a speaker fails to get his message across to the addressee, he does not simply intend harder, or try to intend more clearly (if those things even make any sense). Instead, he switches to another conventional utterance that he feels that the addressee will recognize more readily; alternatively, he might repeat his utterance, for example, with more force, in a louder tone, and so on. For example, an officer directing traffic is in the intersection, clearly visible, that is, meeting all contextual requirements; he utters "upturned palm," fully intending the driver to stop his car. Should the car not perceptibly slow, he might continue to utter "upturned palm" and, in addition, utter "tweet, tweet" (by means of his whistle). If that does not work, he might try to be more forceful in his utterance, or he might switch to a linguistic utterance such as *Stop!* before finally diving for cover. The officer may intend all he can, but the driver still might not stop his car. Why? There are a number of interesting possibilities. On the one hand, the driver might very well intend to pass the corner without stopping, no matter what. In that instance, the officer's intention may be fully recognized, his utterances well-understood, but nonetheless, the intended result is 'counterintended' and not accomplished. In contrast, it might be the case that the driver did not recognize any of the officer's utterances as 'meaning$_{nn}$' that he should stop his car but, instead, thought they 'meant$_{nn}$' that he should hurry up through the intersection. Here, the intended effect is not realized because the 'meaning$_{nn}$' of the utterance, which is intermediate between speaker and addressee, is either not known or not understood. This case is particularly interesting because Grice would have to argue that the reason for the addressee's failing to grasp the speaker's intentions was that the speaker failed to make his intention clear. But the fact of the matter is that the nonlinguistic utterance used to express that intention is what was not clear. The intentions of the speaker were not sufficient to ensure UNDERSTANDING, as the satisfactory completion of the communication act requires. And that seems to indicate that addressee understanding has something to do with the recognition of intention, thus is of importance to the 'meaning$_{nn}$' of the nonlinguistic utterance in question.

The simplest way to state this is to say that the speaker must expect the addressee to understand his utterance if he is to be said to have the proper intention in using that particular utterance. Donnellan's (1968) suggestion that, in terms of linguistic utterances, intentions are tied to expectations, then appears corroborated for non-linguistic utterances also. For Donnellan argues (1968:212) that "Whether [the speaker] can form [a given] intention, however, may depend upon what expectations he has about his audience and their ability to grasp his intention. . . . And the existence of an established practice may be *usually* required for the speakers to have the right expectations." My suggestion, though, is that expectations are tied to the utterance as well as the intention. In the expression of his intention, the speaker must use a nonlinguistic utterance that the addressee may reasonably be expected to understand as expressing that intention. And the speaker may reasonably expect understanding when he uses an utterance that has been conventionalized (by a given group) as expressing that intention. There is no plausibility in supposing a situation in which a speaker has an intention that is perfectly correct (he has the correct expectations), but the utterance expressive of that intention does not meet the required expectation of understanding. The speaker cannot simply intend, lest we have a Humpty Dumpty theory of meaning; but the requirements of sufficient expectations and expression by means of a conventional utterance effectively rule out such a theory. Without those requirements, given the proper intention, a police officer could stand on his head, then reasonably give a ticket to any motorist who did not stop his car; the conductor could scratch his ear, and reasonably become angry if people kept trying to get on his bus. (In terms of linguistic utterances, the examples are numerous, as Ziff and others have shown.) But in my view, the officer must have the correct expectations AND use a conventional utterance to express that intention.

But it is not simply intending, with the correct expectations and using the conventional utterance, that fills our needs in understanding 'meaning$_{nn}$'; the utterance must occur in the appropriate circumstances. A police officer standing in a doorway, back from the street, out of uniform, and so on, is not in the correct circumstances to carry off the stopping of cars in the street. More to the point, three rings on the bell only 'means$_{nn}$' that the bus is full in a bus situation; at the opera, three rings on the bell 'means$_{nn}$' that the curtain is to rise; at the fire station three rings on the bell 'means$_{nn}$' that the fire is a general alarm; and so on.

Some cases even seem to require a specific context if an exchange is to come off at all, for example, Grice's (1968) case of laying down 43¢ at the tobacconist's. In this case, Grice argues that his laying down of 43¢ 'means_nn' that the tobacconist should give him a pack of his favorite brand, because the tobacconist recognizes Grice's intention to be given a pack of his favorite brand, on the basis of the money laid down. Thus, "laying down 43¢" is an 'utterance' like "ding, ding, ding" or "upturned palm." But the 'utterance' must already be conventionalized—the counter-man must know what "laying down 43¢" 'means_nn'; Grice must have a reasonable expectation that the tobacconist will remember "laying down 43¢"; he must also expect that the tobacconist remembers what is his favorite brand; and so on. If this is not Grice's regular tobacconist, for example, Grice is visiting another city, he cannot simply lay down 43¢ and expect to receive his cigarettes. Even if he is in his regular store, the usual counter-man must be there, the brand must be in stock, the store must be open for business, and so on, or the attempt fails. Importantly, not one of these contextual factors is a matter of intention, and they are certainly not linguistic matters—yet they are all crucial to the happy accomplishment of the communication act.

The plausibility of the suggestion that the utterance is of primary importance in intention recognition is increased by the fact that when an utterance is not understood the speaker may try to change to another utterance, one that he feels will have a better chance of being understood as indicating a given intention on the part of the speaker. Curiously, in most cases of nonlinguistic utterance failure, the speaker will switch to a linguistic utterance. The police officer shouts *Stop!*; the conductor says *This bus is full*, or *Stop pushing, there's no more room*, or the like. This is particularly the case with the artist who, when his representation fails, must resort to ordinary telling, that is, explaining the drawing, saying what it was that he was trying to express by means of his drawn utterance. But perhaps such a switch from nonlinguistic utterance to linguistic utterance is understandable, given the fact that there are usually a very limited number of nonlinguistic utterances that are appropriate in a given case—the conductor has only one, "ding, ding, ding," the police officer two, "upturned palm" and "tweet, tweet." The diversity and uniqueness of expression available with linguistic utterances is simply absent with nonlinguistic utterances.

It is interesting to note, however, that in some cases of failure, resolution of the issue is not aided by changing utterances. If the police officer is in the doorway, switching utterances will be of no help at all. If Grice is away from home, he has only to use a linguistic utterance, for example, *Give me a pack of Brand X please,* to accomplish his purpose. Likewise, if there is a new counter-man. But if the store is not yet ready for business, if Brand X is out of stock, if the price has gone up, or the like, there is no different utterance that will help achieve the desired result.

Also, the heavily intentional cases, such as that of the drawing, seem to rely less on the expectation and context elements. Granted the drawing, or showing of the drawing, must occur in a reasonable context (for example, not in a museum display), the artist must use at least semiconventional means of representation (for example, not rows of blocks), and they must be representations that he has reason to expect Mr. X will be able to understand or interpret. But the role of the artist's intention is heightened because there is not a conventional drawing that will tell the appropriate tale, since every drawing is in a sense unique (as a photograph need not be). The artist is quite unburdened by a group of conventional utterances and is free to make his utterance as he will, in a way that the conductor and especially the police officer are not free to make up their utterances. But again, the failure of the utterance the artist uses reduces his situation to that of the conductor and the police officer. He must resort to other, more conventional means of expression, usually linguistic utterances of a very direct sort. Until that time, he uses his drawing, making it such that he is able to get Mr. X to think what he wants him to think, to infer from the drawing that Mrs. X is being familiar with Mr. Y.

The matter of inference in the drawing case brings us back again to the Gricean distinction we noted earlier, that cases of 'meaning' were those in which direct telling was involved, while cases of 'meaning$_{nn}$' were those in which a speaker tried to get the addressee to think something, as opposed to being told directly. The problem we now see with this distinction is that ANY use of a conventional utterance appears to be a case of direct telling; because the utterance has 'meaning$_{nn}$,' it tells the addressee directly what the speaker wants him to know. But notice that this is done in varying degrees, so that it might be plausible to argue that the distinction of 'telling directly' and 'getting someone to think' is not a clear-cut dichotomy; instead, it is the indication of boundaries for a continuum. Further, its application to the natural-versus-nonnatural distinction is not as described. The cases of natural meaning do in fact seem to consist of instances of direct telling, but they are also clearly subject to degree. For example, spots 'mean' measles, but there are clearly defined spots and early cases that may be difficult to differentiate from, for example, scarlet fever. On the other hand, nonlinguistic cases of 'meaning$_{nn}$' are certainly possible in which direct telling is involved, as in the police officer's uttering "upturned palm," although the nonlinguistic cases run the gamut from here on down to 'getting someone to think'. The more conventionalized the utterance, the more direct the telling, at least in most cases. Thus, learning to distinguish 'direct telling' from 'getting someone to think' is by no means sufficient for enabling one to distinguish cases of 'meaning' from cases of 'meaning$_{nn}$.'

The evidence (shown here, as well as by other writers) that intentions play only a cooperative role in 'meaning$_{nn}$', plus the evidence that 'meaning' and 'meaning$_{nn}$' are not demarcated by 'telling directly' and 'getting one to think', would seem to indicate that the distinction between 'meaning' and 'meaning$_{nn}$' is no longer viable. This is correct if we insist that the distinction be made on Grice's terms. But there appears to be nothing wrong with the distinction as established in other terms. It is the distinction between measles spots and bell rings—between something that signifies naturally, apart from and often contrary to what someone might do with it, versus something that signifies solely on the basis of what an agent does with it.[14] Further, it is, at least in part, a distinction based on the role of intentions in an agent's communication activities. Intentions are not present in cases of 'meaning'; thus, cases of 'meaning' are not cases of communication. Intentions are present, or at least relevant, to cases of 'meaning$_{nn}$'; thus, cases of 'meaning$_{nn}$' are cases of communication (attempted, at least).

What we have seen is simply that there are other elements of the communication situation that are relevant considerations in understanding what message is sent and what intentions the speaker had in sending that message. On this account, however, intentions play only a cooperative role, moderating what the speaker does in a given communication situation, indicating possible choices of 'utterance' and so on. There is also a role for intentions on the part of the addressee to the communication situation. He must recognize a conventionalized utterance as one normally used to convey a message indicating an intention on the part of the speaker; that is, his role is intention recognition. It is just that the intention recognition is not as described by Grice but is, instead, a matter of convention, expectation, and context.

[14] Appropriate to this type of distinction are Wilson's (1970) notion of a 'signal' and Pierce's (1955) notion of 'symbol.'

III

Although I have been discussing only nonlinguistic utterances, as stipulated earlier in the chapter, it has been obvious for some time that points I have been noting as aspects of nonlinguistic utterances are also aspects of linguistic utterances. This apparent sharing of characteristics is seen even more clearly if we look briefly at some of the things other writers have said about linguistic utterances and compare them to what we have said about nonlinguistic utterances.

Searle (1965) argued that there is a role for intentions as well as conventions in the use of linguistic utterances; further, he argued that recognition of intention is achieved by the use of utterances that are associated with the effect intended. This is precisely the point I was trying to make in regard to the use of nonlinguistic utterances. One simply cannot recognize an intended effect unless the utterance used normally expresses that intention.

Donnellan's point (see p. 372) about expectations was in fact first made in connection with linguistic utterances; we have simply shown that it is also applicable to cases of nonlinguistic utterances, and added the point that expectations apply to the understanding of the utterance, as well as the intention.

Lewis (1969) argues that in a language situation (which he calls a signaling system context) coordination is required between speaker and addressee if communication is to take place. My analysis has indicated that such coordination is also necessary in cases of nonlinguistic utterances, although for different reasons than Lewis suggests; I am arguing that the coordination is by the use and recognition of a conventionalized nonlinguistic utterance rather than, as Lewis argues, on the basis of a shared contingency program.

Strawson (1971) argues that linguistic utterance acts ("illocutionary acts" or "speech acts") fit on a continuum that runs from those which are "essentially conventional" to those which are "not essentially conventional." We have noted a similar point in regard to nonlinguistic utterance acts and, further, have shown how the matter of conventionality may be directly related to whether or not a speaker, in using a particular nonlinguistic utterance, tells you something directly or merely gets you to know something (or any of the degrees in between). In addition, Strawson argues that in those cases which are essentially conventional, understanding ("uptake") guarantees success UNLESS a rule is broken, while in cases that are essentially nonconventional, understanding of the utterance may occur, yet the intention is not discovered or understood (it is "thwarted," in his terms). This, too, carries over nicely to the cases of nonlinguistic utterances we have examined. For example, in the case of the drawing, which is essentially nonconventional, Mr. X may simply not come to think what he is supposed to, yet he understands the drawing, knows that it is depicting two lovers, and so on. On the other hand, if the driver recognizes "upturned palm," which is essentially conventional, he will stop his car, unless he is intentionally breaking a rule of that conventional utterance act, that is, disobeying the instruction.

More interesting than these points of comparison is that afforded by Austin's "doctrine of the *Infelicities*." As formulated in Chapter II, and discussed in Chapter III, of *How to Do Things with Words* (Austin, 1965), the "doctrine of the *Infelicities*" consists of classification of rules indicating what has gone wrong when a speech act (use of a linguistic utterance) fails to come off, or is, to use his term, "unhappy." In part, his rules are essentially as follows:

(A.1)   There must be an accepted convention for the act, with specific, conventional effects.

(A.2)   The circumstances must be appropriate.

(B.1, 2) The procedure (utterance) has to be properly and completely carried out.

(G.1, 2) When the procedure requires consequential conduct, the participants must have the proper intentions, thoughts, feelings, etc., toward that conduct and must so actually conduct themselves.

He then goes on to elaborate and describe different cases of infelicities, and takes pains to try to categorize them according to what aspect of the total speech act requirement has not been accomplished.

To see how this works in the case of nonlinguistic utterances, consider again the case of the police officer whose utterance fails (the car does not stop). If he has used the utterance "raised fist," failure would be explained as substantially a matter of (A.1)—there is no accepted convention; if he is standing in the doorway, failure is at least partially accounted for by (A.2)—the circumstances are improper; and so on. And should one take the time to go through my other examples of failure, he will be quite surprised at the fullness of explanation found in Austin's felicity conditions.

It might be argued that it is inappropriate to discuss Austin's felicity conditions at this point, since he was concerned primarily with the so-called "performative utterances." That is no problem, however, for the analogue to performatives if found in nonlinguistic cases as well. For example, saying "Redoubled" in a bridge game constitutes redoubling; raising one's numbered card at an auction constitutes raising the last bid. Saying "Go!" starts a race but so, too, does uttering "bang" (by means of a starting gun). Thus, there are acts that, if not analogues to performative linguistic utterances, are certainly close enough in character to avoid disputing the matter of felicity conditions, at least for the time being. In fact, Austin (1965:120) mentions the possibility of bringing off the illocutionary force of an utterance by means of a nonlinguistic act. By my analysis, it would appear that Austin simply understated the matter, for there appears to be a rather full range of nonlinguistic acts that coincide quite nicely with linguistic acts in that both have the same illocutionary force.

Thus, there emerges a nonlinguistic analogue to the linguistic 'illocutionary act' or 'speech act', which analogue we might, for the sake of art, call a 'nonlinguistic speech act'. Such a label sounds self-contradictory, and may in fact be so. But a significant point is made by that contradiction: Nonlinguistic utterances and linguistic utterances together constitute a class of acts that might be called 'communication acts', with 'speech acts' and 'nonlinguistic speech acts' classificatory names for the two elements of the overall class. Further, the similarities between these two sorts of acts, contrary to the appearance given in such a cursory examination as this, are neither minimal nor insignificant. My brief examination has only begun to scratch the surface of their similarity and has, thus, shown that there is a great deal constituting 'meaning$_{nn}$' of which we know very little. However, the points raised indicate what needs to be done: The 'language' of nonlinguistic speech acts will have to be fully understood, with the eventual development of 'rules' similar to the syntactic and semantic rules linguists are currently developing for ordinary language; the elements of context and expectation suggest that consideration must also be given to matters that Stalnaker (1970) labels "pragmatics" — presuppositions, shared speaker-addressee knowledge, knowledge of possible worlds, and so on. In short, we will have to examine nonlinguistic utterances with the same thoroughness with which we have been examining linguistic utterances. That finished, we will have to compare results, abstracting from both analyses the elements of commonness and, on their basis, begin to formulate a theory of communication acts — all of which is a long-term project, this paper being only a suggested beginning.

Given the understanding, then, that there is a distinction between 'meaning' and 'meaning$_{nn}$' (although perhaps not the original

Gricean distinction), and given that the sense of 'meaning$_{nn}$' that has evolved here has the broad implications just sketched, what have we learned that is of any help in understanding the notion of conversational implicature? Let us turn to that matter before closing.

IV

Initially, it would seem that my work is at odds with the Gricean notion of conversational implicature. For that notion, as described in Grice's papers, "The Causal Theory of Perception" (1965) and "Logic and Conversation" (Chapter 2 of this volume), was formulated explicitly in terms of linguistic acts (speech acts, if you will), while the analysis I have given has been explicitly in terms of nonlinguistic acts. Further, 'meaning$_{nn}$' was never mentioned in either of those two papers. How are we to reconcile this apparent difference?

As a matter of fact, nonlinguistic acts, discussed in my terms, lend themselves very nicely to the theory of conversational implicature (properly modified) and, further, the understanding of 'meaning$_{nn}$' we have gained in this discussion may help us to see more precisely what sorts of considerations are involved in understanding conversational implicature, as well as helping us to understand more completely what aspects of conversational implicature are not a part of actual discourse, somewhat as follows.

Conversational implicature is basically the notion that an 'utterance' may mean one thing as uttered while implying (or meaning) quite another thing as understood. In cases of conversational implicature, what is meant is not what is said. Thus, when the duke says to the butler, *It is cold in here*, the duke means, 'Do something about the temperature in here',[15] although this is certainly not what *It is cold in here* actually means. Or take Grice's case of an apparently inappropriate remark (analogous to an apparently incorrect utterance by the police officer, that is, "hand pointing to the right," in a situation that apparently calls for "upturned palm") that in its inappropriateness indicates a hidden, or underlying, implication (meaning).[16] The case is that of the tutor who, when asked to report on the philosophical abilities of one of his students, replied, "*Jones*

[15] The example is essentially that of Gordon and Lakoff (Chapter 4 of this volume.)

[16] In chapter 2 of this volume, Grice uses the term IMPLIES; but he acknowledges, at the beginning of the chapter that MEANS or SUGGESTS are equally good, IMPLIES being only 'a term of art.'

has beautiful handwriting and his English is grammatical"
[1965:448].*"*

The two papers (Chapter 2 of this volume in particular) are,
then, attempts to understand and codify the pragmatic rules for the
conventional (normal, ordinary) use of language so that when an
addressee is presented with a situation of unconventional usage, as
just described, he is able to 'decode' that usage. He is able to go
through a correct chain of reasoning, using the rules of conversation,
much as one uses inference rules in a deductive system, and process
out the correct (though covert) meaning of the linguistic utterance
in question. If the addressee is unable to get a result that makes
sense, then either he has made a mistake in the 'deduction' or the
utterance is inappropriate, incongruous, irrelevant, or what not. The
difficulties in setting up such a system are many. Initially, we must
determine what of the total event is relevant to understanding the
discourse; then we must determine what may be abstracted from particular cases such that the required rules, or generalizations, may be
formulated; then we must determine how the rules are learned, how
they work, what their ultimate contents should be, and so on. For
what is crucial to conversational implicature is that we recognize a
conventional linguistic utterance as occurring nonconventionally,
that is, inappropriately; otherwise, we will not know to apply the
rules and determine what the covert meaning or implicature of the
utterance should be. Unless we can recognize an utterance as inappropriate, we will not be able to identify possible cases of conversational implicature; but, to recognize an inappropriate utterance, we
must be able to recognize appropriate ones. This is where my modified approach to 'meaning$_{nn}$' comes in. For, at least in part, I have
shown that 'meaning$_{nn}$' is based on (if not a set of) felicity conditions
for communication acts, be they linguistic or nonlinguistic. If conversational implicature requires that we know when any utterance is
appropriate or not, we will have to have this sort of condition in
order to make that determination. And if we view the recognition of
intention, as Grice originally described it, as a type of felicity condition, it is quite plausible to suggest that my analysis of 'meaning$_{nn}$' is
the sort of thing Grice was trying to describe. Further, the detailed
analysis of conditions for the CORRECT use of linguistic utterances
given in relation to conversational implicature is certainly an effort
in this direction. Thus, I am not doing something different from
Grice but, rather, trying to put his work on meaning into perspective
with his work on conversational implicature.

However, we must have a more detailed analysis of 'meaning$_{nn}$';

for if conversational implicature is a covert or implied meaning, the sort of meaning in question will have to be 'meaning$_{nn}$', not 'meaning'. Such analysis will, of necessity, include extensive study of intentions, since we have seen, contrary to Lewis' (1969) argument, that convention is not the sole element of 'meaning$_{nn}$'. At the same time, Lewis' work on convention must be given serious attention if we are to understand the relation of intention and convention for which Searle (1965) argues. Without such analysis, we will be unable to grasp the relations between speakers, utterances, and the world, with the result that we will be unable to understand communication and its implications. In addition, we must know, for the sake of our formal studies of language (syntax and semantics), which elements of the utterance situation are intentional and which are conventional. For the latter elements are those which linguists must formalize and evaluate in establishing the syntax and semantics of language. At the same time, pragmatic elements must be understood for their influence, if any, on that syntax and semantics, especially if they are determining factors (as recent work in semantics seems to indicate).

In short, the work has just begun. Hopefully, the preceding discussion will help to show many of the factors that are to be understood before we will be able to determine when a conventional utterance is occurring in its normal, correct, appropriate usage. Also, the need for a thoroughgoing analysis of nonlinguistic utterances is in order for two reasons: (1) These utterances are an integral part of our normal, everyday communication activities, thus of interest from the view of communication theory; and (2) because of the obvious similarities between linguistic and nonlinguistic utterance acts, analysis of one should give us insights into the elements of the other. But since nonlinguistic utterances seem less complex and less difficult to examine (relative, for example, to the examination of linguistic acts, which involves not only syntax, semantics, and pragmatics but morphology, orthography, phonology, and so on), their study would be quite helpful in understanding linguistic utterances. That is, the study of nonlinguistic acts should give us a clearer picture of various features of linguistic acts, with subsequent payoffs in terms of such matters as conversational implicature.

I should note, however, that the extensive amount of work suggested does not of necessity lead to pessimistic conclusions in regard to understanding conversational implicature (or any other aspect of language use). It is not an argument that discussion of such things be postponed until we know in detail all the facts of standard, nonimplicative usage. Rather, it is only to serve as a reminder that any analysis of conversational implicature must be tempered by the fact that our understanding of the features and functions of our language is limited; thus, our conclusions are up for grabs until such time as our knowledge of the relevant facts is at last fairly certain.

REFERENCES

Austin, J. L. *How to do things with words*. New York: Oxford University Press, 1965.

Donnellan, K. Putting Humpty Dumpty together again. *Philosophical Review*, 1968, **76** (2), 203–215.

Grice, H. P. The causal theory of perception. In R. Swartz, *Perceiving, sensing and knowing*. New York: Doubleday Anchor, 1965.

Grice, H. P. Meaning. *Philosophical Review*, 1957, **66** (3), 377–388.

Grice, H. P. Utterer's meaning and intentions. *Philosophical Review*, 1969, **68** (2), 147–177.

Grice, H. P. Utterer's meaning, sentence-meaning, and word-meaning. *Foundations of Language*, 1968, **4** (3).

Hare, R. M. Some alleged differences between imperatives and indicatives. *Mind*, 1967, **76** (303), 309–326. [On Grice, 1965]

Kashop, P. Imperative inference. *Mind*, 1971, **80** (317). [On Hare on Grice]

Lewis, D. K. *Convention: A philosophical study*. Cambridge, Mass.: Harvard University Press, 1969.

MacKay, A. F. Professor Grice's theory of meaning. *Mind*, 1973, **81** (321), 57–66.

O'Hair, S. G. Implications and meaning. *Theoria*, 1969, **35**, pt. 1, 38–54.

Patton, T. E., and Stampe, D. The rudiments of meaning; on Ziff on Grice. *Foundations of Language*, 1969, **5** (1), 2–16.

Pierce, C. S. Logic as semiotoc; the theory of signs. In J. Buchler (Ed.), *Philosophical writings of Pierce*. New York: Dover Publications, 1955, 98–119.

Schiffer, S. R. *Meaning*. London: Oxford University Press, 1972.

Searle, J. What is a speech act. In M. Black (Ed.), *Philosophy in America*. Ithaca, N.Y: Cornell University Press, 1965, 221–239.

Stalnaker, R. C. Pragmatics. *Synthese*, 1970, **32** (1/2), 272–289.

Strawson, P. F. Intention and convention in speech acts. In P. F. Strawson, *Logico-linguistic papers*. London: Methuen, 1971, 149–160.

Walker, D. D. Linguistic Nominalism. *Mind*, 1970, **79** (316), 569–580.

Wilson, N. L. Grice on meaning: The ultimate counterexample. *Nous*, 1970, **4** (3), 295–304.

Ziff, P. On H. P. Grice's account of meaning. *Analysis*, 1967, **28** (1) 1–8.

THE SOFT, INTERPRETIVE UNDERBELLY
OF GENERATIVE SEMANTICS

JERROLD M. SADOCK
University of Chicago

I wish to establish, as a pretheoretical notion, a relationship between a sentence spoken in context and a semantic proposition. I will label this relation INVOLVEMENT and try to explain by illustration what it means for a sentence in context to involve a proposition. I want this relation to be quite general. Very roughly, I would like it to hold between a sentence in context and any proposition that is part of the literal meaning of any sentence or sequence of sentences that adequately get across the sense and force of the uttered sentence in the same context.

Let me bring in a few examples. First of all, if X_c is a sentence uttered in context and p is a proposition that functions in the literal meaning of X on the reading it has in context, then the involvement relationship, $I(X_c, P)$ holds. (The sentence form X obviously can get across what it does in a certain context.) But the involvement relation is neutral as to whether P is part of the meaning of one reading of X or not. Thus, in all cases in which there has been argument in the literature over whether a particular proposition is directly a part of the literal meaning of some sentence, the involvement relation will hold. One instance of this involves semantic decomposition. Regardless of whether the proposition, ALIVE (Harry), functions in the literal meaning of the sentence *Bill killed Harry* (see Lakoff, 1970a, and Fodor, 1970, for two sides of the issue), the involvement relation holds. This follows from my rough-and-ready characterization of the relation and from the fact that some compound sentence such as *Harry was alive some time ago but he no longer is, and this state of affairs was brought about directly because of something John did, and . . .* could accurately capture the sense and force of the original sentence. There can be little question that the proposition ALIVE (Harry) is part of the meaning of the compound sentence. Similarly, any sentence involves any of its presuppositions as well as any proposition that is a component of any of its presuppositions. This is due to the fact that presuppositions can be 'factored out' in an adequate paraphrase. Thus, in place of a sentence that presupposes a constituent clause, for example, *John realizes that Bill is a philosopher*, we could have *Bill is in fact a philosopher, which I assume you knew. Moreover, John shares our belief that Bill is a philosopher.*

There has been some discussion in the literature as to whether or not the conveyed force of sentences such as *Would you please close the door* is an aspect of the meaning of these sentences (See Gordon and Lakoff, this volume, for a negative opinion and Sadock, 1972, for the positive stance). Again, though, such a sentence INVOLVES its conveyed force whether this turns out to be an aspect of meaning or not.

Now, a total explication of our ability to communicate via language will include—indeed, will consist largely in—an account of the infinite set of ordered pairs of sentences in context and the semantic propositions they involve. In a semantically based grammar such as that developed by Lakoff, McCawley, Ross, and others, there are roughly three ways of accounting for the fact that a particular sentence in context involves a particular semantic proposition.

First of all, the entire explanation can be relegated to the grammar. The explanation for the fact that $I(X_c, P)$ holds is, in such a case, that P is to be found in the syntactic history of X (on the reading it has in the context in question). In the most trivial case of all, P (or, more precisely, its linguistic correspondent) appears in the surface form of X. In the more interesting cases, however, grammatical rules alter or even eliminate P entirely. There are many fairly uncontroversial cases in which this mode of explanation has been invoked. Take, for instance, a time-honored example such as *Lions frighten John more than me.* It has been argued (Lees, 1961) that there is a grammatical rule of comparative simplification that serves to delete those parts of a comparative construction which are identical to earlier material. The fact that the example sentence here can involve the proposition, FRIGHTEN (Lions, I) (presuming for the sake of discussion that this is a semantic proposition, which it most likely is not), would be traced to the fact that there is a clause in the underlying syntactic structure of the example that can be identified with this proposition. Generative semanticists have claimed that it is the grammar that is solely responsible for a much larger percentage of involvement relations than had previously been thought. The arguments that were given in favor of this contention were all on the model of earlier syntactic arguments, and the conclusions were therefore thought to be incontestable. The grammatical account of the involvement of P by X_c is schematized in Figure 1.

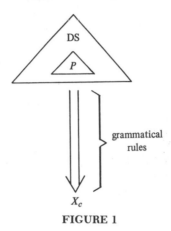

FIGURE 1

Here a triangle represents (underlying) syntactic (= semantic) structure and a triangle within a triangle a substructure thereof.

While it is tempting to describe as much as possible of the understanding of a sentence in context in terms of syntax alone — there exists, after all, a formalism for such descriptions — it is clear that not every case of the involvement of a proposition by a sentence can or should be handled in this way. Consider the following example. Suppose that, in some English-speaking society, families with three or more children are required to pay the government a certain penalty. In this society, one might respond to a question about whether he is subject to the penalty by replying, *I have two children.* In this context, the uttered response clearly involves the proposition FEWER THAN $(N, 3)$ — or whatever the atomic structure of this proposition turns out to be — where N refers the number of children the speaker has. But in this case, it would be absurd to blame the involvement of P by X_c on the grammar. First of all, the number of children the government considered undesirable could be any number whatsoever. Therefore, by saying that the grammar of English accounts for the involvement relation, that is, that the involved proposition is a proper subpart of the underlying syntactic structure of X, we would be claiming that X is infinitely ambiguous. This result runs counter to a field-defining assumption about ambiguity which can be found stated explicitly in Chomsky (1965), and counter to intuition.

Worse still, an attempt to handle involvement relations such as the one just given entirely in terms of the grammar would result in the building of independent cognitive systems—in this case arithmetic—into the grammar. Notice that while the sentence *I have two children* can involve FEWER THAN (*N*,3), the sentence *I have four children* cannot. An entirely grammatical account of the involvements in question would therefore have to include an account of the fact that *two* is less than *three* while *four* is not less than *three,* and so on, thus duplicating in all essentials the independently needed logical account of the fact that two is less than three but four is not. An entirely grammatical account of the involvement in this case would also seem to make the false claim that there could be a language with a slightly different grammar in which *I have four children* could involve the meaning of *I have fewer than three children,* while the meanings of *three* and *four* are otherwise the same as they are in ordinary English.

It is clear that, in cases like this, cognitive systems independent of language mediate between the meaning of a sentence in context and the involved proposition. Thus, we have the second sort of account of an involvement relation; I call this the logical account (for lack of a more general term) and schematize it in Figure 2.

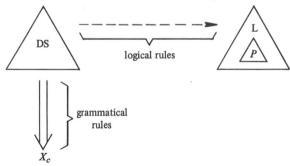

FIGURE 2

This diagram assumes that the output of all of the various sorts of rules of inference (for example, arithmetical laws, logical laws, and conversational principles) is of the same form as underlying syntactosemantic structures, but this assumption is not crucial to my discussion.

The third scheme for describing involvement relations which has been suggested within the context of generative semantics is what I shall call the logicogrammatical treatment. While the grammatical treatment involves grammatical rules (transformations, derivational constraints, and so on) and the logical treatment involves logical rules (rules of inference, mathematical equivalences, conversational principles, and so on), the logicogrammatical treatment requires a new mechanism—transderivational constraints (see Gordon and Lakoff, this volume; Lakoff, 1970b, 1973). Not every device that has been labeled a transderivational constraint produces a logicogrammatical treatment: Some use only properties of syntactic structure in their application.

As an illustration of a logicogrammatical account of an involvement relation, consider the following discussion, adapted from Gordon and Lakoff (this volume). The sentence *Why paint your house purple?* involves the meaning of the sentence *You should not paint your house purple.* Gordon and Lakoff assign to the sentence the meaning of a question about a reason for painting the house purple. They suggest that any question about a reason for doing something can conversationally entail a suggestion on the speaker's part that there is no reason for doing it and, hence, that it should not be done. But whereas this conversational entailment need not go through for every *why* question, the sentence *why paint your house purple?* ALWAYS carries this entailment. Gordon and Lakoff therefore provide a transderivational constraint that makes the deletion of the second-person subject and the tense morpheme dependent on the entailment. Thus nongrammatical processes (conversational principles) play a crucial role in the involvement, but the surface form of the sentence shows some direct reflections of this extrasyntactic process. Schematically, the logicogrammatical account of the involvement of *P* by *X* would be something like Figure 3.

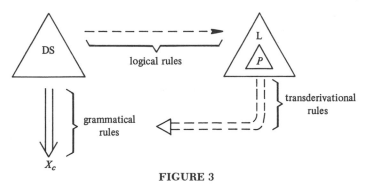

FIGURE 3

The transderivational constraints that have the property of producing logicogrammatical treatments are just those which make a syntactic derivation partially dependent on logical deductions based on meaning, or those which make logical deductions depend to some extent on aspects of syntactic derivations.

Given these three distinct treatments for the involvement of a proposition by a sentence in context, how are we to decide, in any given instance, which to apply? Before transderivational constraints were proposed, argument forms were developed which were designed to show that a particular involvement relation was to be accounted for solely within the syntactic derivation. Indeed, arguments of this sort were used to demonstrate the reasonableness of doing semantically based syntax. There are a great many sorts of arguments of this kind, and a discussion of them all is well beyond the scope of this chapter, but I will describe one typical example.

Ross (1970) wished to show that the performative propositions that declarative sentences involve in context are present as higher clauses in the underlying syntactic structure of declarative sentences. He argued, in other words, that this particular sort of involvement relation was to be handled by the grammar of the language. One typical argument in favor of this position involves the distribution of spurious reflexives, as in the sentence *Peter said the book was written by Mary and himself.* Ross showed that such spurious reflexives are grammatical in dependent clauses only if there is a coreferent antecedent in a higher clause. But he noticed that sentences like *This book was written by Mary and myself* are also grammatical. Here, though, the reflexive must be first person. (There are dialects for which the facts are somewhat different, but I will not bring these into consideration, since I am interested mainly in the form of the argument here.) Ross concluded that a unified account of the distribution of these spurious reflexives could be given only if an abstract higher clause were postulated for declarative sentences that contained a first-person noun phrase. Given this hypothesis, a single statement—the one already needed to account for spurious reflexives in dependent surface clauses—would take care of all spurious reflexives, including those in highest surface clauses. Without abstract higher clauses, two separate grammatical statements would be required, one for highest surface clauses and one for embedded surface clauses. Unfortunately, the availability of a logicogrammatical mode of explanation for involvement relations weakens—I might even say vitiates—this particular argument schema.

Given transderivational constraints of the kind I have discussed, the facts concerning the distribution of spurious reflexives can be handled logicogrammatically without the loss of a generalization. Instead of postulating a higher performative clause for declarative sentences, we propose a conversational principle that operates on underlying syntactic structure and interprets these as having a higher performative clause. This is not a rule of grammar but a rule of conversational logic. It mirrors exactly, and at the same time makes unnecessary, all of the well-formedness conditions required under the abstract performative hypothesis which guarantee that every well-formed semantic structure contains a highest performative clause whose subject refers to the speaker of the sentence and whose indirect object refers to the addressee. Under the performative hypothesis a performative deletion rule is required in order to get rid of just those underlying performative clauses that either obligatorily or optionally fail to surface. Conversely, the conversational rule must supply a performative clause in just those cases in which the performative deletion rule would have applied.

According to this view, the underlying syntactic structure of a sentence that contains a spurious first-person reflexive in a highest surface clause would be roughly that given in Figure 4.

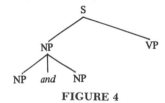

FIGURE 4

To this, the conversational rule that appends a performative clause to the underlying structure of declarative sentences would apply. Now, the generalization that Ross was able to capture syntactically can also be made by referring to any point in the series of logical steps based on the meaning of sentences AFTER the performative insertion rule has applied. A transderivational constraint can be written which says that a spurious reflexive can arise just in case there is a higher coreferent noun phrase IN A CONVERSATIONALLY ASSOCIATED STRUCTURE. For spurious reflexives in surface dependent clauses, the performative addition rule is irrelevant. The structural properties that allow the spurious reflexive are naturally unaffected by the addition of a performative clause to the top of the structure. Figure 5 illustrates the logicogrammatical account of spurious reflexives in highest surface clauses, and Figure 6 the account for dependent surface clauses.

One attempt that might be made to show this transderivational constraint to be invalid and, thus, to rescue the arguments in favor of

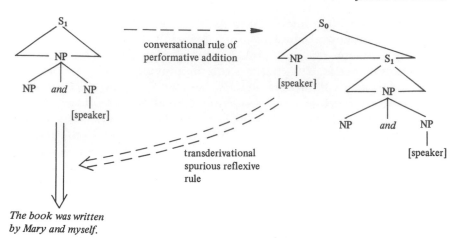

FIGURE 5

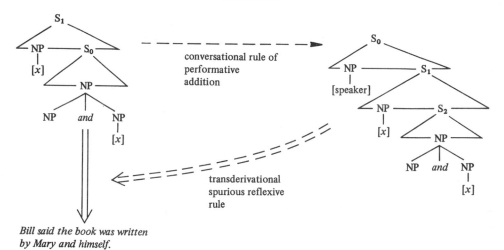

FIGURE 6

the performative hypothesis would involve showing in some way or another that the spurious reflexive rule must be a syntactic rule.

Let us suppose that it is agreed that the spurious reflexive-forming rule is a purely syntactic process. Then Figure 5 will not do as an account of the facts for independent reasons. But transderivational constraints have been endowed with the power not only to modify a syntactic derivation on the basis of logically (rather than linguistically) associated structures but also to modify one syntactic derivation on the basis of another where some sort of relationship exists between the two derivations (Lakoff, 1973). Therefore, it is possible to give a logicogrammatical account of the distribution of spurious reflexives without postulating abstract performative clauses and still retain an entirely syntactic rule of spurious reflexive formation. This is a consequence of the fact that logical calculations on a logical structure that underlies a sentence of a natural language will yield structures that could themselves yield sentences of the language. There might be something about the resultant sentence that violates rules of the language (lexical insertion rules, for the most part), but a good deal of syntactic processing can always be done on these associated logical structures, since generative semantics assumes that logical structures underlie sentences. The required transderivational constraint in the case at hand would state that a spurious reflexive can be found if there is a higher (syntactic) antecedent or if, from a structure associated with the underlying form of a sentence by the interpretive rule of performative addition, a spurious reflexive could arise. This treatment is represented schematically in Figure 7 (the syntactic case) and Figure 8 (the logicogrammatical case). For a discussion of an instance in which just this sort of treatment has been suggested, see Sadock (1975).

It should be obvious that there is no possible argument in favor of an abstract syntactic explanation for an involvement relation that cannot be gotten around by an appeal to some sort of transderivational constraint using logically associated derivations. They allow one to avoid the overt repetition of a syntactic process in the form of

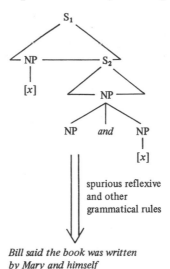

Bill said the book was written by Mary and himself

FIGURE 7

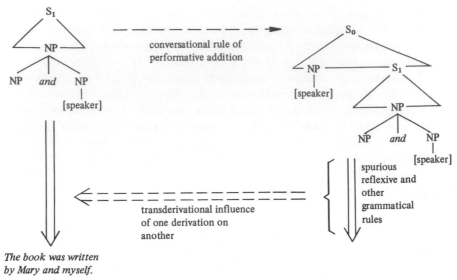

The book was written
by Mary and myself.

FIGURE 8

an extrasyntactic process and, thus, allow one to state any syntactic
generalization that is correlated with the involvement of propositions
logicogrammatically. For example, one of the most persuasive argument types that generative semanticists have employed has to do
with the general constraints on transformations of certain kinds, discovered by Ross (1967). Consider the following argument. Geis
(1970) argued that the understanding of the word *before* as com-
paring two times was to be handled by the syntactic component of a
grammar of English. He argued, in other words, that the involvement relation that can hold between a sentence such as *John came
before Bill left* and the proposition PRECEDE (t_1, t_2) AND AT $(t_1,$
COME (John)) AND AT $(t_2,$ LEAVE (Bill)) deserved an entirely syntactic treatment. Geis' principal argument concerned the observation
that if the underlying syntactic structure of sentences containing
before includes the involved proposition containing the predicate
PRECEDE, then relativization would necessarily be one step in the
derivation of such sentences. But, because of its nature, relativization
is subject to Ross' constraints. Therefore, the understanding of *before*
ought, on this theory, to be governed by Ross' constraints, and this
turns out to be so. A sentence like *John came before Mary claimed
that Bill left* has two understandings. It can involve a proposition
that is true if John came before the time at which Bill was claimed to
have left, or a proposition that is true if John came at a time prior to

Mary's making some claim. But the sentence *John came before Mary made the claim that Bill left* has only the latter understanding. These facts are predicted on the basis of independently established theory (Ross' constraints) and Geis' syntactic theory of *before*.

But again, given transderivational constraints of the type I have been discussing, a logicogrammatical explanation of these facts that does not miss the generalizations of the grammatical theory is possible. First, let us suppose that there is an atomic predicate BEFORE that is to be found in the underlying syntactic form of any of the sentences just given. Let us suppose, in addition, that there is a rule of conversational logic (in this case a meaning postulate) that relates propositions with BEFORE to propositions containing the (atomic) predicate PRECEDE, as in Figure 9.

As Figure 9 shows, this meaning postulate is not complete, since S_4 and S_5 are not filled out. But the relationship between S_4 and S_1 and between S_5 and S_2 can be stated in syntactic terms. For example, S_5 can be any structure such that, after relativization and other syntactic processing, the surface form of S_5 is the same as the surface form of S_2. In this case, then, what is needed is a transderivational constraint that controls a rule of conversational logic on the basis of syntactic derivations. Such mechanisms have been suggested to me in personal communications by several investigators. The constraint in question would allow the meaning postulate relating BEFORE and PRECEDE only if the proper syntactic correspondences exist between S_4 and S_1, and S_5 and S_2. These syntactic correspondences will be partially handled by ordinary grammatical rules such as relativization.

I have argued at length that whatever involvement relations can be explained grammatically can also be explained logicogrammatically. But the reverse is also true. In all cases in which transderivational constraints that take into account deductions in conversational logic have been proposed, a purely grammatical account can be given. In general, what this involves is, first, the hypothesis that what had been looked upon as a structure deduced from the logical form of a sentence is, in fact, a part of the logical form. Next, those aspects of the logical processes which were responsible for the involvement relation in the logicogrammatical account must be looked upon as syntactic operations. If the logical processes can be stated explicitly, then so can their inverse syntactic counterparts.

Lakoff (1969), for example, proposed a transderivational account of the involvement of propositions like SAME (mayor, Irishman) by the sentence *The mayor is a Democrat and the Irishman is honest, too*

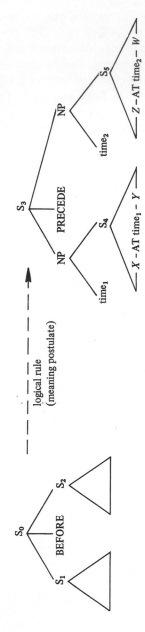

FIGURE 9

when it is read with low stress on *Irishman* and high stress on *honest*. Lakoff claimed that the literal meaning of the sentence is much like its surface form, that is, something on the order of DEMO-CRAT (mayor) AND HONEST (Irishman). Destressing *Irishman* would take place through the operation of a transderivational constraint sensitive to whether there is a presupposition in the context of the utterance that equates the mayor with the Irishman.

But since anyone hearing the sentence would know that the speaker is behaving as if he believed that the mayor and the Irishman were the same individual, it could just as plausibly be supposed that the equivalence of mayor and Irishman is directly part of the meaning of the sentence. In that case, no transderivational constraint, but only a purely syntactic rule of destressing, would be required. It is not obvious which treatment is to be preferred.

The only cases in which this procedure would clearly be in error would be those in which there is no interaction between a rule of logic and the grammar, that is, where no transderivational constraint is needed. Conversely, the only cases of syntactic analysis that could not be handled in terms of a transderivational constraint are those in which the syntactic process has no influence whatsoever on the involvement of propositions. In the vast middle ground, however, where the explanation of most of our ability to communicate lies, there is a serious methodological dilemma. I believe that a failure to appreciate this dilemma is at the heart of a good deal of controversy in modern syntax. Not only disagreements within orthodox generative semantics, such as the one concerning the analysis of indirect speech acts, but even the lexicalist–generativist debate can, I think, be traced to the same source.

Two methods for removing this arbitrariness from linguistic theory suggest themselves. One would eliminate transderivational constraints that state an interaction between logic and language, and the other would REQUIRE a logicogrammatical treatment in terms of transderivational constraints wherever it is possible to provide one. The result would be two radically different definitions of sentence meaning—one very shallow and one very deep. I am not sure that anything at all rides on this difference.

ACKNOWLEDGMENTS

This work was partially supported by a grant from the Mathematical and Social Sciences Board of the National Science Foundation. I wish to think the conferees at the formal pragmatics workshop in Ann Arbor during the summer of 1973, the faculties and students of the University of Chicago and The Ohio State University for helpful criticism, and especially Arnold M. Zwicky, without whose help the title of this chapter would not have been possible.

REFERENCES

Chomsky, N. *Aspects of the theory of syntax*. Cambridge, Mass.: MIT Press, 1965.

Fodor, J. A. Three reasons for not deriving 'kill' from 'cause to die'. *Linguistic Inquiry*, 1970, 1, 429–439.

Geis, M. L. Adverbial subordinate clauses in English. Unpublished Ph.D. dissertation, MIT, Cambridge, Mass., 1970.

Lakoff, G. The role of deduction in a grammar. In C. Fillmore and T. Langendoen (Eds.), *Studies in linguistic semantics*. New York: Holt, Rinehart & Winston, 1969.

Lakoff, G. *Irregularity in Syntax*. New York: Holt, Rinehart & Winston, 1970.   (a)

Lakoff, G. *Linguistics and natural logic. Studies in generative semantics. 1.* Ann Arbor: The University of Michigan, Phonetics Laboratory, 1970.   (b)

Lakoff, G. Some thoughts on transderivational constraints. In B. Kachru *et al. (Eds.)*, *Issues in linguistics. Papers in honor of Henry and Renee Kahane*. Urbana: University of Illinois Press, 1973, 442–453.

Lees, R. B. Grammatical analysis of the English comparative construction. *Word*, 1961, 17, 171–85. Reprinted in D. A. Reibel and S. A. Schane (Eds.), *Modern studies in English*. Englewood Cliffs, N. J.: Prentice-Hall, 1969.

Ross, J. R. Constraints on variables in syntax. Unpublished Ph.D. dissertation, MIT, 1967. Mimeo by the Indiana University Linguistics Club, Bloomington.

Ross, J. R. On declarative sentences. In R. A. Jacobs and P. S. Rosenbaum (Eds.), *Readings in English transformational grammar*. Waltham, Mass.: Ginn, 1970, 222–272.

Sadock, J. M. Speech act idioms. In P. M. Peranteau, J. N. Levi, and G. C. Phares (Eds.), *Papers from the eighth regional meeting of the Chicago Linguistic Society*. Chicago: University of Chicago Department of Linguistics, 1972, 329–340.

Sadock, J. M. *Toward a linguistic theory of speech acts*. New York: Academic Press, 1975.

AUTHOR INDEX

Numbers in italic refer to the pages on which the complete references are listed.

A

Alston, W. P., 305, 306, 307, 318, 321, 325, 346, *359*
Anderson, S., 166, *184*
Anscombe, E., 354, *359*
Antinucci, F., 137, *141*
Austin, J. L., 1, 10, 18, 26, 28, 29, 30, *38*, *106*, 233, *255*, 305, 306, 317, 318, 319, 323, *359*, 377, 378, *382*
Ayer, A. J., 305, 318, *359*

B

Bach, E., 356, *359*
Bell, Q., *184*
Binnick, R., 137, *141*
Bloomfield, L., 318, *359*
Bolinger, D., *106*, 107, *141*
Bouton, L., 166, *184*
Butters, R., 130, *141*

C

Cartwright, R., 306, *359*
Chapin, P. G., 235, *255*
Chomsky, N., 386, *396*
Christensen, N. E., *359*
Cohen, L. J., 5, *38*
Cole, P., 288, *288*

D

Davidson, A., 145, 163, *184*
Davidson, D., 321, 322, 323, 324, 330, 356, *359*, *360*

Davis, S., 310, 312, 315, 329, *359*
Donnellan, K., 330, *359*, 372, *382*

F

Ferrars, K., 180, *185*
Fillmore, C. J., 255, *255*
Fodor, J. A., 383, *396*
Fraser, J. B., 189, *210*, 234, *255*
Frege, G., 357, *360*

G

Garner, R., 324, 328, 333, *360*
Geis, M. L., 214, *230*, 392, *396*
Gleitman, L. R., 230, *230*
Gordon, D., 145, 177, 180, 181, 182, *185*, 238, *255*
Green, G., *106*, 145, 160, 179, *185*
Grice, H. P., 200, 308, 325, 326, 327, 329, 330, 331, 332, 333, *360*, 363, 365, 367, 368, 369, 373, 379, 380, *382*

H

Hare, R. M., *382*
Harman, G., 319, *360*
Heringer, J., 115, *141*, 143, 145, 149, *185*

J

James, D., 295, *303*
Jones, M. T., 330, *360*

K

Kashop, P., *382*
Katz, J., 112, *141*

Klima, E. S., 265, 266, 268, *288*
Kripke, S., 306, 330, *360*

L

Labov, W., 274, *288*
Lakoff, G., 84, *106*, 132, *141*, 145, 177, 180,
    181, 182, *185*, 215, 230, *230*, 236, 238,
    255, *255*, 268, *288*, 383, 387, 390,
    393, *396*
Lakoff, R., *106*, 110, 137, *141*, 153, *185*,
    212, 215, *230*, 255, *256*, 269, *288*
Langacker, R. W., 112, *141*, 218, *230*
Lees, R. B., 265, 266, 268, *288*, 384, *396*
Lehrer, K., 27, *38*
Lewis, D. K., 376, 381, *382*
Liberman, M., 158, *185*
Linsky, L., *360*

M

MacKay, A. F., 328, 333, *360*, 364, *382*
McCawley, J. D., 17, *39*, *256*, *360*
Moore, G. E., 320, 321, 342, 344, *360*
Morgan, J. L., 132, *141*, 294, *303*

O

O'Hair, S. G., 363, *382*

P

Parisi, D., 137, *141*
Partee, B. H., 32, *39*
Patton, T. E., *382*
Perlmutter, D. M., 249, *256*, 266, *288*
Peters, S., 215, 230, *230*
Pierce, C. S., 375, *382*
Postal, P. M., 112, *141*, 249, *256*, 337,
    360

Q

Quang Phuc Dong, 230, *230*
Quine, W. V. O., 305, 352, 353, 354, *360*,
    361

R

Reibel, D. A., *231*
Ross, J. R., 3, 17, *39*, 170, 171, 172, *185*,
    216, 217, 218, *231*, 241, 247, 248,
    249, *256*, 269, *288*, 292, *303*, 336, 356,
    361, 388, 392, *396*
Ruhl, C., 214, *231*
Rundle, B., 355, *361*
Ryle, G., 305, 317, *361*

S

Sadock, J. M., *106*, 107, 131, *141*, 145,
    152, 178, *185*, 269, 273, *288*, 384, 391,
    396
Schane, S. A., *231*
Schiffer, S. R., *106*, 328, 333, *361*, 364,
    382
Schmerling, S. F., 230, *231*, 301, *303*
Schreiber, P. A., 17, *39*
Searle, J. R., 3, 4, 5, 7, 10, 12, 14, 15, *39*,
    60, 71, *82*, 93, *106*, 163, *185*, 189, *210*,
    239, *256*, 320, 325, 330, 355, *361*,
    376, 381, *382*
Stalnaker, R. C., 378, *382*
Stampe, D. W., 5, 36, *39*, 307, 308, 309,
    315, 328, 329, 335, 345, 349, *361*,
    382
Steinberg, D. D., *361*
Strawson, P. F., 190, *210*, 306, 318, 330,
    361, 366, 368, 376, *382*

T

Tajtelbaum, A., 354, *361*
Tarski, A., 321, 322, *361*
Thrasher, R., 301, *303*

W

Walker, D. D., *382*
Whiteley, C. H., 354, *361*
Wiggins, D., 321, 323, 330, *361*
Wilson, N. L., 375, *382*
Wittgenstein, L., 305, 318, 319, 328, 330,
    339, *361*

Z

Ziffi, P., *361*, 366, *382*
Zwicky, A. M., 214, *230*

SUBJECT INDEX

A

Action, speech and, 1
Adverbials
  reason, 162–164
  speech acts and, 161–162
Ambiguity, Cooperative Principle and, 54
And, in asymmetric conjunctions, 211–227
And then, in temporal sequence, 227
Anger, in indirect speech acts, 150–151
Asserted Intention, principle of, 205–206
Asserting acts
  list of performative verbs in, 190
  two groups of, 191 n.
Asymmetric conjunction, 211–230
  and conjuncts in isolation, 224–225
  Coordinate Structure Constraint in, 216–220
  De Morgan's Laws and, 273
  examples of, 214–215
  Gricean analysis of, 215–225
Asymmetric logical structures, surface conjoined structures and, 213

B

Basic meaning formula, 320–333
  "syntax" of, 346–348
  use of, 335–346
Be going to, as hedged performative, 205–207

C

Can, as hedged performative, 199–202
Categorizing phrase consumption, 336

Ceremonial performative, 190 n.
Commands, as imperatives, 179–180
Committing, performative verbs in acts of, 193
Communication
  conversation and, 83
  performative preface in, 2
Complex NP constraint, 293
Conjunction
  asymmetric, 211–227
  conversational implicature and, 212
Conjuncts
  in asymmetric conjunction, 224–225
  priority in, 228–229
Constativism, 18–33
Constraints on Variables in Syntax (Ross), 292
Contextual meaning, lexicalization of, 276–277
Conversation
  implied or conveyed meaning in, 84
  logic and, 41–58
  primary or literary meaning in, 84
  rules of, 211–230
Conversational entailment, 386–387
Conversational implicature, 45, 50
  clear case of, 260
  conjunctions and, 212–213
  criteria for, 260
  defined, 379
  language change and, 273–276
  meaning and, 363–382
  speech acts in, 181
  synchronic and diachronic status of, 257–288
  syntactic evidence of, 263–271
  "utterance" and, 363–366

399

Conversational maxim, 213
Conversational meaning, literal meaning and, 273–275
Conversational postulates, 83–105
  defined, 84
  entailments in, 84
  in grammar, 94–104
  here in, 99
  list of, 84–94
  may in, 102–103
  please in, 98
  problems of, 101–104
  reasonableness conditions in, 89–91
  sincerity conditions and, 84–89
  transderivational rules in, 104–105
Conversational rule, performative clause and, 389–390
Cooperative Principle (Grice), 45, 258, 277
  conversational postulates and, 91–92
  maxims and, 49
Coordinate Structure Constraint, 216–220, 293, 296–299
Could, in indirect speed acts, 78–79

D

De Morgan's Laws, asymmetric conjunction and, 223
Derived force rule, 235–236
Descriptions, speech acts as, 158–159
Dialect, definitions of, 254
Direct speech acts, 143
  inversion in, 176
Doctrine of Infelicities, 377

E

Efficiency, Principle of, 195
Entailments, conversational postulates and, 84
Evaluating acts, performative verbs in, 191
Exercising authority, performative verbs and acts in, 192–193
Explicit performatives, as oratio obliqua sentences, 22–25
Expressed Ability, Principle of, 201–202
Expressibility, Principle of, 5, 7
Expression of Desire, Principle of, 203

F

Factive-agentive verbs, 348–349
  mean as, 307–308
  that clauses following, 349–351
FA-t verbs, 349–351
Felicity conditions, words and, 233
Force, meaning and, 4–11
Fracturing, whimperatives and, 114–115

G

Generative semanticist thesis, 7
Generative semantics
  conversational principles in, 84
  grammar and, 384
  "soft interpretive underbelly" of, 383–396
  transderivational constraints in, 387–389
  whimperatives and, 131
Gordon–Lakoff rule, 245
Grammar
  conversational postulates in, 94–104
  generative semantics and, 384
  as pragmatically transparent, 292

H

Hebrew, *let's* sentences in, 278–285
Hedged performatives, 187–209
  be going to as, 205–207
  can as, 199–202
  could as, 207–208
  explanation and, 193–208
  intend to as, 205–207
  might as, 207–208
  must as, 193–199
  Principle of Asserted Intention in, 205–206
  Principle of Efficiency in, 195
  Principle of Expressed Ability in, 201–202
  Principle of Expression of Desire in, 203
  Principle of Obligation Fulfillment in, 194
  Principle of Permission Seeking in, 203–204
  Principle of Time-Qualified Ability in, 200

Hedged performatives (*Cont.*)
  Principle of Unspecified Time in,
    194–195
  shall as, 205–207
  should as, 207–208
  will as, 205–207
  would as, 207–208
Here, in conversational postulates, 99
Hereby, in *I hereby promise* phrase, 4,
  8–9
Hints, in whimperatives, 128–130

I

I ask you, as postposed tag in indirect
  speech acts, 172–173
Identity statements, meaning and,
  357–359
Idiomatic speech, in indirect speech
  acts, 76
Ifid (illocutionary force-indicating device)
  constativism and, 18
  meaning of, 4
  overt, 15
  promise and, 13
  semantic functions of, 11
  sublimation of, 3–4
I hereby promise, 4, 8–17
  as performative utterance, 30
Illocutionary act, 1
  convention or rule in, 11
  intent of speaker in, 189
  meaning in, 323
  nonliteral primary, 62
  performative verbs in, 190–191
  preverbal modifiers of, 190–193
  primary versus literal, 62
  so pronominalization and, 164–169
  saying and, 33–38
  sentence and, 6, 33
  sincerity condition in, 79–80
  taxonomy of, 189–193
  utterance and, 378
Illocutionary act rules, versus semantic
  rules, 14–15
Illocutionary force
  disjunctive imperative in, 14
  indirect speech acts and, 145, 180–181
  masquerade and, 234
  meaning and, 4–11
  of whimperatives, 135

Illocutionary-force-indicating device,
  see Ifid
Illocutionary verb, 17
Imperative(s)
  grammatical form of, 125
  question and, 107–108
  range of, 179
  suggestions and commands as, 179
Imperative force, sentences with, 107
Implicate, say and, 43–44
Implicature, 43–57
  conversational, 45, 212–213
  conventional, 50
Impositives
  let's sentences and, 259
  whimperative, 125
Indirect directives, sentences used in
  performance of, 64–67
Indirect questions
  as information request, 151–152
  Slifting and, 170
  speech acts and, 146
Indirect speech acts, 59–82, 143–184
  anger and rudeness in, 150
  defined, 143
  descriptions as, 158–159
  versus direct speech acts, 158–173
  dissimilarities in, 157
  felicity conditions in, 71
  generalizations in, 72, 81–82
  idiomatic sentences or speech in, 69,
    76
  illocutionary force of, 158, 180
  irony in, 151–152
  linear sequence in, 178–179
  may I in, 152–153
  negative questions in, 174–175
  performative verbs in, 155–156
  politeness in, 149, 153–154
  putative facts in, 67–71
  reason clauses and, 163–164, 177
  replies as, 160
  sample case of, 61–64
  sarcastic mode in, 152
  semantic properties of, 145–158
  sentence adverbials and, 161–162
  and sentences used in performance of
    indirect directives, 64–67
  Slifting and, 170–173
  so pronominalization in, 164–169
  structure of, 184

Indirect speech acts (*Cont.*)
　syntactic structure in, 157
　theory of speech acts in, 71–79
　transderivational constraints in, 183
　would and *could* in, 78
Indirect statements
　informative, 146–148
　opinion in, 148
Infelicities, doctrine of, 377
Information
　indirect questions and, 151–152
　in indirect statements, 146–148
Intend to, as hedged performative,
　205–207
Intrusion, in indirect speech acts,
　153–154
Irony, in indirect speech acts, 151–152
I tell you, as postposed tag in indirect
　speech acts, 172–173

L

Language
　as communications system, 292
　pragmatic component in, 289
　syntacticosemantic component in,
　289–290
Language change, conversational impli-
　cature and, 273–276
Let's sentences
　literal versus nonliteral, 274–275
　in modern Hebrew, 278–285
　nonliteral use of, 261–263, 277
　as second-person imperatives,
　264–265
　in Swahili, 286–287
　syntactic evidence in, 263–271
　syntactic properties of, 271
　tag endings in, 264–265
　use of in impositives, 259
　in Yiddish, 286–287
Lexical idiosyncrasy, whimperatives
　and, 133–138, 140
Linear sequence, in indirect speech
　acts, 178
Linguistic utterances, 363–366
Literal meaning, versus conversational
　meaning, 273–275
Locution, truth or falsity of, 324
Locutionary verb, versus illocutionary,
　17

Logic
　conversation and, 41–58
　implicature and, 43–57
Logical structure of sentence, 257
　content and, 290
　meaning as, 289 n., 323
　rule of grammar and, 272–273

M

Manner, Cooperative Principle and,
　46–47
Masquerade
　illocutionary force and, 234
　performative utterance and, 233–234
May
　in conversational postulates, 102–103
　in whimperatives, 140
May I, in indirect speech acts, 152–153
Mean
　as factive-agentive verb, 307–308,
　348–349
　as middle verb, 307
　semantic treatment of, 313–316
　as "stative" verb, 313
　uniqueness of, 348–352
Meaning, 305–359
　see also Basic meaning formula;
　　Mean; Meanings
　basic formula in, 320–324
　categorizing phrase consumption in,
　336
　changing the subject in, 316–320
　as classification of utterances, 369–370
　conversational implicative in, 363–382
　contextual, 276–277
　conversationally implied or conveyed,
　84
　evidence in, 374–375
　identity and, 340–341
　identity statements in, 357–359
　illocutionary force and, 4–11
　of incomplete utterance, 328–329
　literal versus conversational, 273–275
　as logical structure, 289 n.
　objectionable phrase removal in, 336
　paradigmatic, 367–369
　primary or literary, in conversation, 84
　quotation and, 352–357
　simplest cases of, 59
　tell in, 343

Meaning (*Cont.*)
  theories of, 316–320
  understand in, 342–343
  understanding and, 371
Meanings
  rejection of, 305–307
  syntactic considerations against,
    307–312
Might, as hedged performative, 207–208
Modals, hedged performatives and,
  193–208
Morpheme, definitions of, 254
Must, as modal performative, 193–199

N

Negative questions
  as indirect speech acts, 174–175
  restrictions on, 182–183
  as whimperatives, 137
Niching, in indirect speech acts, 171
Nondetachability implicature, 58
Nonlinguistic acts, 379
Nonnegative questions, 174
Nonrestrictive relative clauses, 175–176
  restrictions suspended in, 182

O

Obligation Fulfillment, Principle of, 194
Oratio obliqua sentences, explicit performatives as, 22–25

P

Penthouse Principle, 248
Performatism, 18
Performative addition, conversational
  rule and, 392
Performative analysis
  ifid and, 3
  I hereby say and, 31
  Searle's account of, 15–18
  syntactic properties in, 16
  truth-value and, 25–26
  whimperatives and, 130–133
Performative clause, conversational rule
  and, 389
Performative preface, 2, 7
Performative prefix, in speech acts, 2
Performatives
  ceremonial, 190 n.

Performatives (*Cont.*)
  hedged, 187–209
  as oratio obliqua sentences, 22–25
  sentential complement in, 28
  truth-value of, 24–26
Performative utterance, 233–234, 377
  I hereby promise as, 30
Performative verbs
  in acts of asserting, 190
  in acts of evaluating, 191
  in indirect speech acts, 155–156
  reason clause and, 163
Perlocutionary acts, meaning and, 323
Permission Seeking, Principle of, 203
Phoneme, definitions of, 254
Please
  in conversational postulates, 97–98
  preverbal, 238–240, 245
  in whimperatives, 121–122, 126, 129
  in indirect speech acts, 149, 153–154
Pragmantax, as study of mixed compo-
  nents, 252
Pragmatics, syntax and, 289–302
Preverbal modifiers, in illocutionary
  acts, 190–193
Preverbal *please*, 238–240, 245
Principle of Asserted Intention, 205–
  206
Principle of Efficiency, 195
Principle of Expressed Ability, 201–202
Principle of Expressibility, 5, 7
Principle of Expression of Desire, 203
Principle of Obligation Fulfillment, 194
Principle of Permission Seeking,
  203–204
Principle of Time-Qualified Ability, 200
Principle of Unspecified Time, 194–195
Promise
  convention and, 19
  force of, 9–10
  illocutionary force and, 3–4
  meaning and, 6–7
  truth and, 21
Pronominalization, *so* in, 164–169
Proposition, eight positions in, 189–190
Punctuation, syntactic form and, 144 n.

Q

Quality, Cooperation Principle and,
  46–47

Quantity
  Cooperative Principle and, 45–47
  maxim of, 52–53
Quasi-requests, 245–247
Questions
  negative and nonnegative, 137,
    174–175, 182–183
  tag, 174, 182
  whimperatives as, 137–138
Quotation, meaning and, 352–357

R

Reasonableness conditions, in conversa-
  tional postulates, 89–91
Reasonable request, defined, 90
Reason adverbials, indirect speech acts
  and, 162–164
Reason clause, 163
Reason clause test, in indirect speech
  acts, 177
Redefinition I (Grice), tree represen-
  tation of, 333
Reflecting speaker attitude, performa-
  tive verbs in acts of, 192
Relation, Cooperative Principle and,
  46–47
Relative clauses, nonrestrictive, 175–176
Replies, speech acts as, 160
Representation, semantic, 32–33
Requesting acts, performative verbs in,
  192
Requests, sincerity of, 84–89
R.S.V.P., in whimperatives, 137–138
Rudeness, in indirect speech acts,
  150–151
Rule of grammar, logical structure and,
  272–273

S

Sarcastic mode, in indirect speech acts,
  152
Saying, illocutionary acts and, 33–38
Semantic properties, of indirect speech
  acts, 145–158
Semantic proposition
  grammar and, 384
  and sentence in context, 383
Semantic representation, of sentence, 32
Semantic Rule (Searle), 11–18

Semantic rules, versus illocutionary
  rules, 14–15
Sentence
  illocutionary act and, 6
  imperative force of, 107
  logical structure of, 257–258
  semantic representation of, 32
Sentence adverbials, indirect speech
  acts and, 161–162
Sentence lifting, *see* Slifting
Sentence meaning
  see also Meaning
  defined, 321–322
  illocutionary act potential and, 325
Sentential subject constraint, 293
Shall, as hedged performative, 205–207
Should, as hedged performative,
  207–208
Sincerity condition
  as conversational postulates, 84–89
  in illocutionary act, 79–80
Slifting (sentence lifting), 170–173,
  241–244, 247, 250–252
  Penthouse Principle and, 248
  as syntactic transformation, 252–253
So pronominalization, 164–169
  statements and questions in, 168–169
Speaker, intent of in illocutionary act,
  189–190
Speech acts
  conventionalist or performativist view
    in, 1–18
  in conversational implicature analysis,
    181
  direct versus indirect, 59–82, 143–144,
    158–173
  "felicitous performance" of, 60
  illocutionary force and, 145, 178
  impositives in, 125
  indirect, 59–82, 143–184
  meaning and truth in, 1–38
  nature of, 1
  obligations and questions in, 180
  performative prefix in, 2
  replies as, 160
  sincerity condition in, 89
  so pronominalization in, 164–169
  theory of, 71–79
  unsolicited, 157
Speech Acts (Searle), 12

Spurious reflexive-forming rule,
    389–392
Squishes (matrices), 247 n.
Stipulating acts, performative verbs in,
    192
Suggesting acts, performative verbs in,
    192
Suggestions, as imperatives, 179–180
Surface conjoined structures, asym-
    metric logical structures and, 213
Swahili, *let's* sentences in, 286–287
Syntactic evidence, *let's* sentences in,
    263–271
Syntacticosemantic component, of lan-
    guage, 289–290
Syntacticosemantic derivation, defined,
    289
Syntactic transformation, Slifting as,
    252–253
Syntactic evidence, status of in conver-
    sational implicature, 271–273
Syntax
    constraints on variables in, 292–294
    pragmatics and, 289–302
    traditional definition of, 253–254

T

Tag questions
    in negative questions, 174
    restrictions in, 182
Tags
    niching and, 171
    in whimperatives, 114–116
Tell, in speech acts, 148
Tell deletion analysis, 249 n.
Time-Qualified Ability, principle of, 200
Transderivational constraints or rules
    in conversational postulates, 104–105
    in indirect speech acts, 183
    spurious reflexive and, 391
    whimperatives and, 130–131
Transparent predicates, 158 n.
Truth-value, of performatives, 24–26

U

Understanding
    believe in, 344
    meaning and, 371
Unspecified Time, Principle of, 194–195

Utterance
    changing of, 373
    conventionalized, 375
    conversational implicature and,
        363–366
    illocutionary acts and, 376
    inappropriate, 380
    as instance of meaning, 368–369
    performative, 377–378

V

Verb
    factive or agentive subjects of,
        348–349
    middle, 307
    performative, 155–156, 163
    stative, 313

W

Want to, as hedged performative,
    202–204
Whimperatives
    abstract performative analysis and,
        130–133
    cross-linguistic distribution of, 139
    defined, 108
    fracturing of, 114–115
    generative semantics and, 131
    illocutionary force of, 135
    imperative content of, 117–118, 179
    imperative force of, 118
    implications and consequences of,
        126–140
    impositives and impostors in, 125–126
    intonation of, 127
    hints in, 128–130
    lexical idiosyncrasy and, 133–140
    logical structure versus meaning in,
        132
    may in, 140
    may you in, 134
    meaning of, 118
    must you forms in, 134–135
    negative questions as, 137
    in other languages, 138–139
    please in, 121–122, 126–129
    quasi-transderivational rule and,
        130–131
    as questions, 107–141, 179

Whimperatives (*Cont.*)
  response to, 111
  R.S.V.P. in, 137–138
  semantic structure of, 112–113
  synonym cases in, 135–137
  "tags" in, 114–116
  underlying structure of, 126–127
  as ungrammatical questions, 126–130
  universality of, 138–140
  why don't you as, 121–124
  why not as, 123
Will, as hedged performative, 205–207
Will you tag endings, with let's sen-
    tences, 265
Wish to, as hedged performative,
    202–204

Words
  felicity conditions with, 233
  getting people to do things with,
    120–141
  infelicitous conditions with, 233
Would
  as hedged performative, 207–208
  in indirect speech acts, 78–79
Would like to, as hedged performative,
    202–204
Would you, indirect speech acts,
    149–150

Y

Yiddish, *let's* sentences in, 286–287